UNIVERSITY OF
GLOUCESTERSHIRE
at Cheltenham and Gloucester

Oxstalls Library
University of Gloucestershire
Oxstalls Campus, Oxstalls Lane, Longlevens,
Gloucester, Gloucestershire GL2 9HW

Attachment handbook for foster care and adoption

Gillian Schofield and
Mary Beek

This publication has been
produced with the kind
support of Esmée Fairbairn
Foundation

SUPPORTED BY

Published by
British Association for Adoption & Fostering
(BAAF)
Saffron House
6–10 Kirby Street
London EC1N 8TS
www.baaf.org.uk
Charity registration 275689 (England and Wales) and
SC039337 (Scotland)

ISBN 978-1-903699-96-6

British Library Cataloguing in Publication Data
A catalogue record for this book is available from the British Library.

Project management by Shaila Shah, Director of Publications, BAAF.

Cover photographs by John Birdsall Photography, posed by models
www.johnbirdsall.co.uk

Designed by Andrew Haig & Associates

Typeset by Avon DataSet Ltd, Bidford on Avon, Warwickshire
Printed and bound in Great Britain by TJ International

Acknowledgements

This book arose from a working partnership between John Simmonds and Julia Feast (British Association for Adoption & Fostering), Jeanne Kaniuk (Coram Family), Dr Miriam Steele (New University, New York, previously University College, London and the Anna Freud Centre) and ourselves, Gillian Schofield and Mary Beek in the Centre for Research on the Child and Family at the University of East Anglia. We would like to give a very special vote of thanks to Jeanne Kaniuk. Her enthusiasm for the project, her patient reading of the text and her wise, detailed commentary have been very helpful and heart warming.

As part of the project we set up a reference group which included foster carers and adopters, fostering and adoption social workers, child care social workers, trainers, and a Children's Guardian. We are very grateful for their time, expertise and commitment to the project. Their comments and their encouragement have helped us to see how best to make attachment theory both accessible and useful.

The work on the book and the associated training materials and DVD/video was funded by the Esmée Fairbairn Foundation. The Calouste Gulbenkian Foundation contributed funding towards the publication of the book. The Nuffield Foundation funded the foster care research project from which we developed the parenting model that is described in the book. We are extremely grateful to our funders.

Key to the project has been the children, young people, foster carers, adoptive parents and social workers who have contributed their views and their accounts to the project. It is their stories and their voices that have brought so many of the ideas in this book to life – and we thank them.

Gillian Schofield and Mary Beek
March 2006

About the authors

Dr Gillian Schofield is Co-Director of the Centre for Research on the Child and Family at the University of East Anglia. She is Chair of the BAAF Research Group Advisory Committee. An experienced social worker, she practised for some years as a Guardian *ad Litem*. Her research and teaching interests are in attachment theory and family placement practice, the impact of maltreatment on children's development and the role of long-term foster care as a positive permanence option.

Mary Beek is Team Manager (Family Placement, Recruitment and Assessment), Norfolk County Council, and has more than twenty years' experience in adoption and fostering. She has a special interest in training and supporting foster carers and adopters of older children. From 1997-2005 she was a Senior Research Associate in the Centre for Research on the Child and Family at the University of East Anglia and was involved in studies of foster care, adoption and divorce.

This book is accompanied by a training programme and a DVD/video, Beek M and Schofield G (2006) *Attachment for Foster Care and Adoption*, London: BAAF. These are designed to help foster carers, adopters and practitioners to use the theories and ideas from the book in understanding and caring for children.

Also by the same authors

Beek M and Schofield G (2004) *Providing a Secure Base in Long-Term Foster Care*, London: BAAF

Howe D, Brandon M, Hinings D and Schofield G (1999) *Attachment Theory, Child Maltreatment and Family Support: A practice and assessment model*, Basingstoke: Macmillan

Schofield G (2003) *Part of the Family*, London: BAAF

Schofield G, Beek M, Sargent K with Thoburn J (2000) *Growing up in Foster Care*, London: BAAF

To our families

Contents

Foreword

For children unable to be raised by their birth families, foster care and adoption represent a radical intervention. They provide children, many of whom have suffered difficult and often damaging relationship histories, with another set of parents, another family. Carers and families generate the most intense and potent of social, emotional and relationship environments. And it is these relationship experiences that have a deep impact on development, for good or ill. So for children whose experiences of parenting and family life have not always been good, it is particularly important that they are placed in high quality caregiving environments. Of course, this advice is rather obvious but we know that children who have been deprived and hurt, and who have suffered loss and separation bring to their new placements batteries of behavioural and psychological strategies that have helped them survive difficult and troubling caregiving experiences. This adds an extra challenge even for the most experienced and skilled foster carers and adopters. So, we need new carers not only to look after placed children, but also to help them find their way back to pathways of development that lead to brighter futures.

Over recent years, the developmental sciences have expanded our understanding of how the self forms. Their story is one of evolution and behaviour, genes and environment, relationships and early brain development. They have thrown light on both normal and abnormal development. What they have to say is directly relevant to all of us who work with children, particularly children in need. Modern attachment theory is recognised as a key component in the way we understand the development of the person. As a framework of understanding, it helps integrate the way we think about social cognition, the emotions and their regulation, and children's relationship skills and behavioural competence. Attachment is intuitively attractive to those who work with adopted and fostered children because it seems to make sense of so many of their behaviours and interactions. However, although attachment has a simple appeal, in its detail and engagement with other developmental experiences, it is both more complex and revealing. In this present volume, Gillian Schofield and Mary Beek provide a wonderfully accessible and compelling account of attachment theory and its relevance to foster care and adoption.

Attachment Handbook for Foster Care and Adoption guides the reader from theory to practice. But if this is all that it did, the book would be worthy without being exceptional. However, the authors achieve something more rare. Their remarkable knowledge and understanding of both the children and their carers allows them to paint a picture of hope and humanity. Using an attachment perspective, we are invited to think about why the children behave as they do, and to plan how they can be helped to engage and connect with those around them. At the heart of the book is a sequence of key chapters that describe how carers can provide a secure base. It is within the context of sensitive, thoughtful, reflective relationships with their carers that children learn to feel safe, explore, make sense and grow. So step by step, carers are encouraged to be emotionally available so that children can trust; respond sensitively so that children can manage their feelings and behaviour; accept and value so that children might build self-esteem; develop co-operative caregiving so that children feel able and effective; promote family membership so that children know they belong. And if difficulties are met, advice is offered on how to deal with some of the more demanding behaviour problems that can occur.

Brightening each page are the foster carers and adopters themselves as they talk about their children. Their wisdom and skill speaks of great emotional intelligence. They emerge as warm and gifted. Gillian Schofield and Mary Beek are to be congratulated on giving the parents their own, very special voice. The authors' obvious respect for both the carers and the children has allowed them to write a book that combines clarity with compassion. There is so much good sense and sound advice in this *Handbook* that I have every confidence that it will quickly establish itself as the core text for all those who care for and work with fostered and adopted children.

David Howe
University of East Anglia, Norwich
March 2006

Introduction

The importance of close, loving family relationships to the healthy development of children has long been recognised and lies at the heart of foster care and adoption. Children's strengths and difficulties have developed in the context of previous family relationships, so their strengths need to be nurtured and difficulties resolved in the context of new family relationships. We turn to attachment theory because it offers a rich and powerful explanatory framework, both for understanding the histories and behaviours of children who need family care and for defining the special therapeutic potential of new relationships in foster and adoptive families. Warm and committed close relationships are not only important in ensuring that children feel loved and valued within the family; they affect the extent to which children go on to fulfil their potential for success and happiness at school, with friends and later, in work, as parents and as active participants in their communities. The caregiving offered needs to be focused not only on meeting the child's current needs, but on healing the past and building for the future.

There is no more "intensive treatment" than the provision of a responsive family environment that offers therapeutic care 24 hours day. That is the key message of this book. However, offering this care to children who are finding it hard to trust that anybody can care for them and love them is a complex and demanding task, which cannot be undertaken without a good understanding of what is going on in the minds of troubled children and what they need from foster carers and adoptive parents.

In the years since John Bowlby first developed attachment theory (Bowlby 1969, 1973, 1980), his original and influential framework for understanding the power of relationships has been elaborated, extended and applied through the work of many distinguished researchers and clinicians. During that same period, social work practice in fostering and adoption has also developed and has needed to respond to changing legislation and fluctuating social and organisational demands. Fostering now takes many different forms within local authorities and in the independent sector. Adoption of relinquished infants is now rare and in the UK adoption of children from care has become the most common form of

1

adoption. More often than not, foster carers and adoptive parents are now offering family care to similarly troubled children. The significance of attachment relationships has remained at the very core of family placement practice, but it has not always been easy for social workers to keep pace with the changes and developments in attachment theory and research, nor to fit them easily into these new placement patterns and sets of professional expectations. Although 'secure attachment to carers capable of providing safe and effective care for the duration of childhood' is the stated policy aim of children's services in the UK (Department of Health (DH), 1999, Department for Education and Skills (DfES), 2004), "security" and "attachment" are not simple or commonsense terms; they need to be used with accuracy and care. The misuse of attachment theory in assessment and decision-making can have unhappy and even dangerous consequences for children. We owe it to both children and their birth, foster and adoptive families to work towards a well-informed professional approach to the use of attachment theory in practice.

The primary aim of this book, therefore, is to provide practitioners, foster carers and adoptive parents with an account of attachment theory and research that will enable them to use the concept of attachment in more accurate and constructive ways, whether in undertaking assessments, writing reports and making decisions or in providing the quality of day-to-day care and relationships that can help turn children's lives around. Attachment theory helps to make sense of what we know from the detailed information available on files and in reports, but, as importantly, it helps us to make sense of what does not make sense in the behaviour of children who need family placements. Children who smile when they are unhappy, cling to parents who have abused them, or behave in new families in ways that provoke the rejection they most fear, can be better understood with the help of attachment theory.

Knowledge of theory and research on attachment and development can inform and help caregivers to understand children's behaviour and to plan a helpful response, but this response must always be in the context of sensitivity to the specific strengths, difficulties and needs of the individual infant, child or adolescent. The challenge is how to use theory and research about *patterns* of thinking, feeling and behaviour to improve the therapeutic nature of caregiving, while remaining attuned to the thoughts, feelings and behaviour of *the particular and unique child*.

As important is the fact that attachment theory can help foster carers and adoptive parents to understand what is going on when their own reactions to troubled children may not seem to make sense. Carers and adopters bring a range of experiences to their parenting role, but even the most experienced, sensitive or well-prepared may be surprised by the powerful range of feelings that children can stir up in them. A powerful urge to love and protect a child can co-exist with equally powerful feelings of sadness and anger. The interaction between children's minds and behaviour and caregivers' minds and behaviour is at the very centre of attachment theory and of this book.

The book will offer an account of attachment theory and research viewed through the lens of family placement practice – how can the theory be useful in working with and caring for children? Because the book aims to be of practical benefit to social workers, families and children, the theoretical models offered to explain children's behaviour are accompanied by *models of caregiving* that offer a practical framework for promoting security and resilience in children and for enabling children to meet each new developmental challenge with increased likelihood of success. It will be important to think about and understand each child's and each caregiver's strengths and vulnerabilities in order to target help and support most accurately.

At its simplest, attachment theory is most powerful and relevant for family placement work in offering a framework for understanding the impact of the past on the present. Throughout their lifespan, children and adults carry the impression of past experiences in all areas of their lives, but particularly in their close relationships. Even ecological models that stress the role of the macro systems of culture, political processes and the social environment (Bronfenbrenner, 1979) and feature as part of the assessment triangle (Department of Health, 2000), have at their centre the micro-systems of intimate relationships where outer worlds and inner worlds meet (Schofield, 1998a). It is the meanings attached to experiences by the individual as well as the experiences themselves that shape choices and developmental pathways. Attachment theory is entirely compatible with such psychosocial and transactional models and, indeed, Bowlby was radical for his time in believing in the importance of real world contexts. But nevertheless, experience in close relationships for children and adults remains at the heart of most social work assessment and planning, especially in fostering and adoption where children's needs and parents' capacity to meet those needs are of fundamental importance in family placement choice and family placement support.

Part I of the book begins with an outline of the origins of attachment theory, the process of attachment formation and the differences that result in secure and insecure attachment patterns. The focus here is on presenting the language and core concepts of attachment theory. There then follows a chapter offering a detailed account of secure attachment patterns; describing what promotes security in infancy and how we might expect securely attached children in the school-age years and into adolescence to think, feel and behave.

Subsequent chapters outline the three insecure patterns of attachment, with a developmental pathway from birth to adulthood described in each case. In the chapters which discuss both secure and insecure attachment, attention is paid to the implications for these children and their caregivers when children come into new families, whether on a short-term basis (for respite, assessment or bridging), or on a permanent basis in long-term foster care and adoption. The focus is on children's experiences in attachment relationships, but the consequences of security and insecurity are set in the broader context of children's social, cognitive and moral development as they move from infancy, through the toddler and pre-school years, into middle childhood and finally through adolescence to adulthood. One key aim here is to use theories of attachment formation in infancy to identify core mechanisms and processes that can be extended to promoting security and attachment formation for older children. Each developmental stage and each move of placement presents challenges, but also opportunities for growth. Throughout, the emphasis is on how children's minds and behaviour change in the context of interaction with the minds and behaviour of adult attachment figures. But this relationship dynamic will always be understood as set within the range of other key environments, such as playgroups, schools and activities outside the family home, which can also interact to enhance or diminish the likelihood of healthy development.

The book then moves on in Part II to explore what kind of parenting, given this developmental framework and in particular given the impact of abuse, neglect, separation and loss, is most likely to assist children in moving towards security, reshaping both their internal worlds and their relationships with external worlds. Here we draw on both attachment theory and family placement research to develop a model of the parenting dimensions which can work together to provide the child with a secure base. This model is based on the apparently simple, but actually quite complex, application of what we know contributes to secure development in intact parent–child relationships to relationships between children from backgrounds of adverse care and foster carers and adoptive parents. New families need to offer therapeutic levels of care, based on ordinary parenting but with additional tasks to compensate for children's previous experiences, in order to heal the effects of past psychological damage and to promote mental health and resilience.

In Part III, the book considers how attachment theory can be applied to key practice issues: understanding and managing common behaviour problems of fostered and adopted children; the practice of children's social workers in assessing, matching, listening to and working with children; the practice of family placement social workers in assessing foster carers and adoptive parents and supporting placements; and the management of birth family contact.

Because the book is about the full range of foster care and adoption, we have for convenience often used the term "caregiver", which is commonly used in the attachment literature and has the advantage of including fathers as well as mothers. But at times we have also used the words "carer" or "parent". We hope that foster carers and adopters will be comfortable with all of these terms.

The book supplements the references to theory and research by the use of case material from a range of sources. Some examples are from research interviews with foster carers, adoptive parents, children and young people, social workers and other professionals. Others are from more diverse sources – cases from our own practice and stories given to us by a range of families and professionals who were involved in discussions about this project. They will be "recognisable" in the sense that many of the dilemmas they present will have echoes in readers' personal or professional experiences, but all these cases and narratives are anonymised, both in terms of names and identifying details. Some foster carers, adoptive parents, fostered children, adopted children and social workers who shared their experiences with us may recognise their stories or their words. We have treated all we were told about the lives of children and families with the greatest of respect and hope that they will feel that the purpose for which they gave us those stories is met in the publication of this book.

The reality of parenting fostered and adopted children is a complex business; it is challenging, demanding and hard work. But when children, against all the odds, make even small steps forward, it is exciting, rewarding and worthwhile. The moment a child first smiles spontaneously or reaches out for a helping hand is very special. The time when a child successfully negotiates a birthday party without upset or manages and even enjoys the first day at school will be a real triumph for the child and the whole family. These encouraging signs of progress in the ordinary things of childhood are what we are looking for and aim to highlight in this book. When we began talking to practitioners about what they wanted from a text of this kind, they wanted it to be rooted in practice, realistic but, above all, hopeful.

Part I **Attachment theory**

1 Attachment theory – core concepts

It is now almost taken for granted that the quality of a child's early experiences in close relationships will shape development in significant ways. But this is a complex process and many ideas that have helped to make sense of the important interaction between *children's development* and *the care they receive* come from the work of John Bowlby (1969, 1973, 1980) and the framework provided by attachment theory.

Since Bowlby first introduced the concept of *attachment*, researchers and practitioners across the world have continued to test, develop and apply his ideas in ways that have enriched our understanding of attachment and human relationships across the lifespan. Attachment research has explored patterns of relating from infancy to adulthood, both the continuities and discontinuities that can occur. Just as the relationship environment can change for better or worse, so children can change in the way they feel about themselves and other people. They can become more secure or less secure. It is this potential for change in children's thoughts, feelings and behaviour in the context of new relationships that needs to be understood in order to promote successful adoption and fostering practice. But the mechanisms of change are not simple. Attachment theory has provided a rich source of ideas that help explain how children's previous experiences in adverse family conditions affect their minds and behaviour, how children struggle to manage separation and loss, and just why bringing about positive change in the context of a new caregiving environment can be so challenging but so successful.

This chapter outlines the core concepts of attachment theory, the process of attachment formation, secure and insecure attachment patterns and the various tools that researchers have developed to measure secure and insecure attachment patterns in children and adults. The following four chapters explain each pattern in much more detail and explore how each develops through childhood and adolescence into adulthood. This detailed account of attachment relationships takes into account the significant social contexts, the families, peer groups, schools and communities in which these relationships and children's development falter or thrive.

Bowlby and the origins of attachment theory

When John Bowlby was working as a psychiatrist and psychoanalyst in the 1940s, he became interested in and concerned about the emotionally deprived backgrounds of juvenile delinquents and in particular the impact of early experiences of maternal separation (Bowlby, 1944). In further exploring the impact of separation, Bowlby was assisted by the work of James Robertson (1952), who shed light on this question by filming young children's experiences of separation when in hospital or when in residential nurseries and other settings. These films charted the different stages of protest, denial and despair which occurred for children separated for even a brief period of days. Bowlby's focus on the importance of early close relationships and separation led to a clear statement of the link between mental health and the quality of early relationships.

> *What is believed to be essential for mental health is that an infant and young child should experience a warm, intimate and continuous relationship with his mother (or permanent mother substitute – one person who steadily "mothers" him) in which both find satisfaction and enjoyment.* (Bowlby, 1953, p. 13)

Note here that it is the child's experience of a 'warm, intimate and continuous relationship' rather than who is providing it that is key to mental health.

In seeking the explanation of this link, Bowlby drew not only on psychoanalysis and his own observations and clinical experience, but also on studies of animal behaviour, biology, systems theory and evolutionary theory as a way of making sense of how human beings develop into social beings through their relationships. Bowlby concluded that it is the quality of early experiences in relationships with caregivers, and the experience of separation and loss of those relationships, that shape the self and the quality of later relationships in distinctive ways. This core idea has become an important part of our understanding of individual differences in relationships, not only within families, but also in peer relationships and relationships of all kinds. It has a particular meaning for children in foster care and adoption. As Bowlby put it (1951, p. 114):

> *Children are not slates from which the past can be rubbed by a duster or sponge, but human beings who carry their previous experiences with them and whose behaviour in the present is profoundly affected by what has gone before.*

Previous experiences in relationships undoubtedly affect relationships in the present and are central to our understanding of children's strengths and difficulties. In successful family placements, the child's past is taken into account, thought about and understood in order to accurately target the sensitive, available and responsive relationship experiences which can bring about change. An important goal for children is to make sense of the past and resolve their feelings about it, via a lived experience of being understood, held in mind and cared for, so that a more secure and resilient sense of self can develop and be taken into the future.

Proximity seeking and the significance of a secure base

The starting point of Bowlby's theory is an evolutionary one, in that infants are seen as having a biological drive to *seek proximity* to a protective adult, usually the primary caregiver, in order to survive danger. The goal of this drive for closeness in the *attachment system* is to feel safe, secure and protected. This leads to a range of proximity-promoting *attachment behaviours*. These can be signals to the caregiver, such as in infancy, vocalisation, crying, smiling and reaching out. In the toddler years, attachment behaviours will include more direct actions, such as approaching, following, clinging and other behavioural strategies that can achieve proximity to the attachment figure. Attachment behaviours may attract attention in a positive way, for example, calling and smiling. Aversive attachment behaviours, such as crying, will also bring the caregiver closer in order to soothe the child and end the behaviour.

Attachment behaviours are most in evidence when the infant feels 'threatened, endangered or stressed' (George, 1996, p. 112), as an evolutionary perspective would predict. The infant needs to know where protection will come from and to be confident in their own ability to communicate this need and bring about comfort from the caregiver when anxiety strikes. The caregiver, in turn, needs to be tuned in to the specific signals of the infant and then respond in an accurate and timely fashion. The quality of the *caregiving system* therefore has a major part to play in the outcome for the infant. Between the infant and the caregiver, a *synchrony* is established, like a rhythmic dance in which both partners are *attuned* and in step with each other. There is a cycle of arousal and relaxation (see Figure 1) in which needs are experienced by the infant, the infant's anxiety is raised, needs are expressed and are satisfied in the context of the relationship.

The caregiver's raised concerns for the child lead to action that restores the *equilibrium* of both the child and the caregiver. But key to this cycle is the caregiver's capacity *to think about the meaning* of the child's behaviour and to be interested in the child's mind in order to respond in a way that will both meet the child's needs and give messages about the caregiver's availability. Equally important, therefore, is the fact that the child's experience of having needs met and then of relaxation and well-being is also a learning experience at a

Figure 1

Arousal–relaxation cycle

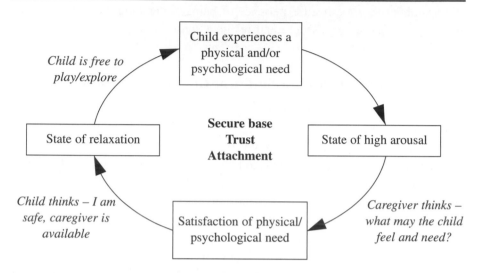

(Adapted from Fahlberg, 1988, p. 63)

psychological level. It shapes the child's beliefs and expectations of the caregiver, increases confidence in the world around them and increases the likelihood that the child will start to communicate those needs more openly as the cycle goes round again and again throughout the day. The caregiver and the child communicate what is in their minds through their behaviour.

The nature of the attachment relationship can best be understood by emphasising the highly significant role of *anxiety about the availability of caregivers in the face of stress or danger* which drives the infant's behaviour (Goldberg, 2000; Howe *et al*, 1999). If caregiver's responses are predictable and accurately meet the needs of the infant – in the form of physical and emotional care, protection and availability – then the infant can feel safe and can relax, physically and emotionally. Anxiety about hunger, cold, loud noises, loneliness and other risks and dangers will not overwhelm the infant, and her faith in the attachment figure as a source of security will be established.

Although anxiety about physical and emotional availability is the key to the early development of an attachment relationship, over time and in the context of sensitive caregiving the infant learns *to trust,* to wait for needs to be satisfied. The infant can begin to have confidence in the attachment figure as available, to manage a degree of anxiety and tolerate brief separation. Winnicott's notion of 'the good enough mother' highlighted the fact that it is how the infant learns to manage the gaps – the inevitable delays in the mother getting to the cot to pick the baby up, for example – which forms the basis of the infant's growing capacity to trust the caregiver and manage their feelings (Winnicott, 1965). So "good enough" means caregiving that is reliable and available, with some gaps in which the child begins to trust that caregivers will return, and begins the slow but critical process of learning to manage their anxiety for themselves.

A key attachment concept here is the capacity of the infant to use the attachment figure as a *secure base* (Ainsworth *et al*, 1978; Bowlby, 1988) who can be relied on and called for or returned to in times of stress. If the infant has developed confidence that their attachment figure is reliable and can be depended on in time of need, then the infant is liberated from anxiety and becomes free to explore, be interested in, enjoy and learn from her environment. Thus there are important developmental consequences of this sensitive and synchronised caregiver–infant interaction. When the caregiver is trusted by the infant to be available and there is no immediate source of threat and no unmet needs, the *attachment system* is not taking up energy and the *exploratory system* becomes the focus of feeling, thinking and activity. The attuned caregiver will not only permit but will actively support and promote exploration, remaining available as a *safe haven* for the child if anxiety or threat arises.

Just as infants' brains are programmed to seek proximity, they are programmed to explore their environment. From an evolutionary point of view, it is essential for even the dependent infant to learn about the environment and begin to understand how the physical world works – for example, the difference between a nice pink ice lolly and a nice pink piece of soap, the danger that a hot tea pot represents. But the infant also needs to begin to understand how the social world works, the difference between mums and dads, sisters and grandmothers, family and strangers. Each person will represent different sources of safety or anxiety, fun or uncertainty. Even at birth the infant is hyperalert to signals about physical and emotional environments and is getting ready to learn the important lessons that pave the way to becoming a competent explorer and social actor.

Although this learning has a serious underlying purpose (at its most basic this is about survival), for infants who can rely on a secure base provided by a caregiver, their environment in all its sensory and social variety is an exciting and stimulating source of pleasure. Most importantly, infants learn that they can have an effect on their environment, not just in summoning up their caregiver when distressed, but in shaking the rattle to make a nice noise or pushing the mobile to make the fluffy animals dance. If there is one clear difference between the sensitively cared for infant and the neglected or abused infant, it lies in the presence or absence of curiosity, interest and joy in the world and the presence or lack of a sense of *agency*. Maltreated infants will often need to become close observers of their unpredictable and frightening world, and the taut facial expression and lack of physical energy and enthusiasm of the wary infant will be quite distinctive. Learning through exploration for these infants will be narrowed down to learning to survive and feelings of anxiety and helplessness will predominate.

Although the attachment and exploratory systems and the extent to which they are in balance are critical to development, Bowlby (1969) also suggested the existence of a *sociable* or *affiliative* behaviour system, which is less commonly emphasised in accounts of attachment theory. The importance of peer relationships and relationships beyond those with the child's attachment figures can also be understood in evolutionary terms, as important for survival. Sociability through the group can provide additional sources of security, companionship and opportunities to learn about the environment. We know that even young babies are very interested in other babies and by the age of three years children frequently have close and sustained friendships (Dunn, 1993). Vygotsky's notion of the *zone of proximal development* (1978) makes a useful connection here between attachment figures and others in the child's network of relationships. He proposed that in a social context (i.e. with the help of others) children have the potential to reach areas of development which they cannot achieve by their own efforts. The direct teaching, supported learning or modelling that makes this possible can be provided by more skilled and competent adults or children, inside or outside of the family.

As with exploratory behaviours, however, the success of the child's sociable behaviours within wider networks is likely to depend on the satisfactory resolution of anxieties through the secure base provided within the attachment system. The child's energy and mental focus need to be free from anxiety in order to share activities and learn with and from older siblings, friends and adults outside the family. Children's capacity to join Brownies or a football team, to make new friends while learning new skills, will depend on a complex interaction between self-esteem and self-efficacy, and on their confidence in the likelihood that others will be friendly towards them outweighing their anxiety that they will be rejected. All of this will be closely related to their sense of security and capacity to rely on their attachment figure as a secure base. As Bowlby put it:

All of us, from the cradle to the grave, are happiest when life is organised as a series of excursions, long or short, from the secure base provided by our attachment figures. (Bowlby, 1988 in Holmes, 1993, p. 61)

Mind-mindedness and the regulation of affect and behaviour

The benefits of sensitive, available and attuned caregiving can be seen in a range of sociable, confident and competent *behaviours* from infancy to adolescence that derive from exploration in the context of an available secure base. But in order to understand the processes involved in promoting security and to help foster carers and adoptive parents to parent children who have lacked these experiences, it is essential for social workers and caregivers to grasp the importance of what is going on in the *mind* of the child – and in the *mind* of the caregiver. Where, for example, caregivers use language in talking to or about their infant that indicate that they can *see things from the baby's point of view*, such *mind-mindedness* strongly predicts security of attachment (Miens *et al*, 2001).

Attachment theory has been described as a theory of affect regulation (Fonagy *et al*, 2002) and this places at the centre of children's development the child's ability to appropriately experience and express, but also regulate or manage, their emotions. It is easy to see why this idea is key to an attachment based view of development, when we consider the behaviour of those troubled foster and adoptive children who become overwhelmed by distress when they feel over-looked, or who turn to aggression when they cannot manage the uncertain world of the school playground, or who are so frozen and traumatised that they cannot tolerate the intimacy of family life.

Infants and children must be able to experience and express the full range of emotions, including the most negative such as rage and anger, while behaviour is kept safe and within limits. But children also need to *manage* or *regulate* strong feelings of happiness or sadness, delight or anger in their everyday lives, so that they do not feel overwhelmed or overwhelm others. They must learn to recognise, name and distinguish between different feelings and to express them in behaviours which get their needs met, are compatible with comfortable close relationships and are socially acceptable. From the enraged or incandescently happy infant, to the furious or joyful toddler to the jealous or proud school-age child to the upbeat or depressed teenager, the capacity to reflect on and process both negative and positive ideas and feelings about the self and others is of great significance in relationships. In particular, the capacity to acknowledge the possibility of mixed feelings (I can both love and be angry with my mother/ sister/best friend) is key to flexible thinking about emotions and is related to attachment security (H. Steele *et al*, 1999). This acceptance of mixed feelings is hard for insecure and maltreated children, whose caregivers have often given the message that there are clear splits between good and bad (If you loved me you wouldn't do that), and that angry feelings are too dangerous to express or repair (If you say that, I will never forgive you).

The benefits of secure attachment can therefore be understood quite specifically as not only about reducing anxiety about danger in the context of a secure base (although this is the central starting point), but also about developing the quality of the child's thinking and their capacity to reflect on minds and behaviour. As Howe *et al* (1999, p. 21) put it, "felt security" grows out of the child's increasing capacity to "mentalise". Key to the child's successful engagement with the social world is the emerging ability to think about or reflect on his own mind, but also the minds of other people (Fonagy *et al*, 1997, 2002). The core concept here that needs to be understood is the link between the way in which children *think* and the way in which they can *regulate emotion and behaviour*. Understanding the impact their behaviour has on other people, for example, is a prerequisite of prosocial behaviour – sharing rather than grabbing that last bar of chocolate or putting a protective arm around a friend who loses a game rather than laughing at their discomfort – such behaviours require a mind that understands what the other will be thinking and feeling as well as some ability to control the emotion behind the impulse to grab or laugh.

Developing such mind-mindedness (Miens, 1997) is rooted in the fact that the availability of the mother, as stressed above, is most significantly the *availability of her mind*. This is most obvious when the infant gazes into the smiling face and interested eyes of the caregiver, but it is significant in many aspects of the caregiver–infant interaction. An attuned mother communicates in complex ways, verbally and non-verbally, throughout a feed that she understands exactly how hungry, how angry at the wait, how eager and then how satisfied the infant is – and that she accepts each of these feelings as legitimate. She uses her voice to calm the infant, her smile to reassure and a stroking hand to help the baby relax. Caregivers initially regulate infants' emotions for them, but with important lessons being learned that will help towards self-regulation.

> *The infant learns that arousal in the presence of the caregiver will not lead to disorganisation beyond his coping capabilities. The caregiver will be there to re-establish equilibrium.* (Fonagy *et al*, 2002, p. 37).

The sensitive and available caregiver's mind is thinking about the infant or child's mind and helping the child think about his own mind and intentions and the mind and intentions of the caregiver and other people. This apparently complex and abstract process can be seen not only in the rhythm and regulation of the infant's feed and the naming and acceptance of his feelings, but very much in the ordinary everyday commentary by caregivers to children of all ages. So, for example, after rain prevents a trip to the park a mother might say to her three-year-old son:

You seem rather grumpy this morning. I think maybe you are a bit cross and disappointed that it is raining too hard to go the park and play on the new swings. I'm disappointed too as I was looking forward to a breath of fresh air. Why don't I put on a video? We can have a cuddle on the settee and we'll both feel better. Perhaps we can go to the park tomorrow.

Such simple communications are rich in messages that help the child mentalise and regulate his feelings. For example, this communication suggests:

I'm interested in what is in your mind and lies behind your behaviour. I need to help you name your feelings. I also need to let you understand what's in my mind, how I feel and why, because mums have feelings too. My feelings of disappointment are rather like yours, but we have different reasons/goals i.e. your loss of a chance to play on the swings compared to my loss of a chance for a breath of fresh air. As your mum, I'd like to make you feel better. Mums too need to feel better. The solution to grumpiness and disappointment is to share some pleasure. We can help each other feel better. There is hope for the future – trust me.

A less confident, competent, available or sensitive caregiver may simply say, 'Stop making a fuss. It's bad enough that we can't go out without you being naughty.' This response gives the child a very different message, 'Your feelings of anger are unreasonable and expressing them is naughty and upsetting. My anger is your fault. Nothing can be done to make you feel better and you will make me feel better if you suppress your feelings.' Such a response may arise because of the mother's inability to take the perspective of the child, but other factors, such as having other children to care for, having a husband who works nights and is trying to get some sleep, having debts so that getting the latest video is out of the question, can also contribute to the stress that affects the mother's response. Nevertheless, whatever the cause, a negative and insensitive caregiver response increases the child's anxiety and reduces the child's capacity to make sense of and manage feelings. It also increases the likelihood that the child will cry, have a tantrum or tear round the house. In cases where a more constructive kind of commentary is provided, as in the first example, the child can make sense of what is going on and develop flexible thinking about the minds of self and others, which in turn enables him to elaborate on the reasons for behaviour and to regulate his feelings. The response is more likely to reassure and calm the child and provide support for play and exploration. Verbal and non-verbal *scaffolding* (Vygotsky, 1978) of this kind can help children to reach areas of development, both in exploring and in mind-mindedness, which they otherwise could not reach.

A further simple example might be a parent helping a young child succeed in completing a jigsaw puzzle. The first step is making sure that the puzzle is of the right degree of difficulty for the child, then sitting with the child, discussing the picture and nudging the right pieces in the general direction of the gaps for the child to discover and use. But simultaneously the adult is naming and helping the child to express and manage feelings of frustration and excitement by encouraging, praising, wondering, consoling and celebrating as each piece fits, fails to fit or completes the puzzle. Here we see attunement, a secure base and support for exploration in action.

Part of this process of learning to be mind-minded is for the child to understand that others are intentional, goal-directed beings. The mother recognises the child's goal of finishing the jigsaw puzzle, but may communicate her own goal that after the puzzle is finished she will have to stop playing in order to put the dinner on. Assisted by open communication about these different goals, the timing of the play has to be negotiated – the basis of the stage in attachment formation described by Bowlby as a 'goal corrected partnership' which becomes possible when children are around three years of age (discussed further later in this chapter).

But it is important for children to be able to distinguish between intentional/deliberate actions and accidental actions, since goals and intentions are a significant part of what gives *meaning* to actions in relationships i.e. what is in the other person's mind at the time. If, for example, a father accidentally catches his young daughter's finger when doing up the zipper on her coat, it is necessary both for the relationship and for the child's social and moral "education" that the child understands that this is an accident. The father knows in his mind that he was trying to help his daughter and that it is an accident, but has to reflect on the likely content of the child's mind and understand that she may be frightened as well as hurt, angry as well as distressed. He will need to hug the child, say sorry in a caring tone, name her mixed feelings, explain what happened, kiss the finger better and perhaps offer to put some special cream on the finger to make sure it heals. He may make a little game of doing up her zipper with her so that she feels more competent as well as trusting him. The child then gets the message that her mental representation of her father as loving, available and protective can be maintained, in spite of the hurt, by distinguishing the intention or lack of intention behind the behaviour.

The child also learns another very important lesson through this modelling i.e. how to make things better, how to make reparation if someone is hurt by their action. When next the child accidentally runs into her mother on her tricycle or tears a page in the story book, the mother signals and names her feelings, so that the child understands that even accidental actions have consequences for other people, but soothingly reinforces the child's understanding of "accident". If the action is deliberate, that too can be discussed and named. In either case, the child has a model (based on the zipper incident and many similar others) of how to think about another's feelings, make reparation, win the forgiveness of the other person and accept that we all make mistakes.

These incidents, which provoke strong feelings in the child, start to have a shape and a meaning when accompanied by the appropriate commentary or scaffolding. They make sense to the child and assist in a rich emotional education which also empowers the child. It is thus the caregiver's ability to think, to reflect on her own, the child's and other people's feelings and behaviour in this complex way and *to help the child to do the same*, which enables the child to regulate his emotions and become a more effective operator in managing his behaviour in the social world.

Understanding that other people – adults and children – have thoughts and feelings that differ from your own *and* need to be taken into account is a necessary part of negotiating relationships inside and outside of the family. If your brother also wants a share of that cake, this needs to be negotiated and you need to manage your own feelings – which may include desire for the whole cake, anger and resentment or wanting to please your brother. If a new girl at the nursery is crying because her mummy has just left her for the first time, empathy suggests she may need your help and you may decide to lend her your favourite toy. If at school you want to get your ball back from another boy in the playground, you need to manage your anger and anxiety and select from a range of possible behaviours the one that will be the most effective strategy in meeting your goals. Hitting the child and grabbing the ball *or* suggesting you play ball together will have very different outcomes, and all options need to be thought through. The *pause for thought* is a critical moment when children who can mentalise reflect like a high-speed computer on what they think will be the consequences of their actions, both what will bring rewards and avoid punishments, but more subtly, what the impact of various options will be on other people's and their own minds (avoiding shame and guilt for example).

This perspective taking requires a developmental shift that generally occurs at around the age of three to four as children develop what is known as *Theory of Mind*, an awareness of other minds that will be the foundation of mind-mindedness across a range of situations and relationships. At this stage, children's mental representations start to include an understanding that other people have minds which will have different thoughts, feelings, goals and intentions than their own. This enriches their sense of the uniqueness of their own minds, as they realise that their thoughts and ideas are not automatically shared by or known to others – hence the magic of discovering the capacity to *lie* successfully or *keep a secret* for the first time. You know that you took the last biscuit, but your mother may not. More straightforwardly, if you prefer strawberry yogurt you will need to say so – you know but your grandmother may not.

Although this is a developmental shift for most children at age three – four, children in secure relationships are developing preliminary understandings of other minds from infancy. The foundations for empathy and perspective taking are being laid in the way in which secure children are parented and feelings are mirrored, named and taken into account even in the first year of life. In contrast, where children are not receiving sensitive care in the early years of a kind that promotes the capacity to take the perspective of others and to be co-operative, children remain overwhelmed and muddled about their own and other minds, often assuming the worst (e.g. that other people are hostile) when anxiety remains high.

The themes of "mind-mindedness" in children and caregivers and the regulation of feelings and behaviour are important in all sections of this book, as we focus on the way in which minds and behaviour interact in secure and insecure children. In helping fostered and adopted children to change their more difficult and troubled behaviours, foster carers and adopters need to focus hard on offering caregiving experiences and relationships that put children in touch with what is going on in their minds and in the minds of others. For fostered and adopted children this will often mean an emotional and cognitive re-education that requires very targeted parenting, using opportunities in many aspects of the child's day-to-day care, from getting up in the morning to going to bed at night. In particular, it suggests the need for conscious use of *reflective commentary* and the introduction of specific strategies, such as reading story books that explore and name a range of different and mixed emotions and offer opportunities for joint reflection on the minds of others. These strategies occur spontaneously in many families, but they need to become part of training for carers and adopters, who often have to adopt such strategies when children appear too old for them or may be initially reluctant or too anxious to allow themselves to think about other people's minds or their own. Lack of perspective taking and lack of the capacity to mentalise are very real barriers to building relationships and regulating emotions and behaviour for insecure and previously maltreated children.

Adaptation, mental representations and internal working models

Because different children in different environments will be developing differently, we need to think from an attachment perspective, using some of these core concepts, about the sources and routes of children's diverse developmental pathways.

Key to the process of development is that the infant and child learn to *adapt* to the specific relationship environment in which they find themselves. They need to *organise* their behaviour around the way in which they are treated, the way in which needs are met and the response that they get to their attachment and exploratory behaviours. The *mental representations* that they form on the basis of experience help them make sense of their environment. From infancy, aspects of the environment, including important people in their lives, are felt about, thought about, assessed or appraised. Appraisals give a positive or negative value to objects, experiences, people and the self – such as "yummy porridge", "nasty hair wash", "funny daddy" and "lovable baby". The processing of such information into mental representations of the environment leads to the child's *anticipatory* behaviour – greeting the porridge with joy, yelling when hair washing is imminent, becoming excited when daddy wants to play and snuggling in confidently for a cuddle when picked up by a fond grandparent.

The infant's information about and appraisals of what to expect from other people are centred initially on the relationship with the primary caregivers. Over time and as the infant matures, the secure base provided by attachment figures becomes internalised through this process of mental representation. The child develops an *idea* of their caregiver which can be held in the mind, so that the continuous physical presence of that caregiver becomes less necessary as the child moves through the toddler years. This is a simple concept yet complex in its implications, since the mental representation of the caregiver is not only of the *person* of the caregiver but also the *associated feelings and ideas* about that caregiver – in particular, whether or not the caregiver makes the child feel safe and lovable, and whether the child believes that the caregiver will be available if needed in times of stress.

Particular experiences in the caregiving relationship lead to the development of core sets of mental representations of self, others and relationships, referred to by Bowlby as *internal working models*, which become the framework for expectations, beliefs and behaviour.

It is a presumption of contemporary attachment theory that working models become so deeply ingrained that they influence feelings, thought and behaviour unconsciously and automatically. They do this, according to Bowlby, by directing the child's attention to particular actions and events in his world, by shaping what the child remembers and does not and thereby guiding his behaviour towards others and thus theirs towards him. (Belsky and Cassidy, 1994, p. 379)

The child whose signals and needs are consistently responded to by the parent thinks of the parent as available and loving and the self as effective, valued and loved; Whereas the child whose signals and needs are not reliably responded to or are rejected by the parent develops the model of a parent as unavailable or hostile and the self as both powerless and unworthy of love. These mental representations are then used to predict the likelihood of how other people will behave and how the self might feel, think and need to respond. The toddler, the school-age child, the adolescent or indeed the adult will *anticipate* the positive or negative reactions of a new person they are meeting for the first time, in the light of stored memories based on previous experiences and laid down in internal working models.

Although the internal working model that derives from the attachment relationship with specific primary caregivers is highly significant in forming expectations of self and others, children may have different experiences, expectations and therefore working models in relation to different attachment figures. So, for example, a young child might learn that 'If I fall over I can always go to my father who will be concerned and comfort me', but 'If I fall over my mother will tell me not to make a fuss'. It is more accurate, therefore, to think in terms of children having a number of internal working models which influence their perceptions and behaviours during childhood.

It is important to bear in mind that, while for some children the prediction of how others are likely to behave will mean learning about the availability of a sensitive parent, for other children it will mean learning about the likelihood that a caregiver will become unavailable or violent when they have had too much alcohol to drink. Thus, the *particular relationship environment* will determine the exact nature of the learned emotion (say joy or fear) as it interacts with the cognitive appraisal of the person (loving or dangerous) and the appropriate behavioural response (approach or avoid). Internal working models thus draw on past experiences in relationships and lead to sets of likely behavioural responses that are strategies to achieve some sense of safety and security. Most difficult of all for children is to adapt or organise a response when the behaviour of the caregiver is unpredictable and may at times be frightening (discussed further below and in Chapter 5 on disorganisation). For these children, as Mary Main's (1991) classic paper suggests, multiple working models of the self and the other person in the same relationship, as often happens in cases of abuse and neglect, can confuse children and leave them with an incoherent model of both self and others.

Memory and internal working models

The role of memory is very important here, as 'internal working models involve defensive processes that influence how the individual perceives and remembers his or her experiences' (George, 1996, p. 413). This is a helpful theme for making sense of the ways in which fostered and adopted children process their experiences. In particular, memories of experiences influence internal working models, but *internal working models also influence how experiences are perceived and stored as memories*. Thus the experience of sensitive or neglectful caregiving influences the child's expectations of whether adults will be available and supportive, but those expectations also influence what the child takes note of and remembers, priming their expectations for future events and experiences. We tend both to see *and* remember what we expect to see. It seems easier for the human mind to seek and find confirmation of our expectations of other people, to fit them into our existing boxes, than to use new "information" based on different experiences to change the boxes. This is the challenge for caregiving in adoption and foster care, where the goal is to create secure experiences/memories which alter negative expectations and models of the world.

Memory takes a number of forms, but three in particular are helpful in making sense of children's attachment experiences (Crittenden, 1995; Diamond and Marrone, 2003). First there is *procedural* memory, which is a memory of experiences of a non-verbal kind or that happen at a pre-verbal stage in the child's life. It can include simple memories of learned "procedures" like how to use a spoon or ride a bicycle, which become automatic and do not require conscious thought. But it also includes memories of experiences in caregiving relationships. Typical here might be the early sensory "memories" of feeling warm, safe and loved or, in contrast, memories of harsh treatment, fear and anxiety. These early procedural memories exist at an entirely unconscious level, but are nevertheless stored in the brain and have the power to reassure or unsettle children for reasons that they would be unable to explain in words. These memories and the feelings they provoke may be sparked off by sensory experiences, such as a particular smell or sound, or a chance incident in a television programme.

In fostering and adoption, knowing the power of such memories can help us to understand how children who have had difficult or traumatic experiences will not always be able to talk them through nor be able to say why they behave in the way they do. This is not necessarily because children do not want to talk about their past or their feelings, but may simply be because they may not be able to link their behaviour and ideas to specific experiences or aspects of past relationships. (This may also be because the memories of traumatic experiences have been defended against and the child had a dissociative reaction that leaves the memory out of reach.) The connections that might explain *why* children feel what they feel and behave as they do are often as much a mystery to them as they are to those who care for them. Asking a child "why?" is appropriate, but the child who cannot answer that question – which is many children much of the time – needs the caregiver to help them make connections.

A child's need from a new family is to have fundamentally different procedural experiences that begin to change internal working models – experiences of physical care, predictability, love and safety that make sense and feed into their memory system, changing these unconscious expectations and beliefs. These experiences need to be reliable, predictable and repeated over years before they can start to become internalised as part of a new internal working model.

Other kinds of memories form what is described as the *autobiographical memory*, which makes up the more conscious life story that we tell to ourselves and about ourselves. One kind of autobiographical memory is known as *episodic memory*. Out of all our diverse experiences in life we selectively remember key events, generally those incidents which have some significance for our view of ourselves and our world. These become markers which define our histories and feed directly into how we develop and sustain our ideas about ourselves and key people in our past, even into adult life, as this young adult who grew up in foster care shows in recalling her birth mother:

> *My mum would just forget, because of the alcohol, she would just forget to pick me up from school and I'd always know if there was a police car in the car park that it was there to collect me to take me home.* (Donna, 24)

Here are two further examples from the same study of adults who grew up in foster care (Schofield, 2003). They give starkly different memories, the first positive and the second negative, of an early episode of distress and a birth mother's response.

> *We kept very close, just my mother and me. She used to sit me on the back seat of her bike and take me back and forth to playgroup. I remember that and we had a show and tell and at the time I had a black and white panda bear that went everywhere with me and I'd left it at home and I was distraught through the day and the school phoned my mum at work and she went home to get it*

and brought it into school. That is my first real memory. (Leo, 24)

I can remember one incident when my mum gave me a 50p piece to get her some sweets from the shop, and I was about five years old, something like that. I went out and lost it down the drain. I went home and she said, you're not going to come in this house until you find that 50p piece . . . I can remember that very clearly. I came back and it was pitch black dark and the doors were locked and the windows were locked and . . . I was five and I slept outside underneath the hedge and the next-door neighbour found me. (Claudia, 18)

Even in retelling, "remembering" these stories in adult life, it was apparent that the very different emotions – the affection and gratitude in Leo, the fear and anger in Claudia – were still present. Leo's mother died when he was six years old and he went on to experience physical abuse from his stepfather before coming into a foster family at age 11. Claudia was taken into care in her foster family soon after this incident, but she remained scared of her birth mother throughout her childhood in foster care. Although both young adults had had stable foster placements, it is perhaps not surprising that as a young adult Claudia was emotionally fragile, but Leo had been able to use therapy and probably draw on his early secure foundations, as well as the continuing security offered in the foster home, to establish a successful and stable adult life.

The existence of such episodic memories and the meaning that becomes attached to those memories over time have a part to play in shaping expectations of self and others in relationships. They are conscious and can be accessed and made sense of, with help. Many foster and adoptive children then also delight in the special family moments that give them new memories to store into adult life. As Beverley recalled in describing the foster mother who was now grandmother to her children:

I mean if you had a graze on your knee, she was always there for you . . . cuddles . . . plasters on your legs and that. She always used to welcome us with open arms when we used to come out of the infants school. (Beverley, 28)

This memory continues to offer a model that helps her with her own caregiving role as a parent.

A second type of autobiographical memory is referred to as *semantic memory*, and consists of the memory of language used to define the self and others, the messages that get stored, often from significant others such as parents, grand-parents or teachers. These messages contribute to the child's mental representations and internal working models. The child is putting together their memories into a narrative. Autobiographical memory tries to give a shape to this history of the self, so that semantic memories and key episodes start to get linked. 'I remember my Dad saying he was really proud of me in my new school uniform and when I did well on sports day.' Or 'I remember feeling humiliated in class and my Gran used to say I was stupid.' On the other hand, there can be contradictory memories: 'My Gran said I was stupid, but I passed my exams and my maths teacher said I was good at maths.' Such complexities are not uncommon.

For children coming into new families, early memories of being treated and referred to as "bad" or "useless" need to be countered by memories of foster and adoptive parents referring to them proudly as "kind", "helpful", "lovely" – though these may need to be delivered indirectly (e.g. in a conversation overheard by the child) as it is only when children have started to trust the intentions, the mind, of the caregiver that they can risk hearing and starting to believe these new messages – a theme discussed throughout this book. All children screen these negative and positive memories for patterns that can make sense of experience, but fostered and adopted children with complex and contradictory stories need active help from adults to manage memories and build a realistic, balanced but generally positive sense of self. Even brief exposure to a more positive care experience in short-term, respite or supported lodgings can offer different memories that sow the seed of the need to revise familiar and negative expectations. But these positive messages and memories need to be frequently (though sensitively) talked about and reinforced for children who have deep-rooted negative ideas about themselves that are resistant to change.

For foster carers and adopters, it is important to think about how new and more positive memories of all kinds are being generated, stored and reflected on as family stories. But it is also important to think about how more difficult memories may resurface unexpectedly at moments of stress and challenge. Sad, traumatic and frightening memories of all kinds may be present but unconscious or suppressed, and can continue to influence behaviour. Children may eventually allow positive new experiences to reshape in a fundamental way their internal working models, but will continue, even in adulthood, to need to manage the troubling feelings and memories that may emerge at unexpected times in response to certain triggers or may persist in dreams. It is acquiring the strategies for managing these moments that is the real gift of foster and adoptive family life. In particular, carers need to promote *the co-construction of new narratives* (Grossman *et al*, 1999), in which children are helped to put memories, ideas and feelings into words and then use these to develop the coherent accounts of their histories and themselves that are the hallmark of security.

Developmental pathways: continuity and change in internal working models

As this account suggests, new experiences may confirm or challenge our expectations and beliefs; internal working models are not seen as fixed in early childhood and can change. They are "working" models and may adapt over time, as experiences fit with existing models or require them to be revised. Such ideas are central to the usefulness of the concept of internal working models for fostering and adoption, both in terms of the persistence of certain mental representations and in terms of the potential for change, since it is on this possibility of change in the context of different family environments that hope for children relies.

It can be helpful to think about the diversity of routes through childhood and adulthood in terms of developmental pathways. Bowlby (1973) conceptualised these pathways as train tracks. Over time and in response to different experiences interacting with the individual's characteristics, the train may branch away from the main line that leads to mental health. But there is the possibility that it can be brought back to the main track by events, by other people (e.g. therapeutic help, new relationships) or by the action of the individual (e.g. striving to fulfil academic potential). Pathways are always a result of interactions between individuals and their environments, between inner and outer worlds. The further the train track moves away from the main line the harder it is to get back on the main track, but there is always the possibility that lines will later converge. This model includes the notion of junctions or *turning points* when different choices might have very different consequences, an element of the model that links well with theories of resilience (Rutter, 1999).

Sroufe (1997) used the analogy of a tree to describe developmental pathways, with each person starting from the base and making their way through the trunk and along different branches that lead to different outcomes at the leafy extremities. This model is also transactional, as different environmental factors interact with one or more factors in the child or some aspect of the system around the child (e.g. health or education) acts as a catalyst for change in other factors. The troubled child discovering a talent for sport needs a teacher who can see past difficult behaviours. The child who finds pleasure in playing with and caring for younger children needs a foster or adoptive family who can support and gradually trust the child. The more damaged the child and the further away from pathways to health, the more the environment needs to support and redirect the child. The changes of direction that count will be those that last and have an effect on improving core aspects of self and relationships, such as self-esteem, self-efficacy, pleasure in closeness and affect regulation. Primarily, change that is likely to have a lasting effect is where the child's state of mind shifts and new, more constructive and coherent internal models begin to outweigh old models of self and others.

Although children's pathways are not fixed for better or worse and internal working models can adapt and change, as these metaphors of a journey and of organic growth suggest, it is necessary to recognise that there will be a *degree of continuity and resistance to change* arising from the fact that beliefs and expectations of self and others can prove *self-fulfilling*. If we take as a simple example the child entering the primary school playground for the first time, we can think of the diversity of outcome depending on what the child brings to this developmental challenge. Where her belief is that she is a lovable little five-year-old girl who is good at making friends and her expectation is that others will like her and want to play with her, then the signals she gives, through her facial expression, body language and initial warm reaction when approached, will be welcomed by other children as a safe invitation to joint activity and a relationship. In contrast, where the child enters the playground believing, on the basis of experience, that she is not lovable and has expectations that others will be indifferent or indeed a threat, her signals through her facial expression and body language will be either needy and helpless or wary, aggressive and defiant. Other children seeking playmates and mutual companionship will steer clear of a child who may overwhelm them, whether by being needy and making too many demands or through aggression. Thus, the anxious child who anticipates rejection finds the further rejection that she most fears, but also finds confirmation of her internal working model of the self as unlovable and others as hostile, reinforcing her expectations and behaviour for the future.

This tendency to act in ways that produce confirmation of our internal working models extends though childhood and adolescence into adulthood. Troubled, anxious and angry birth parents who approach professional agencies for help, whether through the doctor's surgery or the social services office, can produce the same response of rejection in those professionals as children produce in other children and children produce in foster carers and adoptive parents. As with children, this intensifies anxiety and may increase distrust and anger. Of course, foster carers, adopters and social workers are not immune from such downward spirals. When stressed we are all capable of resorting to defensive strategies that alienate others, prove counter-productive and require a sensitive, concerned other to help us stop digging and get out of the hole.

Making sense in this way of the likely persistence of relationship patterns is an important part of our understanding of what children bring into foster care and adoption from their diversely troubled backgrounds. Fostered and adopted infants, children and adolescents who are wary, suspicious and feel unlovable often behave in ways that provoke and perpetuate rejection. They bring with them the strategies that helped them to adapt and survive in adverse family conditions. As Stovall and Dozier (1998, p. 65) have described in their study of infants in foster care, even babies who come into new families from neglectful or abusive backgrounds are often not able to elicit sensitive care nor respond to it. Infants may be very passive and shut off or very fretful and angry. They cannot signal when they have needs and lack the usual responses to a caregiver's smiling face or a gentle touch. They may appear independent and resist care. Such babies are not rewarding to care for nor easily comforted and so can make even experienced carers feel as if they are failing (see Chapters 3, 4 and 5 on insecure patterns of attachment).

The major difficulty for maltreated and troubled children in entering new families is a profound lack of trust and the fact that survival adaptations make them highly resistant to accepting or learning from new and different experiences of caregiving. Maltreated children in particular often find it difficult to process new information about reality (Crittenden, 1995), to believe that loving foster carers or adoptive parents are not like previous adult caregivers and that perhaps the mental representation of "adult caregivers" in their internal working model might need to be changed. When driven by anxiety about survival and needing to stay in control, it is familiar, easier and perhaps safer for children to believe that this new experience is just a *trick* – these new caregivers are just more clever at concealing their true feelings and hostile intentions. Thus carers who attempt to provide a secure base may be viewed with distrust and suspicion as people to be controlled, as sources of anxiety rather than sources of security.

> *The individual may so distrust both affect and cognition that even discrepant information may not trigger the mind to re-explore reality. Instead the mind may determine that this too is trickery and deception or that the risk of mistakenly responding as though it were true is too great to be tolerated. In such cases, the representation of reality is like a false, inverted mirror image in which good and bad, true and false are reversed.* (Crittenden, 1995, p. 401)

Important, then, is the idea that working models can change to accommodate new experiences, which suggests a *window of opportunity* for shifts towards security in the context of subsequent relationships, whether in the birth family or in a substitute family or residential care. However, the persistence of internal working models and defensive strategies that are associated with adverse early experiences and lack of trust explains why such shifts can often prove so difficult to achieve and require skilled care, patience and, often, professional support. Some children can be so averse to the intimacy of family relationships that every day is a battle and progress is very slow. In contrast, other children may make rapid and dramatic progress in the first weeks and months of placement – like thirsty young plants who are ready to soak up and use the nourishing care they receive. The challenge for foster carers and adopters is to remain equally available, attuned and committed to both kinds of children – and all those in between – when it is impossible to predict with any degree of accuracy prior to placement the rate and extent of progress that a particular child will make.

Attachment formation and development: key stages

From these core concepts, we move on to think about the stages in building an attachment relationship as it occurs in infancy and develops through childhood. This section builds on the core concepts and sets out an age-related framework that forms the basis for subsequent chapters on secure and insecure patterns of attachment.

It is important at the outset to distinguish between the infant *forming an attachment* to the caregiver and the caregiver *bonding* with the infant. Since, as has already been described, attachment formation is derived from the drive to seek proximity to a figure who provides safety, protection and a secure base, it can only be appropriate for a dependent infant to seek this from an adult caregiver rather than the other way round. It is therefore not accurate when applying attachment theory to talk of a parent's "attachment to the child". Bonding, in contrast, is about the caregiver's sense of commitment, concern, responsibility and love for the child. Although the caregiver–child relationship *is* like a mutual dance in which it is the interaction between the two partners that produces the quality of relationship, the *contribution* of each partner is different. Although secure attachment relationships are often described as reciprocal and, if secure, are indeed attuned and mutually pleasurable, the child should be gaining love, companionship *and* care and protection from the caregiver, but the caregiver gains love, companionship *and* a sense of satisfaction and reward from the child's happiness and progress. The roles are quite distinct and it is helpful to make this distinction when using the term "attachment".

Secondly, it is important to bear in mind that even from conception and certainly at birth the child is not a "blank slate" and will be a unique individual with many characteristics to bring to the new relationship. Genetic factors, ranging from temperament to chromosomal abnormalities, will have an impact on the early relationship, as will pre-natal environmental factors, such as maternal rubella or alcohol and drug misuse. Babies exposed to drugs *in utero*, for example, frequently have difficulties in settling physically or emotionally even when offered sensitive care (Phillips, 2004). Parents need to adapt to the child's different characteristics and needs, just as the child is adapting to the parents. In a transactional model, the child will be shaping the parent's behaviour as the parent is shaping the child's, and both will be operating within influences from a wider ecological system of family, community and culture.

The process of *attachment formation* begins at birth, when newborn infants are seeking care and protection through proximity to the attachment figure, but are also alert to the messages they receive about themselves and the world around them. These messages are reflected in the face of the caregiver and in the infant's experience of the way in which urgent needs for care and comfort are met. Pre-birth experiences of all kinds have some contribution to make here. Parents will have anticipated the birth with a range of expectations and infants build on pre-birth exposure to voices by rapidly showing a preference first for the mother's voice and then her face, with preference for the father and other primary caregivers following as experience shows that they too are sources of care and safety. Such sensitivity to the detail of the environment is protective in helping the infant to tune in to its potentially most protective aspects, just as caregivers are tuning in to the infant in order to meet her need for protection and care. On the other hand, such infant sensitivity will mean that even small changes in the nuances of behaviour, tone of voice or routine may cause the child to react with anger, distress or withdrawal. Infants can recover and learn to cope with occasional "breaks", but find it very distressing when a flat, inexpressive caregiver's face consistently fails to respond to their facial expressions, an important part of our understanding of the impact of post-natal depression on children's cognitive and emotional development (Murray and Cooper, 1997).

From the *first minutes after birth* infants are processing information about their environment and will be attempting to make sense of the world around them and in particular the world that is reflected back to them through the face of the caregiver and represented through the accuracy and timing of their caregiver's responses. The process of *mirroring* enables the child to experience their feelings as reflected back to them by the face of the caregiver. An angry or sad or surprised facial expression in the infant will be imitated by the caregiver. The infant's eyebrows may be raised, the forehead has a little frown or the mouth opens wide and the caregiver's face, quite unconsciously, does the same – and may even exaggerate the expression momentarily. But the caregiver's face will then subtly change – the eyebrows come back to normal, the forehead clears and the amazed mouth dissolves into a smile. The infant's feelings are acknowledged and empathised with, but then softened, managed and contained through adjustments in the caregiver's face. Thus anxiety can be turned into something bearable. This non-verbal exchange is often accompanied by commentary (even including the momentary exaggeration) that has the same purpose and effect – though again is quite spontaneous. 'Oh dear, you are hungry! You poor thing – you must be starving – Mummy took so long. I know, I know, I know, there there, it won't be long now. Here we go . . . let's just get you comfortable . . . there . . . that's better isn't it?' Difficult feelings are acknowledged to be as legitimate as positive feelings, but difficult feelings are made safe so that the infant begins to understand that such feelings need not overwhelm them. At this age it is only the tone and rhythm of the voice that helps to contain and settle the child but in time the words will have meanings that become important messages for the child. This is the infant's first experience of the *co-regulation of emotions*, part of the synchrony and the dance that starts at birth.

By *three months* or so, the baby is increasingly selective, already beginning to smile less readily for strangers and targeting attachment behaviours more accurately to significant caregivers. From this point on, the caregiver–child relationship is increasingly in synchrony, with the infant and caregiver timing their responses and regulating their behaviour to fit each other and the infant becoming an increasingly active partner. Not only is the sensitive caregiver treating the infant as a distinct whole person with ideas, beliefs and intentions, but the infant also can begin to distinguish primary caregivers from other people and to predict how familiar caregivers, in particular, will respond.

By around *six to seven months*, infants will generally show a clear-cut attachment to one or more caregivers. The infant actively behaves in ways that attract the attention and concern of the caregiver or caregivers to whom they are selectively attached and sensitive caregivers tune in accurately to the infant's communications and needs. Most significantly, the infant protests and shows distress and anxiety about being separated from their preferred caregiver or caregivers, with an attachment hierarchy of parents and other key people starting to form. Around that time, the baby is also likely to show signs of anxiety about strangers, becoming less likely to tolerate being handed to other people to hold, for example.

There follows a period in which securely attached infants and toddlers build on this preferred attachment relationship as they become increasingly interested in *shared exploration* with toys, play and peers, although their primary attachment relationships will remain key to their healthy development. Relationships with fathers develop in parallel to relationships with mothers, although the paternal relationship seems particularly geared up to promote and support exploration and play (Grossman *et al*, 1999). Key to the process of secure attachment formation with both parents, or indeed other attachment figures, is the fact that the secure child will be able to use those attachment figures to provide a *secure base* for exploration.

But it is also important to note that the sensitive care and interpersonal experiences between infant and caregiver as attachments are built in these early months will have had an impact on the physiology of the brain, 'generating the circuits that are responsible for affect regulation and stress recovery mechanisms' (Diamond and Marrone, 2003, p. 25). Schore (1994) has shown that, in attachment relationships, early interactions can lay down the foundation in the brain for the child becoming able to reflect on the self and learning to regulate feelings, both of which are crucial, as we have seen, for mutual and successful social relationships. On the other hand, abuse and neglect negatively affect the ability of the infant brain to organise emotions and regulate stress (Perry *et al*, 1995).

As children move through *the toddler and pre-school years*, increasing individuation and sociability drive development as children learn to define themselves and others in more sophisticated ways. Developments in locomotion (the ability to walk and run towards and away from people and things), in the cognitive capacity to represent others and ideas, in communicative and negotiating abilities, in self-knowledge and understanding and in the knowledge and understanding that come from perspective taking all help children build on the secure foundations of infancy.

The child will then move towards the next major transitional stage in the relationship with the attachment figure, a development Bowlby (1969) described as a 'goal corrected partnership'. At this stage, children who have had their minds and behaviour thought about and understood and have been given access to the caregiver's thoughts and feelings through a process of open communication, become more sophisticated in understanding their caregiver's mind and behaviour. This is, in turn, reflected in their ability to adapt their own behaviour and goals to the goals of the other within the attachment relationship and to regulate their feelings and behaviour. The child understands, for example, that the caregiver has their own needs and moods and that demands are more likely to be received positively at one time than another, e.g. not when dad is cooking a meal or mum is rushing round looking for the car keys. There is thus an increased likelihood of negotiation and co-operation between caregiver and child, a model of mutuality in relationships that will assist the child in meeting her needs for care and proximity within the family, but also in making constructive relationships with peers and with a wider group of adults outside the family.

From the age of four or five, children take their secure and insecure internal working models into the new challenges of school. The balance between the attachment and exploratory systems is still important as secure and insecure primary school-age children manage anxiety in different ways and attachment difficulties and preoccupations impact on learning and friendships. The need for a secure base, stored mentally during the school day and available in person at the beginning and end of it, is essential for successful coping, although some children can find elements of a secure base in the sensitive teacher or lunchtime supervisor, who as secondary attachment figures can make potentially risky environments seem more manageable. Here, the notion of attachment hierarchies is helpful (Kearns and Richardson, 2005) with different figures inside and outside the birth family performing a range of aspects of the function of the primary attachment figure and being significant figures in their own right in the child's life.

At this age and stage, anxiety about separation and loss of the attachment figure is joined by anxieties about self-esteem and fitting in with their peers – key developments at this age. These anxieties are interwoven, as anxiety about the self is increased where children lack confidence in the availability and support of their attachment figures and decreased where children have stored memories and positive internal working models that help them recover from rejections and setbacks. If we think of the range of responses to a disappointing result in a spelling test or not being invited to a popular child's party, we can see the way in which the school-age child needs to find *strategies* to protect the self. Secure constructive strategies in these examples would involve acknowledging the feelings of disappointment and reflecting on the situation in terms of maybe needing to work harder for the test or having other parties to go to. Insecure defensive strategies might include denying the feelings – tests and parties don't matter – and/or become angry, aggressive or helplessly sad.

In *adolescence*, the move towards degrees of separation from attachment figures and the assumption of independent adult roles challenge the adaptive capacity of all children. This challenge is managed more straightforwardly by securely attached children who have achieved and preserved high self-esteem and a sense of competence alongside their representations of others as available and supportive. In adolescence, the secure base offered by attachment relationships continues to support exploration, but attachment figures are also actively involved in the stage-specific task of enabling teenagers to regulate the powerful emotions that impending separation will provoke. Furthermore, the change in thinking patterns in adolescence enables teenagers to begin to integrate internal working models that relate to specific attachment figures into a more coherent, single yet flexible model (Allen and Land, 1999). Thus, the teenager may think (quite realistically), 'I can get help from some people when I'm hurt but not others, so I have to be careful which people I get close to'.

In later adolescence and adulthood, attachment relationships in the family of origin persist, but new attachments can be formed in romantic relationships and in friendships. These more mutual systems of support, in which each partner is providing a secure base for the other, will nevertheless have many of the same characteristics of earlier attachment relationships e.g. proximity becomes more important when stresses arise; anxiety about separation and loss is common; open communication is important for relationships to be secure.

These developmental processes are explored in detail in subsequent chapters, both those that focus on children's attachment patterns and those focussing on parenting/caregiving dimensions. However, the key message from this outline of developmental stages is that progression through childhood to adulthood will follow some broadly defined stages, but that each stage will be affected by experiences in relationships that interact with the child's own characteristics to shape the quality of future relationships. Cross-cultural studies confirm the fact that, although similar patterns can be identified in other cultures (van IJzendoorn and Kroonenberg, 1988), different cultural practices around parenting and child care will also contribute to the quality of relationships and the outcomes for the child in terms of security and insecurity.

Secure and insecure patterns of attachment

Having described some of the core concepts in attachment theory and outlined attachment formation, it is necessary to outline the *different patterns* of secure and insecure attachment that emerge in the context of *different caregiving experiences*. Attachment theory is built on the premise that the different behaviours that children show in their relationships with others and the different internal working models that drive those behaviours are to a significant extent attributable to the different kinds of caregiving they have received. Subsequent chapters describe in greater detail the developmental route through each secure and insecure pattern.

Dimensions of caregiving

Dimensions of caregiving that are associated with different outcomes in terms of security and insecurity in infancy were identified in research by Ainsworth *et al* (1978) and seem particularly helpful in understanding the roots of attachment patterns. These dimensions, availability, sensitivity, acceptance and co-operation are presented here in a framework that is later used to make links with the caregiving likely to promote security for children in foster care and adoption. Key to this model is the fact that these are *dimensions*, with caregivers falling some-where along the range from, for example, available to unavailable, sensitive to insensitive, accepting to rejecting and co-operative to intrusive.

- **Being available – helping children to trust** Essential to lowering the anxiety of the child is the caregiver's ability to remain available and accessible to the child when the child should seek proximity for care and protection. The child learns that lines of communication with the attachment figure are open and the caregiver will keep the child in mind and respond if called upon for help. This offers the child a secure base from which he can safely venture out to explore, play and learn.

- **Responding sensitively – helping children to manage feelings and behaviour** Sensitive caregivers are able to see the world from the child's point of view and treat the child as having a mind that needs to be understood. They tune in to the child's signals of need and expressions of feelings, using their understanding to respond in ways that reduce anxiety and help the child to manage feelings and behaviour. They provide scaffolding for experience, naming as well as responding to feelings and enabling the child to reflect, to pause for thought when strong feelings need to be managed.

- **Accepting the child – building self-esteem** Caregivers who accept and value the whole child, understand that each child is a unique and complex being who has particular characteristics, strengths and difficulties. Children who receive the message that they are accepted and valued for who they are by important people in their lives develop a balanced, realistic but positive self-concept and raised self -esteem.

- **Co-operative caregiving – helping children to feel effective** Co-operative caregivers not only understand that children from birth onwards need to assert themselves, but actively promote the child's effectiveness and autonomy. They form a co-operative alliance with the child, following the child's lead rather than intruding, allowing the child to direct play and supporting their choices. They provide safe boundaries within which behaviour can be negotiated and children can cope with failure and enjoy success.

Additional to the four dimensions identified by Ainsworth, we have added a fifth dimension that captures the psychosocial dimension of family membership, an important factor in providing a secure base that is particularly relevant in family placement.

- **Promoting family membership – helping children to belong** Children need to grow up knowing that they have a secure place within a family where they belong. Children learn that they have both rights and responsibilities in relation to other family members. This experience of belonging in the new family needs to be actively created, alongside supporting the child's sense of belonging to the birth family. The balance between families will be different depending on the plan for permanence, but even in short-term and respite care placements children can expect to feel that they belong during their stay in the foster family. Feeling part of the family is an important foundation for emotional and behavioural progress.

If we use these dimensions to think about ways in which infants and children develop strategies to feel safe, then we can see how attachment patterns emerge.

- **Secure:** Secure attachment occurs when the infant is cared for sensitively, has available, accessible and *flexible* caregivers, feels understood, accepted and valued and is helped to make choices and be effective. Taking these strengths into childhood, the child builds on high self-esteem, self-efficacy and the capacity to think about and manage thoughts, feelings and behaviour in order also to become effective and successful outside the family. In later adolescence and adulthood, this pattern is referred to as *autonomous, free to evaluate*.

- **Avoidant:** When the caregiver finds it difficult to accept or respond sensitively to the infant's needs, the infant may find their demands are rejected, their feelings minimised and that the caregiver tries to take over in an intrusive, insensitive way. Although the *rejecting* caregiver's overall role in providing care and protection continues, the infant or child learns to shut down on her feelings in order to avoid upsetting the caregiver and provoking rejection or intrusion. It is more comfortable to be self-reliant and this also makes it more likely that the caregiver will stay close. In later adolescence and adulthood, this pattern of minimising the importance of feelings and relationships is referred to as *dismissing*.

- **Ambivalent:** In contrast, where the caregiver responds to the infant's demands, but only in a sporadic, unpredictable and at times insensitive fashion, the infant finds it difficult to achieve proximity in a reliable way. Care and protection are sometimes available, but the caregiving is *uncertain* and ineffective. Initially, the infant may simply make demands almost constantly to attract and keep the attention of the caregiver or may become rather helpless in the absence of an available strategy. Over time, the infant becomes a preoccupied, demanding, clingy but distrustful and resistant child. In later adolescence and adulthood, this pattern is referred to as *preoccupied and enmeshed.*

- **Disorganised:** Where the caregiver is rejecting, unpredictable *and* frightening or frightened, the infant is caught in a dilemma of 'fear without solution' (Main and Hesse, 1990). Caregivers abdicate the caregiving role, representing themselves as out of control and are *hostile/helpless* to protect the child. The infant's drive to approach the caregiver for care and protection results in fear and increased rather than decreased anxiety. The absence of a strategy in infancy leads to confused and disorganised behaviours, but over time the child starts to develop controlling behaviours to enable them to feel some degree of safety. However, feelings of anxiety and fear remain unresolved and reappear at times of stress. In later adolescence and adulthood, this pattern is referred to as *unresolved.*

One of the key messages for the *accurate use of attachment theory* and *attachment patterns in practice* is that professionals need to focus first on the *distinction between secure and insecure patterns* of attachment. It is unhelpful and can be positively dangerous to think in terms of "strong" or "weak" attachment and to use this language in assessments. For example, an ambivalent child who displays extreme feelings at separation is no more "strongly" attached than an avoidant child who conceals them. Disorganised children who have been abused still maintain powerful ties to their abusive parents. Both secure and insecure attachment relationships have developed in the context of a powerful drive for proximity, care and protection and although the behaviour strategies and relationship patterns that emerge differ, the "strength" of the relationship is not a helpful indicator of the impact on the child's development or the value of the relationship. The danger is that, when "strong" attachments are referred to, they tend to become synonymous at a common sense level with "good" or even "secure" attachments. This can, in turn, become, for example, an argument for reunification with the birth family, for high levels of contact or for not pursuing a plan for adoption. This is particularly true where children have become caregivers for their drug and alcohol misusing, learning disabled or mentally ill parents. Children may deny any problems and express strong views about their wish/need to return home (Forrester and Harwin, 2004). In such cases, inaccurate use of attachment theory could put children at risk of further abuse and neglect or of missing the opportunity for an appropriate permanent placement.

The second important message is that practitioners need to distinguish between *organised and disorganised* patterns of insecure attachment. Avoidant and ambivalent insecure patterns are organised strategies which "work" to some extent e.g. the avoidant infant/child does succeed in keeping the caregiver close by not demanding too much and the ambivalent infant/child does succeed in getting some attention from the caregiver by displaying feelings.

In contrast, the *disorganised* infant lacks any strategy that can manage the experience of a caregiver who increases anxiety rather than provides protection. Even when disorganised children start to develop controlling strategies, these are not coherent attempts to achieve a relationship, but rather ways of staying safe. Maltreated disorganised children may also show symptoms of dissociation – cutting off from experience and again creating distance rather than relationships. It is disorganisation rather than insecurity itself which represents the most significant risk for development. (See Chapter 5 for further discussion of maltreatment and disorganisation.)

Attachment disorders

Some children who experience extreme attachment related difficulties are said by a range of professionals, carers and parents to have an *attachment disorder*. Attachment disorder is, however, a medical diagnosis which should only be made by a clinical practitioner. Two sub-types of attachment disorder are recognised, *inhibited* and *disinhibited*.

> *The inhibited subtype is marked by hypervigilance and fear that is manifested by withdrawal and ambivalence. The disinhibited subtype is distinguished by indiscriminate friendliness and the absence of a selective attachment to a discriminated figure who is sought for comfort.* (Greenberg 1999, p. 470–71)

But the concept of "attachment disorder" remains difficult to use in practice, at least in part because there is no agreement as to assessment or appropriate treatments.

> *We must acknowledge that there is as yet no systematic evidence-based approach for treating children with attachment disorders. Moreover, the very concept of attachment disorders is a controversial one because of the substantial remaining questions about assessment and diagnosis.* (Steele 2003, p. 219)

In this context, Howard Steele's recommendation is that the starting point for any intervention using attachment theory must be Bowlby's concept of a secure base (Bowlby, 1988).

> *The emphasis is on the fundamental need for the therapist to provide a secure*

base from which the patient's internal working models of relationships, regarding the present and past, may be explored. The need for the client to feel understood and respected is a precondition to the updating of these internal models and the experience of positive change. Throughout, the therapist must hold in mind or be sensitive to the patient's present and past, conscious and unconscious, emotional worries. (Steele 2003, p. 219)

For "therapist" here we can think of the foster carer or adoptive parent, since a sensitively and respectfully provided secure base for exploration is also what needs to be offered to children in the context of family relationships in foster care and adoption. Mind-mindedness and the capacity to reflect on the thoughts and feelings of the child will be difficult but essential for even the most troubled children.

The premise in this book is that just as the child's insecurity, trauma, dysregulation and controlling strategies originated in family relationships, so affect regulation and organisation, security and resilience need to be built in new therapeutic family relationships in foster care and adoption. The concept of providing a secure base through availability, sensitivity, acceptance and co-operation is at the heart of therapeutic family relationships. The expectation must be that these processes take time, that there are no quick fixes, and that change will be seen in small incremental shifts in the child's thinking and behaviour. But time alone will not be enough to achieve change and healing – parenting must be targeted and focused around *actively* resolving feelings about the past and *building* strengths for the present and the future. For many children and families this will require access to multi-disciplinary support and advice.

Measuring security/insecurity of attachment

There are a number of measures of attachment security used by researchers internationally, but here it is intended to focus on outlining those key measures that are most widely quoted in research relevant to family placement and which will be used during the book to help explain aspects of secure and insecure attachment patterns at different ages and stages.

The Strange Situation

From the outset, attachment theory was developed by Bowlby in an attempt to explain psychopathology as well as health (Bowlby, 1944, 1951). The use of attachment theory to understand individual differences in relation to security and insecurity was greatly enhanced by the work of Mary Ainsworth, a colleague of John Bowlby at the Tavistock Clinic in the 1940s. Her observational studies with mothers and infants in Uganda, in particular the infants' responses to separation, were followed by the development of the "Strange Situation" in the USA (Ainsworth *et al*, 1978). The Strange Situation is an experimental procedure which measures *in infancy* (12–18 months) the secure and insecure patterns of attachment, as described above, that develop in the context of different kinds of caregiving.

In an unfamiliar playroom setting, infants are taken through a series of brief events of separation and reunion which are designed to activate the infant's attachment behavioural system. Each part of the sequence lasts a maximum of three minutes – with the caregiver returning more quickly after a separation if the baby continues to show distress. The researcher (and the caregiver during separations) can observe the child through a one-way mirror. The sequence of events is as follows:

- Caregiver and baby: caregiver is inactive and infant is free to explore.
- An unfamiliar female adult enters room – sits, then talks to caregiver, then attempts to engage infant.
- Caregiver leaves.
- The stranger and infant are left together.
- The caregiver returns and the stranger leaves. The caregiver settles infant and leaves.
- The infant is left alone.
- The stranger returns.
- The caregiver returns again and the stranger leaves.

The infant's behaviour is video recorded, coded and analysed to examine what has been revealed about the infant's mental representations from the way in which they react to the play materials, to separation and to reunion. As Steele and Steele (1994, p. 95) have described it, the Strange Situation is a 'window on the child's internal working model of the child–caregiver relationship'. Each child's behaviour pattern in the Strange Situation can be understood in relation to the quality of caregiving that has been experienced and its consequence for the child's state of mind, internal working model and behavioural strategies. Thus the secure child may be distressed at separation, but at reunion trust in the caregiver is quickly restored and the child returns to play, whereas the ambivalent child who doubts the availability of the caregiver is clingy but also angry and resists comfort, and does not easily return to play. (More detail of each pattern is given in Chapters 2–4.)

Thus, the balance between *attachment and exploration* can be judged in terms of how easily the child is able to manage these different separation events and return to play, and the *specificity* of the attachment relationship is understood in terms of the infant's reactions to the caregiver and to the stranger. It was through the Strange Situation research, that Ainsworth (1978) identified three patterns: secure (B); insecure–avoidant (A); and insecure–ambivalent/resistant (C). The disorganised pattern was not initially recognised when Mary Ainsworth developed the Strange Situation during the 1970s. There were, however, a group of children who did not fall into the three secure and insecure patterns that she had identified. When tapes of these infants and some from other samples were re-analysed by Main and Solomon (1986), they were found to show diverse and often contradictory behaviours, but behaviours which could be seen as demonstrating the approach/avoid dilemma that is a result of seeking comfort from a caregiver who is frightened or frightening – such as crawling towards the caregiver but then freezing, or crying as if wanting contact but simultaneously backing away with eyes averted.

When infants are classified as disorganised in the Strange Situation, they are in most cases also given a "best fit" secondary classification. Thus, a child might receive the classification of disorganised/avoidant, disorganised/ambivalent or disorganised/secure. Infants will show disorganised behaviour at separation or reunion i.e. the points of greatest stress, but otherwise may show characteristics of avoidance or ambivalence/resistance or security at other points in the procedure. This suggests that there is a collapse in the child's strategy when stressed and fearful. Thus a child may play like a secure child, protest at separation, appear to be returning to play as a secure child would at reunion, but then lie flat and still on the floor instead.

> *Disorganised attachment can be described as the breakdown of an otherwise consistent and organised strategy of emotion regulation.* (van IJzendoorn et al, 1999, p. 226)

This use of a dual classification (disorganised *and* an organised secure or insecure pattern) may appear to be an unnecessary complication for practitioners to under-stand. But, in fact, it is helpful in making sense of the range of different behaviours shown by children who have experiences of maltreatment and behavioural signs of disorganisation. When infants and children who are classified as disorganised are not stressed, they may show behaviours more typical of those discussed in one of the next three chapters on secure, avoidant and ambivalent/resistant children. Although, as van IJzendoorn *et al* (1999, p. 226) also point out, 'in some cases the disorganisation of attachment is so prominent that a secondary, organised strategy cannot be detected.'

Story stems

As children move from infancy to pre-school and early middle childhood, it becomes necessary for researchers to use other methods of gaining access to the child's internal working model and attachment patterns (George, 1996). A widely used measure in research for children aged 4–8 is the story stem completion test. In this procedure, a child is presented with a doll family or, in some cases, an animal family, and the beginning of a hypothetical story about an event in the doll figure's family life. Children are then invited to show and tell the researcher what they think will happen next. The use of story stems of this kind was first seen in the MacArthur story stems and they have provided a particularly rich source of material which, by giving access to children's mental representations, can enable researchers to classify children in secure and insecure patterns (Bretherton et al, 1990; Solomon et al, 1995). They have also been used specifically with adopted children (Hodges et al, 2003) to trace associations between children's and parents' attachment patterns (Steele et al, 2003; Hodges et al, 2003). Other researchers have developed similar instruments such as the Manchester Child Attachment Story Test (MCAST) (Goldwyn et al, 2000; Green et al, 2000). Although most commonly used in research, story stems are also sometimes used by clinicians, practitioners and in court-ordered assessments to help in the understanding of the mental representations, the internal working models of individual children. Story stems should only be used to classify a child's attachment pattern by someone who is qualified to do so by undertaking the appropriate training.

As in the Strange Situation, the content of the story stem is designed to create some kind of attachment-related anxiety for the child which activates the attachment system. This will prompt the child to complete the story in ways which reveal their mental representations of the relationship between self and caregivers. For example, one story is of a child spilling a drink while the family are watching television and another is of a child falling down in the park and hurting his knee. Separation and loss, illness and fear are often represented e.g. parents who go away for a weekend or a child lost in a shopping mall. In the analysis of the child's stories, there is particular interest in 'the degree to which the child represents adults as comforting and capable of caregiving as compared to injuring or neglectful' (M. Steele et al, 1999, p. 20). There is also interest in the extent to which feelings are acknowledged, dramas and crises in the narrative are resolved and the overall coherence of the story is sustained. (Further discussion can be found in Chapters 2–5).

Adult Attachment Interview

The instrument most commonly used in research for classifying the attachment patterns of *older adolescents and adults* is the Adult Attachment Interview (AAI) (Hesse, 1999; Main and Goldwyn, 1984). The AAI asks questions about relationships which also raise anxiety levels to a certain degree and 'provokes a discourse of attachment-related memories'. This reveals how the adult is organising thoughts and feelings and using 'different strategies or rules to access, process and express attachment-related material' (Main, 1995, p. 420). It is a semi-structured interview which, although asking apparently simple questions about childhood and significant relationships up to the present day, has the effect of 'surprising the unconscious'. Adults are asked, for instance, to respond to the question: 'Can you give me five adjectives to describe your relationship with your mother in childhood?' They are then asked to give examples for each word. This is then repeated with questions about the father. The ability to provide examples that support each adjective is key to the interview. There are also specific questions about separations, losses and abuse in childhood.

Coding of the interview transcript relies less on the *content* of the story than on the *manner* of its telling, in particular its coherence. The responses are rated on whether they are relevant, appropriate in length and detail, and suggest that the subject is able to collaborate with the interviewer. It is through the lengthy analysis of the fine detail of the language used and the pattern of response and conversational interaction with the interviewer that it is possible to classify individuals according to the different secure and insecure patterns. This is an extremely complex process of analysis as manner and content are separated out. For example, adults who have experienced loss, neglect or abuse in childhood will not necessarily be rated as insecure on the AAI – a fact that may be very relevant in thinking about the life histories of prospective foster carers and adoptive parents. What matters is how those experiences have been processed, at the time and since. It is this which will be determining the current internal working model, the mental representations of self and relationships, and the behaviour that results. For some adults there may be evidence in the interview that it has been possible to reflect on and evaluate difficult or even traumatic experiences in a coherent and relatively non-defended way (Main and Goldwyn, 1984; Hesse, 1999). These adults may then be rated as secure autonomous/free to evaluate, because they demonstrate what is described as 'earned security' (Pearson *et al*, 1994 cited in Howe *et al*, 1999).

The AAI is very time-consuming to administer, transcribe and rate, and to qualify to undertake the AAI rating requires a lengthy training process taking up to two years. In research, each interview would be independently coded by two qualified raters. The interview is not, therefore, a means for *classifying* adults which could be used by social work practitioners in their everyday work. Although some agencies use the core questions in their assessment interviews with foster carers and adopters, they need to take great care not to present the outcome as a formal classification. However, even though the AAI will rarely be used in practice, it is important for practitioners using attachment theory to understand the principles of the AAI, since it has been the basis of so much attachment research. Understanding the AAI also helps us to understand aspects of how adult states of mind in the different patterns are reflected in the way they construct a narrative of their lives. It helps us think about how to make sense, for example, of accounts where parents – whether birth, foster or adoptive – seem to have idealised their childhood and their parents or find it hard even in adult life to get beyond preoccupying anger with their attachment figures.

To appreciate the use that has been made of these measures of attachment in research we can consider, for example, their value in establishing evidence of a correlation between the adult attachment pattern of caregivers and the attachment pattern of their infants. This has been very influential in our understanding of intergenerational links. Fonagy *et al* (1991) found that a mother's attachment pattern, as measured in the AAI during pregnancy, predicted their infant's attachment pattern in the *Strange Situation* at 12 months in 75 per cent of cases. This is not a perfect correlation i.e. not 100 per cent (suggesting that other factors can intervene, such as the quality of support for the mother), but it has helped to provide good evidence of the way in which attachment patterns are passed from mother to infant. As Hesse (1999) puts it, what is most striking about this research is that the *discourse*, the way in which in which the mother *talks* about her life and relationships (regardless of the life content) predicts the *behaviour* of the infant in the Strange Situation at one year in highly specific ways. So, for example, the combination of internal coherence, consistency and collaboration in the secure mother's attachment interview seems likely to predict her infant's secure behaviour in the Strange Situation. (Further discussion can be found in Chapters 2–5).

Summary points

- Infants are biologically programmed to seek proximity to attachment figures for care and protection
- The available and sensitive caregiver provides a secure base that liberates the child to explore and learn.
- Mind-mindedness in the caregiver promotes mind-mindedness in the child – which helps the child to regulate their feelings and their behaviour.

- The infant adapts to the particular kind of caregiving experience in order to maximise chances of care and protection and to feel safe.
- Infants form internal mental representations of other people, of themselves and of relationships. These lead to internal working models – sets of beliefs and expectations that influence behaviour.
- Separation and loss of attachment figures causes grief which needs to be resolved.

Some key messages for practice

- An attachment relationship in childhood is *not* necessarily a close or loving relationship – children form attachments to caregivers who offer sensitive care, but also to caregivers who are insensitive or who abuse and frighten them. These may be equally "strong" attachments – a term that must be avoided in practice in favour of "secure" and "insecure" attachments.
- The quality of caregiving (and the presence or absence of a secure base for a child) will have an effect on the way in which the child's mind, internal working models, exploration, behaviour and relationships develop.
- There is a process of ongoing adaptation to caregiving environments that leads to identifiable secure and insecure patterns, but within each pattern there will be a range. So, for example, even among secure children, some, when stressed, will be more likely to show their upset than others.
- Attachments can form at any age and stage but are likely to be affected by previous relationships.
- There is a degree of continuity of attachment patterns from infancy to early childhood and to adolescence, *but* a major feature of this continuity is likely to be the continuity of care from caregivers who continue to reinforce the child's pattern (to be more or less secure or organised) by their style of caregiving.
- Where children experience life events that disrupt that pattern of caregiving, whether for better or worse, in the direction of more or less sensitive caregiving, then the child's attachment pattern may change. Secure infants may become insecure children; insecure infants may become secure children.
- This potential for change for the good provides the window of opportunity for sensitive foster and adoptive parents to make a difference to children's development, their security and happiness.

2 Secure–autonomous patterns

Infants whose caregivers are sensitive and responsive learn that they are thought about, loved and can readily get their needs met. Because discomfort and anxiety are relieved by their caregivers, babies can pay attention to the world flexibly, being interested in their caregivers and other people, and enjoying the exploration of toys and new experiences.

Being thought about and knowing from experience that problems can be resolved, children go on to become flexible thinkers themselves. As toddlers and pre-schoolers, they develop a range of strategies for coping with each new social and practical situation they face. They can express the full range of positive and negative emotions, happiness and sadness, joy and rage, but learn to regulate these emotions and their behaviour constructively, selecting options that manage situations co-operatively and in a pro-social manner. Their strategies work increasingly well as they become able to anticipate, read and take into account the thoughts and feelings of others, as well as appropriately asserting their own right to get needs met. Secure children are likely to feel confident in themselves and their environment. Socially competent and emotionally intelligent as pre-schoolers, they enter middle childhood with interest and enthusiasm, keen to make and keep friends and happy to learn. As adolescents they face the threat of separation with appropriate anxiety, but with some degree of confidence in their own resources and their ability to access the resources offered by other people, in particular their continuing secure base attachment figures. Key here is the continuing role of *mastery*, *emotional regulation* and *capacity for interpersonal closeness* (Weinfield *et al*, 1999).

This progress through childhood is by no means guaranteed based on early experiences. Continuity of secure pattern attachment is likely to arise because of the continuing security offered by the secure base attachment figures, who lay these foundations in infancy, but then continue to support the child with availability and sensitivity through to adulthood. Where the quality of care changes, children's security will be affected.

It is important for social work practitioners to think about what security means at each stage of the child's development. Although only a minority of children entering foster care or adoption will have a secure attachment pattern, there are some children who have experienced good enough care but who can no longer be looked after in their birth family, for example, following parental illness or if a child's disability can no longer be managed. Even for children with very troubled histories, there may have been protective elements, such as an emotionally supportive aunt, grandparent or family friend, who laid the basis for some aspects of security in the child's mind. Additionally, there will be children moving into a permanent family from a secure attachment relationship in a short-term or bridging placement.

It is also essential to understand the development of secure attachment, since throughout this book we will be building on knowledge about what promotes security in intact birth family caregiver–child relationships in order to construct a model of therapeutic parenting which promotes security for children in foster care and adoption. Using Ainsworth's caregiving dimensions, it is possible to see the way in which at each developmental stage *availability*, *sensitivity*, *acceptance* and *co-operation* work together to promote the child's competence, sense of security and resilience.

Infancy (birth–18 months)

At birth (if pregnancy and labour have gone relatively smoothly), the infant arrives in an alert state, ready to engage with the world. The voice of the mother is already familiar, but now a face can be put to the voice and other faces – dad's, big sister's, grandparent's – can become extra sources of delight and information about the self and the world. The importance of these early interactions should not be underestimated in understanding the power of attachment relationships to influence development during these first months.

As soon as their child is born, the *sensitive* caregiver is seeing and thinking about the child as a whole person with a mind. One father was heard saying to his newborn son, 'I wonder what you're thinking? I bet you're thinking, who is this big man then? I'm your dad!' Quite spontaneously, parents try to find out about and make sense of the mind of the infant. They communicate interest and affection. They can only speculate on what the baby is thinking, but the assumptions are positive and joyful, anticipating that the child is going to want to know and love them. This process of thinking about, valuing and *accepting* the child as a unique person with a mind of his own forms part of the subtle and powerful foundation for relationship building.

Perhaps most striking is the way in which, from the first moments of life, these interactions between the infant and the sensitive caregiver are structured around turn-taking "conversations". These are focused on the infant's behaviour and rhythms to which the sensitive caregiver becomes *attuned*. The slightest murmur from the baby is met with a responding murmur from the caregiver. The smallest movement of an eyebrow or wriggle of the body is met with an adult raised eyebrow or a calming stroke. Sometimes the baby leads, sometimes the parent leads. Within minutes of birth the infant will copy an adult action, for example, by poking his tongue out. The caregiver's *mirroring* of facial expressions will help the child to recognise and manage emotions. The child's small frown of annoyance at a toy going out of view is met by an exaggerated frown from the caregiver that acknowledges the child's annoyance but then melts into a reassuring smile, often accompanied by an empathic comment – 'Oh dear, where's that toy gone? You are fed up about that, aren't you? Has your big brother taken it? Don't worry- we'll find another one.'

The rhythm of this sensitive responsiveness is clearly giving messages to the infant about the *availability* of the mother or father, about the way in which emotions can be expressed and managed, and about the *effectiveness* of the infant him or herself. From the infant's point of view, the ability to produce a reaction in the parent at a timing to suit themselves makes them not only confident that their needs will be met and comfort will be there for them, but that they are able to bring this response about. This leads to a *co-operative* interaction, such that if the infant chooses to pause in a game of mutual cooing, the caregiver will also pause rather than insist on the child continuing the game. The accurate *timing*, appropriate level of *intensity* and *reciprocity* of these interactions leads to a state of *synchrony* in which the caregiver–baby dyad creates what is often referred to as a dance, with the steps of the dance being unique to each couple. Children with disabilities, particularly sensory but also intellectual, will need extra help to establish this synchrony, with creative use of all the senses and very focused predictability and rhythms. But the goals of empowerment, reciprocity and attunement will be the same for all children.

Where caregivers are accepting of the child's *need for autonomy* and able to negotiate a *co-operative relationship* with the child, key experiences, such as feeding, become opportunities for developing the child's self-esteem and self-efficacy alongside the satisfaction of a physical need. For breast- or bottle-feeding, the importance of tuning in to the infant in terms of the infant's own natural rhythms (suck – then pause – have a think and a look round – then suck some more) will be an important part of sensitive care. The rhythm may vary from day to day depending on the state of the baby; with hunger, tiredness, illness, teething, and distractions from other people in the room all having an effect, alongside messages coming to the baby about the mood and mental state of the caregiver. Adjusting in a flexible way to the infant around feeding is essential for the caregiver to give the message that not only is the infant able to "choose" to feed through signalling hunger, but that the infant can then control the amount of food, the pace and the intensity of engagement with the caregiver during the process. Caregivers have, for example, to be aware that infants vary in the degree of continuous eye contact or the closeness of holding that they like and that helps them relax. Genetic factors such as temperament can make a child more adaptable or more fussy. Prenatal experiences and the circumstances of the birth may also have an impact on the infant's responses. This diversity is why each baby needs to be treated as unique. Parents often comment, for example, on how different feeding is with different children in their family, even when they appear as parents to be doing very similar things. Feeding, therefore, has potential tensions, risks and rewards, for both the infant and the caregiver, that need to be managed. But through the caregiver's close attunement it also provides opportunities for promoting security, autonomy and effectiveness in the infant and for building the adult's sense of competence and enjoyment of the parenting role.

Where the caregiver has been able to offer this kind of active and sensitive availability in the early months, the infant learns that the presence of the caregiver will restore their *equilibrium* after upset and anxiety. The hunger or the need for comfort become powerful feelings for infants which can be overwhelming and those needs must be met in order for the infant to be able to mentally and physically calm and either slip into a comfortable sleep or move back to play and exploration. This core idea is at the heart of Fahlberg's arousal–relaxation cycle, in which the meeting of the aroused child's needs by the parent enables the infant to relax (Fahlberg, 1994) and forms the basis of trust and security.

This notion of the child as a balanced or settled system that can become unbalanced and unsettled is a helpful way of thinking about the value of certain aspects of the caregiver–child interaction. The caregiver monitors, anticipates and manages the inevitable points in the day when the child becomes unsettled and takes a range of steps (feeding, changing, cuddling, playing, putting on a cardigan) to restore a comfortable balance. But, as emphasised above, the arousal–relaxation cycle needs to include the minds of the caregiver and the child. The satisfactory sequence of events, and the secure attachment that Fahlberg describes as resulting from the frequent repetition of the cycle, relies on the caregiver first *thinking about and reflecting on* what the child's needs may be or the child's signals may mean. Meeting the child's needs may involve trying a number of options that this reflection process in the caregiver's mind suggests could be helpful to the child. The *meeting of the need* for a cuddle, for food, for reassurance, helps the infant to relax and restores equilibrium, but the *security of attachment* comes from the messages taking root in the child's *mind* – my caregiver is available, cares about me, understands me and what I need and I can trust that this will continue to be the case and can enjoy my play and exploration.

An infant's day is full of potentially anxiety-provoking or unsettling events that require the sensitive monitoring and responsiveness of the caregiver. These range from sudden and alarming noises from the road outside through to the regular patterns of sleeping, waking, being hungry, being moved from cot to bath to lap to car seat. Some of the more frequent disruptive events, such as nappy changes, can easily disturb an infant's peaceful composure or disrupt their play and fun. Even with the most careful physical handling, nappy changing involves removing a baby's clothes, exposing skin to different temperatures and sensations and getting small arms and legs out of and back into often rather awkward baby clothes. Babies sometimes enjoy the fresh air on their bodies and the full attention of their caregiver, but nappy changing can cause even a much loved and secure baby to protest with a combination of anger, disappointment and distress if this is not what they wanted to happen at the time. The sensitive caregiver has to find ways of helping the child with this experience and will often use a range of multi-sensory strategies that between them have the effect of forming an alliance with the baby and lowering anxiety. The smooth nappy change is accompanied by a running commentary, which begins from the point the child is picked up through to the child being resettled for a feed, a cuddle, a sleep, a chat or a play. The caregiver may first take the baby round the room picking up creams, the clean nappy, and the clothes, commenting on each item. Once placed on the changing mat, the baby can be given a chance to have a little fun while she gets accustomed to this new angle on the world. The caregiver's stroking, touching and gentle moves to change the nappy are accompanied by a range of facial expressions and vocal tones that hold the baby's attention as the awkwardness of getting the clothes off is acknowledged, the dirty or wet nappy exclaimed over, the washing becomes a jolly game, the nice feeling of the cream being applied is celebrated and the relief and relaxation after getting it all done is shared.

This moment is often the cue for a chat, as the infant and caregiver have a strong connection at that point – putting the baby straight back in the cot would be a missed opportunity. Just two to three minutes of baby-led conversation at exactly the right time after a feed or a nappy change can be key learning points from the early weeks of life. With a totally available carer and when totally relaxed, the child can make big strides in communicating more actively. Those well-timed interactions may only occur a few times in each 24 hours, but they can be rewarding landmarks for both infant and caregiver.

The pattern or shape of such everyday events provides an opportunity for the baby to feel and express strong feelings and to have them anticipated, understood, accepted and soothed. Smiles and protests are treated as equally legitimate. The scaffolding provided by the caregiver physically, facially and vocally in each individual event of this kind becomes most powerful through its regular repetition during the day, so that predictability, as in a familiar mutual game, becomes itself another factor in lowering anxiety. Each experience is a richer learning opportunity for the fact of the infant's angry protest, since this allows the infant to test out the safety provided in the relationship and to find a way, with the caregiver's help, through difficulty to relaxation and recovery. This is at the heart of the process referred to by Donald Winnicott as "good enough" parenting (Winnicott, 1965). The most available and sensitive parenting cannot take away pressure points in the infant's day, such as having to wait a few minutes for a caregiver to rush through from the kitchen in response to a cry, but it is only through managing the wait, mastering the anxieties and challenges in the context of a relationship, that children learn to face new challenges with confidence. It is also the case that, on the inevitable occasions when even the most sensitive caregiver misreads the child's signals, the child has to learn how to work harder to make the signals more accurate and comprehensible. In that moment of misunderstanding or misattunement, though, also lie the seeds of a realisation that the mother cannot share the baby's mind, but has a mind of her own that needs to be understood and communicated with in the interest of closer co-operation. Thus, the mother's capacity to repair the damage done by a misjudged response is matched by the infant's growing capacity both to tolerate the gaps in the understanding and availability of others and to signal more accurately.

Although the nappy change is an apparently passive process, relying on the infant's confidence in the care and competence of the caregiver, the child's co-operation in putting out a hand to go through the sleeve, allowing her body to relax so that removing the nappy is easier, joining in a humorous tickling game, can all give the baby some sense of her own effectiveness in this shared enterprise. By the end of the first year, the child can be given a range of different experiences that build even more active participation. Feeding, in particular, becomes a more active and enjoyably messy experience, once holding a spoon becomes possible and is encouraged by the caregiver. The child having lunch in the high chair then has the experience of choosing between the relative benefit of using the spoon to eat the food (nice taste, I'm not hungry anymore, I feel competent, I am praised) compared with the game of throwing it on the floor and laughing (makes parent laugh, it's naughty but exciting, I feel in control). The child, of course, needs to trust that the parent is not going to take the food away or get angry, for such choices to be possible. In a well-functioning and attuned feeding relationship, the business of eating is best dealt with calmly first, so that the message is clear that eating and playing are both pleasurable, but that it is better to separate the two to some degree. If the feed starts with an uproarious game, then the child gets too excited and has the wrong message about what sitting at the high chair is supposed to be about. Again, this is another form of scaffolding that needs to be provided by the caregiver and relies on clear verbal and non-verbal communication.

Developing self-efficacy around play is a major part of security in the first year. Choosing toys to play with, enjoying banging or building, pat-a-cake or peek-a-boo, sitting still or crawling around, all offer exciting possibilities within the context of a relationship in which the child experiences the caregiver as offering a secure base and the caregiver promotes and facilitates exploration and activity. A key shift during the first year is that, in the second six months, as the child starts to take more of the initiative in expressing their intentions and goals, the caregiver role shifts towards affirming the child's developing sense of self through promoting competence and through play and exploration (Diamond and Marrone, 2003, p. 137). It seems that in play the child and caregiver, at this stage, turn from facing each other to facing the world side by side, as books, toys and games become central to shared exploration.

It is at around six to seven months that the child starts to show clear-cut selective attachment to primary caregivers, a development which parallels the cognitive move towards *object permanence*. The infant understands that objects and people do not disappear when they go out of view, but have a continuous existence and can be thought about in their absence. Trusted attachment figures can be held in mind, so that although the secure child protests about separation from much-loved attachment figures, the child is moving step by step towards managing the idea of the parent's continuing existence during an absence.

By the second half of the first year, the secure infant will be developing an *internal working model* of the self as lovable and effective and others, in particular the primary attachment figure, as available, loving and a haven of safety. At this age this is largely based on procedural memories of the quality of care received. Children with learning disabilities appear to go through a similar route, although there may be some delay. Studies of children with Down's syndrome suggest that they too can construct a secure relationship, with 'most children with Down's syndrome using their primary caregivers as a secure base for exploration and a haven of safety by the time they have reached the developmental age of 1–2 years' (Goldberg, 2000, p. 117).

In Ainsworth's *Strange Situation* (Ainsworth *et al*, 1971, 1978) as described in Chapter 1, used between 12 and 18 months to measure attachment security, the secure infant will typically begin by playing with interest in the unfamiliar play-room while keeping an eye on the availability of the mother, especially when the stranger enters the room. Secure infants will vary in the degree to which they cry on the departure of the mother, though some protest and movement towards the door is likely. But when the mother returns they will show the distinctive reaction to reunion of greeting the mother with joy and relief, seeking comfort in a cuddle or a reassuring word, but then rapidly settling back to play. The infant will not be engaged in play or be comforted by the stranger, showing a clear preference for the mother. The speed with which the infant settles to play at reunion with the mother after separation demonstrates the infant's sense that the mother's comforting reappearance simply gets things back to normal, *restores equilibrium*, confirms the infant's *trust* in the mother's availability and frees the infant to play again. It is like a light going back on in the mind of the child, which switches her from attachment concerns back into pleasurable exploration.

Joining a new family in infancy (birth–18 months)

Secure infants who come into a new family (whether from a birth family or from a previous foster family) will feel a powerful sense of loss. The loss is not only of specific attachment figures, but also of the predictable and familiar physical environment and the routines that make a young child feel trusting, comfortable and confident. The new environment is a very different sensory experience, with different sights, sounds, smells and kinds of touch. Separation from the person or people who have come to represent a secure base can sometimes be managed in the short term – as infants do when in nursery care or with a babysitter. However, as it dawns on the child that they are starting to feel anxious and upset, but their crying is not producing their familiar caregivers panic may start to set in. The infant may go through the processes of grieving.

It is not easy to predict exactly how separation will affect a particular child, with protest, anger, denial, despair or resolution occurring in different forms and within different timescales. Because of such differences, it may not be easy to tell from a child's initial reactions to the separation too much about the quality of the previous relationships, although social workers are often asked to draw conclusions in this way. For example, children newly placed in a foster family who are initially withdrawn and appear to be in denial may be secure or be anxiously avoidant and accustomed to suppressing their feelings. Very obviously distressed children may be secure or anxiously ambivalent and likely to show their feelings. Secure children will be employing a range of strategies to cope with their loss, but it may be that what is being observed at a particular point of assessment is simply one stage in a succession of rather different behaviours as the child attempts to process these new experiences and manage their situation. Their success in managing this experience and sustaining a secure internal working model will depend on their age, their past caregiving experiences and the quality of the caregiving they receive in the new family.

Although the placement of a child who is deemed to have an existing secure attachment in a bridge foster family is sometimes referred to as 'transferring the attachment' to the new family, it is almost certainly more helpful to think about the child as appropriately mourning the loss of one caregiver alongside forming a new attachment relationship. A secure attachment relationship cannot be "gifted" but must be earned by the new caregivers. The secure infant will have developed an internal working model of sensitive available others, but at this age this is based very much on the specific attachment relationship. Positive memories and messages about self and others will have been laid down very much in the context of that relationship. So the child's expectations of the world will have taken a severe knock with the loss of those relationships and it will take time for the child to build a new set of positive memories and expectations of the new caregivers. However, the experience of secure relationships in the past may enable a child to "take the risk" of accepting care and committing to this new relationship, a risk that insecure children will find harder to take. It is also the case that the child may more rapidly become rewarding to care for than an insecure child and thus set up a more positive cycle of mutual warmth. However, it is still likely to be a slow process and the child's security could be put at risk if the new carer is unable to take the time to be completely available, practically and psychologically, to the infant.

Depending on the circumstances, it is likely to be helpful for the child to have contact with previous caregivers to convey the very important message that significant people do not just disappear as soon as you learn to trust them. Where a previous caregiver has moved abroad or contact is impossible or very infrequent, photographs can be useful, even for children of 12–18 months. The important thing is for the child's core belief that the world makes sense to be preserved if at all possible. The child may need transitional objects from their previous life, the teddy or the blanket, to reinforce the message that they have a continuous existence and to protect their emergent sense of self.

The core parenting message for new caregivers is to carry on providing consistency, availability, and sensitive responsiveness, even though the child may treat them initially with anger, uncertainty, distress and even suspicion. If we think of how the stranger is completely unable to comfort the secure child in the Ainsworth's Strange Situation when the mother leaves even briefly, it is possible to understand that the grief and anxiety that is being expressed may be deep-rooted. It is nevertheless still distressing for new caregivers eager to comfort the child and requires exceptional patience to remain available, supportive and accepting of the child.

Talking to the infant through difficult moments and putting the infant's feelings into words, alongside being available and caring, may be helpful; for example, 'I know you don't really know me yet and this must all seem very strange to you and I guess you must be missing your mum / brother / foster carer, but I'm going to be doing my best to make you comfortable. You will feel happier in a while.' This is an important way for carers to begin the process of communicating an empathic response even to non-verbal children. Expressing these ideas keeps the carer focused on the infant's mind and psychologically attuned. Over time, the child will start to pick up on these messages and even the tone of voice will be calming and reassuring. This flow of talk that creates a meaningful story has the additional benefit of reassuring other children and indeed adults in the family circle that the baby's upset is reasonable in the circumstances and will be gradually resolved. The new primary caregiver needs to be able to contain everyone's anxiety and build hopefulness – so it is critical that she or he has access to a secure base in the form of a partner or friend or social worker to enable this to happen.

When looking after separated infants there is the advantage that their dependency on caregivers for food, comfort and play provides numerous opportunities to parent in ways that provide a totally available nurturing environment, alongside supporting exploration and autonomy. The balance between the child's need for attachment and for exploration will need to be maintained. Moving between caregiving appropriate for the chronological age and for the emotional needs of the child is a key part of caring for all fostered and adopted children, but requires a subtle balance even in this young age range. Thus, building the confidence of the separated infant means providing support for exploration and facilitating pleasure in everything, from food to toys to soft, comfortable clothes. The child's inner and outer worlds need to form a coherent experience, aided by this kind of holistic approach. It is important to remember that foster carers and adopters are not only building a new relationship, but also shaping the healthy development of the infant's mind and brain.

Early childhood (18 months–4 years)

Through the toddler and pre-school years, children's range of relationship possibilities grows as siblings are born and children start to develop friendship networks (Dunn, 1993). From the second year of life, the child starts to develop some key skills that can help them to explore the world and contribute to relationships in more subtle ways. The simple ability to walk towards and away from situations and people increases the potential for making choices. You can find the toy you want or approach the uncle who is fun to play with or run away for a joke when dad wants to put your coat on.

Developments in the cognitive capacity to represent others and ideas, in communicative and negotiating abilities, in self-knowledge and understanding and in the knowledge and understanding of others that comes from perspective taking, all enhance the quality of the secure child's experiences at this age. Secure young children who have confidence in their own abilities and in the environment will be able to make maximum use of these possibilities for pleasure, play, growth and learning. They will and do protest loudly if angry or disappointed, but they can learn from these experiences and from their own mistakes. Each move they make brings the child new information to process about objects and people. This information can be assimilated into existing mental representations and models or bring about change in these models

This process of learning and cognitive development is common to all children (Piaget and Inhelder, 1969), although the timing and detail will vary, especially if children have a learning disability. As their world becomes more complex, children's thinking also becomes more sophisticated. Young children's concepts need to become more varied and more complex to accommodate their new learning. The horse with a hump on its back is discovered to be a camel. Existing concepts broaden and have to be related to more complex behavioural choices. For example, a child starts by learning what a dog is and that it goes "woof". Gradually, the child learns that you can have big and small dogs, and that woofs vary from loud barks to little yaps. Most importantly, some big dogs that look and sound scary are actually cuddly and some small dogs that look and sound like toys are actually fierce biters and must be avoided. The more elaborate meanings of "dog" can inform the decision about whether to use new toddling skills to approach or to avoid a particular dog. These important distinctions apply to people too. Big and small brothers and sisters may also need to be divided into those who fight and snatch and those who cuddle and protect – and how to tell by their facial expressions and voice which they might be about to do next becomes important.

One of the challenges of this age period for caregivers and children is that the toddler can sense an exciting ability to be *more active and autonomous*, to do so much more, and yet needs to be kept safe and contained. They can toddle towards the fire or the gate, but need to be prevented from endangering themselves, with "No!" becoming an increasing part of parental vocabulary. Parents now ask them to do things and so the child discovers the pleasure and consequences of asserting themselves by also saying "No!" Thus new potential for conflict develops alongside exciting developmental possibilities for the child. Nevertheless, as Fahlberg (1994) suggests, when children are having difficulties in the toddler years, the advice to caregivers should be to keep them safe, but to do whatever will *help them to feel more competent*. One of the many apparent paradoxes of child development is that the secure child who is given most encouragement to be appropriately autonomous and effective within safe boundaries will also be the most co-operative. Similarly, it is through parenting the child co-operatively that competence is promoted. As mentioned in the previous chapter, children are described by Vygotsky (1978) as having a 'zone of proximal development', an area of potential development that can only be reached in a social context, with the help of more knowledgeable adults or peers. Although Vygotsky talks in terms of children *learning* and being *taught* in a social context, the notion of *co-operation* is intrinsic to a psychosocial model of parenting that builds not only skills, but also self-confidence.

The development of *language competence*, the second major breakthrough in this age period, allows children to understand the talk of others with more subtlety, to communicate their needs more accurately and to participate in verbal humour and other games with adults and other children. They now have semantic memories, as they soak up messages about themselves and the world. The development of language also enables children to begin some direct learning about how to name feelings and how to think about the minds and feelings of others – and the consequences of those feelings. The caregiver can explain to a child the fact that if she takes the toy of another child he'll be upset and may cry or if she pulls the cat's tail, the cat will be hurt and may bite her. For secure toddlers this helpful commentary about feelings, behaviour and its consequences will have been going on from birth in different forms, but the move towards proper conversations is significant; for example, when the mystified toddler says after taking the toy, 'Boy crying?', she can receive an explanation of what has happened, why the boy is crying (i.e. what might be in his mind) and practical advice on how to make it better. The child is just beginning to learn a key lesson of this period, that other people have minds and feelings that have to be taken into account – a lesson in *mind-mindedness* (Miens, 1997; Miens *et al*, 2001) that depends almost entirely on the quality of relationship experiences.

Peter Hobson (2002, p. 147) explains that the child's capacity to recognise and act upon the alternative perspectives of another person, to have a capacity of empathy, is connected with a caregiver's sensitive responsiveness, which in turn affectively informs the child's sensitivity. The more finely attuned the sensitive quality of the caregiver's response to the infant is, the more the infant can emotionally understand him/herself and this is the basis for a potential for empathy. (Diamond and Marrone, 2003, p. 130)

A further significant ability developing during the toddler years is the ability to *pretend*, which contributes to this growth of "mind-mindedness" in the secure child. Not only can the child play symbolic games, with imaginary cups of tea offered round, but toddlers can use pretence to tease other children and adults. The infant in the high chair who used to tease the caregiver about whether they will drop the sticky biscuit on the carpet can now, as a two- to three-year-old, pretend not to know where the biscuit is, even when they are holding it rather obviously behind their back, and can even put on a false look of concern to help the game along. Significant here then is the fact that children, through their facial expression and behaviour, learn to pretend to feel and think something other than what they actually feel and think. This has only become possible once children realise that other people cannot actually know what is in their minds. Children therefore begin to learn how to use the expression of emotion, in looks and words, as a way of deceiving adults. They may look angry at being accused of something they have in fact done or shake their head reproachfully. This kind of deception, like lying, is an important social skill – family special occasions and social life in general would be impossible without a certain amount of social "lying". 'This present is just what I wanted' and 'I like your new dress' oil the wheels of relationships throughout the lifespan and from the toddler years onwards children learn to admire, praise, conform, say and look sorry in strategic ways.

Secure toddlers need to learn these skills and will play with, tease and at times deceive caregivers. However, what distinguishes secure from insecure children is that through their relationships with their caregivers, secure children begin to learn that direct and truthful communication is a quicker and more effective way of getting their needs met. Their caregivers communicate openly and truthfully with them and respond in a sensitive, contingent and constructive way to their direct requests or explanations. So, for example, the child learns that admitting that he accidentally broke a toy leads to opportunities to say sorry, accept the feelings of shame, get help to pick up the bits, be forgiven for the damage and be comforted for the loss. This is preferable to the consequences of deceit that would arise from a lie, such as 'My little brother did it', which would leave layers of guilt and sadness, whether the little brother gets told off or the lie is discovered. As with other kinds of openness, it relies on the child being able to trust that the caregiver will accept that it may be an accident or, if it was deliberate, will be able to separate the behaviour from their view of the child as fundamentally a good person and be able to combine censure with forgiveness and advice for the future. Acquiring the capacity to forgive as well as the capacity to repair is critical to the self and future relationships, and starts very much in the pre-school years, in the context of open communication and acceptance of mixed emotions such as love and anger.

Direct communications from young children can be about factual events – how the toy got broken, for example, but also about feelings – 'I love Grandma, but I don't like my cousin who's rough with me'. Straightforward communications of distress, shame, love, anger and jealousy can be tolerated and managed by the caregiver, so pretence is not required. There is a presumption by the child that they have the trust of their caregiver. The caregiver in turn communicates, names and manages their own feelings of anger, upset, joy and pride in the child truthfully and within safe boundaries, thus modelling for the child and enabling the child to feel more confident in expressing their own feelings and managing them. Discovering feelings of shame about one's actions is a particularly painful but necessary part of this process, since secure young children are likely to "steal", lie or hit smaller children as they learn about and test the boundaries. Managing shame is an important step towards regulating behaviour and links feelings about oneself and others in order to establish moral standards. This process is just getting established in the pre-school years and needs consolidation as children move towards and into middle childhood. However, empathy in these open relationship contexts develops as the first stage of moral development, when children begin to imagine the consequences of their behaviour and develop a propensity to make pro-social choices.

By the age of three or four, secure children will have developed a sophisticated ability to understand the feelings, ideas, humour, goals and intentions of others (Dunn, 1988, 1993). This is aided by the child's interest in and close attention to behaviour, tone of voice, facial expressions, direct explanations and, with familiar people, their prior knowledge of how this particular person might be expressing anxiety, pleasure or anger. Thus, a general understanding that other people have minds is accompanied by particularly skilled understanding of the mind and behaviour of important people. It is this development that leads to the move towards what Bowlby called a 'goal corrected partnership' in the attachment relationship. The understanding of the caregiver's feelings and goals allows the child to "negotiate" with the caregiver, for example, thinking, 'My mum's a bit tired after work and needs to sit down for five minutes, but if I wait a little and approach her in the right way she will give me a cuddle and then help me set my train/doll's house/computer game up'. The secure child has learned that the interpersonal world is meaningful and goal-directed, and to be effective it is necessary to understand and negotiate with other people's meanings, feelings and goals.

These are family-based lessons in management of the self and negotiation with others that the socially intelligent, secure child takes out into the world of playgroups and nurseries. For example, the secure pre-school child will know, 'If I want to get the interest, attention and liking of nursery staff, I need to pick the right moment to approach (i.e. not when they are talking to someone else) and use the right tone of voice' (i.e. polite, friendly and appropriately assertive). The secure three- to four-year-old is socially competent and in day care settings, nurseries and playgroups maximises not only the benefits of the relationships with adults, but also the development of collaborative friendships and the learning and fun from exploration and play opportunities. They learn the new *behaviour scripts* that matter in the particular pre-school setting – taking turns to give out the biscuits, hanging up your coat on the right peg – as they busily process all the information they need to meet their attachment needs, explore and maintain their own equilibrium under these new challenges and in the absence of their secure base attachment figure.

The separation from the caregiver that day care involves is managed through the process of mental representations and in particular an internal working model of the self as lovable and competent and the caregiver as available and to be trusted (reinforced by the caregiver reliably appearing at the end of playgroup or nursery). In this environment, as at home, the full range of feelings can be expressed, though there are some subtle differences. Secure children will display both joy and some of the more risky negative feelings of anger and distress, but are not likely to give free reign to dangerous feelings when only authority figures are available, instead displaying them in a rather modified way. Children are more likely to feel safe enough to let rip with emotions at home and in the presence of the attachment figure, a familiar experience when children get home from nursery and playgroups. But this is an appropriate distinction between social situations, relevant throughout our lives. It is the secure child's ability to discriminate between different environments and to manage their feelings and behaviour flexibly that makes them successful social actors, whether at home, at the playgroup or indeed at the library or in the supermarket.

From the age of about four it is possible to see, through the use of story stems (Bretherton *et al*, 1990; Solomon *et al*, 1995; Hodges *et al*, 2003; Green *et al*, 2000) the model that secure children have of their world, and in particular the anticipated availability and protectiveness of parents. Secure children when faced with the story stem of the child who fell and hurt her knee while with her parents in the park, would immediately acknowledge the feelings about the hurt knee and may use their imagination to develop the story's theme, even increasing the drama of the situation by involving ambulances and hospitals. The child in the story may be seen as active in seeking help, but the parent figures are available and attentive, comforting the child and making sure the child's hurt knee was responded to sensitively and competently. The secure child tells a coherent story, creating a narrative that develops logically from the starting point provided and leads to a resolution that depends on the availability and responsiveness of parents, but also often includes the child's own resourcefulness.

Joining a new family in early childhood (18 months–4 years)

For the secure toddler or pre-schooler, leaving familiar birth or foster family caregivers and coming into a new and different family home is likely to cause immediate distress, although it may initially prompt some children to use their new skills in social relationships. They may play constructively, for example, and accept food from these strangers, particularly if they are familiar with being cared for outside the family. However, when they start to realise that this separation is not just for a brief interlude, and that they are expected to sleep there without access to their previous secure base caregiver, their normal coping strategies are likely to be overwhelmed. Apart from showing feelings of distress, recently-acquired areas of competence, such as toilet training, may lapse, a distressing and difficult experience for young children.

Eighteen months to four years old is a wide age range, of course, and so although children may share a similar secure internal working model, secure toddlers at the younger end of this age range are likely to feel more immediately and extremely anxious and will also have fewer skills and strategies to manage their feelings and behaviour than the secure four-year-old. In particular, the different level of language ability, both to understand explanations and to express feelings, will affect their attempts to cope. Other factors will also have an impact on coping; some are child-related factors, such as being with older siblings who offer comfort, and others are placement-related, such as the practical and emotional availability of the caregiver. It is also very important to bear in mind that, within the range of children broadly defined as secure, some will be more inclined to shut down on feelings when under extreme stress and others will be more inclined to seek comfort or make demands, so new caregivers will need to tune in to children's specific ways of coping.

The new caregivers may have a positive foundation to build on in terms of the child's early care and the resulting secure internal working model. But the child's confusion and distress at the separation and loss will mean that helping him to accept the new relationships and care on offer will require considerable time and sensitive care. Above all, it will require an ability to restore the child's faith in their own competence and lovability. The overall parenting task is to provide a very intensively nurturing environment, to build a relationship of trust and gradually build in support for exploration and fun, enabling the child to achieve a gradual return to previous levels of competence. It is important to remember again the secure child's response to the stranger in the Strange Situation – the healthy response is one of wariness and it will take time for the caregiver not to be a stranger.

The child of this age also is likely to benefit from contact with previous significant people. They may also need transitional objects from their previous life, such as the duvet, the favourite video or the photographs, in order to experience continuity with their past self and to regain some degree of cognitive and emotional equilibrium after the initial period of crisis. They need help to feel that the world makes sense and for young children this will need to be offered in a fairly practical way as part of daily care. For pre-school children, such tools as wall calendars to plot the activities of each day and the days of the week and patterns of contact can help with this. Protests and tantrums need to be managed within an overall and visible framework that offers predictability and consistency and promotes mastery.

Middle childhood (5–10 years)

Security during this middle childhood period moves further towards being a characteristic of the self rather than a characteristic only of specific attachment relationships, for example, with mother, father, grandmother and others. In this age group, children commonly have a hierarchy of attachment figures who meet different needs and the self is also increasingly differentiated, as children think about what kind of person they are in different contexts (Kearns and Richardson, 2005). Self-esteem and identity become linked to environments outside of the family, such as school, friends, the Brownie pack, the football team. Although parental approval will always be the most important motivator for most children, these other environments can boost or diminish self-esteem significantly. This is an exciting period of opportunity, but also a time when anxiety around separation and loss of the attachment figure is joined by anxiety about threats to the self, through not coping with new situations, not matching up to expectations or not being recognised as the person you think you are and want to be.

For the secure child, it is therefore important that the mental representation of the caregiver as available and loving is accompanied by a model of the self as not only worthy of love but also as competent. Raised self-esteem and a sense of self-efficacy enable children to engage in the full range of social activities and can sustain the child in the face of normal anxieties about both separation and performance. Their competence is reflected in the way in which they are treated by others. For example, because secure children tend not to be emotionally needy, teachers treat them warmly but "matter of factly", offering help when it is needed but with the focus on promoting educational progress (Sroufe, 1989).

Secure children entering school will have many of the skills required to cope not only with the structure and learning demands of the classroom, but also with the rather different demands of the playground, where friendships and fun have to be negotiated in the context of power hierarchies, the in-crowds and out-crowds that dominate peer group politics. As the child stands in the playground and has to negotiate their way into a game of football or skipping, the ability to approach with confidence has to be matched by the preparedness to cope with a refusal and the capacity to take a deep breath and try again elsewhere. Here, in particular, having social skills and being competent at approaching others needs to be supported by a self that provides their own internal and constructive running commentary when turned away; for example: 'Not to worry – I'm OK. I expect they had enough children in that game. Or perhaps they are just being a bit mean and would not be good fun to play with anyway. I'll just try to get into a different game – or perhaps start one myself.' As children process each experience of success or failure, they need to call on this sense of who they are – drawing very often but quite unconsciously on all the messages they have received from others, the procedural, semantic and episodic memories that make them feel themselves to be a lovable, valued, competent child.

This age period is dominated by the developmental task of learning a number of different kinds of *rules*. These vary from the school rule about waiting in line to go into class through to informal rules about how to approach older and younger children, how boys and girls are supposed to behave and the general moral rules of fairness and justice. Primary age children insist on the rules of games being strictly followed and get particularly angry at any signs of cheating, even though the parallel pressure to be a winner rather than a loser at games means that most children cheat at some point – taking off two layers of paper in a game of Pass the Parcel, perhaps, in the hope of getting the prize.

More secure children, because of their trust in others, their self-esteem and their ability to negotiate, are likely to find the process of learning and following rules a fairly comfortable one, although their tendency to seek autonomy and assert themselves often leads to rules being tested out first. Because many of the informal but essential rules around managing social relationships require children to be able to take into account the feelings of others, secure children are likely to be particularly competent in this area. *Managing the self* is a key developmental task for this age group and takes place in an interpersonal and social context which has to be thought about, reflected on and understood. *Moral choices* that are pro-social derive from this ability, as children become better able to *pause for thought* and reflect on and choose options that avoid hurting others or put themselves second if a younger, upset child needs help. There will continue to be times when secure children make mistakes, act selfishly and become overwhelmed by feelings. Thus, they continue to need support after a difficult day at school or a sleep-over party with friends that may not have gone so well, in order to re-establish their confident sense of who they are and to restore their equilibrium. Each episode is an opportunity for learning about how the social world works, but children need help with making sense of why things don't always work out the way they want.

Outside of school, activities and interests are frequently playing a major role for this age group. A key part of available parenting is often facilitating, supervising and supporting children in school and in activities. During this age period, children become increasingly responsible for planning their time and negotiating boundaries, such as walking to a friend's house but only in daylight. The secure base is still playing an important role here, as children sample karate club, Brownies, dancing or football and cope with success and failure in both activities and social relationships. Caregivers constantly juggle the need to support exploration and praise achievement with the need to minimise the impact of failure. Secure children receive constant feedback on their performance which needs to be reflected on and processed in order to shore up their sense of self as they face an inevitable diet of 'Well done!' mixed with 'Never mind – better luck next time'. Flexible thinking in parent and child and open-communication will help to maintain a reasonable level of self-esteem and emotional regulation.

Joining a new family in middle childhood (age 5–10)

Secure children joining a new family during this age period may be coming from an extended period with a birth family carer who is no longer able, through perhaps illness or changed circumstances to care for the child. Some children with severe disabilities come into foster care at this age from caring families who can no longer cope. It is less likely, though possible, for secure children to come into care from abusive families. However, as with other ages, there are children in this age group who have had a good start in life, but stress in the primary caregiver or a new stepmother or stepfather leads to the home becoming neglectful or abusive. Another important group are children who move into new families from a short-term or bridge foster home where secure relationships have been established.

Whatever the circumstances, this move into a new family and a new home is not only an emotional challenge due to the anxiety of separation and loss, but is also likely to be a challenge to children's understanding of the "rules". Children previously cared for in the birth family will understand the expectation that children "normally" grow up in birth families and that this new family setting is not, by those social rules, "normal". This is not their "real" mum and dad. Children moving from a foster family where they had become secure will have focused on fitting in and belonging in that family and, even if prepared for a new long-term foster or adoptive family, will find this move to include the acutely difficult loss not only of close relationships but also the loss of a familiar family culture with familiar rules (Lanyado, 2004). Where the move is to another temporary family, it is even more difficult for the child to make sense of what is going on.

Each move will generate issues to be dealt with. For example, moves that are from or to transracial or transcultural placements require children to make certain adjustments. When a white child moves from a black foster family to whom he is attached to a white permanent family or a black child moves from a white foster family who have become his secure base to a black foster family, anger and confusion at the move can come out in varied ways. One black foster carer reported how initially her black foster child, who had come from a placement with white carers, hurled racist abuse at her and eventually said, 'Do you like being black?' When the carer explained how proud she was to be black, it started a positive shift in their relationship and in the child's perception of his identity. These reactions suggest how all issues about self and others, including ethnicity, get caught up in the complex experiences of moves even for secure children. Such reactions are not arguments against such moves, but simply show how important it is for carers, whatever their circumstances or ethnicity, to feel confident and comfortable with themselves, to understand the child's mixed and difficult feelings, to help them access their thinking capacity and to be able to seek help if needed.

Changes of school and neighbourhood also require the child to start from scratch in terms of making sense of what are often obvious "rules" to others: the street or school culture; the local social hierarchies; the favoured TV programmes; the pop music and the clothes that are deemed to be "cool" in the new peer group. This age group can be particularly rigid about their new-found rules; for example, what is gender or age or ethnically appropriate behaviour. So for the child, who has to adapt to a new group, and the group, who need to accommodate the new child in their midst, there will be a process of negotiation. Even previously competent children need a significant amount of help and support with this process of adaptation and integration. In particular, children in this age range need a story to tell to help them get past the questions about who they are and where they come from, questions which any new child in a school will need to answer, but which fostered and adopted children in this age range may struggle with. Children need tactful and straightforward answers for themselves and they need ways of presenting their story to others.

For secure children in this age group, who will tend to be more sophisticated language users and thinkers, it may be possible for them to be helped to understand something about the reason for the move and gradually accept the routines of the new household, school and community. Maintaining previous sources of self-esteem and self-concept through contact and continuing familiar activities can also help. With these children, as with children of all ages, secure or insecure, caregivers need to start as far as possible where the child is at in terms of routines in day-to-day living, as this is going to be the least unsettling. Equally important is the need to accept for a while the child's defensive strategies, which even secure children may use when stressed and away from familiar attachment figures. Children who tend to bottle up difficult feelings should not be challenged, but encouraged to find ways of expressing them unthreateningly – perhaps simply by writing them down in a special private notebook. Children who feel safer being self-reliant or making cups of tea for the caregiver should be allowed to do this, even if the caregiver wants to be the one doing the nurturing. The basic principle of starting where the child is can get overlooked in the wish to help the child move forward, but it remains the best, most sensitive and most respectful strategy if reducing anxiety is the first goal.

However sensitive the new caregivers, the experience of loss and change is still likely to strike at the heart of the child's sense of self at times. Even intelligent, sophisticated children of 10 may need, and will in time accept, some primary nurturing that builds sensory security through soft duvets and cuddly toys, treat foods, nice bubble bath – alongside their familiar age-appropriate clothes and music. They can then begin to feel secure enough again to access their thinking capacity, in order to reflect on and work through difficult feelings more openly with the caregiver or the social worker.

We should also bear in mind the fact that, for some children who have been waiting in a foster home for a permanent new foster or adoptive family for some time, the chance to get fully settled in their "own" room with their "own" safe and loving parents and to feel that this is where they will be staying is a very great relief. Although we should never underestimate the difficulties that some children will have with a move of placement, for many children this will be a very positive step for which they have prepared and to which they are ready to commit. As ever, each child must be thought about as a unique individual, with no preconceived ideas about the "inevitable" reaction to a placement move getting in the way of understanding the feelings and thoughts of this child. Tuning in to children in middle childhood is helped by the fact that they have a greater capacity to express their wishes and feelings, even if those feelings are complex and their expression at times indirect (Schofield, 2005).

Adolescence (11–18 years)

The period of adolescence takes the child through a range of physical, mental, emotional and social changes as they prepare for the move into adult roles. This is a process of increasing independence and impending separation from parents. It presents opportunities but also challenges and risks. Taking advantage of these opportunities, alongside anticipating and managing the separation and the potential anxiety associated with it, is going to be more straightforward for more secure children. They are more likely to be able to rely on their raised self-esteem, to draw flexibly on their ability to think things through, to seek and find help when they need it and to trust that future environments – at work, at college and with friends – will provide, on balance, positive experiences.

Anxiety about separation is accompanied by many other pressures in adolescence, with the competition to succeed in school work, for example, being accompanied by the challenge of establishing an identity, making intimate relationships and finding sexual partners. Here the developmental tasks of adolescence include being able to reflect on success and disappointment, to process both kinds of experience without losing the sense of self and indeed to allow the mastery of each difficult experience to become a source of additional strength and to broaden their sense of identity as a person. Difficulties and conflict are not inevitable in adolescence but there are few adolescents, even among the most secure, who do not experience many moments of self-doubt and uncertainty.

The circumstances surrounding a teenager will certainly contribute to the developmental pathway they take. A child of average intelligence, for example, may be deemed very successful in one school, but a failure in another, higher achieving, school. Although felt security and support from the family may moderate the impact of being deemed a failure at school, the child's self-esteem and sense of self are likely to take a significant knock. Thus adolescents need to be regularly built back up after setbacks by the continuing availability of a secure base and the kind of active parenting that can help them find success and restore their self-esteem. Being secure at 11 is no guarantee of being secure at 18 – just as being insecure at 11 does not rule out the possibility of developing new secure base relationships during the teenage years. Sustaining a secure internal working model through adolescence to adulthood will rely on an interaction of the previous and current quality of life experiences and the continuing support of sensitive caregivers. Even for secure teenagers, the viewing of self as practically grown up and of parents as equals is likely at times to switch to a need for practical and emotional support more reminiscent of previous more "dependent" stages. The two steps forward, one step back progression of development continues in adolescence, but for secure adolescents, movement is broadly in the direction of autonomy in the context of reflective selves and co-operative relationships.

One of the subtle consequences of shifts in cognitive development is that adolescents become better able to reflect on the varied relationships in their experience and to begin to integrate internal working models that differ e.g. 'I can rely on my parents to support me'. 'My teachers seem rather critical' (or vice versa) to a model that says, 'Some people can be relied on to support me in difficult circumstances and I need to be alert to the signs and flexible in my strategies in order to get the best from other people and to maintain my self-concept/self-esteem' (Allen and Land, 1999, p. 320). This process of reflection brings about a degree of distance, as young people stand back to reflect on the failings as well as the virtues of their parents. This can be rather unnerving for parents, especially as it may be accompanied by a process of testing out the extent to which parents are prepared to get into a dialogue about their own strengths and weaknesses as well as those of their sons and daughters.

Secure older adolescents in the Adult Attachment Interview (AAI) are those who demonstrate their ability to offer a coherent, relevant, sufficiently detailed and balanced view of themselves and others. For example, when asked, 'Can you give me five adjectives to describe your relationship with your mother (or father) in childhood?' they are likely to offer a mixed picture – such as 'loving, kind, available, a bit bossy, proud'. Whichever words they choose, they will be able to come up with examples of incidents in childhood that accurately support those words, both the more positive and the more negative. The list could be very negative, "angry, mean, hurtful", etc, where adolescents have had adverse experiences of parenting in childhood. However, if they use appropriate examples, if they are able to talk about these experiences without denial or preoccupying anger, and if they have been able to face up to/reflect without defensive exclusion or angry preoccupation on the facts of their childhood (in the likely context of subsequent more secure attachment experiences), then they may be classified as secure or "earned secure". These young people will take this secure state of mind into parenthood, and there appears to be no difference in the level of security among children parented by secure and by earned secure caregivers.

The "earned secure" category is particularly important in social work practice for a number of reasons. First, it demonstrates that attachment theory is not deterministic but allows for the possibility of recovery from adversity and change in the internal working model in the direction of security. This reinforces the potential benefit for insecure, vulnerable children of offering secure family environments in foster care and adoption that can help them reshape their mental representations of the world, their expectations and beliefs about themselves and the support and care they can expect from other people. The move towards increased security can be offered not only by the secure base in a new family, but also by relationships offered by friends, teachers and, for some teenagers, therapists. These new experiences can be offered at any stage from early childhood to adulthood – adolescence is certainly not "too late" for building new relationships and increasing security (Schofield, 2003). As one of the earliest pieces of research on unexpectedly positive outcomes from childhoods of adversity by Quinton and Rutter (1988) suggested, for some the turning point may be the point of marriage.

Joining a new family in adolescence (11–18 years)

Much that has been said about children of primary school age joining new families will be true for older secure children. Loss of friends, disruption to schooling and moves of neighbourhood hit teenagers particularly hard as identities are developing but not yet firm. Even secure adolescents coming into short-term or permanent new families will be coping with feelings of anxiety about whether they are lovable enough and whether they should trust people who say they will care for them.

For new carers, there is the need to accept the coping strategies that teenagers adopt, such as retreating to their rooms, alongside patient attempts to offer nurturing and concern. Forming an alliance needs to be attempted, as with all adolescents. With secure adolescents, it may be possible to parent them within safe boundaries while building on their capacity to be reflective, their capacity to regulate emotions and their basic trust in self and others (see later chapters for examples).

Even where teenagers are not putting their feelings into words, it is important for carers to offer the kind of running commentary that anxious children of all ages need to help them make sense of what is happening. At this age, children will be involved in discussions about their future and in decision-making, and will need carers to facilitate this process but also to give a clear signal that adults will make sure that where options are offered to children (e.g. levels of contact) none of them will put the child at risk.

Difficult here for fostered adolescents in new families is the social work practice context that emphasises "independence" at a point when the young person still needs to build new relationships in this family and may need a supportive relationship that lasts into adult life. If the adolescent has no other secure family base available, then, regardless of age or apparent competence, that young person will need to build that base in the new family. Adolescents of 15 and older may in fact be better able than younger teenagers to appreciate what they need from a family, as they face the reality of what will be expected of them once the school years end. Although this issue of premature expectations of independent living is not specific to secure adolescents, it needs to be acknowledged that even the most competent fostered or adopted teenagers need continuity and support from a secure base into adult life.

Adulthood and parenthood

As secure adolescents move into adulthood, their positive sense of self, flexible strategies for managing feelings and behaviour and their capacity to plan for the future, will all facilitate their routes through work, further education and into establishing independent households. The use of families as a secure base continues, but work colleagues, friendship groups and romantic partners can provide alternative sources of emotional support, new identities and a sense of belonging. Here the giving and receiving of support becomes increasingly mutual, as adults both offer to others and experience from others available and committed concern.

For secure adults who grew up in foster or adoptive families, there may still be special challenges as they take up adult roles. For adults who grew up in care, this part of their history may need explanation to new partners, friends and employers. Some fostered and adoptive adults will be managing contacts with both foster and birth families. For those young adults who were adopted without contact or without good information about their histories, questions about their families of origin may lead to a decision about tracing and reunion (Howe and Feast, 2002; Trinder et al, 2004). Such challenges, even for secure adults who feel competent and comfortable with themselves and their identities, may yet raise anxieties that need to be managed.

Parenthood provides the ultimate challenge as adults move into the caregiving role, a transformed role in which they are providing care and protection in their relationship with their children rather than seeking it (George, 1996). This role transformation is most comfortably achieved by adults who not only have mental representations of available others, but have the actual support of partners, friends or parents who provide them with a secure base. Winnicott's model of fathers facilitating the intimacy of the mother–infant relationship offers a powerful image of a caregiving triangle (Winnicott, 1965), but the principle can equally be extended to the need for any adult who is providing care for a baby or child to feel that they have their own emotional back-up. For some parents who lack informal support systems, it may be that professional support is needed to provide the secure base, even for parents who are themselves secure. If a secure mother is isolated for any reason or if the child presents specific challenges through illness or disability, then the availability of a knowledgeable and supportive health visitor or social worker may be necessary to enable the mother to remain fully emotionally available to the child.

Through adulthood and parenthood external stresses, whether chronic, such as illness or marital difficulties, or significant life events, such as sudden bereavement or financial collapse, may jeopardise the equilibrium of the secure, autonomous person. The notion of the secure, resilient person who is sufficiently robust to withstand whatever fate throws their way is not helpful. No person is invulnerable to the impact of a sudden bereavement or a major illness, for example. In thinking about what secure parents, whether in birth, foster or adoptive families, can provide for a child, the role of social support in sustaining or restoring their capacity to parent successfully from infancy to adulthood will be important.

Summary points

- Secure infants and children have experienced secure base parenting that is:
  - available, mind-minded, attuned and sensitive to their needs;
  - supportive of exploration, effectiveness and co-operation;
  - builds self-esteem.

- Secure infants and children have an internal working model of self as lovable, others as loving and available and relationships as reliable.

- Secure children, as they develop:
  - trust in attachment figure(s) as a secure base for exploration;
  - display a full range of negative and positive emotions;
  - understand mixed emotions in self and others;
  - can manage/regulate emotions and behaviour;
  - are mind-minded/reflective/empathic/emotionally intelligent;
  - can think flexibility;

- are not too impulsive – can pause for thought before acting;
- are sociable/socially competent;
- are co-operative;
- have raised self-esteem/confidence;
- have raised self-efficacy;
- display pro-social behaviour;
- are hopeful/optimistic;
- show capacity to rebound/resilience.

3 Avoidant and dismissing patterns

From birth, all infants make demands on their caregivers. They communicate their need for food, comfort and closeness; their feelings of sadness, anger, anxiety, joy and excitement. However, some caregivers find it difficult to tolerate, accept or respond sensitively to their infants' emotional demands and, in particular, their expressions of negative emotions, such as distress and anger. Crying, for example, may be experienced as unnecessary and unreasonable, rather than as a normal part of communicating a normal range of needs. Signals of need and negative emotion, "making a fuss", can be experienced by the caregiver as critical, ungrateful or hostile. The infant's need for physical contact and closeness in particular is resisted. The caregiver needs to preserve an image of herself as a "perfect" parent, an image which requires the baby to be a "perfect" baby. If the baby is restless and demanding, even after the parent has done all the "right" things in a practical sense, then it must be the child who is the problem.

Rejection of the infant's signals of need may be expressed in terms of turning away from or ignoring the infant when they make demands or are making a fuss; more actively attempting to terminate the infant's behaviour by getting angry; or using intrusive parenting behaviour that is not in tune with the child. In infancy, insensitive and intrusive caregiving of this kind may focus around practical tasks such as feeding or a dismissive response to distress. For older children, intrusive parenting may include taking over the child's play and reshaping it or redefining and minimising the child's worries and experiences e.g. 'you have not really hurt yourself', 'you can't really be hungry', 'there's no reason to be anxious about going to the new school' and so on. These parenting behaviours reflect the caregiver's *dismissing* approach to the importance of feelings and are symptomatic of the caregiver's inability to see the world from the child's point of view – but they are also symptomatic of the caregiver's need to defend against her own feelings of anger and fear of rejection by the child in order to protect her sense of self.

Infants rapidly learn that expressions of need or distress do not get their needs met or bring about the desired comforting closeness. Even infants need to find ways of *adapting* to this caregiving behaviour, *shutting down on their feelings, deactivating attachment behaviour* and *relying on themselves* in ways that are acceptable to the caregiver. This achieves the best kind of relationship that is available, one based on emotional distance and reason. It is important to think of this as an *organised* strategy, adaptive to a fairly predictable if insensitive kind of caregiving. Infants are *not avoiding a relationship* but achieving the best relationship they can by *avoiding direct expression of emotions and demands*.

However, the *anxiety about rejection* and the underlying feelings of *anger* which are denied and suppressed by children in such a relationship may spill out from the pre-school years onwards as aggression, often in relation to their peers, but increasingly also in relation to the caregiver and other adults. The child whose feelings have been dismissed as unimportant grows up to dismiss the importance of the feelings of others – a combination that can lead to a lack of empathy and even bullying, in some cases, when others are perceived to be weak or in distress. *Dismissing* is the term used to describe this pattern in adulthood, but it captures something of the quality of the child's response even in the pre-school years and certainly as children move through childhood to adolescence.

The internal working model is of a self who is unloved and self-reliant and others as rejecting and intrusive (Howe *et al*, 1999). Avoidant children and young people range from those who function reasonably well and are merely rather cool, reserved and with a tendency to focus on things rather than people, reason rather than emotion, to those who struggle to maintain relationships and who become angry, isolated and, in more extreme cases, turn to aggression and anti-social behaviour when stressed.

Infancy (birth–18 months)

Where caregivers show this lack of sensitive responsiveness and emotional availability for an infant, it can be expressed in a range of parenting behaviours. It is important though to bear in mind that, although the caregiver appears to distance herself and reject the baby's emotional demands, she wants to be a successful parent for the child. A mother or father may, for example, have a range of theories about what it takes to be a good parent and how children are supposed to develop. However, the parent–child relationship can only feel comfortable when it fits rather an idealised (and therefore distorted) view of a successful relationship as smooth, rational and not stressful, one in which the child does not make too many demands. Time is invested in the role of caregiver, but there is a failure to respond to the child's cues. The *rejecting* caregiver continues to offer care and protection, but with a focus on their own goals, while dismissing and devaluing their child's attachment needs (George and Solomon, 1999).

Lacking the ability to tune in to the infant's experience of the world, which includes anticipating and making allowances for potential anxieties, the caregiver may approach the infant in ways that startle and upset him. For example, a mother may briskly wash a baby's face with a flannel, approaching from behind and taking the baby by surprise, so that the baby feels under attack and protests loudly. From the mother's point of view the infant is behaving irrationally – she is doing a necessary and correct parenting job and is not, after all, going to hurt him. She does not take into account what it feels like to be very small and to be ambushed by a big person with a wet flannel. Thus his reaction is defined as excessive and the caregiver may get angry and frustrated at the difficulty in completing a simple task. She can also become anxious that the baby is making her fail as a parent. His need to have his feelings anticipated, responded to and managed is misunderstood as him being "difficult" or "naughty" or, most painful, not loving her. The problem is exacerbated because the mother is not in tune with the infant and so does not provide the kind of helpful scaffolding, reassuring commentary and tone of voice that hold the child's attention, contain anxiety, build an alliance and raise self-esteem. A more sensitive approach to face washing might be 'Come on then let's see how much porridge is left round your mouth. I'll just give it a little wipe with your special flannel. It won't take a minute. Here we go – there, nice and clean, all done. Good boy!'. Instead, the dismissing mother may give mixed messages, for example, saying nothing as she approaches, smiling when the infant protests and then switching into anger, 'What's the matter with you?', which casts doubt on and minimises the child's feelings and makes them seem unreasonable. This adds to the infant's confusion about emotions and increases his lack of trust in his feelings and the response that they get.

The lack of attunement in infancy and potential for intrusiveness can be seen significantly around feeding. All feeding infants tend to have a spontaneous suck-pause-suck rhythm which both breast and bottle-feeding caregivers need to learn to adjust to, letting the infant take the lead on the whole. One hungry baby may guzzle away solidly for several minutes before taking a little rest. Another hungry baby may have been crying as if desperate for a feed, but still starts with a couple of sucks and then has a think and a gaze round. If the caregiver sees the feed as entirely a rational and functional task of getting food into the baby, these pauses can easily be misinterpreted as 'the baby's not really hungry' or worse, 'the baby is messing me about'. There may be anxiety that the baby is taking charge of or manipulating the mother, alongside some genuine concern that as a mother she is failing to feed the baby successfully. This may lead to the feed being either forced or abandoned and the child's subsequent protests seen again as unreasonable.

If the caregiver either withholds food when the infant makes a fuss or tries to persuade him to feed when he makes no demand or pauses for breath, the lesson is soon learned – if the infant wants to feed comfortably in accordance with his own natural rhythms, it is better to feed himself. As soon as it is possible for the infant to engineer getting the bottle to hold or the spoon to dip in the carrot dinner, then this will be achieved. Such signs of autonomy and self-efficacy are to be valued in the context of a warm and co-operative feeding relationship, but in these relationships, the child's self-reliance can leave the caregiver out of the feeding experience altogether. Self-feeding signals competence and self reliance of the kind valued by the caregiver, avoids intrusive feeding and allows the child to both conform and be in charge; but it means that the cuddles, togetherness, co-operation and playfulness associated with feeding can be lost. It is important to remember, again, that the child's behaviour is an organised defensive strategy that can fairly consistently ensure some kind of proximity (i.e. the caregiver is not driven away by "fussing") as well as satisfying hunger. The child is thus *not* avoiding a relationship but on the contrary protecting the self by avoiding being intruded on and avoiding the expression of negative emotion in order to maintain relatively comfortable physical if not emotional closeness with the caregiver. The selective attachment that has formed by six–seven months may not be obvious to an observer of an avoidant child when so many of the usual expressions of feeling are suppressed, but it is nevertheless a clear-cut attachment.

The most powerful way to illustrate what is underlying this strategy is to consider how the avoidant infant from 12–18 months old behaves in Ainsworth's Strange Situation. The infant will settle to play in the presence of the mother, but not in such a rich way as the secure child; rarely, for example, taking toys to show the mother. The child *appears* relatively indifferent to the position of the caregiver in the room and to both the caregiver's departure and the reunion. This is striking in such a young child. The child may even show some preference for the stranger. However, physiological tests which test levels of cortisol, skin response and heart rate (e.g. Spangler and Grossman, 1993) suggest that, far from being indifferent to the presence or absence of the attachment figure, the child is anxious and highly aroused by the separation, but uses the familiar strategy of not showing distress, being self-reliant and retreating to play with objects.

Although avoidant infants shut down their feelings in this complete way in the particularly stressful circumstances of the Strange Situation, when seen in home settings, they are more likely to show some of their anger in attacks on the mother – even though they run the risk of provoking rejection (Ainsworth *et al*, 1978).

Joining a new family in infancy (birth–18 months)
Attachments are being formed during the first six–seven months, so the youngest infants in this age range who have experienced caregiving of this kind may be

more open to accepting a different and more sensitive style of caregiving in a new family, although even at a few weeks old, infants may have learned to turn their head away to avoid a previous caregiver's intrusive gaze.

But older infants who have a more fully developed avoidant strategy will have formed a set of beliefs and expectations of the world, an internal working model that states: 'If I need my caregiver's company or attention, I must not express negative feelings, cry or make a fuss but be well behaved. I need to be competent and self-reliant.' Note that these infants will be having to cope with the loss of familiar sensory and relationship signals that have helped them to make sense of the world and some infants will already have been moved more than once between different environments. This in itself may make it difficult to be self-reliant and intensifies simply closed, defensive survival strategies. On the other hand, the organised strategy may break down, with feelings of anxiety and anger surfacing.

It is very important to remember that some infants may have developed avoidant strategies in their birth family, become more secure in previous placements, but then revert to avoidant strategies when stressed by the move to a new family. This may be particularly upsetting for new carers or adopters who have observed the infant in the previous foster home as responsive, but find that the infant shuts down and excludes them after a move to their care. New carers' feelings of inadequacy or even guilt about the move can be alleviated to some extent at least by explaining why the baby may respond in this way. Indeed, new carers may be helped by knowing the child's history and being advised in advance that this reaction is possible – but can be managed constructively.

Initially for new caregivers, the well-behaved (but withdrawn) baby may seem like a "good" baby compared to more fretful, difficult, demanding infants. There may even be a suggestion that this absence of expressed grief means that there was "no attachment" with the birth mother or other previous caregivers, which in most circumstances would not be the case. However, if over time the infant does not express the normal range of emotions, it makes it difficult for the new caregiver to get to know the infant or to feel successful in their familiar task of soothing distress and meeting needs. The infant may seek proximity, but it will be in indirect ways, such as leaning against the chair where the caregiver is sitting, but being apparently preoccupied with building a tower. In contrast, the caregiver's direct offer of play or comfort may be rejected.

There is a risk that the new caregiver will start to feel rejecting toward the "indifferent" infant for making her feel like a "bad" parent whose attention and care are unwelcome, thus repeating the child's previous experience. Support staff need to give caregivers the message that the child's internal working model is producing behaviours based on expectations learned in relationships with previous caregivers. If the new caregiver has a tendency to be dismissing, this needs to be recognised. The "match" may mean that the distance in the relationship is initially comfortable for both caregiver and child, but it will be important for the caregiver to be encouraged to help the child communicate more openly about emotions, even if such behaviour is not part of the caregiver's usual repertoire (Dozier *et al*, 2005).

For all new caregivers, the challenge is to offer nurturing care to avoidant infants, but in ways that are not experienced as intrusive. Starting where the infant is comfortable and going at the infant's pace are particularly important. It is not helpful to be extra jolly in order to warm the child up and get communication going as this will be experienced as intrusive and resisted. Only the most gentle of approaches and careful handling will be acceptable to the infant and initially even this degree of closeness may be met either with a flat expression and passivity or with some more active protest. It will take time before the infant will be able to relax enough, physically and psychologically, to respond with a smile or to show an appropriate range of emotions. Tuning in to the child in terms of identifying and responding to the smallest of signals and getting the arousal–relaxation cycle going is central. Using objects, sharing stories or toys, playing the child's own indirect approach game, may offer the best chance of unthreatening closeness and also support exploration.

During this time it may be that the child can also use transitional objects, such as teddies or blankets, to help them to connect with previous family experiences and to tolerate the move. Continuity of a sense of self needs to be promoted, even if infants are coming from adverse parenting experiences or have defensive strategies that attempt to keep people at bay. The caregiving strategies of the foster or adoptive parents will need to be thought through, and built on an attuned understanding of this particular infant. Knowledge of the kind of strategies that attachment theory suggests could work should always be accompanied by careful observation and sensitivity to this particular baby.

This is a challenging time for infant and caregiver, but the young age of the child, the inevitable dependency on the caregiver to satisfy hunger and other needs, and the frequent opportunities for reassuring physical touch and non-verbal messages of availability, should provide many opportunities to offer a secure base in ways that, over time, will build trust and help the child learn to express and then go on to regulate their emotions without suppressing or defending against them.

Early childhood (18 months–4 years)

As we have seen, in the toddler and pre-school period the child develops a number of important new skills, but also has some significant tasks to tackle, such as achieving greater autonomy and self-regulation, in order to get to grips with the social world outside of the family. Even the family itself may be changing as younger siblings are born. However, the role of attachment relationships in providing a secure base continues to be important as each new challenge and potential danger (physical and emotional) is faced and risks are taken. For the avoidant child, tight control over revealing feelings, self-reliance and compliance persist in order to achieve some sense of security and predictability. Focus on activities may produce some productive learning, but play may be rather concrete and repetitive. This is a period for making early relationships outside of the family, but difficulties in expressing and managing feelings can lead to problems in peer relationships in particular.

The total shutting down of emotions as seen in the Strange Situation starts to give way to greater anger and negativity, including displays of negativity towards the caregiver, during the preschool years. This is an important issue across the patterns i.e. although we learn about secure and insecure patterns in their "pure" form in the Strange Situation, a developmental and life span approach is necessary to see how these behaviours and strategies evolve. The pre-school years are a particular focus for the evolution of behavioural strategies in new contexts and as new age-appropriate skills develop.

As with other secure and insecure patterns, once the toddler becomes mobile, verbal and generally more competent, the steps of the relationship "dance" between the child and the caregiver become more elaborate in some key respects. However, the rhythm and the function of the core moves remain fundamentally the same. For example, the dismissing caregiver's redefining of the baby's experience as "not hungry" when the baby merely pauses in a feed was followed in infancy by the physical removal of the bottle. In the toddler and preschool years, such insensitive responding and redefining of experience are also communicated verbally in messages that the child can understand and will learn from. The toddler who falls over and hurts herself and cries now understands the verbal message when the caregiver says, 'It's nothing serious. You are not really hurt. Don't make a fuss.' This dismissing, minimising approach both protects the caregiver from having to recognise and respond to the child's distress and reinforces the previous pattern for the child of not experiencing physical concern and comfort. These incidents feed into the child's now verbally structured knowledge base about the world – the semantic memories. They lead the child to distrust what they feel – am I hungry or not?

Do I hurt or don't I? It adds general uncertainty about who knows the truth of the child's own feelings and suggests that feelings in self and others are not to be trusted, reinforcing the notion that seeking help leads to rejection. Self-reliance is the answer.

As children mature, they become increasingly competent in directing their behaviour and using language, and so become more skilled in avoiding rejection and fending off intrusion while achieving safe proximity. For example, an avoidant child can toddle over to play unobtrusively with jigsaw puzzles in the vicinity of the caregiver or can conform by taking their plate into the kitchen or can smile and give the signal, 'I'm OK', in order to reassure the caregiver that it is "safe" to stay close to the child because no emotional demands will be made. The child's involvement in constructive activity becomes a useful escape, while also pleasing and reassuring the caregiver – though the caregiver's tendency to interfere at times with the child's play, to help the child get it "right", may still cause difficulties and affect the child's creative exploration.

Although the child may have been led to avoid the expression of emotions and to value reason and self-reliance, the anxiety and need for closeness persists. These are important and subtle factors in assessments. Secure pre-school children will only actively approach adults when their own competence (emotional and practical) is insufficient for the task of getting needs met and maintaining their equilibrium. Avoidant pre-school children may sometimes appear similarly self-reliant, but will be less able to ask openly for or to use help flexibly and creatively.

The avoidant pre-school child's experience in attachment relationships and their adaptive but defensive responses get played out in their developing relationships outside the family and in the peer group. In nurseries and play-groups, where separation from attachment figures raises anxiety to some degree for all children and initially increases the need for defensive strategies, insecure children may display a range of behaviours that derive from primary attachment experience. Rather reserved avoidant children may find themselves quite comfortable in more structured pre-school environments that allow them to focus on activities when stressed and to maintain a comfortable and controllable distance in relationships. They can use the newly acquired skills of pretence and their realisation that positive facial expressions are pleasing to adults to smile, stay safe and keep adult approval. But peer group relationships can be problematic for all avoidant pre-schoolers. More anxious and more aggressive avoidant children will be both cut off from the rewarding friendships with peers that should be available by the age of three or four *and* also find themselves rejected by staff.

With staff, children are likely to behave in ways rather similar to the strategies found to work at home. Children who are avoidant in the Strange Situation at 12 months, at age three–four are likely to meet their need for a sense of safe proximity in an indirect way. In order to monitor the parent and maximise the possibilities for comfortable closeness, it became necessary to read the parent's behaviour and the child will now monitor the nursery nurse or playgroup worker in the same way. Fear of rejection and anxiety about being intruded on may jointly keep the child well behaved at times and conforming to expected rules, while continuing to minimise the expression of emotion and to dislike and distrust displays of emotion in others. Such children, when they become anxious in pre-school settings, may retreat to predictable objects for comfort, even become obsessive about keeping things in order, for example, lining up hangers systematically by colour in the dressing up corner rather than using their imagination to dress up and become a fairy or a police officer in a role play with others.

Pre-school avoidant children aged four–five tend to be more restless and to get into conflict, showing anger and frustration in play themes and roles, then finding it harder to resolve conflict with other children in the way that secure children generally manage to do. One factor may be that they are more likely than secure children to show a 'hostile attributional bias' (Dodge *et al*, 1990), a tendency to assume hostility even in the neutral acts of others. Research with cartoons suggests that they do not seem to accept, for example, the concept of one child *accidentally* breaking another child's favourite toy.

Social relationships in the peer group are thus tricky for these children, since in the nursery environment there are many opportunities for shared activity and displays of excited and pleasurable feelings by other children, which may seem strange to them, but also many potential sources of stress, rivalry, anger and unsettling aggression. Research suggests (Sroufe, 1989) that avoidant pre-school children may become bullies when paired with more anxious, ambivalent and dependent children. They lack an understanding or proper appreciation of the emotional life of others. Empathy is a key developmental goal of this age period but avoidant children are made anxious by signs of distress in others (just as their parent was made anxious by signs of distress in them). The very neediness and displays of emotion in a more vulnerable child that might provoke concern in a secure child will provoke anxiety, anger and rejection in an avoidant child. Contributing to this behaviour, which may amount to bullying, is also the opportunity to identify with the rejecting and powerful attachment figure, to project into the victim the anxiety and vulnerability which they themselves have experienced but suppressed, and to express some of the anger which they have hitherto had to keep tightly controlled. Even weaker, more anxious adults/members of staff may find themselves treated coolly and contemptuously or effectively feel as if they are being bullied by young children.

In *story stem tests*, children with an avoidant strategy tend to minimise the anxiety in the situation and the story they offer is generally brief. They may name the child's expected feeling in an appropriate way, but then indicate by their narrative that parents are unresponsive and that the child can look after himself. The child figure with a hurt knee, for example, may be ignored by the parent figures, but the child jumps up as if nothing has happened or sorts his own bandage out.

> *Their stories suggest that they immobilise the attachment system by system-atically scanning, sorting and excluding fear, pain, and sadness from conscious awareness.* (George, 1996, p. 415)

Joining a new family in early childhood (18 months–4 years)

Children coming into a new foster or adoptive family at this age will bring with them both the strengths and the difficulties of the strategies that they have used to feel safe and secure in the past. As for infants with this avoidant strategy, toddlers and pre-schoolers may seem very quiet and rather subdued, easy to care for initially but not easy to reach. Foster carers and adopters talk of feeling shut out by children who are self-reliant and insist on looking after themselves. Small children who fall and hurt themselves even quite badly will declare that they are all right and don't need a bandage, thank you. Some children may be able to express their anger through imaginary play, using toy soldiers to play out battles, or may simply retreat into safe havens behind wardrobes or under tables.

Forced to be dependent on foster carers or adoptive parents in some respects, if only because they are not able to provide their own food or run their own bath, they may nevertheless attempt to demonstrate their competence and/or their lack of need for parenting in as many areas of their lives as possible. At the extremes, and among the older children in this age group, this may mean not simply rejecting offers of care but treating them with contempt. Although this can seem very sophisticated and unlikely behaviour for young children to display, it is behaviour that has been learned in order to protect the self and is part of a drive to survive. They are unlikely to experience themselves as being "rescued" when taken from birth caregivers and are far more likely to think of themselves as "kidnapped" or, alternatively, "given away" by the parent (Fahlberg, 1994, p. 157) and taken to a new and potentially dangerous environment where they need all their wits (and defensive strategies) about them.

Tuning in to these children is a challenge, as they will already be skilled concealers of emotion and will withdraw the moment they sense intrusion or fear rejection. The messages might be mixed, as the child may linger in the caregiver's vicinity, but then resist attempts to engage. Given this lack of trust, it will be important for caregivers to observe the pre-school child carefully in order to understand how the child is managing his or her anxiety. If the child is only relaxed and allows physical closeness not when actually upset or stressed but over a shared puzzle or watching television in silence together, then this is a sensible first step. As in infancy, caregivers need to be aware of their own strategies for managing emotions, as their reaction to the child's minimising, withdrawal and occasional aggression may appear to confirm the child's working model of others as rejecting and intrusive.

It is likely that the avoidant child will lack both the understanding and the language of emotion. So one of the first and most important tasks of caregivers will be to help children who are at an age when developmentally they should be learning empathy and language to develop both the concepts and the labels for feelings. Developing perspective-taking skills and emotional intelligence in young children needs to be an active focus that takes into account the avoidant child's view that acknowledging feelings and thinking about them is a source of rejection. A range of "teaching" strategies can be involved. It may be through the caregiver modelling the expression and labelling of their own feelings or through using story books or television characters to discuss feelings that children will begin to see that the full range of feelings are safe and can be trusted and managed. Indeed, some children's emotions will then flood out.

When Nathan first came (age 3) he wouldn't hug or cuddle. He was more attached to dolls and soft toys. The dolls had become his mothers. Now, at the age of six, if I don't give him a cuddle and a kiss at night he will become very upset. (Foster carer)

The advantage of this age period is that it is a time of rapid developmental change and this developmental drive to play and to communicate can be capitalised on to provide therapeutic change. On the other hand, the difficulty is that time for bringing about necessary change is often tight, as children may start school soon after their fourth birthday. Enabling the child to build on their school-appropriate strengths, such as their liking for structure and focus on activity, while reducing the likelihood of anxiety, aggression and relationship problems before that first day in the playground and the classroom, is a major parenting task.

Middle childhood (5–10 years)

School, like nursery and playgroup, provides children with a mixture of opportunities and challenges. For some avoidant children, school may provide the chance to develop their reasoning powers and use their preference for focusing on activity both to escape from emotional turmoil and to achieve academically. However, we should never forget what we know of the avoidant child in the Strange Situation: although the infant may appear to be quietly playing during separation from the mother, physiological tests suggest that they are nevertheless highly aroused and anxious. Just as the play of the avoidant infant is less rich than that of the secure child and anxieties are unexpressed in the Strange Situation, so it is likely that the avoidant primary school child who is quietly getting on with their work may nevertheless at times be struggling to screen out anxieties about intrusion and rejection by others. Where children have additionally been exposed to abuse and neglect, it is also likely that their capacity to think and to fully use their intellectual potential in a classroom setting will have been limited by the disorganising impact of fear (see Chapter 5 on disorganised patterns).

Children tend to repeat their experiences in primary attachment relationships in their relationships with teachers and with other children. Research suggests that teachers quite unconsciously treat children according to their attachment pattern, and that avoidant children of five or six tend to be ignored, rejected and thought of as "mean" (Kestenbaum et al, 1989). This should not be surprising when we consider the way in which the avoidant child is likely to be managing the school situation. First, the child may give non-verbal and verbal signals that he or she does not need help from the teacher, may keep the teacher at such an emotional distance that the child is hard to get to know – and yet at times requires that the teacher intervenes in a conflict. In a busy primary school classroom, the child who is neither showing their pleasure and excitement nor seeking help academically or emotionally can easily get overlooked. Secondly, if the child moves into aggressive or bullying mode with other, more apparently needy children, then this will anger the teacher, provoke rejection and may, over time, identify the child as a discipline problem rather than a focus of the teacher's sympathy and concern. The child may become somebody to protect other children from and this research (Kestenbaum et al, 1989) does suggest that teachers are most likely to be angry with and rejecting of avoidant children. Finally, if when challenged about their aggressive behaviour the child denies the significance of the other child's distress, and may even treat the teacher's more sympathetic appeal to his emotions, his better nature, with contempt, it can seem as if this child is beyond help – is a "bad" child. The school's involvement of parents in trying to change the child's behaviour may be necessary but risks reinforcing the parents' rejection of the child, as the dismissing parent will find it hard to see the situation from the child's point of view and such public incidents threaten their need to be a successful parent with a well-behaved son or daughter – and in worst-case scenarios the circle of labelling and negativity is complete around the child.

Although insecure and anxious about the self, the child has to defend against vulnerable feelings. Key here are the mental representations that the child has developed of others and the self. Although the avoidant school-age child is anxious about rejection, the suppression of *expressions* of negative feelings becomes associated with the denial that such feelings *exist*. If they can be screened out of consciousness, then it is easier not to express them. This process of screening out feelings can lead to a polarisation of beliefs about feelings, so that, for example, children are unable to think flexibly in terms of *mixed emotions* about people and situations (H. Steele *et al*, 1999). Thus in a reflection of the parent's own strategy, the child's representation of the mother may be of an idealised, perfect mother and the representation of the self may also be defensively idealised, often in terms of achievement – 'I'm the best at football in the school', 'I'm brilliant at maths'.

As children move through the middle childhood years (aged 5–11) these grandiose ideas can lead to new and often even more counterproductive strategies for managing the self in relationships. With an internal model that defines the self as self-reliant and without doubts, children can become *boastful* and *bossy*. They may publicly *claim* that they are the best at football or the cleverest at maths, even when there is evidence to the contrary. Nobody likes children who boast and other children as well as adults will be drawn into cutting this apparently arrogant (but actually anxious) child down to size.

When linked with the tendency to be rather cool, controlling, unempathic and aggressive, such behaviours make it hard for these children to be liked or to make easy friendships and reinforce their experience of rejection. As Weinfield *et al* (1999, p. 78) put it, these elements interact and highlight the difference between anxious – avoidant and secure children in terms of the link between aggression and lack of empathy.

Empathy is in many ways the complement or counterpoint to aggression. Whereas aggression often reflects an alienation from others, empathy reflects an amplified connectedness, and where aggression reflects a breakdown or warping of dyadic regulation, empathy reflects heightened affective co-ordination. In fact in many ways, aggression is dependent upon a lack of empathy or emotional identification with others.

Joining a new family in middle childhood (5–10 years)

When children who have developed these avoidant and defended strategies join new families during the primary school years, they will show these emotionally closed behaviours and aggression to varying degrees, depending on a number of factors, including the extent to which separation and loss intensifies their defensive behaviour. Children may, for example, have had at least some good experiences at home, or in a previous foster family, or at school prior to this placement or they may have particular talents, such as a genuine ability at football or school work, that has produced some reduction in their anxiety and facilitated more comfortable relationships with adults or with children. They may have rational coping behaviours which, though characteristic of this attachment pattern, are not too disruptive and may even be productive and can be valued, such as writing a diary or keeping lists.

Troubled avoidant children who have experienced birth family rejection in circumstances that were neglectful or emotionally abusive, will take a long time to allow degrees of closeness that involve sharing emotions and accepting comfort from caregivers, as these carers' descriptions of three different children in placement suggest.

One time he got stung by a wasp – it had got inside his pyjamas. He was in pain. But I'm trying to hug him and he's stiff as a board. I thought, I can't even cuddle him now.

He can't bear to show any emotion, so he cries when he thinks you can't see him. If you see him showing emotion he clams up.

He has friends but he can take or leave them. In certain situations he turns away from people – he cuts people out. If he's a little bit cross with you he will cut you out.

Varied sources of distress go unacknowledged. For example, children who are clearly upset by difficult contact with birth family members where they have re-experienced rejection, will resist the offer of a cuddle when they return to the foster or adoptive family home and may prefer to turn to a game or play on a computer or sit frozen in front of the television, not really following the programme, or become angry and aggressive.

Bullying and bossiness in the family home may also make it difficult for foster carers and adoptive parents, who need to be in charge and also need to protect other children in the home, to remain emotionally available and to keep faith in the child's potential for good. However, caregivers can often see beyond the child's apparent arrogance.

> *Well if you listen to him he's the bee's knees. But . . . I just get the feeling that it's only surface. He was in tears at school.*

> *He likes to be the boss. He's a real know-it-all – but that's his Achilles heel because he doesn't really know it.*

An *emotional education* for these children has to be built on developing their confidence that they will not be rejected. Caregivers need to acknowledge feelings in the child and model/comment on appropriate displays of their own and other people's feelings. In the beginning, sharing their own feelings of pleasure, anger or sadness with the child has to be low key, as it may be experienced as overwhelming or seen as a sign of weakness and met with contempt. These anxious but controlling children need caregivers that are well supported them-selves and able to maintain their sensitivity and empathy in the face of apparent indifference or attack. The goal of parenting, as for all secure and insecure children, is to reduce anxiety and enable children to manage feelings without suppressing and denying them or acting them out. For avoidant children, this will mean allowing them the space to retreat when stressed if they need it, without criticism, but in the context of building a warm environment, in which consistent messages of availability and acceptance are given and children can be helped to step out of the hole rather than digging themselves further in.

Many stories offered in the parenting chapters (Chapters 6–10) provide examples of how school-age children can be helped to relax, warm up, be more affectionate, accept comfort and express anger. But it is important to bear in mind that the emphasis is *not* on eliminating self-reliant strategies, but on building in *additional and more flexible ways of coping* with difficulty that include seeking help, trusting relationships and valuing open communication in order to reduce the child's tendency both to withdraw and to be aggressive.

Adolescence (11–18 years)

Adolescence is a time of physical, cognitive, emotional and social change. Often referred to as a time of almost inevitable conflict, for most young people it is also a time of opportunity as they seize their new freedoms with pleasure, as well as some anxiety, and develop their identity and skills in readiness for adult life.

Adolescence can be a trying time for children who find close relationships difficult. Avoidant/dismissing teenagers who struggle to manage or value relationships have to cope with age-appropriate expectations that adolescent friendships will be more confiding and that intimate relationships with partners will emerge. Adolescence also sets the major challenge of coping with impending separation from parents, a transition which heightens anxiety and may increase the use of defensive strategies. Secure adolescents actually consolidate, renegotiate and build on prior attachment relationships at this stage in preparation for adult life, but for dismissing adolescents who are likely to have dismissing attachment figures, these sources of support and opportunities to share adolescent dilemmas and feelings may be limited.

Anxiously attached teenagers, even in the avoidant group, are actually more dependent than secure teenagers. Although the model of the self is self-reliant, the fear of intrusion and rejection, and need for approval are still strong. This can lead young people in the complex social world of adolescence to shift their behaviours in order to be accepted. Just as the pre-schooler learned to follow the rules of the family and the nursery in order to avoid rejection, so the adolescent tries to learn the varied rules of the different social groups in which he finds himself. The attempts to fit in, rather like a chameleon, as Howe *et al* (1999) put it, may leave the young person with no coherent sense of self.

The link between dismissing feelings, fear of rejection and aggression or bullying seen in middle childhood continues to affect some young people in this group. They receive higher peer ratings for hostility and report more loneliness and less social support from their families than other attachment groups (Goldberg, 2000, p. 144). It seems that avoidant/dismissing adolescents experience more negative feelings of both anger and sadness than they express, but that the message to other young people and adults is nevertheless only one of anger and resentment. Feelings of weakness and vulnerability must be suppressed in favour of being in control.

There have been a number of attempts to identify possible links between specific insecure attachment patterns and particular emotional and behavioural problems in adolescence. It seems that avoidant/dismissing teenagers are more likely to engage in externalising disorders (such as anti-social behaviour, aggression) whereas ambivalent/resistant adolescents (see next chapter) are more likely to be at risk of internalising disorders (such as depression). However, some problem behaviours, such as drug and alcohol misuse, are not so clearly linked to attachment patterns. One issue here is that different kinds of substance misuse can be linked with different mechanisms: for example, drinking alcohol to inhibit/block out feelings compared to drinking to disinhibit/display feelings. Even the use of different types of drugs serves different functions and for avoidant teenagers this is likely to be to block out painful feelings.

It therefore seems more useful to think about the *function* of particular behaviours as strategies for managing feelings and behaviours and as derived from different internal working models and different strategies. This kind of assessment needs great care. For example, a young person who has many sexual relationships, may seem to be the very opposite of avoidant and dismissing and yet promiscuity allows physical intimacy without the need for sustained emotional expression or true mutuality and may be accompanied by a lack of feeling or even contempt for the other – all potentially characteristic of avoidant young people. On the other hand, the search for the perfect partner who can offer unconditional love and meet the excessive emotional demands of an ambivalent/preoccupied adolescent (see Chapter 4) can lead to a succession of brief and unsuccessful relationships, which may look like a similar pattern, but has very different functions and roots in the state of mind of the young person.

In the *Adult Attachment Interview* (AAI), which can be conducted with older adolescents, the dismissing pattern is shown in a tendency to idealise early family life, but to find it difficult to recall much detail. So the five adjectives to describe the mother or father could be 'Very loving, generous, very caring' and so on, but little can be offered to support those words accurately. They may report such things as falling off a bicycle as a child, but holding on to the painful broken arm for a long time before seeking help from a parent. Sometimes stories that are offered of "perfect" family life may be contradicted later in the interview by accounts of parenting that was cold or rejecting. This inconsistency is indicative of a lack of the coherence that characterises the accounts of secure/autonomous adults. Incoherence here generally reflects the difficulty in reconciling actual (but suppressed) memories of rejection with an idealised (but unsupported) view of parents. It is often simpler not to remember.

Joining a new family in adolescence (11–18 years)

When adolescents come into a new family, whether leaving the birth family for the first time or after a number of previous moves, the common experience of difficulties in building new relationships is compounded by the developmental challenges of impending separation. Nevertheless, as this age period is one of general change and the development of adult identities, it can still be an opportunity for teenagers to learn new lessons about the self and relationships in the context of available, responsive, accepting and co-operative caregiving.

It is important for caregivers to start by building on any areas of successful functioning, whether this be computer skills or sport or affection for animals. One fostered teenager who shut down on his feelings and would not communicate with his carers described how he loved calling to their dog to come to him when they were out walking or letting the dog snuggle up to him in front of the television (Schofield *et al*, 2000; Beek and Schofield, 2004a). Any areas of activity that raise self-esteem, increase self-efficacy or make the young person feel less isolated can be the basis for lowering anxiety and building relationships.

Within the avoidant/dismissing pattern in adolescence there will always be a range, from young people who are rather reserved, but can be successful at school and maintain some friendships, to those young people who find themselves increasingly isolated or get involved in anti-social behaviour. The extent to which teenagers are cool or aggressive will be having an impact on their social relation-ships. Genetic factors, such as intelligence and temperament, will be interacting with environmental factors, such as the history of abuse or neglect in the birth family, the quality of relationships and caregiving in the foster or adoptive family and other factors such as school provision and contact with birth family members.

Nina (now 13) was a rather cool nine-year-old when placed with her foster carers but they were able to accept her and be patient. Although Nina accepted foster family life, it took a while for her to begin to feel and show feelings of affection for her foster mother – feelings for her foster father started earlier. School was an area of success for her as was her football. Contact was the subject of some negotiation but worked well. Her birth mother had opposed the Care Order, but later accepted this placement as in her daughter's best interest and was supportive. Nina was thriving.

Sean (15) was scapegoated in his birth family and was rejected at the age of 10. This rejection was reinforced during contact. He was placed with foster carers who focused on controlling his behaviour and lacked understanding of his difficulties. In his foster home he was deeply anxious but bossy and boastful. He was of average intelligence, but not able to accept authority at school. He started to steal.

Although both teenagers had been rather dismissive of relationships and reluctant to share any feelings or accept comfort, they differed in some key respects. Nina had an overall sense that, although her mother had neglected her, her mother's drug addiction problem explained this and she was now proud of Nina. Nina had an exceptionally stable foster family who were able to respond to her strengths and help her gain more flexible careseeking strategies. Sean, in contrast, was distrusted and unloved in both families. This rejection was intensifying his avoidant and controlling strategies and leading him towards anti-social behaviours.

Whatever an avoidant teenager's behaviour, there will be some opportunities to use the caregiving relationship to bring about change. However, where adolescents are especially cool, defiant and contemptuous of attempts to offer concern and care, new caregivers will need a great deal of support to avoid getting into a cycle of disappointment, irritation, anger and rejection. For caregivers, the capacity to think through the origins of the young person's behaviour, to understand the consequences of the young person's experiences in terms of their defensive strategies, and to bear in mind what in the young person's behaviour triggers a negative reaction in them as carers, is essential.

For many avoidant teenagers, years of negative experiences will have left a legacy of suppressed emotional turmoil and cognitive confusion. As with children in middle childhood, adolescents will need to have their own space to retreat to – a choice that is often seen as more "normal" and indeed necessary in adolescence. More shared experiences in the family can be contrived around ordinary everyday things, such as shopping for clothes, having meals or occasionally watching television together. Opportunities to parent the child in ways that start to open doors to more open communication can arise through times when the teenager is particularly upset or unwell. In these circumstances, providing cups of tea in bed and special nurturing becomes more acceptable, more valued and is stored away as an episodic memory. Even aggressive, anti-social adolescents value carers who advocate for them, go the extra mile for them, stay up waiting when they are out late and demonstrate their availability (Walker *et al*, 2002). This kind of authoritative parenting, characterised by high expectations, nurture and concern, disconfirms the adolescent's negative internal working model and builds in the possibility that caregivers can be trusted and that the adolescent can feel competent as well as worthy of love and support.

Adulthood and parenthood

For insecure adults, as for insecure children and adolescents, the challenge remains one of balancing dependency and attachment needs with the ability to explore – which in adult life will be around establishing satisfying roles in the worlds of romantic relationships, family, further education and work. In any of these environments there are possibilities for success and failure, pleasure and pain, and although adults continue to need secure base relationships on which they can rely, there are expectations that adults will manage their feelings and behaviour competently.

Different pathways will bring different risk and opportunities and so factors in the dismissing adult's history and current circumstances will make a big difference to outcomes.

Pete (28), married with one child, spent much of his childhood in two foster families, following domestic violence, neglect and rejection in his birth family. He described how he had survived his difficult childhood by never letting anyone get close to him, until he met his wife. However, he had been encouraged by one foster family to use his intelligence and, after leaving school, he had become a scientific assistant for a fishing company, testing the mineral content in fish brains. The job allowed him to focus on the minute detail of his task, but he explained how much he enjoyed working in a team of people as 'I need a bit of a push to be friendly'. (Schofield, 2003)

Adults who have experienced more significant and direct abuse in childhood may find it harder to take the opportunities of work environments or adult relationships. Jack (22) had experienced physical and sexual abuse in his birth family and had continued to cut himself off from close relationships during an otherwise stable foster placement that was still a family for him in adult life. He could not sustain relationships in adult life and his capacity to think logically had been damaged, so that he had difficulty remembering instructions in order to hold down a job.

For dismissing adults who have grown up in foster or adoptive families, parenthood can provoke powerful feelings about loss and rejection alongside some particular issues around how to tune in to their children's emotions. Dismissing adults tend to suppress memories and idealise childhood and yet for parents who have experienced poor parenting or neglect and abuse, there are some hard-to-deny realities around the circumstances that led to them coming into care. As with all developmental challenges across the lifespan, the taking on of a parental role may lead to a continuation of problematic patterns of relating or can offer opportunities to revise relating patterns in the context of support from secure base adults.

Summary points

- Avoidant infants and children have experienced parenting that is:
  - rejecting of emotional demands;
  - intrusive and insensitive to their needs;
  - rational and minimises/devalues feelings;
  - giving the message – don't make a fuss, be self-reliant;
  - not supportive of exploration, effectiveness and co-operation;
  - not conducive to building self-esteem.

- Infants and children adapt to this kind of caregiving by shutting down on their feelings, deactivating attachment behaviour and relying on themselves.

- Avoidant infants and children are not avoiding a relationship – they are achieving the best kind of relationship that is available, by *avoiding direct expression of emotions and demands*. This is an organised strategy, adaptive to a fairly predictable if insensitive kind of caregiving.

- Avoidant infants and children have an *internal working model* of the self as unlovable, others as rejecting and intrusive and relationships as reliably distant and unavailable.

- Avoidant infants and children, as they develop, show the following characteristics:
  - anxious, dependent but shut down on feelings;
  - deactivate attachment behaviour, but anger can burst through;
  - do not understand emotions, especially mixed emotions, in self and others;
  - poor at perspective taking, empathy;
  - cannot reflect on/manage/regulate emotions and behaviour;
  - rational but rigid thinkers;
  - can be awkward socially;
  - can be bullies – when anger at rejection and a lack of empathy for other people combine;
  - low self-esteem/confidence but can be boastful and grandiose;
  - low self-efficacy but can be controlling;
  - risk of antisocial behaviour/conduct problems.

4 Ambivalent / resistant / preoccupied patterns

Infants who make the normal range of emotional and other demands but who experience *inconsistent* caregiving find it difficult to trust their caregiver or to organise a strategy that enables them to gain a predictable response. Variable caregiver responses to similar behaviour (crying, seeking proximity) mean that infants lack reliable information about what behaviour will be effective in obtaining comfort or reassurance. Caregivers who are insensitive to specific needs and communications leave infants with a different kind of dilemma to that faced by avoidant infants, who have experienced a negative but consistent response. Their infants learn the lesson that it is necessary to increase their attachment behaviours, to display their emotions and to make persistent demands in an attempt to increase the predictability of their caregiver or at least to produce a more frequent response. However, their lack of trust in caregiver availability makes them *resistant* to comfort.

As these infants move through the toddler and pre-school years, they develop either into rather passive, dependent, anxious children or into anxious and angry children who use a combination of alternately coy and threatening behaviour to *coerce* the caregiver (and increasingly their peers) to pay attention to them. *Preoccupied* with the lack of availability and concern of others and their own need for relationships, in the school years they become more sophisticated in trying to engage adult and peer attention, but feel disappointed and increasingly angry at what they perceive to be relationships and a social world generally that lets them down by not loving them enough. The questions they persistently ask (directly or indirectly) are: 'Do you really love me?' 'Are you really angry with me?' as they anxiously demand attention and seek reassurance from others. They often define themselves as and can become victims. In adolescence, dependent helplessness or stormy relationships tend to be the norm, as anxieties surface both about separation from the family and the difficulty in sustaining intimate relationships with friends and partners.

Ambivalent children range from those who have a tendency to display emotions and be preoccupied with relationships, but can keep their feelings within reasonable bounds and function fairly effectively, through to children who are either highly anxious and dependent or who swing in a more extreme and unregulated fashion from needy to angry in ways that alienate others and detract from an age-appropriate focus on play, school and work. For children and young people coming into foster and adoptive families, who are likely to have experienced quite significant abuse, neglect and loss, it is these more extreme forms that are likely to be the more common. The internal working model is of a needy, ineffective and dependent self, and of potentially loving but withholding others, who are unpredictable, cannot be relied on and may let you down.

Infancy (birth–18 months)

In contrast to the mothers of avoidant infants, mothers of ambivalent infants respond at times to the infant's demands and expressions of emotion – but not sensitively or predictably. George and Solomon (1999) describe these caregivers as *'uncertain'* and 'unable to integrate positive and negative, good and bad, desirable and undesirable'. They appear to overemphasise their caregiving role and describe being concerned about their availability for the child, but are actually unable to understand or respond consistently and flexibly to the child's cues.

In the more extreme cases that might feature in the history of children who come into care, these are likely to be rather neglectful families. The caregiver is too preoccupied with their own anxieties, anger and emotional concerns, often struggling with their own entangled relationships with family and friends (and perhaps other more practical concerns that they find hard to focus on and solve), to be mentally or physically available for or in tune with the infant. As with the mothers of avoidant infants, these mothers want to be good mothers to their babies – indeed they may have a great deal invested in the idea of being a loving mother and having a baby who loves them. However, because of their own distractions and preoccupations, in response to the same signals from the infant, a mother may sometimes be comforting, sometimes angry and sometimes unresponsive. Thus, in the context of such a lack of focus and attunement, the crying infant may one minute be swept up and cuddled, but another minute be shouted at or left to cry until he gives up and falls sleep. This presents a major difficulty for the baby in learning what to expect from his relationship environment, how to feel reliably safe and how to get his needs consistently met. This is a mental and emotional struggle, since the baby needs to get to the point where he can learn how to shape his behaviour, to *organise* his behaviour, to get specific responses in order to reduce anxiety, restore equilibrium and regulate his emotions and behaviour.

A number of behavioural and emotional consequences for the infant follow from this experience. First, the young infant *may cry and make a fuss* almost constantly in the hope of getting attention from the attachment figure. Even if this proves to be negative attention at times, at least some attention tells the infant that the caregiver is there and provides some recognition of his existence. For the infant, this fundamental *existential* anxiety – not only, do I matter?, but do I exist? who am I? – is critical and becomes difficult to manage without the available presence of a caregiver to reflect consistently back to the infant a sense that he exists as a whole person in the mind of the caregiver. Without some form of reassurance, he is *overwhelmed by anxiety*.

Secondly, the infant fairly rapidly gets to feel rather *helpless* and *ineffective* if there is no predictable way, no behaviour within his power, by which loneliness, hunger and anxiety can be resolved. This increases the infant's sense of dependence, but in the context of an unreliable other person. Thus the internal working model starts to be shaped in particular ways from early on, as the infant tries to make sense of their environment. The self is not felt to be lovable enough to keep the caregiver's attention reliably.

Thirdly, and almost simultaneously, the infant starts to get increasingly *angry*, raging against the fact that the mother will not come when she is needed or when her presence and care are asked for. This combination of anxiety, anger, helplessness and lack of trust means that when the mother does finally respond the infant is likely to *distrust* and *resist* comfort and so continue to cry and fret. The infant has learned that the mother is too likely to go away, physically or psychologically, for it to be safe to cease the emotional demands. The mother in turn may feel that, having made the effort to return and comfort the child, the child is rejecting and unrewarding – and she too will become angry, disappointed and resentful of the excessive and unfair demands placed upon her. Her defensive tendency to split the world into good and bad people, who do or do not meet her needs, may force the label of "bad baby" on to this child in order to preserve her own identity as a "good mother".

The cost to the child of the caregiver's lack of availability and preoccupation with relationships is most clearly seen in the lack of support for the infant's competent exploration and play. These insecure infants often experience not only too much anxiety to play, but also mothers who tend to interfere when they do start to explore. As Grossman *et al* (1999, p. 764, citing research by Cassidy and Berlin, 1994) describe:

Mothers of ambivalent infants were not only less consistently available to their infants when the infants were distressed, but also interfered when their infants

regime that, above all else, signals to the baby their *predictable availability* for nurture and safety. *Being* available is not enough – clear signals have to be given and familiar, reassuring structures to the day established. The infant needs help to learn to trust in that availability, in spite of previous experiences and in spite of existing mental representation of others. Infants from neglecting environments will not, as Stovall and Dozier (1998, 2000, Dozier *et al*, 2005) have described, be very good at eliciting nurture in the usual way. Their signals will be more persistent but less specific, and their resistant responses will make them often unrewarding and frustrating to feed, hold and comfort.

The accuracy and timing of sensitive responses to signals of need will be very important. Even for older infants, this may need to match the closely contingent timing of the first few weeks of life, rather than the more comfortably delayed and trusted timing possible with the secure 12–18-month-old. Using baby intercom systems, for example, may minimise delay in responding to signals of distress and need for proximity. The voice will calm the child and will primarily signal the caregiver's availability on demand. Such strategies can help to establish the kind of predictable synchrony whenever the child is upset that should have occurred in the first weeks of life and will build trust. It does, of course, suggest that foster carers and adoptive parents need to be able to make that time available in order to bring about therapeutic change in the infant's beliefs and expectations, revising their internal working models.

Responding in a way that is timely and accurate needs to be accompanied by the caregivers' ability to reflect back to the infant through their facial expression, their eyes, their words, their voice and their touch, that the world is a safe place. Caregivers can mirror the infant's primitive anxieties through facial expressions, for example, a frown of uncertainty or the raised eyebrows of shock and surprise, but reflect them back in a processed, contained and safe form. Unlike a newborn infant, however, the older insecure infant does not only need to learn about the caregiver's containing mind through this experience, she needs to *unlearn* previous sets of expectations and beliefs and replace them with expectations of a caregiver who reliably acts as a safe haven and a secure base for exploration. The task is to regulate the infant's emotions and release them from the fear of being overwhelmed by anxiety.

Signs of progress will not only be a moderation of the child's level of emotional demands, suggesting the beginnings of trust and self-regulation, but also evidence that the secure base effect is starting to liberate the child to explore and enjoy their world. Given these children's tendency to be dependent and to feel helpless, direct and targeted support for exploration (e.g. through play and promoting self-efficacy – see Chapter 8) will be of key therapeutic value, alongside offering indirect support for exploration though secure base availability. The two work together in promoting security and age-appropriate development.

Early childhood (18 months–4 years)

Since one of the challenges of this age period is to establish a balance between autonomy and dependency, managing neediness, closeness and distance while benefiting from opportunities for exploration and play will not be easy for these more anxious children. The ups and downs of toddlers' moods and behaviour are common, since all young children are managing in different ways the excitement and the stress of becoming a separate and independent person. But for ambivalent/resistant children whose caregivers continue to be insensitive and inconsistently available, high levels of anxiety about being let down and a resultant need to insist on the carers' attention will often intensify the more volatile, stormy aspects of early childhood.

Lack of trust and lack of parental support for play can mean that full enjoyment of their physical environment is also less likely. In neglectful families, the constrained, unsafe or unstimulating physical environment may itself be preventing productive learning and play. But as we have seen in infancy, caregivers may interfere with rather than support play and exploration. The care that children's bodies receive, feeding and toileting processes in particular, can also become affected by the lack of sensitive attention and the battles that ensue when infants both demand and resist comfort. Physical symptoms of anxiety and stress may start to appear, as painful emotions start to become experienced and expressed by these young children as painful headaches and tummy aches.

By the end of the second year secure children will have a range of new physical and psychological skills that will affect how they manage the self in relationships and the progress that flows from this as they move towards the school years. But the likely development of these abilities in ambivalent children must be understood in the context of their insecure internal working models and coping strategies. Their walking skills, for example, should enable them to seek comfort or avoid danger more effectively. But needy preoccupied insecure children may cling to the caregiver and not explore in the way their new-found mobility allows. In contrast, they might use their mobility to test out the commitment of caregivers and gain their attention, for example, by running off in the supermarket or hiding under the clothes racks in the department store. The element of cat and mouse game-playing that all toddlers enjoy is not in itself a problem; indeed, it is exciting to run off or hide and very reassuring to be found. But if taken to extremes, as it may be for these children, the range of attention-demanding behaviours can mean significant risk-taking, such as rushing out of the store. The coercive testing can also wind the caregiver up to such a pitch of anxiety and anger that this in turn forces the child to resort to their most seductive, coy, penitent behaviour in order to avoid punishment – and the cycle continues.

Similarly, the new-found ability to pretend, and in particular to display false positive or false negative emotions through facial expressions, is an important part of social learning; for example, smiling when receiving a present regardless of whether you like it, or appearing enthusiastic about an activity which your dad wants you to enjoy. For both secure and insecure children, pretence can be part of the necessary repertoire for managing social relationships. But for anxious–ambivalent children in this age group, pretence may come from both deep-rooted *distrust of others* and lead to *distrust by others*. False facial expressions, for example, can be used to reassure, placate, threaten and manipulate the responses of others, adults and children.

The growth of language skills, another key area of developmental progress in this age range, enables secure children to become more flexible and sophisticated in managing relationships comfortably and getting needs met in a co-operative way. For ambivalent/resistant children, language can be an important development in expressing their needs and in building relationships, but it can also become an extra tool in the struggle to win the attention of the caregiver or other adults. Language can be used selectively and strategically, for example, speaking in a babyish voice to gain comfort or placate an angry caregiver or using language and a threatening tone of voice to coerce others. If the core anxiety is that the self is unlovable and there is a need to ensure the concerned attention of others, then more sophisticated tools for communication can be enlisted to the cause and can be (temporarily) effective. On the other hand, caregivers, other adults and friends may start to feel increasingly weary and irritated when faced with the demands from the young child's needy and angry selves as expressed through these various new skills. There is then an increased likelihood that the child will get caught up in a spiral of lengthy battles or be emotionally rejected and abandoned.

One further relevant characteristic of this developmental period will be the tendency for pre-school children to become more sophisticated in their behaviour and relationships as they start to become better able to judge the responses of others. Young children gradually come into contact with a wider range of behaviour in a wider range of other people, but they also develop greater perspective-taking skills which help them to make sense of the thinking behind different behaviours. By the age of three or four, secure children will have become better readers of other minds, better able to experience and show empathy and better able to plan their own responses. However, insecure children exposed to unpredictable parenting will find it more difficult than secure children to both read and make due allowances for the feelings and needs of others. If raised feelings do not predictably bring about attentive caregiving, and other coercive or even needy strategies sometimes produce the abandonment they are meant to avoid, then it will be hard to learn productive lessons about how to make relationships work successfully If the main strategy for the child is to keep the attachment figure close through use of emotional demands, then the challenge is how to prevent that person from getting too angry and abandoning them. Using some sense of what is in the mind of the caregiver becomes another tool for forcing attachment figures to pay attention. But it does not lead to the goal-corrected partnership in which both caregiver and child negotiate in a co-operative way to ensure that the goals of both "partners" are achieved.

Thus, for example, think of the scene at the supermarket checkout, in which a three- or four-year-old child with her mother tries to get the packet of sweets that she wants. If the mother says no, the child may begin by a persuasive, 'But I've been a good girl'. Then if this is unsuccessful, the child may start to escalate the demand from increasingly insistent requests, 'But I want it, now!' to a high-volume 'Give it to me!', and on into a threatening rage and tearful tantrum, 'Give it to me or else . . .!' If the mother starts to get angry rather than giving in, the child may match the raised temperature and volume of the mother's mood and voice, in order to force her to resolve the situation by giving in to avoid further embarrassment. Alternatively, the child could switch to a placatory, seductive tone, suggesting again that she does deserve the sweets, 'Just a small packet, please . . . go on . . .' If this reduces the mother's anger, but still does not produce the sweets, the 'but you promised' theme might build into a tantrum, as the child moves into coercive mode again.

This strategy has thus become a much more subtle and sustained variation on the behaviour in the Strange Situation, when the child both demands and resists proximity. Although not an unusual strategy for all pre-school children, the swinging from coy to coercive is more intense and persistent in ambivalent children. The ambivalent child has learned something of what is in the mind of the caregiver (embarrassment, guilt, distress), but uses it to develop a coercive rather than co-operative strategy, reflecting the parent's own likely difficulty in sensitive responding and co-operative thinking and also the parent's own tendency to resort to extremes of emotion. This coy-coercive strategy may produce short-term gains on some occasions with some people (i.e. it might work with dad but not mum, granddad but not uncle), in terms of achieving attention and perhaps the sweets. But the model that the mother or other attachment figure is building of the child is that of a troublesome, unreasonable, demanding, and embarrassing and now powerful person, who while still small appears to have control over the family. The lesson learned by the child is that this strategy "works" at times, but almost certainly the child feels as drained and disappointed as the caregiver. The big scene, with others watching, the caregiver getting angry and upset and the incident reported to other people as further evidence of what a naughty child she is, is far from reassuring for her self-concept or self-esteem.

The caregiver–child relationship can therefore be quite a roller-coaster experience for this emotionally demanding, needy but angry dyad. Both parent and child have needs to be met by the other, with angry exchanges alternating with some moments of contrasting sentimental closeness, when making amends by either parent or child may be on the agenda. Demonstrations of feeling are the currency in this relationship, but their unpredictable quality means that the child's world does not make a lot of sense. There is no *reason* or *logic* behind the cuddle or the absence of cuddle, the anger or the lack of interest that appears to connect with their behaviour. On the other hand, more extreme behaviours do seem to allow the child to take control and may start to be favoured.

For some ambivalent children who may not be quite so anxious, it is possible to observe in the playgroup or nursery setting, how they use their displays of emotion in ways that replicate this coy/coercive switching, but in a more moderate, less destructive form. The child may recruit allies among the peer group, for example, by making them their best friend and by offering privileged status in their game – 'You can be the baby' or 'You can have the princess outfit'. They may be controlling other children, but the seductive element, for example, following a command with a conspiratorial giggle, is persuasive – often matched with an implicit or explicit threat that failure to co-operate or failure to love them enough, could lead to being cast out in the cold. These small children may also be controlling staff, by using cheeky and engaging smiles to distract attention from the fact that they did not do as they were told at tidy-up time. There is a fine line here between the secure pre-school child's confident managing of social situations and testing of boundaries and the more insecure child's controlling behaviour. Key here will be the extent to which the child is too preoccupied with relationships, with peers or adults, to settle and complete play tasks and to pay attention/find pleasure in a flexible way with people and with materials.

More anxious, needy and angry ambivalent children in pre-school settings may demand and need too much care or control, so that other children start to peel away and find more congenial, reciprocal friendships, leaving the anxious child declaring, 'Why isn't anybody listening to me?!' Often the last resort for anxious–ambivalent children is to claim a physical need, to which staff have to respond. After a period of unsuccessful demands to get the company or concern of other children or staff, the child may collapse on a cushion saying to staff, 'I've got a tummy ache!' This may be a learned behaviour to gain attention – adults cannot ignore it – but it can also reflect a real sense of physical stress when emotional needs are not met and the child feels overwhelmed.

More dependent ambivalent children may lack the skills or capacity to manage relationships in any sense and can become the victims of bullies. Cries of 'He's hurting me!' and 'It's not fair!' may be used to gain attention and sympathy, but they may also be genuine symptoms of victimisation by avoidant aggressors (Troy and Sroufe, 1987 cited in Weinfield *et al*, 1999, p. 79). When children are repeatedly appealing for support and blaming others, it is not easy to respond accurately and with justice, so that caregivers in family or nursery settings may gradually ignore their pleas with the hope of reducing the "attention-seeking" behaviour – but this may increase anxiety, leave children vulnerable and lead to more insistent cries for help.

Joining a new family in early childhood (18 months–4 years)

Children coming into care at this stage may be rather passive and helpless. If they are more demanding and angry, they may be seen as simply showing a rather extreme form of the expected "terrible twos" or, if a little older, as perhaps not having had appropriate boundaries set during that period. They may even be thought of as "spoiled", because previous caregivers have "given in" to them. But it is important to help new caregivers maintain empathy and child focus by understanding the likely source of the child's behaviour in the context of uncertain or neglectful care – intensified by a reaction to anxiety and loss. It is hard to maintain faith in the idea of anxiety when children seem so defiant and the family's boundaries for behaviour are challenged.

Ambivalent/resistant children may initially treat carers with suspicion or with enthusiasm, or may show some of the more clingy, dependent and seductive approaches. However, it will not be long before saying no to the child produces the kind of rages that reflect their anger and anxiety about abandonment. As when caring for the infants in this group, predictability and availability in order to reduce anxiety and build trust will be key, but so also will be some attempt to engage the child co-operatively within safe boundaries, to avoid every situation becoming a battle. Accepting and acknowledging feelings, but explaining and putting feelings clearly into words, can give the carer and child some foundation of open communication on which to start building *confidence in reason* rather than relying solely on outbursts of emotion.

Sensitive physical care will be part of the message of availability and concern, but toileting, feeding and sleeping may all cause the child and the family difficulties in the early days. It is important to bear in mind that older children in the family will also have to tolerate the young child's various kinds of unregulated physical and emotional messes and may need to be enlisted in the cause of helping the child to relax and settle. Young children will need physical care and comfort, such as sitting on the caregiver's lap and sharing a bedtime story. Restrictions on physical affection in the name of "safe care" are not in the child's interests (for further discussion see also Chapter 11).

One of the particular challenges for caregivers of ambivalent/resistant young children is that they are likely to be jealous of attention paid to other children in the family or even attention that the parents may pay to each other. The tendency to split people into love/hate camps will affect even these young children, who may, for example, be highly seductive and endearing with one parent, but hostile and resistant with the other. This requires a maximum degree of co-operation and partnership between those who will be caring for the child – including, where relevant, grandparents and older children of the family. Even social workers will have to take care not to be drawn into the 'I love you, but I hate them' game. The child may show very different strategies and appear to be a very different child with different caregivers – another feature that can lead to anger and anxiety among caregivers, as well as a sense of being manipulated and even controlled by a young child.

The feelings that made the birth caregivers anxious and angry and disappointed can easily surface in foster carers and adopters. It is at this point that it is most important to hang on to a firm understanding of where these behaviours come from and an awareness of the need to raise the child's self-efficacy and self-esteem, even if it appears that they are too powerful and too big for their boots already. Later chapters (6–10) will give more examples of these parenting behaviours, but it is essential to use support from social workers to sustain a belief in the child and in the potential for resolving this dilemma i.e. it is a learned behaviour pattern that can be unlearned. The child needs help to change their behaviours, but also to believe that they can be loved and lovable. Young children are not going to change until they are able to trust both the boundaries and the availability of carers. Small changes need to be noticed and celebrated, as it takes time for that trust to develop.

Middle childhood (5–10 years)

Developing and valuing a sense of self, learning the rules, concentrating on academic work and other competitive activities, managing feelings and regulating behaviour in the context of the social world, are all key tasks of this age group –

and all tasks that can prove challenging to insecure–ambivalent/resistant children. The social world is rapidly changing as school, peer group activities, competition and performance anxieties require each individual child to adapt in ways that strengthen the sense of self, but also facilitate fitting in to the group. If the value and effectiveness of the self is already in doubt, the playground, the classroom, the football team and the Brownie pack can present major challenges.

As in the younger age group, for some children this defensive strategy may mean that they are rather dependent and overemotional. Teachers were found to "baby" ambivalent children in the early years of school, recognising the signals of neediness (Sroufe, 1983). As in the nursery stage, some school children may achieve a degree of social acceptance and find friends to look after them through their displays of emotion and neediness, though the quality of these friendships will depend on how extreme and, in particular, how coercive they have started to become. Crittenden (1995) suggests that in this middle childhood period the coercive element in the ambivalent child's behaviour starts to increase. The determined and strategic toddler having a tantrum at the supermarket checkout may now, as a school-age child, have become a dictator of family life, with increased cognitive complexity facilitating greater powers of control and growing physical size making it more difficult to physically move children who are behaving defiantly.

There are social expectations that children once at school should no longer be having tantrums and be such a control problem. The "terrible twos" are well known – the terrible sixes or sevens are less common and are less publicly acceptable. Parents and children feel that this cannot be right but are locked into battle lines. Because the caregivers themselves are likely also to be anxious and preoccupied with relationships, both parties to this wrangle will be angry and needy, with some caregivers likely to threaten abandonment, 'I'll go home without you then' through to 'You can go into care then, I'll ring them now' or 'You'll be the death of me' as the ultimate threat, even though such threats increase the child's anxiety and demanding behaviour.

Through this age period and as part of identity development, all children are very conscious of how they are being labelled and how they should label themselves. Although as Harter (1987) has suggested, self-esteem will derive from a number of different aspects of performance (e.g. academic, sporting, friendships), this is the period when a more global sense of self-esteem develops. Ambivalent children's attachment preoccupations make it less likely that they will be successful in activities. The experience of being difficult and demanding, and the parent's response to it, can leave children feeling bad and labelling themselves as incorrigible in ways that reflect the anger, anxiety and possibly negative language of the parent. Lengthy sulky silences may grow into angry battles and sustained feuds, inside and outside the immediate attachment relationships.

In school, the preoccupation with self in relationships continues to dominate the children's minds as they sit in class, but need to actively monitor the relationship environment – Am I missing out on something? Is somebody getting more praise/attention/love than me? Restlessness that attracts an investigation of attention deficit hyperactivity disorder may be disguising a firm focus of attention, but their focus is on the availability of teacher attention or friends rather than on the assignment. This limits the child's capacity to concentrate on and find success in academic work. The child's emotional life is full of drama as the playground world revolves around who is friends with whom. There are switches between who is considered best friends or sworn enemies, in-crowds and out-crowds, which raise anxieties further and make it harder to focus on the requirements of maths or geography. Difficulties in playing by the rules of games, taking turns and learning to lose as well as win create more drama. In contrast to secure children, insecure children try to conceal their feelings of loss with bravado but give up more readily if they see losing as inevitable.

Children's relationships with their bodies also continue to be significantly affected by their attachment experiences, with one study finding that boys aged six with resistant histories were more likely to have somatic complaints than secure children (Lewis *et al*, 1984 in Weinfield *et al*, 1999, p. 81). It is difficult to be sure about the connection here, but it seems likely that, even for these children who appear to express their emotions to excess, many anxieties remain unresolved and are expressed through their bodies.

Joining a new family in middle childhood (5–10 years)

When these anxious, dependent children come into new families in the primary years, they may appear quite open at first, showing feelings of sadness and happiness in ways that give carers some confidence that at least they know what the children are feeling. They can sometimes be very appealing children, putting on a show full of energy and excitement. They are often described as "like an open book" and "bubbly" (Schofield *et al*, 2000). Sometimes this openness and bubbliness spills over into clearer expressions of neediness, asking for constant physical contact with the carer perhaps, showing and respecting few personal boundaries. Switches between open/affectionate and stormy/challenging behaviours are likely to emerge, however, with the degree of explosiveness depending on the kinds of separation, abuse, neglect and trauma the child may have experienced.

Children who, in addition to experiences of inconsistently available and insensitive parenting, have been at some point frightened, assaulted sexually or physically or emotionally terrorised may be very extreme in both their neediness and in their rage, throwing chairs through windows, for example, when distressed and out of control. Foster carers and adopters describe children "going berserk". The "bubbliness" then seems less like champagne and more like a volcano. Those children who have experienced frightening caregiving in their birth families may be described as disorganised with ambivalent as a secondary classification (see Chapter 5), but their controlling behaviour when stressed and upset can be helpfully understood in terms of an extreme form of needy/angry, coy/coercive ambivalent switching (Crittenden, 1995).

Calming these children and enabling them to be less extreme in their excitement, their need and their anger is the key task for caregivers. Providing security through availability and sensitive responsiveness will help children to build a secure base and to make sense of the world at an age when they are looking for "rules". These children are used to a lack of predictability and logic so they need extra help to shape their past and present life into as logical a narrative as possible. But this reflective process needs to be paired for more chaotic and distressed children with practical strategies for keeping them safe and preventing damage to other people and to property. Children can frighten themselves as well as others by their rages and may start to split off this wild person from the real person they want to be. One such foster child talked about herself as having 'a nice inside but a nasty outside' (Beek and Schofield, 2004a). This can be a scary notion, which requires the carer to help the child understand that good and bad impulses exist in all of us, on the inside (in our minds) and on the outside (in our behaviour), but that these impulses can be talked about, understood and managed – and that reparation is possible. Thus, coy and coercive behaviours can shift to a more constructive and co-operative pattern, with more open and honest communication that promotes pro-social and positive behaviour, reduces anti-social behaviour and offers the possibility of repairing the consequences of bad behaviour when it has occurred.

A major challenge for caregivers of ambivalent children in middle childhood is to enable them to regulate their feelings and behaviour well enough to manage not only in the home but also in their school and community environments. Anxious children's tendency on the one hand to become victims and on the other hand to be such demanding friends and pupils that both peers and school staff become irritated and rejecting, can send children into a downward social and academic spiral. Increasing the child's felt security in the new family takes time and may need to be accompanied by a degree of engineering of the external social situation. This can mean working with school teachers, gymnastics clubs and Brownie leaders to try to hold the child's anxiety and prevent victimisation long enough to allow the therapeutic relationships in the foster or adoptive family to have an impact on the child's internal working model. For some children who are most desperate for comfort but most distrusting of close family relationships, it may be that skilled teachers and activity leaders or family friends are initially the best able to offer a child sources of self-esteem, for example, prior to a warm and trusting relationship in the foster or adoptive family developing. Positive experiences in a range of contexts can then form the foundations of calming and reassuring the child about their own worth and help them to use the sources of support inside the family.

The range of children who show these difficulties is very wide and the extent of their emotional, behavioural and social problems will depend on genetic factors, such as intelligence and temperament, as well as environmental factors, such as past experiences of abuse, current experiences of birth family contact and the quality and availability of the care being offered in the foster or adoptive family.

Leah (10) was of average intelligence. She was placed at the age of five with her older sister who had provided her with a sense of security in her neglectful birth family. Her anxiety was contained by the foster carer's availability, sensitivity and love for her. Contact was relatively unproblematic. Leah started to find success at school and was able to channel her "bubbliness" and tendency to dramatise into dancing classes.

Neelam (10) had an IQ of 60 and struggled to cope with her anticipated move to a mainstream comprehensive school. She had contact with anxiety-provoking birth family members who had emotionally abused and neglected her. She was placed in a very busy foster family with a carer who loved her but had unresolved trauma from abuse in her own childhood that made her angry and emotional at times. (Case material from Beek and Schofield, 2004a)

The insecure and ambivalent behavioural strategies of Leah and Neelam were similar. Both were also more secure at the three-year follow-up than they had been at the point of placement, but Leah was making good progress, while Neelam retained many of the kind of troublesome symptoms that Leah had lost e.g. high anxiety, being clingy, dependent and volatile, a victim of bullying and finding it difficult to regulate her feelings or to learn how to manage relationships.

In providing a therapeutic environment, whatever the child's specific circumstances, it is best, as ever, to start where the child is at. But for these children, balancing emotion and reason, meeting dependency needs but promoting autonomy within safe boundaries is a complex task. The goal here is not to get rid of the child's defences and end the child's use of emotional display strategies (genuine liveliness and emotionality can be appropriate and appealing), but to enable the child to be more flexible, and at times to think quietly before acting while at other times to display upset and seek help. The goal of security and autonomy is to reach this flexible (but not roller coaster) position, a position in which the child can begin to regulate their emotions, become a more active problem solver and find satisfaction in play, exploration and learning.

Adolescence (11–18 years)

The important shift in thinking abilities that marks the onset of adolescence permits more flexible and abstract thinking. Flexible thinking is key to the adolescent task of adapting to the many varied actual and potential environments – but for this ambivalent/resistant and preoccupied group of adolescents there are clearly barriers to this development. Although adolescence is a period of affirming a unique identity, adolescents learn that they can and are required to be different people in different circumstances and that, for example, in planning their futures, they have to include a range of possible future selves. This kind of thinking requires an ability, which tends to be lacking in this group, to reflect on the self and to plan with some degree of self-confidence for future routes in which a range of relationships will develop alongside a focus on work and activity. Reflecting on the self means facing up to anxieties about lovability, about fitting in, about getting your share of attention in the family or the classroom or the youth club. These persistent anxieties make it unsurprising that there is an association between ambivalent/resistant attachment histories and anxiety disorders in adolescence (Warren *et al*, 1997 cited in Weinfield *et al*, 1999, p. 81).

For this group of adolescents, a preoccupation with, but anxiety and anger about, themselves, their bodies and their relationships is played out in family environments which anticipate moves to independence and also in peer group environments where developing skills in selecting and building relationships with potential partners is going to be the norm. The prospect of either being alone or being in committed close relationships with others who might be expected to let them down, raises further anxieties about their lovability. Even when, or especially when, their birth family caregivers may have been unpredictably available, teenagers continue to seek reassurance from them that they are loved enough and to be coercively insistent on material things and their rights.

As in the toddler years, when becoming your own person is also an issue, needy but demanding behaviour is not unusual in adolescence – nor is a focus on material possessions. But for these young people, whether their behaviour is more coercive or more dependent, the strategic switches from angry to disarming are played out in the light of serious anxieties about academic and social performance and in the context of the psychosocial risks presented by alcohol, drugs, anti-social behaviour and sexual relationships. For example, a degree of recklessness, a tendency to rush into new situations without thinking of the consequences, may seem not untypical of adolescents, but for these children risk-taking may take more extreme forms as part of the way in which they become disinhibited, express feelings and gain attention.

In the Adult Attachment Interview (AAI, Main and Goldwyn, 1984), also used with older adolescents, the distinctive feature of this pattern (referred to as *preoccupied* or *enmeshed* in adults) is the combination of preoccupying anger and rather rambling, incoherent narratives. These are often lengthy interviews in which the person finds it hard to give relevant and concise responses to questions. The emphasis then is on angry feelings that still bubble up in response to questions about early childhood relationships with attachment figures. What is significant is that these are not just accounts of anger in early childhood – the anger is still live, current and preoccupying in the mind of the adolescent. Anxiety and anger seem to be closely linked for these young people and, of course, amplify each other – anxiety makes you angry, anger makes you anxious.

Joining a new family in adolescence

Adolescents coming into new families, whether from birth or previous foster or adoptive families, are inevitably bringing with them not only long-standing patterns of behaviour but also a powerful sense of loss and separation. The usual psychosocial challenges and opportunities of adolescence have to be faced in the context of new possibilities in family relationships, but also with the necessity of reworking mental representations based on previous relationships.

For those ambivalent and anxious children still in contact with entangling birth family members it can be very difficult to be free enough to establish a new life. Teenagers often feel responsible both for younger children at home and for parents and grandparents who are perceived to be dependent on them. For example, reported illness in the birth family and implicit or explicit messages to the young person that they are either partly responsible for the illness because of their behaviour or that they are needed to support the family can prove an irresistible pull. Such highly-charged communications can arrive at a fostered teenager's mobile phone during a school lunch break. In one case, a mother reported (falsely) to her 15-year-old daughter, whom she had consistently rejected and failed to protect from sexually abusive partners, that she had just been diagnosed with a terminal cancer. In another case, a mother (falsely) told her 13-year-old son that his grandmother had died and the foster family comforted him with his grief – but he then received a birthday card from his grandmother. Not all contact is this complex, but teenagers will need help to make sense of these relationships.

Adolescents with a tendency to be demanding, challenging and stormily emotional may not fit easily into new families, and the fact that the young people continue to be drawn back to birth families that will reject them and hurt them can make it harder for caregivers to cope with the young people's anger and distress. However, many caregivers who are experienced with adolescents become expert in seeing beyond the behaviours. They offer security by being available, setting boundaries, parenting co-operatively and accepting that risks have to be taken when preoccupied and entangled adolescents are learning some painful lessons. The children have to learn to manage their membership of two families. They need to learn that neither family is perfect, but to start to think in a more rational way about the risks and benefits of the two families in order to prioritise for the future.

Contrasting cases may help to clarify the range of children in this group and some of the differences where entangled relationships with birth families need to be managed. Charlene (13) and Vicky (12) had both had neglectful early child-hoods and came into care at between the age of five and six. They were both bright and bouncy children in the early days. Both had contact with mothers with significant personality problems.

Charlene (13) was encouraged to engage in a wide range of activities that built her self-esteem and channelled some of her energy. She was much loved by the foster carers who had enjoyed her energy as a primary school child and were still enjoying her achievements as an adolescent. Contact with her mother had always been difficult for a number of reasons. Her mother would sometimes have drunk too much alcohol for the contact to proceed. Charlene would wet the bed and become very upset before and, on occasions, at contact. Her mother subsequently had a baby whom she had kept, so contact was complicated emotionally.

Charlene's foster mother was very understanding of Charlene's complicated feelings and was active in helping her think in a balanced way about her mother. The carer also built a relationship with the birth mother. Finally, she took control of all contact arrangements and was able to achieve contact that was comfortable and even pleasurable for both Charlene and her mother. This process contributed to the fact that Charlene became much calmer and more settled and had not wet the bed since.

113

Vicky (12) had lost her sparkle and was subdued, without this being associated with any moves towards constructive, reflective thought. She had little interest in her school work and her foster carers were disappointed that 'she wouldn't make an effort'.

Vicky had taken on the role of confidante to her mother even as a small child and this role was getting more pronounced as Vicky became an adolescent. Contact with her mother was unsupervised and outings as well as phone calls were fraught, with emotional appeals to Vicky to love her more.

Vicky's carers found it difficult to understand why Vicky was so preoccupied with her mother when her mother had let her down so much. They felt unable to do anything about the situation and tended to blame both Vicky and her mother for the fact that the placement had not gone as well as they had anticipated.

Outcomes for all children will be a complex interaction of factors in the child, the birth family, the foster family and the social work service. In these cases, it is possible to see how children with similar starting points and similar attachment patterns can take very different pathways depending on whether the child can become less anxious and more secure, whether the entangling relationship in the birth family can be managed and whether a new more secure and stable relationship in the foster or adoptive family can be established.

Adulthood and parenthood

As adults, the preoccupying anger with childhood attachment figures who let you down continues, as does the search for unconditional love and for the perfect relationship. Neighbours, friends, partners and social workers come into the frame as people who might be "the one". Adult life can be an emotional roller-coaster rather as childhood has been, as the playground is replaced with the workplace or the neighbourhood, but the feelings of anxiety and the expectation of being let down by those around you interferes in establishing relaxed rewarding relationships. As with ambivalent patterns in children, preoccupied adults may present very brightly and openly, chatting at length about themselves and their past. This is very appealing to social workers, as is the message you might get on a first or second visit, 'You are the perfect social worker, you really listen and understand me – not like the last one, she was very unsympathetic and never came to see me or answered the phone.' Inevitably, there are times when you too cannot get to the phone or make the visit when asked – especially if phone calls from the parent are coming in ten times a day – at which point you too will be added to the list of social workers who are not to be trusted. This pattern is a genuine marker for anxious distress in the adult, but engenders irritation and may cause a great deal of difficulty in multi-disciplinary networks when the health visitor is "wonderful" but the doctor "doesn't care" or vice versa.

As parents, the legacy of all that need, anger, hope and disappointment can lead to high expectations, initially, of what the baby will bring into their lives. This may lead to a great deal of anticipation, buying of expensive baby clothes and so on. But this cannot be matched by any consistent sensitivity to the child or commitment of emotion, energy and interest. The child makes demands and inevitably disappoints too. Without intervention with caregiver and child, the cycle is likely to continue.

Summary points

- Ambivalent infants and children have experienced parenting that is:
  - insensitive and only intermittently available;
  - uncertain and unpredictable;
  - sentimental but preoccupied with own emotional concerns;
  - not supportive of exploration, effectiveness and co-operation;
  - not conducive to building self-esteem;
  - preoccupied with anger.

- Infants and children adapt to this kind of caregiving by hyperactivating their attachment behaviour and making constant demands in the hope of getting care and attention.

- This is an organised strategy, adaptive to an unpredictable if insensitive kind of caregiving.

- Infants and children have an *internal working model* of the self as unlovable, others as unpredictably loving, and relationships as unreliable.

- Infants and children, as they develop, show the following characteristics:
  - anxious and dependent;
  - shows of emotion/attachment behaviour;
  - do not trust reason – rely on emotion;
  - cannot reflect on/manage/regulate emotions and behaviour;
  - seek relationships but are socially at risk because they are demanding/ needy;

- can be victims of bullies – when neediness, anger at rejection and a lack of empathy for other children combine;
- show low self-esteem / confidence but can seem bright and lively at first;
- show low self-efficacy – can become coercive during pre-school/middle childhood years, using extremes of feelings to control;
- are at risk of internalising problems, depression.

5 Disorganised, controlling, unresolved patterns

Disorganised infants have had the experience of seeking comfort from a primary caregiver when anxious, but finding that the caregiver is frightening or frightened and a source of anxiety. 'Fear without solution' (Main and Hesse, 1990) is the key to disorganised patterns. The caregiver may be actively frightening the child through their behaviour or may themselves be frightened and unresolved in relation to past or current trauma in their own lives, through loss, abuse or violence. Frightened, frightening and unresolved caregivers abdicate their caregiving role (George and Solomon, 1999), representing themselves as helpless, out of control and unable to control or properly care for the child. The infant cannot experience the caregiver as a haven of safety or as a secure base for exploration. There is no organised behavioural strategy that the infant can adopt in order to achieve security and relief from anxiety through proximity to the caregiver. On the contrary, the infant's mind needs to protect itself from the anxiety caused by the caregiver's behaviour and mind. This is an attachment relationship, but it is binding the child to a caregiver who cannot provide reliable care and protection and leaves the child at increased risk of pathology.

As children grow through the toddler and pre-school years, the need to protect their minds from feelings of fear, to prevent the self from being overwhelmed by anxiety and 'to be or to feel safe' (Crittenden, 1995), leads to attempts to find strategies for survival. *Role-reversing* strategies emerge for *controlling* the relationship environment, either by *punitive/aggressive* behaviour or by *compulsive caregiving/compulsively compliant* behaviour. As Liotti (1999) has described it, the child avoids being the *victim* by becoming either the *persecutor* or *rescuer* of the attachment figure. However, these three roles are constantly shifting. Thus, the child experiences himself as a victim when abused or scared of attack, seizes control in attacking and persecuting the parent, but may then, with the parent in victim role, try to rescue the parent and show concern. Thus, the child's representations of self and others are shifting, often quite rapidly and even within a single incident, leaving the child with multiple and contradictory models of the self and significant others. As Main (1991) describes, it is part of normal development to have different models of different people (e.g. my father is more comforting than my mother), but to have multiple and contradictory models of the *same* person, (e.g. 'My mother loves me and cares about my welfare'; 'My mother despises me and rejects me when I approach her'; 'My mother hurts me') leaves children confused and anxious. For young children in the formative early years "dual coding" (Main, 1991) of this kind makes it difficult to form a coherent set of expectations on which they can rely.

Unresolved and helpless/hostile caregivers may, in turn, become frightened of their punitive/aggressive children, seeing their behaviour as a deliberate attack on them as parents, as beyond their control and as likely to lead to disaster. This may seem extreme, but as social workers often report, there are parents who feel that the child, from birth, is alien to them and find it difficult to touch or be in the same room as the child. For other parents, the feeling of disillusionment, dislike and fear of the child grows more gradually in the early months and years. Then, as young children's behaviour starts actually to become difficult and controlling in the face of fear, rejection and the message that they are unlovable, caregivers (with their own heightened sense of unmanageable and catastrophic fear) can begin to feel that this is not the normal range of naughtiness, but suggests something far more serious. One mother speaking to a social worker said of her distressed, angry five-year-old, 'I think he is going to be a serial killer'. Such mental representations of the child give him the message that he is so bad, so dangerous that he is beyond control by normal means. It places the blame for the breakdown in the relationship and the child's behaviour firmly on something intrinsic to the child's make-up. In some cases, fatalistic talk of the inevitable future of local authority care, secure units and prisons may start quite young, fixing the child as incorrigible in the mind of the caregivers and the child.

Disorganisation and maltreatment

Disorganised and controlling patterns are more common among children who have been maltreated. A meta-analysis of studies suggested that 48 per cent of maltreated children are likely to be disorganised compared to 15 per cent in non-clinical, middle class families (van IJzendoorn *et al*, 1999), but some studies (Carlson *et al*, 1989) suggested that more than 80 per cent of maltreated children are disorganised. However, by no means all children who are classified as disorganised have been maltreated and there will be some disorganised children who have parents who are themselves unresolved in relation to loss or trauma, but who do not neglect or actively harm them.

The most helpful way of thinking about the research on disorganised patterns and maltreatment is that *children who are disorganised in infancy will be particularly vulnerable to later risk experiences and in particular to maltreatment and loss* (Main, 1995). Thus, a child who is born to a mother who has unresolved loss and trauma, who is disorganised as an infant, and who is then exposed to physical ill-treatment from the mother or the mother's partner, is especially vulnerable to more extreme behaviours, such as punitive aggression or dissociative, trance-like states (Liotti, 1999; Howe, 2005). This is not an uncommon pathway for children who come into the care system. Their birth parents' histories and current life circumstances often include multiple losses and trauma and children's experience of maltreatment compounds the effect of disorganisation. We know that, as Lyons-Ruth and Jacobvitz (1999, p. 543) put it:

There is ample evidence that maltreated children experience more negative family relationships and exhibit poorer developmental outcomes on multiple dimensions, as well as having early disorganised relationships.

In summary then, where children are disorganised *and* have had traumatic and fearful experiences, including physical abuse, sexual abuse, emotional cruelty, severe neglect and rejection, there is a higher risk of pathology. Traumatic experiences in early attachment relationships create the need to use defence mechanisms to exclude painful feelings and to avoid introspection and self-awareness. Children's capacity to think and reflect, in order to regulate their feelings and behaviour, to understand the minds and feelings of others and to achieve mutually rewarding relationships, is particularly at risk when experiences are incoherent and feelings are too painful to think about.

The disorganised pattern is the most complex to understand. This is in part because by definition children do not have the more consistent, organised patterns of thinking and behaviour that we have described in previous chapters. But it is also because as disorganised infants grow into toddlers and pre-schoolers they develop a range of very different survival strategies for controlling others in order to cope with the dilemmas of fear and overwhelming anxiety that they experience. Thus, three siblings assessed as disorganised and with apparently similar experiences may be behaving/adapting very differently. *Role reversal* and *control* may be through aggression or caregiving, children may be disinhibited or inhibited. Children may have obviously challenging behaviours, such as soiling and aggression, or the more subtle, trance-like absences of a dissociative response, or both. In broad terms, however, they are likely to develop controlling but highly insecure strategies, which break down at times of stress to leave them out of control and feeling hostile but helpless.

Developmental processes are particularly important here since, as disorganised children mature from infancy through childhood to adolescence, there will be some attempts at adaptation that reflect developmental changes in the child and also the changing expectations of environments at home and school. Children who are fostered and adopted will bring these adaptations – the legacy of their failure to find a secure base in previous environments – into their new families.

Infancy (birth–18 months)

As George and Solomon (1999, p. 664) stress, it is important to understand the disorganised infant in the context of the caregiving relationship.

In order to explain what in the mother's behaviour frightens the child, let us examine the chain of events that we propose is likely to prevail during mother–child interaction in disorganised dyads. Hypervigilant and lacking robust, organised defences, the mother is susceptible to being overwhelmed by helplessness and fear as the result of cues from the baby, from the environment, or perhaps from within (e.g. being flooded by affect). This state of panic or helplessness is disabling to caregiving, because it renders the mother herself closed (impermeable) to the child's attachment cues. Thus the mother is not able to care for or respond to the child's needs or distress for some period of time. Importantly from a caregiving-system perspective, we stress that what frightens the child is the mother's simultaneous abdication of care and impermeability to the child's cues or bids for care.

George and Solomon suggest that the infant's response of freezing in response to fear has the effect of closing down and shutting off (Bowlby, 1980), so that 'Mother and child are left simultaneously vulnerable, mutually impermeable, helpless and afraid, leading to a dialectic cycle of failed protection' (George and Solomon, 1999, p. 665). In maltreating families, the parent's panic and abdication may be associated with neglect or with anger and hostility to the child, leading to abuse when helplessness shifts to hostility.

To understand the early impact of frightened or frightening, abdicated and hostile/helpless caregiving, it is important to remember the significant combination of physical dependency, emotional dependency and cognitive immaturity in the newborn infant. Infants who try to get close to and find safety with their caregivers when they are needy or anxious, but instead find that their caregivers are unavailable, or are an unpredictable source of fear and/or increase anxiety rather than offering a reliable source of care and protection, are left with an insoluble dilemma. The infant is biologically programmed to approach the caregiver for care and protection from anxiety and threat, but finds the caregiver a source of threat, leading to 'fear without solution' as stressed above (Main and Hesse, 1990). The initial reaction to this approach/avoidance problem may be to freeze. Yet a very young infant's physical needs, emotional distress and cognitive confusion cannot be that easily controlled and shut down. So initially at least the infant will instinctively cry out when hungry or afraid in order to attract help. The young infant has a very limited behavioural repertoire and is likely to carry on crying, even when or perhaps especially when confronted by an angry, upset and frightening caregiver's face.

Persistent crying is most likely to provoke both anger and anxiety in the caregiver. Caregivers who are frightening or frightened, for example, in situations of domestic violence or where they have unresolved traumas from their own childhood, find this behaviour unbearable. Unresolved caregivers experience themselves as helpless, but may react to that feeling by becoming hostile. The baby's crying behaviour, especially when the caregiver can see no reason for it, can be seen as suggesting that this is a bad baby, an ungrateful baby, an unrewarding baby and a baby who is accusing the caregiver of being a bad mother or father. In maltreating families, whether caregivers abandon or attack the infant when they become overwhelmed with anxiety, rage and disappointment, it is not surprising that children are at most risk of serious neglect and injury in the first year of life. Young infants cannot help but cry out, they have no strategies to please or appease the caregiver and their very dependence and neediness overwhelms the caregiver with anxiety that can lead to panic and rage.

Although most infants will protest initially, many neglected and frightened infants will become silent and withdrawn quite quickly. They start to switch off and shut down on their feelings. This has a different quality to the shutting down of avoidant infants and is the forerunner of the disengaged and dissociative states that are seen in older children and adults. Chronically neglected and frightened infants will also become out of touch with their physical senses and, in the absence of any demands or protests, may appear, for example, not to be hungry. They may even be reported as quiet, content babies who sleep a lot – a description that in the presence of other evidence of neglect and caregiver unresponsiveness must always be questioned. Here too infant experiences are laying down patterns for the future, since the processing of sensory information is often shut down or distorted in maltreated children in ways that store up trouble for later development. Older children with disturbed early relationships are often unable to distinguish physical from emotional pain, hunger from anger and, for example, eat to excess or not at all without being able to monitor their bodies or ever feel completely comfortable in them.

Neuroscience is playing an increasing role in helping us to understand the impact of maltreatment in early relationships on brain development and, in particular, the capacity to regulate emotions and the storage of traumatic memories (Schore, 1994; Diamond and Marrone, 2003). Howe (2005, p. 25) states that, 'Perry *et al* (1995) are clear that early life maltreatment can adversely alter the organisation, structure and density of the emotional processing parts of the brain'. This can lead to impulsiveness but also to hypervigilance and may contribute to the wide range of difficulties that these infants will experience later in regulating arousal and managing their emotions and behaviour.

In the early months, the infant who is confronted by frightening and helpless parenting, will be unsuccessfully struggling to make sense of their experience in order to find a strategy for adapting to it. In the Strange Situation at 12 months, disorganised infants are distinctive for being unable to shape a coherent response to separation or reunion. As Main and Solomon (1986) found, they may show diverse and often bizarre behaviours, but behaviours which could be seen as demonstrating the very approach/avoid dilemma that has been described in terms of fear without solution. The infant of a frightening or frightened mother feels anxious in the Strange Situation when the mother departs, but the protest at her departure is complicated by doubts about whether crying or proximity-seeking is effective or may even be dangerous and counterproductive. So, for example, a child may start crawling as if to follow the mother, but then crawl in the opposite direction. Similarly, the reunion is going to be complicated by the fact that comfort and reassurance are unlikely to be forthcoming and, indeed, seeking closeness might be ignored or rejected in a scary way. Thus, at reunion the infant may crawl as if to go to the mother, but stop and turn away, or move towards the mother but backwards, or cry as if to seek comfort but remain facing the corner of the room rather than approach. Other typical behaviours may be freezing, trance-like states or idiosyncratic movements, such as waving a hand as if to strike the parent.

In so far as the Strange Situation is 'a window on the internal working model' (Steele and Steele, 1994), it seems that the infant lacks confidence in the self and in the caregiver. The model at this point is of the self as helpless and unlovable with the caregiver as unavailable, unpredictable and to some degree frightening. As described in Chapter 1, when infants are classified as disorganised in the Strange Situation, they are also given a "best fit" secondary classification. An infant might receive the classification of Disorganised/Avoidant, Disorganised/ Ambivalent or Disorganised/Secure. Thus, infants will show disorganised behaviour at separation or reunion i.e. the points of greatest stress, but otherwise show characteristics more consistent with avoidant or ambivalent/resistant or secure patterns at other points in the procedure. This suggests that there is a collapse in the infant's strategy when stressed and fearful. So an infant may be clingy initially like an ambivalent child, but after the separation may freeze and be unable to seek comfort. When infants and children who are disorganised are not stressed or a traumatic memory is not triggered, they may show behaviours typical of those discussed in one of the last three chapters on secure, avoidant and ambivalent/resistant infants/children – hence the importance of a good understanding of all patterns even where the child has been maltreated and disorganisation is the likely primary classification.

Joining a new family in infancy (birth–18 months)

Not all disorganised infants will react in a highly disturbed way in a new family and some will settle more easily than others. But infants who have experienced both unpredictable and frightening caregiving that is associated with maltreatment will often have a significantly distorted relationship to their bodies, to other people and to the physical world around them, that needs to be managed.

The normal developmental process for a secure infant is to have become in tune with his body and his mind through sensitive feeding, physical care associated with a close emotional relationship and access to the safe and containing caregiver's mind. For the disorganised, maltreated infant, this process will have been disrupted and distorted, leaving the infant unable to manage or regulate any of the physical sensations of hunger and discomfort or the need for proximity. Comfortable rhythms of sleeping, waking, feeding, playing, exploration and proximity-seeking are not likely to have been established. The infant may demand chaotically and fretfully without being able to be satisfied by food or comfort. Watching the world around them distrustfully, anxiously monitoring the faces of other people or seeming in a trance and not being good at asking for or accepting nurture (Stovall and Dozier, 1998; Stovall and Dozier, 2000), these are infants with negative expectations that may take a long time to change. This case demonstrates this dilemma:

> *Jasmine (9 months) had been severely neglected by a mother who was herself traumatised by systematic and ritualistic sexual abuse as a child and currently had both drug and alcohol problems. Once in foster care, Jasmine was extremely fretful and difficult to manage. Nappy changing was experienced as an assault and she appeared to prefer the familiarity of lying in a dirty nappy. Bathing and having her hair washed were also experienced as frightening in the context of a lack of trust, so that each attempt to care for her seemed to provoke extreme panic and rage.*

manipulate rather than becoming a foundation on which to build empathy and reciprocal concern. Indeed, when unfamiliar care and concern are offered by others – adults or children – it may be perceived by the child as a sign of weakness to be exploited rather than something to be trusted.

Children may lack a coherent working model of the self or other people (Main, 1991), which reflects the shifting and multiple models in their attachment relationships and affects their other relationships. Research found that children classified as secure, avoidant or ambivalent at 18 months behaved in similar ways at age four with two different peers, but disorganised children showed contrasting behaviours.

> *For example, one child spent much of his interaction with one peer trying to annoy him, shining torchlight in his eyes, using a puppet to try to grab his nose and periodically shoving toy animals in his face. With the other peer, however, the same child did not interact at all and progressively withdrew. By the end of the session, he was lying face down and burying his head under a pillow.*
> (Lyons-Ruth and Jacobvitz, 1999, p. 538 citing Jacobvitz and Hazen, 1999)

Such switches demonstrate incoherent, random and multiple models (Main, 1991); here an aggressive, intrusive, controlling approach switches to social withdrawal and collapse. The contrasts make it difficult for other children or adults to predict the disorganised child's behaviour and therefore collaborate with him, but they also make assessment by professionals more difficult, as there may be contrasting and competing accounts of the child's behaviour.

The link between maltreatment, disorganisation and dissociation becomes evident during this age period. Macfie *et al* (2001, p. 49 cited in Howe, 2005, p. 58) suggest that, 'Maltreated children who are most likely to have disorganised patterns of attachment to their caregivers in infancy and deviant self-development, develop an increasingly incoherent dissociated self during the preschool period'. Behavioural symptoms of dissociation are described by Howe (2005, p. 58) as falling into three main categories.

- *Amnesia: performing actions for which the individual has no memory.*
- *Absorption: becoming engrossed in an activity to the point of losing awareness of one's surroundings, sometimes appearing to be in a trance-like state.*
- *Depersonalisation: experiencing events including what is happening to the self (for instance, physical or sexual abuse) as if they were happening to someone else; the self being disconnected from body and feelings; the self as an emotionally uninvolved observer.*

As Howe goes on to describe, 'Body sensations, feelings and thoughts that cause anxiety are disowned and put outside of awareness'. Maltreated young children distance and detach themselves from their experiences, both at the time and as memories. It is as if those events and those feelings, physical and psychological, are not happening or have not happened.

Maltreated young children's feelings about their bodies are often disturbed and distorted by their experiences of fear and lack of comfort. Although problems around developmental stages such as toileting are common for this age group of children and to be expected, other problems to do with children's relationships to their bodies but less familiarly linked to this age group, such as self-harm, can occur in extreme cases. Young children may scratch away at arms, legs or sensitive parts of their bodies, especially nipples and genital areas (Schofield *et al*, 2000 – see also Chapter 11 on behaviour problems). This behaviour, as for older children, can take on an addictive quality, as children retreat from their fears and social pressures, stimulate themselves and take control at least of the pain and of their bodies.

In story stems, some disorganised pre-school children are too helpless to engage in the exercise of the imagination or too reluctant to face the stress of the hypothetical situation in the stories, just as they dissociate in response to their own stress triggers and experiences. When children do engage in the stories, they reveal their mental representations, their internal working model, of themselves as helpless and caregivers as helpless or frightening, experiencing anxiety and fear in situations that cannot be resolved. Thus, the story of a separation may spiral out of control, with caregivers and children dying in dramatic circum- stances or fights between caregivers and children represented as random and unending. The lack of safe resolution in the story is often compounded by a general incoherence, perhaps with adults falling down dead but then getting up again and hurting each other or the child. Ordinary domestic scenes, such as the story of the child spilling a drink while the family watches television, can lead to punishment, explosions and death. Children who do not communicate these frightening ideas in other ways may reveal them through the hypothetical attachment-related situations of the story stems.

Joining new families in early childhood (18 months–4 years)

Children from backgrounds of maltreatment very often come into care between 18 months and five years old and this is also the main age range when children from care are placed for adoption. It is therefore a critical developmental stage to understand, as the input that families offer needs to build in sources of security and resilience before children face the separation and the social and academic challenges of school. This example demonstrates how even the most troubled child can be helped to make this transition.

Peter (4) had been sexually abused by a number of his mother's partners. He caused several fires in the house when his mother was either under the influence of drugs or had left him alone with his younger sister while out trying to buy drugs. When assessed as part of the plan for placement for adoption, he appeared to have no memory of the sexual abuse or the fires. It was impossible to know where these experiences had gone to in his mind and quite difficult to predict how they or his probable dissociative reaction to them would affect him in the new adoptive family where he was to be placed with his sister. Although social workers and other professionals were pessimistic, as Peter had a number of other persistent problems such as wetting, soiling and brief dissociative "absences", in fact Peter did thrive in his adoptive family, with patient committed adopters, the dedicated help of the adoption agency and a good school placement.

Foster carers and adopters taking a young child like Peter into their family will have been prepared to care for maltreated children and may have cared for troubled children before. The toddler or pre-school child that arrives in their home may still present a whole range of both anticipated and unanticipated behaviours. As one foster carer described, from the outset, her three-year-old cried for hours, resisted being touched, screamed if an attempt was made to bath her and attacked a younger child in the family. For this child, punitive and controlling behaviour was exacerbated by panic at separation from her disturbed mother. In contrast, another three-year-old girl was quiet, well-behaved and seemed like a compliant, unresponsive doll, which her carer found almost equally hard to live with. In both cases the child had an identical sounding history of neglect, fear and sexual and physical abuse. The strategies that each had evolved and the reaction to the placement looked very different, but both had the effect of controlling and keeping carers at a distance.

In the early days and weeks, the child may show varying degrees of prepared-ness to let the caregivers get close, physically and emotionally. Sometimes the more aggressive child may be more reachable, while at other times the more withdrawn, inhibited child will warm up and relax quite quickly. More often though both children need strategies by tuned in and very patient carers to help them relax and accept care, as one foster carer described:

William was a very closed off four-year-old who resisted physical contact with me and slept with the sheet over his face and tucked tightly underneath him. I started by putting a soft toy, Barney, at the end of the bed and kissing Barney goodnight when I said goodnight to William. William gradually moved Barney closer, but it was two months before he asked me if he could have a kiss too.

Children often connect positively or negatively with different objects or people, toys or pets. More constructive and more destructive urges both need to be identified. It could be that a child who is very destructive with the furniture may genuinely be able to be gentle with babies or likes to help feed the cat. Or a child who cannot be trusted with smaller children without supervision, may enjoy helping to sand an old table. Children who find close interpersonal contact overwhelming can sit drawing or building Lego in the vicinity of others, or enjoy helping to cook, as long as they can stir the cake mixture without the caregiver standing too close. Looking for children's strengths may seem difficult at first, but engineering situations to help the child feel more connected, have more fun, feel more valued and become more competent, whatever their behaviour problems, is essential, alongside providing practical and emotional availability and safe boundaries.

Certain areas of development appropriate for this age need to be targeted, in particular around helping children make sense of their own feelings and behaviour and the feelings and behaviour of others. This will be a constant and ongoing task for all the family and cannot be left to chance or to evolve naturally as part of family life. It could include actively talking through incidents involving the child or involving other people in the family or at nursery, reading story books and using television or videos to provide material that helps put names to feelings, encourages a focus on their own and other people's minds, clarifies the ups and downs of relationships and aims to develop some understanding of the existence and normality of mixed emotions (see also Chapter 7).

Even in the context of positive caregiving of this kind, what troubled and anxious but controlling young children will almost certainly do in one way or another is to get under the skin of the new caregivers. Because even young children are very familiar with monitoring and controlling environments, they are likely to be on the look out from the beginning for potential areas of susceptibility in the caregivers. It could be, for example, that a three-year-old child newly placed for adoption becomes aware that eating up all the food on the plate or good manners at meal time are particularly important in this family, so this could be the very time when the child acts up by throwing a plate of food to the floor, accompanied by a contemptuous laugh and a jeer when his adoptive father protests. It is hard then for the father to hold on to what he has learned about the roots of this behaviour in the child's early experiences, because this small child seems to challenge all that the father values and is trying to achieve for the child. It makes him look weak as a father and suggests that the child whom he has taken on as a son has no love or respect for him.

These are painful and testing moments for the father and the family and it requires a high degree of empathy for the child, an understanding of what might lie behind the behaviour, and self-confidence as a parent to resolve the situation calmly and without retaliating in the way the child expects and has tried to provoke. *Staying in charge* as a parent, *showing concern* while also *handing some responsibility* to the child for the plate incident, is necessary. But the child also needs the message that *this behaviour has meaning/makes sense* – he is angry and impulsive and in a new family – but that he is a normal three-year-old who has some problems and they need to work together to help him settle in and communicate his feelings in other ways. The child needs to be offered a realistic appraisal of the situation in which clear signals are given, the feelings of all parties are explored and which neither ignores the incident nor builds it up into a heightened state of disaster, avoiding saying 'No other three-year-olds do this! You are a really bad boy!' Lowering the temperature of the occasion is the only way to lower the child's and the parent's anxiety and prevent the feeling that the situation is irrecoverable, for the child and the parent.

In the early stages of placement, and indeed later in placement, it will be essential for foster carers and adopters to spend time trying to observe the patterns of behaviour of their particular child, making sense of the often confused and anxious thinking and feeling that lies behind it and planning a constructive, caring and therapeutic response. This process almost certainly needs to involve discussions with family members, social workers or other professionals. Using an understanding of the possible strategies of disorganised children as described here can be helpful. It can explain a lot that seems irrational and may reassure foster carers and adopters that they did not cause this behaviour. *But* it should not be a way of simply putting children in boxes and assuming that now the child has a label it will be possible to predict his or her every move. Sensitivity and empathy in relation to *each child as a unique individual* remains at the heart of working out what will help this particular child. The agency social worker or the adoption support service (and other agencies) need to provide both a well-informed sounding board *and* emotional support to help the caregivers stay with the pre-school child through even the most difficult times.

Middle childhood (5–10 years)

During this period, disorganised and controlling children may become increasingly anxious in the face of developmental tasks in the academic and social arena, but they may also become increasingly sophisticated in the ways in which they attempt to miscue and control others in order to cope. Being poor at impulse control and delayed gratification, however, the smallest trigger can provoke an extreme reaction. At age five, children in their drawings and stories depict themselves as victims and caregivers as frightening, but the shifts of role from victim to persecutor to caregiver that occurred in their birth family relationships continue to suggest an incoherent sense of self in relationships, which feels very frightening for the child – a fear that needs to be defended against and denied. This may be additionally complicated by moments when the caregiver is appropriately loving and protective – another conflicting model to be incorporated into the child's diverse and irreconcilable working models.

For maltreated disorganised children, the *role-reversing* aggression, caregiving and manipulation that began in early childhood may develop to the point that birth parents may be feeling increasingly angry, hostile, helpless and hopeless – a spiral that increases the likelihood that children will be rejected or abused, emotionally if not physically. Parents feel that children have got out of hand, are ungrateful, are upsetting and shaming the family and may be so "bad" that they no longer have the right to expect care and concern. At the same time, birth parents and step-parents may also be very anxious about their own potential to harm the child, while lacking any sense of an ability to care for and protect the child. Scapegoating of children with these severe difficulties is possible and indeed likely, especially once the world outside starts to complain about their behaviour or indeed children become the focus of protective investigations by official agencies.

For most disorganised children who have been maltreated, the move into school requires strengths, skills and resources that they lack. Academically they are likely to be underperforming, but as one study of maths scores among disorganised children found, the main causal factor in this underachievement was the children's lack of self-confidence (Jacobsen *et al*, 1994 cited in Lyons–Ruth and Jacobvitz, 1999). Insecure children generally are more inclined to give up than secure children when they become anxious about doing well on a specific task, but maltreated children who give up trying when their self-esteem is so threatened may lash out or switch off in a more extreme dissociative way, such as falling into trance-like states.

From the first step into the playground or the classroom, children need a foundation of self-esteem and competence in order to manage feelings, negotiate access to peer groups, play games, queue for assembly or dinner, wait for the teacher's attention and be able to concentrate on their work. They need to bring to bear social rules learned as pre-schoolers and go on to learn the rules of this new environment – key tasks of this age period. In the absence of these skills and this knowledge, disorganised and controlling children may simply panic and resort to familiar controlling and aggressive ways as their anxieties grow. They also lack perspective-taking skills, which, as discussed above, should have developed in the pre-school years in order to assist in deepening the quality of friendships but are unlikely to have done so. The simple social and moral rules, such as taking turns, being helpful to children in difficulty, helping to tidy up, can be "learned", but to apply them thoughtfully requires the child to be aware of the feelings and perspectives of others. It also requires them to be able to stop and think in order, at times, to prioritise shared goals rather than act impulsively to promote their own goals – stopping and thinking in this way is another behaviour which low self-esteem and raised anxiety would predict is unlikely.

School is a setting in which children are encouraged to be appropriately assertive and make some choices, but in the main children are expected to relinquish power and control to the teaching and supervisory staff. This requires a degree of trust, which for children who feel that life is threatening and unfair and who have previously relied on taking charge themselves can be very difficult. More subdued, compliant children may cope by remaining still, unresponsive and helpless, and some will be more cool and controlling, but others will react more explosively to school environments where high expectations of performance, sociability and impulse control – none of which they can achieve – are the norm. They will find it almost impossible either to sit quietly in class or to respect the rights of other children in the playground.

Where primary age children do manage to settle into some kind of routine with the help of a teacher or classroom assistant, any change may feel catastrophic.

Dwayne (6) had grown up in a very neglectful and chaotic family where he had been physically and emotionally abused. He lived in a very deprived area and attended a local school where behaviour problems were quite common and good strategies for supporting pupils were in place. But from Dwayne's first day at school his inability to abide by the normal expectations of sitting, waiting, working, playing and accepting the teacher's authority was extreme. He had been suspended from school on several occasions in his first year. He seemed in a perpetual whirl of helpless dependency and extreme aggression. He was unable to get pleasure from play or his interactions with peers and only took some occasional comfort from the times when he could crawl on to the teacher's lap at story time. It took the slightest incident with another child to produce volcanic tearful rages and attacks on both children and staff, resulting in injuries which had necessitated hospital treatment – for example, when he assaulted a teacher with a chair and threw a toy that hit another child in the eye. But in particular, Dwayne found any change of environment (e.g. a proposed class walk to the park) or staff (the absence of his usual teacher and the arrival of a supply teacher) unbearable and this sparked off his panic and aggression.

This is an extreme but not unusual story for children whose early years have been dominated by uncontained anxiety and who are totally unequipped for the transition to school. A number of disorganised, maltreated children do not come to the attention of professional agencies in the pre-school years, having stayed at home, racing round the living room day after day or shut in bedrooms. Such troubled children have often become too much out of control or too embarrassing to be taken by parents to the shops or to playgroups and so their world is completely limited to this environment where positive use of time and the development of self-esteem and self-efficacy are not possible. Where previous health or social work assessments have been conducted, they have sometimes suggested that the children were showing just an extreme form of normal pre-school tantrums. However, these children are discovered on admission to school to be not only seriously developmentally delayed, but also wildly out of control and unable to adjust their behaviour to cope with the new environment. The gap between them and their peers is often dramatic – although in some very deprived areas there may be a number of these children entering local schools. The profoundly sad, disconnected, helpless and hopeless disorganised children cause less of a fuss, but the gap between them and most of their peers will be just as significant in terms of their inability to concentrate, learn, explore and enjoy what school has to offer.

As secure children move through the primary school years, their sense of identity and global self-worth develops in a positive direction, but all children become increasingly aware of how they are seen and what label or value has been put on them. Children in this disorganised group have to struggle to manage the label "difficult", "naughty", "stupid" or worse that is often placed on them and have a profound sense of their own "badness" and worthlessness. This deep anxiety may be concealed behind a boastful, grandiose front, with children claiming to be the best at everything – and threatening anyone who says they are not the best at football or maths or having friends. They have understood the importance of being competitive with their peers, but cannot manage a realistic assessment of their abilities or cope with the possibility of not being the best – since this must mean rejection or being controlled by those who are the best.

Sustaining the myth that they are in charge and are the best is wearing, as the truth inevitably can and does come out when people pick football teams or the results of the maths test are known. As discussed in relation to avoidant children, nobody likes a boastful child and the temptation is for family members, other children and even teachers to feel the need to confront children, not only with the reality of their poor performance but the absurdity of their claims. The failure to perform becomes mixed in with the naughty label to produce a self-concept of unremitting failure. Further denial of this painful reality then becomes the only escape, as children head off into fantasies about the kind of people they are/would like to be and perhaps start to make themselves "special", if only for their violence and the outrageousness of their behaviour. On this dimension, avoidant children can be quite similar in that the contrast between the image they need to project and the reality can result in aggression. Both disorganised and avoidant children are less competent in their play *and* then in their ability to resolve conflict, but disorganised children are more likely to go to extremes in their behaviour in ways that frighten others.

Increasingly, disorganised/maltreated children, far from developing an integrated sense of self as secure children in this age range will do, can start to lose touch with reality as they spiral downwards.

Jonathan (6) from a family where neglect, emotional abuse and sexual abuse were his primary experience, refused to wear proper clothes, stopped speaking and started to communicate only through animal noises.

Antoinette (10), also with a history of sexual abuse and violence, who was still wetting and soiling by day and night, seemed to lose her sense of who she was and started to adopt other children's identities, denying her name, putting a paper clip round her teeth as a brace and claiming to need glasses to see the board, in order to be like other children in her class.

This is more than "regression" in Jonathan's case or "lying" in Antoinette's – such behaviours suggest something more profound about the child's existential anxieties – What am I? Who am I? Do I actually exist?

As children grow through primary years to adolescence, their behavioural strategies reflect some increasing sophistication (in targeting weakness in other children and adults, for example) that comes with development, but builds on these core controlling, role-reversing behaviours. However, for maltreated disorganised children, the physical and emotional cost of fear, unresolved anxiety and lack of access to comfort and a secure base, is considerable and can lead towards a range of desperate/controlling behaviours that deny and attack the self (for example, self-harm), hurt less powerful others (such as smaller children or family pets), or damage the physical environment. Children may destroy bedrooms, for example, especially when left alone for long periods or for punishment, sometimes doing bizarre things such as eating wallpaper or chewing wooden beds (behaviours that first appear in the pre-school years). On the one hand, disorganised and controlling children may become coolly calculating in their attempt to protect themselves from hurt, but on the other hand, when anger and distress break through, more harmful and even dangerous behaviour may result. Early and current feelings of hurt and loss remain unresolved.

Alongside the difficulties around control, self-esteem and social relationships, the children's disturbed relationships with their body may mean that traumatised disorganised children are also wetting, soiling, smearing, stealing food, eating from bins and so on. These behaviours can be both a reaction to and a cause of conflict and low self-esteem in the birth family, the school and the community. Each of these difficulties can be seen as signals of current distress, but are deeply rooted in children's earlier difficulties in the context of poor and often frightening care and can persist right through this period and into adolescence if their relationship environment does not change.

It is important to reiterate that not all disorganised or maltreated children will show these extreme behaviours, but given that the majority of children entering and remaining in care or going on to adoption have experienced abuse and neglect, it is important to think about how, in this age group, disorganisation interacts with maltreatment and the range of problems that may result.

Joining new families in middle childhood (5–10 years)

School-age children will have been through a good deal, whether coming into care at this age or having come into care at an earlier stage and now moving to a new placement. Even if these moves are planned, but particularly when they are not, the impact of separation and loss on disorganised/controlling children is going to be significant. Even where children are relieved at some level about a move from a birth family and feel safer, there may be anxieties about the new family and paradoxically, about both leaving and being sent back to the birth family.

Children who have settled quite well in a bridge family and are well prepared for the move, may revert to some of their more extreme early behaviours as they try to anticipate and survive the loss and change. Raised anxiety will create a heightening of defensive strategies that may mean an increase in shut off, dissociative and/or controlling behaviours. Children who anticipate being "given away" or "taken away" again may attempt to provoke it. The muddled thinking and emotional confusion in the mind of the child may appear in such apparently small things as a child's inability to learn to tell the time, remember what happened the previous day or to sequence events in order to plan. This can make it difficult for them to understand the sequence of moves or future placement plans. There may also be a muddle created in the mind of the foster carer and the adopter as they try to make sense of and respond to children's miscuing behaviours. Signals from the child, to 'back off and leave me alone' or to 'come close and look after me' can be equally misleading if the child then demands attention or explodes when closeness is offered.

Hardest to bear for some foster carers and adopters is the atmosphere of wariness and the looks of suspicion that children may cast towards a caregiver as a result of these anxieties.

Michael (age 7 when he came into the placement) used to fix his eyes on his long-term foster carer's face and seemed always to assume, even when she was simply getting on with doing the washing up, that she was upset or feeling cross with him. She had to take a long time patiently indicating her availability and concern for him, but continued to feel even after some years in placement that she was 'walking on eggshells' and that she had to choose her moment carefully before approaching him. She could never rely on him not to withdraw or verbally attack her when he imagined that she was hostile.

An adoptive mother described how her newly-placed nine-year-old adopted daughter accused her of "playing tricks" when she was trying to offer her affection and care. The concept of good care being perceived as a "trick" is exactly how Crittenden (1995, p. 401 quoted in Chapter 1) describes the difficulty of reshaping children's internal working models when children do not feel able to take the risk of believing that new caregivers can be different from those that they have known in the past. The big advantage for this adoptive mother was that her daughter had been helped in her bridge foster placement to be more communicative and was able to bring this idea, and the lack of trust behind it, into the open and put it into words, thus enabling the mother and daughter to talk about it and face it together.

The *delays and difficulties in perspective taking,* and the barriers that this in itself creates to developing relationships, mean that foster carers and adopters have to work extra hard with these older children to take them back to that stage of development and start some basic education.

Claudette's adoptive mother found that although developmentally Claudette (who had been neglected in her early years) was well settled and coping at school as a ten-year-old, her friendships were rather limited and she seemed to have what was an associated difficulty with understanding the perspectives of other children. In reading stories, Claudette could not imagine what people might be feeling or predict what might happen next and this became a focus of her mother's story reading with her – but also a necessary focus of discussion in relation to everyday incidents.

In such situations, children need carers and adopters (with the support of social workers) to identify where the developmental difficulty lies and identify strategies for meeting these needs in ways that are emotionally and chronologically age-appropriate for the child. It is not enough to say that a child has difficulty in peer relationships – steps need to be taken to tackle the component parts of that difficulty.

As with disorganised pre-school children, looking for disorganised older children's strengths may seem difficult at first, but identifying ways of helping each child to feel more valued and more competent, whatever their behaviour problems, is essential. As a starting point, children with such chaotic and unsafe histories need structure to the day and consistency in relationships provided by the foster carers and adopters to help reassure them that the new environment is safe. Within that structure, children with significant histories of abuse are described as enjoying such things as helping with gardening when they feel the need to stay close to caregivers, or joining in family activities such as swimming, which can provide outlets for energy as well as shared experiences to reflect on and celebrate in photographs (Beek and Schofield, 2004a). Not all children will allow themselves to enjoy such events and for some it will take a long time – months if not years – before there are any of these special feelings of closeness. Realistically, some children may never allow this fully – but even the smallest moment, the shared laugh over a television programme, the child's look of concern for another child, the child wanting to make and give a Father's Day card – these moments of connectedness when distancing and control may slip are much to be valued.

Sometimes even the child's wary monitoring of caregivers can take a positive turn.

A long-term foster mother, who struggled in the face of very wary, disturbed and aggressive/contemptuous behaviour by her son, Keith (10), found that he took great pleasure in buying the right present for her birthday, or even when simply wanting to make reparation for an outburst. He knew she liked teddy bears and on one occasion had bought her a tartan teddy bear brooch with his pocket money.

This unexpected strength in an otherwise very challenging child may have been a complicated mix of wishing to please his foster mother, to placate her, to make sure she did not end the placement – even to control and manipulate her. But there was enough in the gesture to make her feel that at least at some level he wanted to please her and knew how to go about it. The gift also made him seem more "normal", given that he had some very serious behaviour problems that had made it difficult to accept and love him, including persistent soiling, verbal abuse and "accidentally" killing the family's pet rabbit.

The initial goal for these children is to help them move towards security, often via more organised insecure and less destructive defensive strategies, and to enable them to value and accept being parented. This could mean that children who tend to be more defended would continue to manage difficult feelings by denying and shutting down on them, but would begin to accept some degree of proximity and care as long as caregiving was not too intrusive or emotionally demanding. Compulsively caregiving children may need to continue to make cups of tea for caregivers, and this could be viewed positively, but they would also accept that caregivers made cups of tea for them. Children may continue to display their feelings and use them coercively at times, but it might begin to be possible for the child to name those feelings and to develop some ability to talk calmly about them with caregivers rather than rage or express those feelings through self-harm. Parenting needs to be very active, focused and purposeful in order to ease children towards more coherent and less controlling ways of thinking and behaving. Managing the different fronts on which this battle may be played out and where children will need advocacy as well as support – family, school, peer group and community – requires considerable energy, underpinned by personal and professional resources.

It should not be forgotten that carers and adopters themselves will bring to their relationship with this child their own tendencies to react to stress in particular ways – perhaps to shut down on emotions and focus on practical care or to show emotions and expect emotional responses from the child or even to feel helpless and walk away. This is an issue for caregivers of all fostered and adopted children, but confused children whose minds have had to adapt to particularly disorienting and frightening care may produce in caregivers some of the most powerful and confusing feelings. It may be, for example, that caregivers get caught up in the victim–persecutor–rescuer cycle of the child and start to feel as if they too are moving between these roles, as they try to take charge of a child who then attacks them verbally or physically. Sometimes it is as if the caregiver no longer recognises the person they have become since taking this child into their home. Feelings of passionate concern, empathy, hope and love for the child become mixed with feelings of anger, frustration, disappointment and helplessness.

Just as multiple models become scary and disorientating for the child, so foster carers and adopters can become deeply unsettled by the shifting feelings and loss of self that such challenges to them as parents and people can cause. They need access to the support of a reflective person who can help them recognise these feelings, determine what belongs to the child and what belongs to the foster carer or adopter, and find a way of containing the anxiety in order to remain available, sensitive, responsive and therapeutic for the child. Caregivers and their supporters need to keep sight of small signs of progress in the child – this can be hard to do without help.

Adolescence (11–18 years)

A major challenge for disorganised, controlling children in adolescence is how to reflect on and regulate feelings and behaviour in the face of high anxiety, and in the context of raised expectations of age-appropriate interpersonal competence and autonomy. The movement from early adolescence and puberty itself, through school and into work and adult life, requires not only these core skills, but also some additional and specific abilities in terms of managing dramatic bodily changes, coping with the move towards intimate and sexual relationships and facing up to the potential for parenthood. In adolescence, changing bodies should be accompanied by developing minds, but for disorganised teenagers, minds are often stuck in rigid, repetitive and counterproductive defensive patterns that do not become more flexible and more reflective as these tasks of adolescence require. Indeed, they may become more rigid, inhibited or disinhibited, despairing or controlling, as new anxieties strike. Difficulties in accepting praise or tackling new situations, for example, may be gradually resolved for some young people, but may actually intensify for others.

As we have tracked through this chapter, defensive and controlling strategies will have started to emerge in the pre-school years and, in the absence of a change in the quality of the caregiving environment, by adolescence these strategies will have become more fixed and more troublesome to the young person and to other people, since their experiences of life are likely to have left them isolated and with low self-esteem. Young people who are still in birth families with unresolved/helpless/hostile caregivers at this stage may have had many years of continuously or intermittently being exposed to unsafe minds and experiences of rejection, intrusion, psychological confusion or emotional entanglement. Additionally, family lives may well have been unstable, both in terms of marital breakdown and moves of house. Where families have been dysfunctional psychologically, but stable socially, young people may themselves wonder what is wrong with them that they are so distressed and their behaviour is so difficult to manage when their family is viewed as "normal". In particular, where children have been sexually abused in the family, the child may be left with a stark contrast between the family's respectable public face and their traumatic private experience. Adolescents will often become more aware of such disparities, but will remain perplexed and left with feelings of guilt and shame.

In the family environment, the young person may be one of several difficult siblings and may or may not be deemed to be the "worst". Where a child is the eldest in the family, there are often additional expectations of caring for younger children and comparisons are made with more appealing, less challenging babies and young children in the family that can make the adolescent feel even more of an outsider and beyond the pale. Sometimes one child, even in a disturbed sibling group, is scapegoated and held responsible for the family's troubles. In some families, one child of different parentage or different ethnicity in the family may have been singled out as "the problem" or a child may be said to have caused the family extra difficulties because of a disability. Often there is no apparent reason for singling out a particular child for rejection, but the family works on a dynamic of splitting and such is the stress within and around the family that if that target child were to leave then another family member would take their place as the scapegoat. These family dynamics can come into play at any age, but for adolescents, tensions and rejection can spill over into anti-social behaviour resulting in abandonment by or expulsion from the family.

In the school environment, difficult behaviour that might have been coped with in a primary school becomes less tolerated as challenging 11-year-olds become physically large and verbally challenging teenagers. Secondary schools, even those with good pastoral care systems, find themselves forced to focus on academic outcomes. Controlling teenagers may turn to bullying and victimising others, building gangs and capitalising on the anxieties of other children. Children may find themselves in the role of bullies, allies or victims. In each case, the more productive and pro-social aspects of adolescence, the enjoyment of more freedom, the satisfaction in academic work and the comfortable companionship of reciprocal friendships, are likely to be lost to them.

Although not strong on reflective function, troubled teenagers are often painfully aware of the hurt they cause and the difference between their lives and the lives of other teenagers around them. Teenagers who are also avoidant/

dismissing will continue to minimise the feelings of others and the harm they cause, as well as their own feelings. The combination of controlling/unresolved and avoidant/dismissing characteristics makes these young people the most likely to be anti-social but the hardest to reach.

In the community, teenagers who have led troubled lives in disturbed families and have not coped well through the primary school stage will often have acquired a reputation for difficult behaviours that impact on others. They may have located a similarly troubled peer group with whom to hang out, with resulting problems relating to smoking, drugs, alcohol and early criminal activity. As adolescents, they are looking for anchorage for their new almost adult selves. Torn between anxiety about and desire for relationships, with the prospect of escape from painful feelings through drugs and alcohol, young people can find it hard to resist the pull towards risky groups and activities. The possibility of being effectively out of school by the age of 14 or 15 through truancy or school exclusion increases the risk for quite a number of these young people. Lacking a secure base in the family, it will only be if professional help can offer an alternative secure base that adolescents will be able to reverse this downward spiral (Schofield and Brown, 1999).

This picture so far has emphasised the externalising and anti-social outcomes that are possible developments in adolescence, but equally important are concerns around internalising and mental health problems such as anxiety and depression. As traumatised and maltreated adolescents will still carry with them from earlier stages (including infancy) problems in relating to their bodies, puberty has particular significance. This may show itself in terms of simple anxiety about whether their bodies are good enough and are developing in the right way – a self-esteem issue and a concern about whether in this way too they are "damaged goods". Girls worry about maturing, gaining weight and being sexually attractive, and boys worry about maturing, gaining strength and showing sexual prowess. Such anxieties are present to a degree for most teenagers, but for these young people they can provoke anger, shame, depression and the need for fight or flight. Managing risks to bodies, selves and reputations is not easy in adolescence and for the young people most likely to come into care the absence of support in the birth family – indeed, what may be abdication of care, anger, mocking and rejection in the family – can leave them very vulnerable to sexual activity, early pregnancy, drug misuse and suicidal thoughts; a difficult mix of mental health and psychosocial risk. Externalising and internalising behaviours may feature together, as violent and aggressive young people with *unresolved* experiences of trauma can also become depressed and suicidal.

Set against this negative picture is the fact that major developmental and social turning points, such as adolescence, hold within them the possibility for positive change. If teenagers are able to find and use a secure kind of anchorage, perhaps through school, activities, friends or romantic partners, they may be able to build an identity and sources of resilience which set them apart from their former selves. The expectation of the young person separating from their families may cause anxiety but it may also be liberating. Of the essence here is the prospect of developing one or more relationships which enable past traumas and self-doubts to be thought about, put in context and to some extent resolved. Although this can happen for young people without professional intervention, it is important to think about how foster care and adoption are able to provide and/or support secure relationships that offer just this window of opportunity for change.

In the Adult Attachment Interview (Main and Goldwyn, 1984), adolescents (and adults) will be rated as *unresolved* (the adult equivalent of disorganised) if they show *lapses in the monitoring of reason or discourse* when discussion of loss (often of an attachment figure) or trauma (such as abuse) occurs. This lapse could be something quite simple, such as talking of a dead person as if they are alive or extended silences in the middle of a sentence about the death and the funeral or about the kind of punishment received as a child. At this point the person is "lost" in their own thoughts and lost to the interview. These "lapses" make sections of the interview incoherent and reflect the person's inability to mourn the loss or resolve the trauma. Such elements in the interview may appear minor, but research suggests that they do indicate a significant aspect of the individual's mental state. For example, when mothers are rated on the AAI as unresolved during pregnancy, their infant is more likely to be classified as disorganised at 12 months (Fonagy *et al*, 1991). As with other measures, adolescents or adults who have an unresolved classification are also given a "best fit" secondary classification of one of the three organised patterns – secure autonomous, insecure preoccupied or insecure dismissing. This dual classification allows us to understand the differences between unresolved/disorganised teenagers who devalue feelings and relationships, for example, and unresolved/ambivalent teenagers who are angrily preoccupied with relationships – these differences can readily be seen in the behaviour patterns of young people coming in to care (Schofield *et al*, 2000; Beek and Schofield, 2004a), although some disturbed children may switch between the two classifications.

Joining new families in adolescence (11–18 years)

Controlling and unresolved adolescents coming into new foster and adoptive families will inevitably have had very diverse histories, both in terms of the quality of birth family experiences and in terms of contact with the care system. Some will be young people coming into care for the first time, while others may have had very chequered careers in multiple short-term foster placements, and still others will have been in long-term foster or adoptive families that have broken down in adolescence. Time is not on their side in terms of repairing earlier damage in preparation for a stable adult life and the emphasis has to be, where possible, on focused and therapeutic parenting in a committed family that offers a secure base and the chance to belong. Adolescence is an opportunity as well as a challenge.

Late placements often have the feeling of a last chance to get it right – an additional pressure but also a real opportunity to focus with the young person on what they need and what can be achieved together. Although challenging, this is preferable to the alternative view in some agencies, which can be expressed when children are as young as 14–15 years old, that it is only a short time to hold on to this young person before he/she can go into "independent living". There is plenty of evidence that teenagers can have their lives turned around in adolescence, even in the later teenage years, by new placements in a family which can help them make sense of the past and can offer hope, help and support into adult life (Schofield, 2003; Beek and Schofield, 2004a).

Melanie (30) came into her foster family at the age of 15. She had experienced neglect, physical and sexual abuse for the first eight years of her life and then was placed with a foster family where she was emotionally neglected and rejected. At the point of this late placement she was on the verge of suspension from school. In the three years that she lived with this foster family, she was helped in many ways, but in particular with her education and her self-esteem, and settled into a stable life. Now married and with a child, she is still part of this family. As she put it, 'They gave me the life I have now'.

The degree of difficulty of the young person in terms of the range of worrying symptoms that they may have developed and their possible strengths needs to be acknowledged. For this age group with histories of disorganisation and likely maltreatment, matching the child with the placement is critical – even though in some agencies placing older children is often the least likely to involve much choice because of shortage of placements prepared to take them. An out-of-control four-year-old or eight-year-old can be managed in a wide range of families, but a drug dependent or sexually active or sexually aggressive or self-harming teenager will need a specific kind of family acceptance, support and boundaries and will not be helped by placements which include young children, for example, or with families that have not been carefully prepared for the adolescent's specific needs.

Controlling/unresolved adolescents need to be given the same kind of caregiving, i.e. availability, sensitivity, co-operation and self-esteem building, as younger children *and* as adolescents with more organised secure and insecure patterns. So the challenge is how to shape this kind of caregiving in ways that are suitable for controlling adolescents *and* work from the basis that young people will be finding most aspects of family, school and peer group life difficult and anxiety provoking.

Role-reversing strategies that are punitive and aggressive are based on a fear of proximity and so children need to be helped to see the adoptive parent or foster carer as a safe person, who will be straight with them and is not going to be overwhelmed by the young person's fears, needs and anxieties. Not all teenagers will put caregivers to the test in extreme ways, but most will test out boundaries to some extent, ranging from coming home late to seeing if stealing from the new family will break the placement. As with younger children, the fear of being unexpectedly taken away or given away may well mean that adolescents appear to work to bring this about in a predictable way.

For some adolescents, significant mental health problems may emerge as they struggle to manage either disinhibited aggression or inhibited withdrawal – with a number of young people swinging in a distorted way between approach and avoidance in relationships, just as the disorganised infant does when anxious in the Strange Situation.

For most adolescents coming into new families, with the possible exception of some from the breakdown of adoption placements without contact, there will be some ongoing involvement with birth families. There may be supportive contact from some family members, but birth family contact may also perpetuate some of the psychological pressures and distortions that have contributed to the young people's problems to date (Beek and Schofield, 2004b). Whatever the circumstances, one of the tasks of the new family will be to help adolescents gain balanced but realistic insights into their birth families and their feelings about them. (See also Chapter 10 on family membership and Chapter 14 on contact.)

Adulthood

There are a number of psychosocial risks in terms of outcomes for unresolved adults. Fonagy *et al* (1996) found that 76 per cent of a group of psychiatric patients were classified as unresolved compared with 7 per cent of the control group. Such figures do *not* indicate what proportion of unresolved adults will have psychiatric problems, but do suggest that unresolved adults are likely to be more at risk. The risk of criminal activity and violent criminal activity particularly increases for those young adults who are unresolved in relation to loss and trauma *and* who are dismissing i.e. minimise the significance of and derogate attachment issues. This is entirely consistent with the pattern described throughout this chapter of poor reflective function and lack of perspective taking and empathy, accompanied by anger, fear of rejection and the tendency to dissociate.

As at every stage, however, there is the potential for relationships – whether with a romantic partner, a close friend or a therapist – to provide opportunities for changes in internal working models that produce a more coherent sense of self and lead to some resolution. The potential for change through reflection and relationships can be supported by other strengths in the young adult's life. It may be, for example, that if for whatever reason a young person leaves a foster or adoptive family without fully resolving their earlier losses and traumas, *but* has been given the experience of a stable home, stable education, involvement in activities, and a set of pro-social norms and values on which they can build, then they stand a better chance of managing employment, accommodation and establishing a stable lifestyle. This increases the likelihood that a normal and independent life will be possible, and that more secure/organised insecure adults who are leading ordinary lives in the community will be willing to become friends and partners (Schofield, 2003). This gift of "a way of living" will be discussed further in subsequent chapters, but remains an important element of what foster carers and adopters should recognise as their invaluable contribution even to very troubled young people, who may not themselves appreciate it until they are in their 20s and beyond, when they can sometimes rebuild their connections to the family (Howe, 1996).

Such developments in early adulthood will make the difference between those adults who go on as parents to be unresolved and be likely to repeat the cycle in producing disorganised children and those who are able to offer their children caregiving that is less likely to be frightening and provide a more secure base than they themselves experienced.

Summary points

- Disorganised infants and children have experienced parenting that is:
  - frightened or frightening;
  - insensitive and unavailable;
  - helpless/hostile;
  - intrusive;
  - not supportive of exploration, effectiveness and co-operation;

147

- not conducive to building self-esteem;
- negative about the child and the self.

• Infants cannot find an effective strategy to feel safe. Caregivers who are frightened or frightening leave infants with an insoluble dilemma – if infants approach their caregiver for comfort and safety, the caregiver is experienced as frightening rather than protective. Thus children experience "fear without solution" (Main and Hesse, 1990).

• In the pre-school years children start to develop controlling and role-reversing strategies e.g. punitive/aggressive and compulsive caregiving/compulsive self-reliance.

• Disorganised children have an *internal working model* of the self as unlovable and helpless, others as hostile and helpless, and relationships as unpredictable and frightening.

• Disorganised infants and children, as they develop, are likely to show a combination of some of the following characteristics (Howe *et al*, 1999):
  - poor emotional scaffolding;
  - verbal deficits;
  - poor affect regulation;
  - low self-esteem/self/confidence;
  - dissociation;
  - poor relationship with peers – withdrawal/aggression;
  - hypervigilance in presence of distress, aggression and violence;
  - fear and aggression;
  - punitive and controlling;
  - conduct disorders;
  - low novelty-seeking;
  - rigid and/or incoherent thinkers when stressed;
  - reading problems;
  - withdrawal and avoidance, especially neglected children;
  - poor sense of humour, low positive affect;
  - unempathic;
  - risk of anti-social behaviour/conduct problems.

• Disorganised attachment is far more common among maltreated children (van IJzendoorn *et al*, 1999; Carlson *et al*, 1989) *but* not all disorganised children have been maltreated. However, disorganisation and maltreatment together present a high risk to children's healthy psychosocial development.

Introduction

We have seen that early experiences of loss, or neglectful or abusive parenting, will cause children to distrust close relationships. All children who are placed in foster or adoptive families will have a sense of loss and dislocation, making them wary and defended for a time. For many, however, experiences of neglect and maltreatment will often have had a more profound effect. These children will transfer negative expectations of adults into their new environments, along with the patterns of defensive behaviour that have functioned as survival strategies in the past. In these circumstances, they will find it hard to let adults come close enough to establish trusting and supportive relationships. The risk, then, is that feelings and behaviours become fixed in destructive loops and the damage of the past will not be healed.

Attachment theory would suggest, however, that exposure to warm, consistent and reliable caregiving can change children's previous expectations both of close adults and of themselves and there is ample evidence from research and practice to support this (Downes, 1992; Wilson *et al*, 2003; Cairns, 2002; Schofield, 2003; Cairns, 2004; Beek and Schofield, 2004a; Schofield and Beek, 2005). The intervention of foster carers and adopters, therefore, is of central importance. They must take on a parenting role for the child but must also become a *therapeutic* parent in order to change the child's most fundamental sense of self and others. In order to achieve this, they must parent in ways that demonstrate to the child, implicitly and explicitly, that they are trustworthy and reliable, physically and emotionally available and sensitive to his or her needs. In addition, they must be mindful of the protective strategies that the child has learned in order to feel safe in the past and adjust their approaches so that their parenting feels comfortable and acceptable to the child rather than undermining or threatening. In these circumstances, children can slowly begin to mentally represent their new caregivers as protective and available and themselves as loved and lovable. The ensuing relationships will provide a secure base from which children can develop and be supported to explore and maximise their potential.

We have found that an understanding of infant caregiving, based on attachment theory (Ainsworth *et al*, 1971) and adapted to include the additional needs of fostered and adopted children regarding family membership (Schofield, 2003), provides a helpful conceptual framework for understanding the process by which children can be helped to move towards security. If foster care and adoption are to be viewed as potentially *therapeutic* interventions for a child, we must think not only of the parenting approach but also of the *developmental benefit* that this approach is likely to have for the child. With this in mind, our framework (see Figure 2) consists of five inter-related dimensions of caregiving, each with an associated developmental benefit for the child.

Figure 2

Providing a secure base

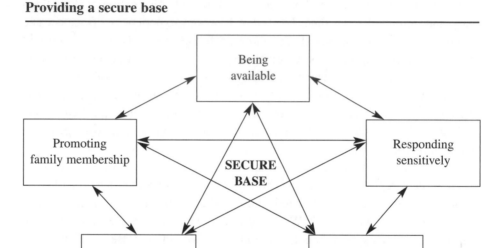

Being available – helping children to trust

This dimension focuses on the caregiver's ability to convey a strong sense of being physically and emotionally available to meet the child's needs, both when they are together and when they are apart. From this, the child begins to trust that he is safe and that his needs will be met warmly, consistently and reliably. Anxiety is reduced and he gains the confidence to explore the world, safe in the knowledge that care and protection will be available in times of need.

Responding sensitively – helping children to manage their feelings and behaviour

Responding sensitively refers to the caregiver's capacity to "stand in the shoes" of the child, to think flexibly about what the child may be thinking and feeling and to reflect this back to the child. The reflective, "mind-minded" carer also thinks about their own feelings and shares them sensitively with the child. The child thus learns to think about his own ideas and feelings *and* the thoughts and feelings of others and is helped to reflect on, organise and manage his own feelings and behaviour.

Accepting the child – building self-esteem

This dimension refers to the caregiver's capacity to convey that the child is unconditionally accepted and valued for who he is, for his difficulties as well as his strengths. This forms the foundation of positive self-esteem, so that the child can experience himself as worthy of receiving love, help and support and (when linked to self-efficacy) also as robust and able to deal with setbacks and adversity.

Co-operative caregiving – helping children to feel effective

Within this dimension, the caregiver thinks about the child as an autonomous individual whose wishes, feelings and goals are valid and meaningful and who needs to feel effective. The caregiver, therefore, looks for ways of promoting autonomy, but also working together and achieving co-operation with the child wherever possible. This helps the child to feel more effective and competent, to feel confident in turning to others for help, if necessary, and to be able to compromise and co-operate.

Promoting family membership – helping children to belong

This dimension refers to the capacity of the caregiver to include the child, socially and personally, as a full family member, at a level that is appropriate to the longer-term plan for the child. At the same time, the caregiver is able to help the child to establish an appropriate sense of connectedness and belonging to his birth family. In this way, the child can develop a comfortable sense of belonging to two families.

As Figure 2 illustrates, each of these parenting dimensions interacts with and reinforces each other, with self-esteem, for example, underpinning effectiveness, and trust contributing to family membership.

If we are truly to understand the therapeutic potential of foster and adoptive parenting, however, we have to examine more closely the interactions that occur between caregivers and their children on a day-to-day, minute-by-minute basis. In earlier chapters, we have seen that the process of shaping the mind and ultimately the behaviour of the child begins in the mind of the caregiver. The ways in which a caregiver thinks and feels about a child's behaviours will determine his or her own parenting behaviours. Parenting behaviours convey certain messages to the child. The child's thinking and feeling will be affected by these messages and there will be a consequent impact on his or her behaviour and development.

We have chosen to represent this process in a circular model (Figure 3). Cycles or circles have often been used to conceptualise parenting (Fahlberg, 1994; Marvin *et al*, 2002) and they capture the essential inter-connectedness of parent–child relationships as well as their ongoing movement and change.

Figure 3

Parenting cycle

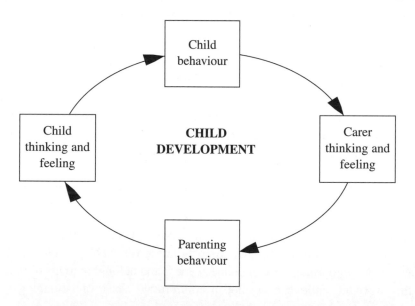

This parenting cycle encompasses the innumerable interactions of family life, ranging from the moment-to-moment exchanges over breakfast to managing major emotional or behavioural crises. Each interaction conveys a number of messages to the child, has an incremental effect on the child's internal working models and so will influence the child's functioning and development.

The following five chapters explore this circular model within each of the five parenting dimensions outlined above. They are underpinned by the wealth of information and research generated by attachment theory (Ainsworth *et al*, 1971; Bowlby, 1969, 1980, 1988; Cassidy and Shaver, 1999; Crittenden, 1995; Fonagy *et al*, 2002; Howe *et al*, 1999; Howe, 2005) and by a considerable number of research studies with foster carers and adoptive parents (Hill *et al*, 1989; Howe, 1996; Dozier *et al*, 2001; Rushton *et al*, 2001, 2003; Sinclair and Wilson, 2003; Sinclair *et al*, 2004; Wilson *et al*, 2003; Beek and Schofield, 2004a). There is a final diagram (Figure 9) which summarises all of the five dimensions.

Together, the chapters aim to define and understand more precisely the nature of therapeutic caregiving and to highlight the additional tasks of building and sustaining a secure base for vulnerable children from infancy to adolescence. It is hoped that they will help social workers and caregivers to conceptualise and celebrate much of the therapeutic caregiving that is already occurring in foster and adoptive families and also to think about ways of developing the skills and potential of foster carers and adopters through training and support.

6 **Being available – helping children to trust**

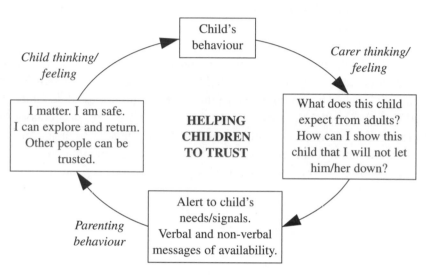

Figure 4

The best environment for children's healthy emotional development is one in which they can take for granted that nurture, comfort and protection are readily available when needed. Such an environment provides a *secure base* for exploration and forms the foundation on which *trust* in the self and others will be built. To provide a secure base, dependable adult caregivers must be *available* but not intrusive, *alert to their children's signals* for closeness and protection and ready to respond with help or encouragement (see Figure 4). When the child is reassured and ready to resume exploration, this, too, must be supported and facilitated by the caregiver. Caregivers need always to *keep the child in mind*, so that even in the absence of signals they will be anticipating and planning ways of meeting needs, both physical, for example, hunger or cold, and emotional, such as supporting the child's first day at nursery.

Children who are nurtured in this way come to expect that their caregivers will be interested in them and to trust that they will provide emotional warmth, care and protection. At the same time, they gain a sense of their own worthiness to receive loving care. They are liberated from anxiety and free to explore, learn and develop. Through infancy, childhood and adolescence, children can move progressively further away from their caregivers, becoming increasingly curious and negotiating greater risks. They can venture forth with confidence, safe in the knowledge that the secure base is there for them in times of trouble.

What children bring to their placements

Many looked after children have lacked consistent care and protection from reliable caregivers. They have often experienced adults who have reacted to their distress with frustration, anxiety and rejection, or have "blown hot and cold" according to their own needs or the external pressures in their lives. Each of these approaches will cause children to have anxieties and uncertainties around caregiving. They will not be able to trust that an adult will always be available or that their needs will be met consistently, safely and kindly. Most detrimentally, previous caregivers may have reacted to a needy child with unpredictable anger or frightening aggression, causing the child to feel deep fear, panic, confusion and helplessness. The child is then likely to associate closeness with feelings of fear and dread and feel panicked by the approach of any potential caregiver, however trustworthy they may be.

Fostered and adopted children, therefore, bring a range of deeply-rooted experiences that may lead them either to distance themselves from their new caregivers, to clamour constantly for their attention, to feel helpless or to be determinedly in control. In some cases, foster carers and adopters find that their parenting approaches actually trigger negative patterns of behaviour. In each of these situations, children are trying to protect themselves from the painful aspects of close relationships, rather than being able to relax and enjoy the benefits of them. Their defensive strategies, which were necessary for survival at an earlier stage, can become problematic, stressful or hurtful to new caregivers who want so much to nurture, soothe and protect their children from further harm.

Tasks for adopters and foster carers

The challenge for foster carers and adopters is a complex one. The eventual goal is to change their children's expectations of adults – to convince them that in this family (and perhaps in others in the future) children can rely on adults to care for them safely and meet their needs. Firstly, however, they may have to disentangle some confusing messages. Through words and behaviour, children may be indicating 'I don't need you, I prefer to look after myself' or 'I need you all the time, but can never be satisfied by you' or 'I can only manage my anxiety by controlling you and everything that happens in the household'. New caregivers may have to remind themselves of the true needs that lie behind these messages and this is no easy task when they are accompanied by extremely resistant, needy or hostile behaviour. They may need additional support, therefore, to help them to *think* about the child's previous experiences and speculate on *what this child might be expecting from adults.* In the light of this, they can think about targeting their trust building interventions precisely and finding ways of showing the child that *they will not let him down, that adults can be trusted.*

Each child will need an individualised approach, according to his chronological and emotional age, his personality and, above all, according to his existing ideas, his *internal working models* of how adults are likely to behave and respond to him. With this in mind, caregivers can begin to be more *alert to their child's signals* and then take opportunities to do and say things that will begin to change the child's expectations of himself and adults. They will give *verbal and non-verbal messages of availability,* but – and this perhaps, is the greatest skill of therapeutic caregiving – they will find ways of doing this that feel comfortable and acceptable to the individual child. This can often involve a certain amount of trial and error and delicate judgement, such as when to move closer and when to wait for a child to make the first move himself. Most important, however, is the capacity of the caregiver to generate *flexible theories* about what is going on for the child (e.g. this behaviour may be caused by a bad experience in early childhood, a difficult day at school or both), to try different approaches and to wait patiently for small changes.

Gradually, as children begin to receive and absorb messages of availability from their caregivers, they begin to think differently about themselves and others. They do not have to worry constantly about whether or not they will be fed, comforted, kept safe from harm and so on. They start to *feel safe* and develop a sense that they *matter* in this family. As children begin to *trust* that close adults are not going to disappear or let them down, anxiety is diminished and the urge to *explore, learn and play* becomes greater. It is at this point that a marked change in behaviour is likely to occur. There will be greater confidence and competence to venture away from the secure base and explore the wider world – but there will also be an increasing capacity to rely on caregivers for comfort and nurture and to enjoy appropriate closeness. Signs of progress in these areas may be painfully slow to appear but they are among the most exciting and rewarding for foster carers and adopters to observe. This chapter explores the complexities and practicalities of building trust for fostered and adopted children of different ages.

Infancy (birth–18 months)

When infants and young babies are placed in foster care or for adoption, they are usually in a state of heightened anxiety and vulnerability. The majority have had an adverse start in life and will have little sense of the world as a safe and predictable place to be. Those who have begun to build secure relationships in their birth families (e.g. where a child is looked after because a parent has died or become ill) or in a previous but temporary foster family, will have their trust shaken as they enter an unfamiliar environment in which their signals cannot immediately be read and responded to in the same predictable way. The aim of therapeutic caregiving, therefore, is to create an environment in which the child can be in no doubt that his or her fundamental needs for proximity, safety and loving care will be met. Once this expectation is established in the infant's mind, anxiety will diminish and learning, play and exploration will become progressively more important.

Patterns of behaviour become established very early and even young babies will have found out how best to survive in adverse conditions. Some have "shut down" their expressions of need. Their attachment behaviours are infrequent and muted and they provide their caregivers with few signals of distress or need or contentment. They may be limp and expressionless, sleep a lot and not wake for feeds.

If a baby is providing little in the way of signalling, the first tasks will be to alert her to her own needs, to wake her for feeds, to hold her closely, talk to her soothingly and provide gentle stimulation, even if she appears content to be left alone for lengthy periods. The caregiver needs to be keeping the infant in mind and fully focused on her needs even when she is not communicating them, as this foster carer describes:

> *When Jasminder came to me at 12 weeks old, she was completely unresponsive, not waking for feeds, not responding to me, not showing any emotion. She had just switched off. I had to stay close to her and respond to even the slightest sound or facial movement and keep talking to her and touching her. It took time, but gradually she started to show different feelings and become more responsive.*

Even at 12 weeks, an infant can have started to withdraw and shut down, especially if emotional neglect is associated with physical neglect and the baby is malnourished. Once in foster care, when there are signals of need, even if they are tentative, a prompt response will help the baby to understand that she can make things happen and that they will happen in ways that are soothing, pleasurable and, eventually, predictable. This can be a stressful journey for carers who may need help in understanding why the infant is taking so long to respond.

Some babies, in contrast, will have developed heightened and excessive attachment behaviours. They may be constantly fretful, signalling needs for proximity and yet being hard to soothe and sometimes even rejecting closeness when it is offered. A great deal of physical time and emotional energy is required to show such infants that their needs will be reliably met. When cuddles and close feeding are hard for the baby to tolerate, the challenge is to find the minimum level of closeness that is comfortable – sitting beside him for a feed, for instance, or stroking a hand or a foot and unobtrusively building on this. For babies who cannot cope with separation from a caregiver, even for a few minutes, a period of maximum availability, permitting physical closeness and reassurance wherever possible, will be demanding for the caregiver but may be the only way of diminishing the child's anxiety sufficiently for a programme of brief, but gradually increasing, separations to be put into place. This may include using strategies such as introducing special soft toys as transitional objects or having another special person in the family to act as an auxiliary safe caregiver.

The overall aim of caregiving will be to demonstrate to the baby that there will always be a warm, familiar adult at hand to relieve discomfort or distress and that closeness is both reliable and enjoyable.

For babies who have experienced trauma, care will need to be taken to ensure that they do not feel alarmed or confused during caregiving routines and to anticipate occasions when this might be the case. For example, the approach of an adult from behind might be startling, thus the positioning of a high chair or cot, the direction from which the carer approaches with food or wet flannel and the signals of approach all need to be considered and adjusted if necessary. Anything that causes confusion or distress should be pre-empted or swiftly dealt with. Key here will often be the main caregiver's voice, which can be used to create a safe climate and to soothe the infant during waiting times and in anticipation of needs being met. As trust builds, the caregiver's voice can also have the effect of "bringing a child to life", inspiring her with confidence to enjoy both the sensory and interpersonal world, as happened for Jasminder (above).

At the beginning of a new family placement, key tasks of caregiving for infants such as feeding, nappy changing and settling to sleep, may need to be restricted to a small number of committed adults in order to help the child to focus on the experience of predictable patterns of care and to develop selective attachments. This may be a time when sharing the care of the baby among a range of people, such as older children and relatives, may not be such a good idea – although such people are very valuable playmates from the outset and over time may help to broaden the child's sense that other people can be trusted.

As anxiety and stress diminish, infants will become increasingly alert and eager to explore their toys and surroundings. Responding to this, the caregiver can provide opportunities for both closeness and distance, allowing time to play alone, but ensuring there are regular checks or reunions with the caregiver and responding promptly to signals for help or company. As trust build over time, the baby can tolerate a certain degree of separation, because she *knows* that the caregiver is keeping her in mind and will return. The foundations of feeling safe and confident to explore the wider world are formed in these early experiences.

When babies are signalling interest in their surroundings, they need an environment which can be explored safely and pleasurably and without too much adult intervention. Soft surfaces, the removal of valuable or fragile items, sufficient warmth and space and the securing of unsuitable areas will reduce the need to discourage exploration or curiosity. Exploration will be further encouraged by toys and materials which stimulate and reward curiosity and can be safely investigated with the mouth. Caregivers can also develop games and activities such as "peek a boo", hiding objects under cushions, gentle hide and seek or calling or singing from another room, all of which can help babies to learn that objects and people continue to exist when they cannot be seen − and to experience their world as a little more safe and predictable as a result. Such games neatly combine messages of availability with the infant's growing capacity to explore how the world works.

These activities and many of the other approaches mentioned above occur spontaneously in most families − but for infants who have had uncertain beginnings in life, their therapeutic value is such that this cannot be left to chance.

Overall, therapeutic caregiving for children in this very young age group involves developing a repertoire of parenting behaviours that actively, consciously and deliberately aim to build the infant's trust both in adults and in himself. Within this broad aim, approaches will be tailored to fit comfortably with the particular needs and preferences of the individual child. It helps to have a good understanding of the child's history.

Case example

Tammy came into care at 10 months old, having experienced consistent physical and emotional neglect from birth. She had been shut away in her bedroom for much of the time or left strapped in her buggy. She was not picked up for feeding. Her mother described her to health visitors and the paediatrician as a "good" baby who never cried and slept a lot. Admitted first to hospital, where she was found to be suffering from the rare vitamin deficiency disease, rickets, Tammy was entirely limp with no muscle tone, laying completely flat and going floppy when picked up. She did not respond to light, sound, toys, or her mother's face or voice. She also did not respond to the nurses. Her only faint response was to her two-year-old sister's voice. Investigations found no evidence of a congenital disorder.

In foster care, it took several months before Tammy began to respond to the carer. It was necessary not only to offer constant availability and consistency around meeting Tammy's physical needs and demonstrating emotional warmth, but also to embark on an intensive and planned programme of gentle stimulation to help Tammy discover an interest and joy in people and her environment which she had lost as a tiny infant. This required getting past the early stages in placement when, as Tammy started to feel physically stronger, her first reaction was to fret and demand without offering much in the way of smiling and rewarding behaviour.

It was not easy for the foster carer to keep faith in Tammy's potential to be a lovable and loving child and she began to sympathise with the birth mother's difficulty in caring for such an unresponsive, difficult baby. The carer had to be helped with feelings of disappointment that the high standard of care that she was offering was nevertheless taking a long time to "work". Tammy was successfully placed for adoption at the age of two, although it was acknowledged that these difficult beginnings might continue to have an impact on her development and that her adoptive parents would also need, for some time to come, to provide a therapeutic level of care.

Early childhood (18 months – 4 years)

When children in this age group enter a new family, whether from a birth family or previous family placement settings, there is a risk that the move and the sense of loss will interrupt developmental progress. But there is also a real opportunity for a well-timed intervention that will help children to feel settled, secure and trusting before the big move into school. Even at the younger end of this range, however, children will bring a set of beliefs, expectations and behaviours in relation to object and interpersonal worlds and these *internal working models* will influence their take-up of sensitive care in significant ways.

Pre-school children need to achieve a comfortable balance between dependency and autonomy as they move towards the full separation of nursery and school. However, developmental processes can be helpful in achieving this goal. For example, the development of expressive and receptive language enables the child to demand or express anxieties about the caregiver's availability and the caregiver to provide information about their whereabouts and their commitment to being available. On the other hand, as discussed in previous chapters, children of this age have learned to pretend to feel things they don't feel. They have a greater potential to give misleading signals, to miscue carers about their needs, so caregivers need particular skills in distinguishing and meeting underlying needs in order to convince the child of their availability.

Some young children may signal their needs directly through clingy behaviour and resisting their caregivers' attempts to promote independence. For others, anxiety about closeness leads them to signal their needs in indirect ways such as false smiles, controlling behaviours or rages and tantrums. Small signals of the need for nurture, therefore, such as the child leaning against the caregiver during a story, may be the best that's on offer – and all that will be accepted by the child in return may be an acceptance of this gesture or a stroke of the child's hand, since to cuddle the child more tightly might be experienced as intrusive and threatening. A child's reactions when care has been given, whether or not in response to a request, can include resisting or ignoring the caregiver. Thus, even apparently minor contacts need to be carefully handled so that trust rather than anxiety is increased. In the following extract, a foster mother describes how she demonstrated her availability to four year-old Charlie, who was deeply distrustful when he came to her following the breakdown of a previous placement.

> *He found it impossible to trust me and watched my face warily all the time. I found that after nursery, if I sat with a drink for him on the settee with children's television on, he would circle the house for a long time dragging his favourite blanket and eventually end up sitting on my lap wrapped in the blanket, drinking his drink. I needed just to be there and he needed to have the confidence that I would wait for him to come to me.*

Often it will be the caregiver's ability to see the needs that lie beneath difficult behaviour rather than direct signals that prompts the caregiver to offer closeness. Charlie could also be extremely unsettled by any change in routine and this needed to be anticipated so that verbal and non-verbal support could be offered.

Children in this age group remain very much dependent on adults to provide basic care and this offers opportunities to provide closeness and nurture through help with feeding, dressing, bathing and so on. Availability offered in this way may be usefully focussed, as in infancy, on the child's sensory and bodily needs – the softness and smells of the familiar blanket, the warmth of the drink, the closeness of the carer's body, the stimulating colours and sounds from the television programme. Significant events, especially those that awaken attachment needs, such as illness, can be consciously built into opportunities for providing the child with distinctive experiences which reinforce messages of care and protection. Extra cuddles, soft pillows, milky drinks in bed, the shared and familiar book and other comforts may be more readily received by an unwell child whose defences are not drawn up as sharply as usual. Most important then, is the opportunity to process these experiences after the event, perhaps through a story about a sick child or animal that needed comfort, or by talking through the events with the child or helping him to tell someone else about them. In this way, the good feelings of receiving comfort and nurture can be stored in the child's memory and perhaps can be drawn on at other vulnerable times.

This may seem to be rather a sentimental process or to be building illness into something to be enjoyed, but such commemoration of getting through difficult times is not uncommon in ordinary family life, where stories of illness or minor accidents are the very stuff of family memories – and often appear in the Adult Attachment Interview (Main and Goldwyn, 1984), for example, as an indicator of whether parents were experienced as loving and available or not. For looked after and adopted children, who are often resistant to the ordinary, everyday offering of availability and concern, it may be that such episodes become helpful turning points. Taking these opportunities and being sensitive to the therapeutic potential they hold can be very valuable for children of any age, but the foundations for secure base availability can be laid in these pre-school years when internal working models are becoming firmed up.

As children move towards school age, the message that the attachment figure can still be available, even when they are not in sight, may need to be made explicit for the child. In the following extract, a short term foster mother describes how she manages the separation from her foster children when they appear ready to stay at the local nursery on their own. She has an open and trusting relationship with the staff and she is confident that they will help her foster children to hold her in mind when they are at nursery and to know that she is available if needed.

I'll crouch down so I'm at the same level as the child, because that's important and I hope the member of staff will crouch down too. And I'll say 'This is Mrs. So and So and she's the person in charge here and she can ring me if you've got any problems. If you want me to come back or if you fall over and hurt yourself, she will ring me, she won't wait until the end of the day, and then I will come back and get you.' And I'll probably say that every day until I think

*the child has got that trust in me and also has started to build trust where they
are, as well.*

This sense for the child that there is a trusting relationship between the caregiver
and the nursery staff, who are now more immediately available for the child,
enables the staff to act as a proxy for the secure base caregiver. It is not surprising
that often even young children sense the powerful ties between their parents and
other extended family members and so they trust in the care of relatives who may
not have had much prior contact with them. If this model of a transfer of trust can
be extended by caregivers to other people caring for the child in their absence,
it will be very helpful. Without this capacity to both mentally represent the
caregiver as an available secure base and to accept the role of playgroup leaders,
teachers and others in offering a safe environment, children will find it hard to
make the next important transitions of middle childhood.

Middle childhood (5–10 years)

The process of building and maintaining trust in the availability of a secure base
remains a primary concern for older children. However, in middle childhood there
is an increasing need for children to move physically away from their immediate
source of security for sustained periods of time as they branch out into the wider
worlds of school, friendships and activities. They cross a threshold for which
good preparation in the pre-school years is of great importance.

Almost all children entering new placements at this age will have experienced
adverse caregiving at some stage but many will also have had some more positive
experiences of adults. A particular teacher, birth relative or previous carer, for
instance, may have been interested, supportive and encouraging, creating
strengths and resilience to be built on. Universally, however, fostered and adopted
children have been separated (sometimes repeatedly) from familiar people, places
and things, making them vulnerable to stress during the normal processes of
separation and exploration. They are preoccupied with the big questions: 'Am I
lovable and will you love me?' alongside the inevitable: 'Why did my mummy
and daddy not love me enough to keep me?'. These big concerns for children
often come out in the small stresses of everyday living.

New caregivers will need to manage children's sense of loss and dislocation,
at the same time working to disconfirm negative and distrustful expectations of
adults and support exploration at the child's pace. Parenting approaches must
again be tailored to the individual child and caregivers will need to take into
account the emotional as well as the chronological age of the child and also the
degree of closeness and distance that the child finds acceptable and comfortable.

As in infancy and the pre-school years, the ways in which children are fed, kept safe, comforted and helped to play and relax are of major significance in the process of building trust. Mealtimes, bath and bedtime routines, playtime and quiet, relaxing time can all be viewed as opportunities to disconfirm negative expectations of the self and others. High standards of reliable and predictable "basic care" provide messages to children that they matter and that they are safe in this family. As Heather's carer put it:

> *When Heather (9) first arrived her life revolved around food. She looked forward to coming home from school and a drink and a biscuit, then later tea. And every week on Sunday she asked, 'Is it roast today'? And I'd say, 'What do we always have on Sunday?' and she'd reply, 'Roast!'*

Care has to be negotiated with older children and tailored to their preferences. When sensitively targeted in this way, such messages of care, concern and respect become embedded in the mind of the child, since they are repeated and reinforced hour by hour and day by day in the normal routines of family life. Mental representations of caregivers as reliably warm, kind and responsive will slowly begin to replace more negative representations of neglectful or abusive caregivers.

Some caregivers sense a strong need in their older children to experience the closeness and nurturing care that they may have missed at an earlier stage and the approach to this is a matter of sensitivity to the child's signals, but also of judgement about when and where it is helpful and acceptable for the child to receive such care.

> *At the age of ten years, Terry still wanted his foster mother, Ann, to bath and dress him. Ann encouraged Terry to feel that it was important for him at his age to do these things for himself, but knowing that he yearned to be nurtured like a younger child she compromised by helping him to put on his top clothes sometimes, 'just to make him feel special' and still tucked him up at night. This gave him reassuring physical contact and care as he was getting ready to set off into the outside world or when allowing himself to drift into sleep, but also helped to keep him focused on developing age-appropriate competence.*

For many children, the provision of "special time", in which the caregiver is alert to the child's signals and fully focused on ways of responding to them, can provide strong messages of availability. Time that is routinely set aside to play, talk, go for a walk or just watch TV together can be mutually rewarding and highly significant for fostered, adopted and birth children alike.

For some children, however, well-meaning attempts by caregivers to get close or show concern may be experienced as intrusive or threatening. Alison recognised that this was an issue for Lizzie (7) when she first came to live with her. After a difficult day at school, Alison observed that Lizzie would tend to take herself off into her bedroom during the evening. Resisting the temptation to follow her and make enquiries, Alison might, instead, make a point of doing the ironing or putting clothes away on the landing outside Lizzie's bedroom:

Not really to entice a conversation, but more to give her an opportunity. And she does seem to sense when I've got time to listen. I mean, they get to know you as well as you get to know them.

The message to Lizzie here, then, is 'I think you may be worried about something and I am here for you, but in your own time'. The fact that Alison had made herself available in this way offered a message of concern and reassurance, even if Lizzie chose not to communicate with her on that occasion.

Sometimes, however, lack of trust leads to behaviours that are deliberately intended to keep adults at bay or provoke angry rather than comforting responses and it is hard to convey messages of love and availability. This was the case for adoptive parents, Sabena and Karim and their son, Kris (6). Sabena and Karim followed professional advice in providing structured "child time" for Kris, which was designed to lead to the kind of attuned relationship that would usually develop in early infancy. This involved a period every evening in which one parent became fully focused on Kris and whatever play or activity he was choosing to do. They were to be alongside him, but not directly involved, and they could indicate their availability and interest by following his lead and briefly describing what he was doing (for example, giving a simple commentary such as 'you're putting the yellow brick on top of the red brick'). Kris loved these sessions and his parents felt that they were highly beneficial in the building of their relationship with him. Karim commented:

You could see that something was going on for Kris (during the sessions). It was comfortable for both of us and he was getting our full attention, which he wanted and needed so much, but he was getting it in a way that was acceptable and enjoyable to us and to him, instead of getting it in negative ways.

When children are signaling need or anxiety with negative and very difficult behaviour, it is understandable that caregivers will sometimes seek to distance themselves from the child, either emotionally (by responding angrily) or physically (by sending the child to his bedroom, or walking away). Although these reactions may be unavoidable at times, a strategy that continues to provide some degree of physical and emotional availability or repairs the incident with a strong message of availability is going to be more effective in building trust.

Such an approach was described by Paula, whose foster daughter, Charlotte (10), frequently refused to do as she was requested. Paula had developed a clearly-defined approach to this form of conflict. She would aim to defuse the situation by removing herself from the argument, but staying within range. Then she would reconnect with Charlotte by offering food or drink, important symbols of comfort for Charlotte that reassure her and help to promote trust and co-operation.

Sometimes, when I've asked her to do something and she won't do it, then I just have to walk away, but then I'll come back into the room and start making a sandwich or a drink and then I turn to her and say, 'Would you like a sandwich or a drink, Charlotte, or do you want to make a sandwich with me? And that's the opening and then we start again and then maybe she'll do what I've asked her to do.

By middle childhood, children spend increasing amounts of time away from their caregivers and without adult supervision. For children who have yet to establish trust, these can be stressful times. Even children who have settled well in their foster or adoptive families may find it hard to *hold in mind* the comforting presence of their caregivers when they are apart from them. Without this mental anchorage, they may easily become overwhelmed by anxiety and be unable to regulate their behaviour or be free to explore and learn.

Aiden (4), for instance, found it hard to mentally represent his foster mother as a source of security when he went for contact with his father. A "transitional object" provided by his foster mother was a source of comfort and reassurance that his place in the foster family was secure, as she described:

When Aiden had contact with his father, he was always very anxious about what might happen and whether I would be here for him after the visit. On one occasion when I took him to a family centre, I gave him my cardigan to hold during his contact visit so that he would know that I would be waiting for him afterwards. On another occasion I gave him a small cushion from the settee at home so that he had something to hold on to, but also so that he would know he would be coming home.

Caregivers who are alert to their children's needs in this area will find various ways in which they can help their particular child to retain a sense of security when they are apart. An adoptive father spoke of leaving a text message on his son's mobile phone early each morning when he was away on a camp. A foster mother used a special painting that the child had done to convey to the child that he was of central importance in her mind when he was at school

> *I said to him 'I'm going to put that up on the wall and every time I look at it, it will remind me of you when you're at school. I shall look at it and think of you doing it and how beautifully you did it and it will make me feel happy to think of you.'*

In each of these examples, the message to the child is the same – *you matter, we are thinking of you even though we are not with you, we are here for you when you return.* When these messages are repeatedly received by the child, there will be small shifts in behaviour as anxiety diminishes and the confidence to learn and explore increases.

Adolescence (11–18 years)

Within Western culture, most young adolescents spend increasing amounts of time out of the family home, away from their secure base. For most young people, the desire to explore and gain new experience becomes more acute and more demanding activities are available, along with peer group pressure to take part in them. Young people begin to make a shift towards friends and partners as significant attachment figures and to think about living independently from their parental home. On the other hand, young people who are becoming more independent often still need actual and symbolic contact and demonstrations of availability.

> *Susi (14) was six when she was placed with the foster mother who went on to adopt her. She had come from a very neglectful family and had already experienced the ending of one foster placement. She had made very good progress in the context of what had been, at times, quite a stormy relationship with her adoptive mother. But Susi would only settle to sleep at night after saying goodnight to her mother. Even if her mother went out for the evening, Susi would, without fail, ring her on her mobile at bedtime to say goodnight.*

This account shows how significant times and transitions, such as bedtimes, remain important even to older children, and how making contact, checking availability and, by implication, sometimes making amends and getting reassurance, are important ways of ending the day. The adoptive mother accepts and understands why this phone call is still important to her teenage daughter.

For adolescents newly placed in foster or adoptive families, there may be only a limited window of opportunity to build trust before the need to break away from the secure base becomes an imperative. Even for those placed at a younger age (perhaps even in infancy), the normal shifts and transitions of adolescence can feel exceptionally difficult, with the risks of exploration seeming too great to manage or the enticements of "independence" offering a form of separation that feels desirable initially but results in a premature or unplanned severance from the secure base. Many fostered and adopted adolescents have a heightened need for reassurance as they also face other issues around their identity and what kind of person they will become. It is hard to anticipate the future and all need reassurance that the family is available for them, even if they make mistakes. As one 11-year-old said to her long-term foster mother:

My social worker says I can leave here when I'm 16 – but if I leave, can I come back?

A central task for foster carers and adopters, therefore, is to provide a strong sense of the availability of the secure base when it is needed, but also to help teenagers to successfully manage movements across the family boundary. When insecure young people are moving towards chronological adulthood and yet behaving in ways that signal their need for dependency, there are dilemmas for caregivers in terms of how to meet these needs while promoting greater independence and self reliance. Often there are concerns that a young person might never be able to "stand on their own two feet" if they are not strongly encouraged to do so at this stage. *Attachment theory challenges this position.* Instead, it promotes the idea that if attachment needs are met, the young person's capacity for development and exploration will be freed up. Thus, caregivers who can build supportive and consistent alliances will enable young people to trust in the current and future availability of their secure base (Downes, 1992). Then they can move away with greater confidence, strengthened by the knowledge that they are not alone and that they can refer back or return to their attachment figures if necessary. The caregiver accepts the young person's need (one that all adults as well as children share) to have someone to turn to, while building confidence and supporting the young person's confidence and exploration.

Many adolescents have the verbal and thinking skills to communicate their needs more accurately. But those who have troubled early lives have also spent longer avoiding and concealing their feelings and have less reason to take the risk of building trust at this stage. Defensive behaviours, such as demanding but resisting closeness or contemptuous responses to care when it is offered, can become barriers to close relationships.

For all teenagers, however, ongoing messages of parental availability are valued at some level, even when they are distrustful or striving for autonomy, and this is especially true for fostered and adopted children. The following young woman, for example, recalls the significance of being held in mind by her foster father when he was away from home.

Fiona (24) had experienced several broken foster placements, separation from her siblings and a failed adoption prior to the long-term foster placement which became her family for life. It took her a long time to trust her long-term carers. She recalled how her foster father used to work away on occasions during her teenage years, but would ring home and speak to each child in turn. She said, 'He could just have asked my (foster) mum how we were, but he always wanted to speak to us'.

Sensitive caregivers seek opportunities to signal their availability in ways that feel natural and unobtrusive to teenagers. Grace, a mother in a busy family of birth, adopted and fostered children, is aware of this issue.

I try very much, if they talk to me, to stop what I'm doing. Because there's a lot of them, I feel it's important, because otherwise opportunities disappear. I create opportunities as well. I mean with Liam (13), in particular, we might take the long road home if I sensed he wanted to talk about something. And if they mention something and I really can't talk about it at that moment, I'll say 'Right, we can't talk about it now, but we can talk about it at such and such a time,' and we will.

Explicit and repeated statements and demonstrations of reliability and consistency can have an incremental effect in trust building for young people. Awareness of this as a parenting goal can direct caregivers to take every opportunity to underline the centrality of the young person in their thoughts and their strong commitment to his or her well-being.

For Sue and Trevor, such an opportunity arose when Cilla (16) said that she felt it unlikely that she would receive a computer as promised through her local authority scheme as things like this never worked out for her. Sue assured her

173

that they would do everything possible to ensure that, this time, it would work out for her and made a point of informing her of the subsequent letters, telephone calls, etc. that they were making on her behalf. The eventual arrival of a computer was therefore significant in a variety of ways.

The provision of nurture, proximity and protection remains significant throughout the teenage years, both as a retreat from the pressures and expectations of growing up and as a continuing process of filling the gaps from earlier times. Again, the challenge for caregivers is to find ways of providing good experiences in ways that are both age-appropriate and acceptable to the young person. It is important, too, that such experiences are unconditional and available to the young person, even through times of angry or rejecting behaviour. Unobtrusive and enjoyable closeness may be achieved in a jacuzzi, during a manicure session or in a game of pool or cards. Important messages can be imparted through the provision of special or favourite foods, bedrooms and bathrooms that feel warm and safe, and a general ethos that suggests that a young person is valued and important.

Nina (14) had a history of violence and had spent time in secure accommodation. It was very difficult to get through to her. Her carer wanted to make bath times a bit special to help her relax. She took her shopping for a nice fluffy towel. Then Nina was invited to choose bath foams and shampoo. They got to the check-out and Nina asked to change her teenage bath products for baby lotions and bath foam. The bathroom and the towel were warmed and once Nina was in the bath, her carer from outside the door could hear her singing and laughing to herself in a way that she had never heard before. (Judith Morris, personal communication)

Such experiences offer a sensory indulgence in private that can release the tight grip on their feelings that many children and young people maintain. At the same time, the role of the caregiver in facilitating the process will not go unnoticed by the child. Special for the caregiver would be the discovery that a challenging teenager has the capacity to laugh and sing.

However, there are many situations when demonstrating availability to adolescents is exceptionally complex and difficult. Signals for both proximity and distance can become highly distorted as young people come under increasing pressure to conform and meet expectations outside the family boundary. Emotional retreat, for instance, can feel hurtful and rejecting to caregivers. Young people who are feeling anxious but finding it hard to communicate their emotional needs can become increasingly passive and unable to take the initiative. They might give little feedback about relationships and feelings and become excessively self-sufficient and hostile to adult approach, however well-meaning. The aim for caregivers in these circumstances is to stay alongside this behaviour and seek the smallest ways in which to encourage and enable the young person to have a safe experience of a less distant interaction.

At the other end of the spectrum, excessive emotional expression – verbal and physical outbursts – can also be hard to deal with, especially when it is carried into the family from other settings, such as school or birth family contact, and then misdirected towards well-meaning caregivers. The aim here is to avoid getting drawn in to hostile patterns of interaction which can undermine messages of availability and trigger fears of rejection (and more negative behaviour) in the young person. Joy, an experienced foster carer of teenagers, felt that Barry (15) had a range of behaviours which were specifically designed to make her do or say things that would confirm to Barry that he was unloved and unlovable. Her response was a pre-rehearsed verbal strategy that she could use when she felt her exasperation rising:

> *My line is something like: 'Barry, a lot of children have been through my home and I have learned over the years that although I don't like these things you do, they don't put me off – I still love you.'*

This approach enabled Joy to normalise the situation; acknowledge and manage her feelings in order to remain calm, in control and available; and at the same time provide Barry with reassurance that he would not destroy his secure base through his bad behaviour.

For many fostered and adopted young people, the realities of increasing separation from the secure base and the prospect of eventual independence create a high level of anxiety. The increasing demands and pressures of coping with school and peer relationships are likely to be especially stressful for vulnerable teenagers and the impact of this may be reflected in difficult behaviours at home. Recognising this link can help caregivers to pick up and respond more accurately to their teenagers' signals and to provide additional support at home. For instance, an adoptive mother recognised that 14-year-old Kira was signaling anxiety about the day ahead when she was repeatedly angry and oppositional before school. She needed closeness and reassurance before setting off for school and yet her behaviour often resulted in argument and emotional distance. The introduction of a baby alarm into Kira's bedroom enabled her mother to wake her by 'speaking to her softly and sweetly', thus avoiding intrusiveness and conflict and demonstrating her physical and emotional availability at this difficult time of the day. The morning routine improved greatly as a result of this and Kira was able to have breakfast more calmly with her mum and leave for school feeling loved and supported.

In some cases, adolescents may need the physical presence of a parent figure to accompany them across the family boundary and into a new, anxiety-provoking setting, for instance, to a new school or a job interview. In her study of adolescent foster placements, Downes (1992) refers to this as creating a 'safe transitional zone' through which the young person is able to experience his secure base at first hand while anxiety levels are heightened. Downes contrasts two cases where young men were seeking employment. One was expected to leave the foster home each morning to look for work and told not to return until teatime. The other, Andy, was accompanied by his foster father to a series of (unsuccessful) job interviews. As a result, this foster father was able to be supportive to Andy (they agreed that some of the jobs weren't worth having) but also realistic about his past mistakes (Andy once got the sack because he was drunk at work). Through this "supportive alliance" with his foster father, Andy was enabled both to take the risk of further job applications and also to address what he needed to do to change things for the better. This also allowed him the possibility of disconfirming some of his negative feelings about himself (he did not lose his job because he was "unlikeable", but because he was drunk). For the unsupported young man, there was no source of security during the anxiety of job hunting and no opportunity for change in his view of himself. It is no surprise that he became "paralysed" and unable to move beyond the family boundary.

For many young people, adolescence is a time in which they seek to explore their birth family relationships, through enquiry, discussion or establishing, increasing or decreasing contact. They may move physically or emotionally to and fro across the foster or adoptive family boundary and into the birth family, requiring caregivers to be especially available and responsive. In all cases, the task is to demonstrate that the secure base is ever present and reliable, that parent figures are available for advice and reassurance and that home is a place of safety and welcome.

In some foster and adoptive families, the adolescent years may be characterised by a good deal of angry, hostile and destructive behaviour, which can leave caregivers burnt out and exhausted and young people feeling that the only route open to them is to "blast out" of their family, often into very undesirable settings. At these times, the capacity of the caregivers to provide continuing messages of availability can be sorely tested, but there is evidence that if even a thread of reassurance and connection can be maintained (for example, birthday and other special occasion cards), there is a chance that this will be picked up by the young person at a later stage (often in the mid-twenties), leading to much more positive and mutually rewarding relationships between foster carers and adopters and their adult children and grandchildren (Howe, 1996; Schofield, 2003).

Conclusion

Caregiving that is physically and emotionally available, warm, consistent, and reliable can help infants, growing children and adolescents to rebuild their trust in adults and their own belief in themselves as competent participants in relationships and in the social world. Foster carers and adopters may need to be particularly thoughtful and sensitive in providing this caregiving in ways that are acceptable to children who are predisposed to be distrustful and wary of their approaches.

Summary points

- The best environment for children's healthy emotional development is one from which they can explore the wider world whilst at the same time feeling certain that nurture, comfort and protection are readily available when needed. Such an environment provides a secure base and forms the foundation on which trust in the self and others will be built. When children can trust that such an environment will be unfailingly there for them, they are freed from anxiety and so able to explore, play and learn freely.

- Fostered and adopted children have often previously experienced adults who have failed to provide consistent, nurturing care (*unavailable*). Previous caregivers may have reacted to the child's distress with anger (*rejecting*), or "blown hot and cold" according to their own needs rather than the child's (*unpredictable*). Or sometimes their responses may have caused the child to experience feelings of deep fear, panic and helplessness (*frightening*).

- Children will develop patterns of behaviour that enable them to feel safe and get their needs met as best they can in these circumstances. These behaviours can become very deep-rooted and may be associated with the approach of any potential caregiver, however trustworthy they may be.

- In order to *change* children's expectations and build their trust in adults, caregivers will need to *think about* the child's previous experiences and how these might be shaping his current responses and behaviours.

177

- Therapeutic caregiving will be directed at demonstrating to the child that, in this family, when he is anxious, he will be soothed, comforted and protected and when he is ready to explore, play and learn, he will be helped to do so. This needs to be the central priority in the caregiver's mind. Each child will need a different approach, depending on their previous experiences and what will feel comfortable and acceptable to them now.

Approaches for helping children to build trust

N.B. It is important to choose only those activities that the child is likely to accept and enjoy.

Day-to-day activities
- Establish predictable routines around mealtimes, getting up and going to bed.
- Ensure that the child always knows where to find you when you are apart.
- Manage separations carefully, with open communication about why it is happening, how long it will be, and clear "goodbyes" and "hellos".
- Use calendar or diary charts to help the child predict and anticipate events.
- Ensure that the child feels specially cared for and nurtured when ill, hurt or sad.
- Be "unobtrusively available" if the child is anxious but finds it hard to talk or accept comfort (for example, suggest a ride in the car).
- Offer verbal and non-verbal support for safe exploration.

Building trust when caregiver and child are apart
- Allow child to take small item or photo from home to school.
- Use mobile phone or text to help child know that you are thinking of him.
- Place small surprise on child's bed when he is at school to show you have thought about him during the day.
- Keep a "goodies tub" in the kitchen and put small treats in it for the child to have in the evening.

Activities that help children to think about trusting
- Ask child to draw a fortress or make one in clay or sand. Child may choose miniature toys or animals to stand for the main people in her life. Ask child to show and talk about which ones she would let into her fort and which ones she would keep out and why (from Sunderland, 2003).
- Ask child to draw a bridge with themselves on one side and someone they trust on the other. Ask them to draw a speech bubble coming out of their mouth and

write in it what they are thinking or saying. Do the same with the other person (from Sunderland, 2003).

Games and activities that help to build trust

- Hand holding games such as "ring a roses"
- Clapping games
- Reading stories with child on lap or sitting close
- Leading each other blindfold
- Face painting
- Three-legged race
- Throwing a ball or beanbag to each other
- Bat and ball
- Blowing and chasing bubbles together
- Rocking, singing, gently holding child
- Rubbing lotion on to each others' hands and arms.
- Brushing and plaiting hair
- Painting nails
- Teaching a new skill or learning one together

7 Responding sensitively – helping children to manage their feelings and behaviour

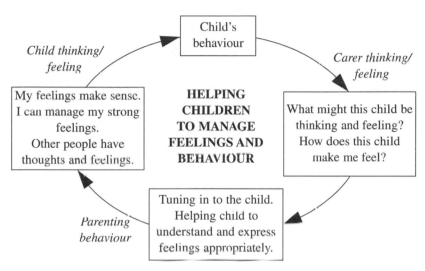

Figure 5

A fundamental task for parents, from infancy onwards, is to help their children to organise their thinking and regulate their emotions and behaviour. Newborn babies arrive alert but helpless in an incomprehensible world. They are dependent on others both to ensure their survival and to help them to make sense of the world and their place within it. In order to do this, the caregiver must have the capacity to *tune in* to the state of mind of this particular child at this particular time, to gauge the child's thoughts and feelings and *respond sensitively* to them (see Figure 5). Thus, from the moment of birth, sensitive parents will be actively *wondering* what their baby is thinking and feeling and why certain behaviours are occurring. They will provide a verbal and non-verbal feedback loop, which affirms the infant's ideas and feelings and yet also provides comfort and reassurance. In this way, infants are provided with a "supportive scaffolding", from which they begin to *organise their thinking* and *regulate their feelings and behaviour*. At its simplest, a hungry baby will be reassured by the voice of the parent talking to him as well as by observing the preparation of the feed. The prompt, predictable and soothing responses of the caregiver will enable him to manage his rising anxiety and thus wait a little longer for the food to come.

Helping children to make sense of themselves, other people and the world around them, to develop *social understanding*, enables them to manage themselves and their relationships. From an early stage, parents begin to introduce the idea that other people have feelings, ideas and intentions. This is the process that promotes *mind-mindedness* in children (Miens, 1997). Parents talk about their own feelings and goals ('Mummy's hungry too', 'Daddy's happy with his present', 'We'd better hurry if we're going to catch the bus') and (often playfully) speculate on those of others ('Does teddy like toast?').

Through this process, young children gradually begin to develop a sense of the content of other minds which also aids the development of empathy. Even a two-year-old can understand that a crying baby in the nursery may need to be soothed in special baby talk or may need a mother for comfort – though at this age their empathy is not entirely accurate and they may offer their own mother. By the age of three or four, children can be quite sophisticated "mind readers", able to think about their own and other people's thoughts and feelings, goals and beliefs. These are vital skills for survival in the family, with friends, in the nursery and then at school. Having acquired them, it is possible for the child to understand that other children may wish to play a different game, that the teacher would like everyone to be quiet for the story, or that her parent will be pleased with the picture she has drawn.

The experience of thinking and talking about their feelings and those of others also enables children to review the origins of a distressing or unsettling event and the effects that it has had on themselves and others involved. Thus, children are equipped to deal with the wide range of social interactions that they will encounter and especially those that are stressful. They can take a step back, think, contain their feelings and plan a response. This *pause for thought* generally leads to more constructive and pro-social solutions, gained through talking, negotiation and compromise.

All of these skills and capacities are required for development into adolescence, when young people move further away from the family environment, have a wider range of relationships and situations to deal with and are increasingly responsible for their self care and presentation – and for restoring their own equilibrium. As they move towards independence, they must increase their abilities to predict and order the world, plan and organise their lives, seek help when needed, successfully regulate their strong feelings and be aware of and responsive to the thoughts and emotions of others.

What children bring to their placements

Insecurely attached children have often lacked opportunities to have their thoughts and feelings acknowledged and understood. They may have been in situations where there was no one able or available to help them deal with strong feelings, so panic, anger or despair may have overwhelmed them at times. Or they may have had caregivers who denied their feelings, distorting their sense of reality to the point where they could not discern the "truth" of what they felt in any situation. Sometimes, they will have been cared for by adults who could not manage and regulate their own feelings and children may have been blamed or feel themselves to blame for chaos or violence in the household. For a range of reasons, previous caregivers may have been too anxiously absorbed with their own distress or too preoccupied with their own needs to attune themselves to the minds of their children. Lacking the resource of a safe and containing adult mind or a supportive scaffolding for managing their feelings, children develop their own ways of coping with them. This might involve *letting them go* excessively, *using them to control* others, *holding them in* or *denying* that they exist at all. Each strategy is problematic in the setting of a foster or adoptive family, where feelings are normally communicated fairly openly, in a managed and regulated way within close and trusting relationships.

When children lack perspective-taking skills and their own thoughts, emotions and behaviours become dysregulated, there will be a range of consequences. Children may have difficulty in predicting the responses or imagining the feelings of others, find it hard to understand and enjoy humour, to engage in play, to express joy or to anticipate, enjoy and then remember a pleasurable experience. There may be gaps in basic knowledge or vocabulary. Children may simply be overwhelmed by feelings and cut off in a dissociative way. Senses may be numbed and bodily signals such as pain, hunger and thirst may not be picked up or correctly interpreted. Children may not recognise or understand the origins of strong feelings in themselves or other people. Friendships, which inevitably require taking the perspective of others, are hard to sustain and children come to expect rejection and isolation.

Tasks for foster carers and adopters

For foster carers and adopters, a primary task is to reflect on and make sense of their children's feelings and behaviours. They must attempt to tune in to their child, stand in the child's shoes and try to imagine 'what might this child be thinking and feeling?' The challenge here, of course, is that new caregivers do not have the benefits of a shared history and a familiar communication pattern with their children. Caregivers must, therefore, be particularly thoughtful about the child's previous experiences and flexible in their thinking about how these might have shaped the child's thinking processes and expression of feelings. Although it is painful to do so, the capacity to project oneself into the mind of a child who has been maltreated is important. It is from this starting point that caregivers can begin to think about the child's beliefs and expectations of herself and others and to speculate on how this might connect with her current behaviours. Opening oneself up to the mind of the child, with its difficult and often very painful memories and feelings, can trigger powerful feelings of sadness, anger and despair in the caregiver. At the same time, new caregivers may find that a child who is wrestling with these strong feelings may unconsciously seek relief by transferring them to those who are close to her. Foster carers and adopters can find themselves carrying intolerable feelings, with the child temporarily relieved and released from them.

The darkness of aspects of the child's history and the impact of her dysregulated feelings on caregivers can, if not fully understood, seem to contaminate the mind of the parent or even contaminate the cheerful and positive family atmosphere that the carer or adoptive parent has so carefully created. In this context, there is really no substitute for a containing relationship with a thoughtful, reflective practitioner, who can bear the pain of thinking about the child's history accurately and without distortion and can allow the caregiver to reflect honestly on the question of *how does this child make me feel?* Feelings of sadness, rage, disgust and, at times, hopelessness need to be acknowledged and their origins properly understood. Although caregivers may have partners and friends to support them, there is real value in being able to leave some of this burden with the social worker. This can provide relief and containment for the caregivers themselves, enabling them, in turn, to provide the warm and containing family environment that their child so urgently needs.

With this supportive framework in place, caregivers can begin to adopt a range of parenting approaches geared towards helping children to manage their feelings and behaviour. An important first stage is that of *naming feelings*, helping the child to reflect on them, recognise them and think about their origin. Often the expression of feelings is either suppressed or excessive and caregivers must help some children to show feelings more freely and others to contain and moderate them. In order to help children to understand and respond to the feelings of others, caregivers need to feel comfortable in expressing and discussing the full range of their own feelings. They are then in a position to model the fact that both positive and negative feelings can be safely managed. In particular they can show children that *mixed feelings* are "normal" and that combinations of love and anger, longing and distrust, anxiety and eager anticipation are part of the human condition – affecting not only them but also their birth parents, foster carers, adopters, friends and social workers.

Linked to the understanding of mixed emotions is the concept that it is possible to repair damage done in relationships, to forgive oneself and other people and to move on. Often fostered and adopted children take extreme and split (good/bad) positions in their expectations of themselves and significant others. They find it hard to make amends or to allow others to make amends to them. The emotional education provided by sensitive care includes a careful process of reviewing past and present relationships. If, for example, children cannot understand and realistically appraise the mixture of concern, personal hurt and neglect that may have characterised their birth parents' behaviour towards them, then it is difficult for them to move on from seeing themselves as irredeemably bad and forgive themselves when they think bad thoughts and do bad things. When children and young people have been helped in these areas, they will gradually begin to resolve the pain of the past and move forward with greater confidence.

Enabling the fostered or adopted child to be increasingly self-aware and sensitive to others means engaging in an educative process. Children need to learn about *cause and effect*, the links between their behaviour and how it makes them and other people feel. Caregivers must draw on their own subtlety of social understanding to develop self-understanding and perspective-taking skills in the child. As this process develops, the child will begin to recognise and think about his feelings. He will become more able to link his feelings to events and thus to *make sense* of them. Over time, the supportive scaffolding provided by the caregiver enables the child to *manage his strong feelings* and to feel confident that the feelings will not become overwhelming to himself or others. Finally, he can be helped to understand that *other people have thoughts and feelings* that must also be addressed and taken into account. As the child's thinking shifts and develops in these small but important ways, there is a likelihood of more constructive relationships, greater empathy and prosocial rather than antisocial behaviour.

Infancy (birth–18 months)

It is likely that babies entering foster care will have had inadequate support in managing their strong feelings. If adults have not been consistently available and responsive, feelings of pain, hunger, loneliness and so on may have become overwhelming and out of control, or showing these feelings may have produced angry or rejecting responses from adults. For new caregivers, the aim is to create an environment in which the infant can learn that the expression of feelings is safe and acceptable and that adults will intervene to prevent difficult feelings from spiralling out of control. The aim is also to help the child experience the full range of positive feelings – love, joy, wonderment and amusement – in order to promote a fuller interest and engagement in the world of things and people.

To achieve this, caregivers must begin by being swift to respond to any signals for food, comfort or sociability, or to provide these things even when signals are weak or absent. When reassured promptly and consistently in this way, the infant can begin to presuppose that the expression of feelings will quickly be met by a soothing response and that a gentle and reliable adult will take action to relieve her discomfort. However, a certain level of anxiety is unavoidable in any caregiving situation – having a nappy changed, waiting for a feed to be prepared, watching a carer leave the room are all anxiety provoking and yet inevitable events. The caregiver who can *take the perspective* of the infant and recognise the impact of earlier, negative experiences, will have a heightened awareness of the need to help the baby to cope with these situations without panic, and restore his equilibrium as smoothly as possible. In this context, availability and sensitivity need to work together.

Case example – Simon

Simon was born during care proceedings in relation to his siblings, aged two and three. Although monitored and supported, it was apparent that his mother, Sarah (who had been traumatised by sexual and physical abuse in her own childhood), spent as little time as possible with him, rarely touched or held him. She often went out, leaving him with neighbours' children who were truanting from school. Simon failed to gain weight and was admitted to hospital for investigations at seven weeks.

Sarah agreed to give Simon some of his feeds in hospital in order to promote their relationship. On one occasion the social worker observed a feed. Sarah arrived late and Simon was getting increasingly distressed. She picked him up but did not move to feed him, instead put him still crying over her shoulder and walked around talking to staff and parents. She then changed his nappy at a slow pace (he was still crying), without talking to him. Finally, she sat down to feed him and he fretted at the bottle, struggled in her arms and took little of the feed. Sarah did not appear to be able to keep Simon in mind as a person and there was no sense of connection between the mother and infant.

Simon was discharged to foster care. One week after placement, the social worker observed a feed. On this occasion, Simon woke in his bedroom and was heard crying. Immediately, the foster carer, who was in the living room, called to him by name and kept talking to him soothingly as she walked towards the bedroom. The crying ceased. She brought him back into the room, stroking him, talking and responding to his vocalisations. The feed was a calm affair, with her taking his lead, meeting his gaze and holding him comfortably close to her body. After the feed, she changed his nappy, again in constant but not intrusive eye contact, using her voice to make the nappy change into a positive and enjoyable experience. She then sat him in a layback chair where he could kick freely and wave his arms about. She sat on the floor in front of him, within his range of vision, and they had a lengthy conversation of lively vocalisations, in which Simon became at times very excited, but the excitement was kept within comfortable, calm boundaries by the tone, timing and intensity of the carer's response. Simon seemed like a completely different child, alert and engaged with the body, person and mind of his carer.

Striking in this example is not only the impact of responsive caregiving but the way in which Simon's age had made it possible for a much speedier beginning to the recovery process than even older infants of 10/11 months are capable of. This process may also have been helped by the fact that there was a key nurse system on Simon's paediatric ward, so that a familiar nurse had perhaps given him not only adequate nutrition, but also some preliminary experience of sensitive care and access to an available mind.

The provision of structure and ritual not only gives a strong message of consistent availability, but helps a child to see how the intervention of the caregiver moves them from being unsettled to settled again in a predictable way. A gentle *commentary* on events and the feelings associated with them can thus help babies to see the shape of experiences and to identify and manage the feelings and sensations in their minds and bodies. For example, during an everyday routine, such as getting the infant dressed, a caregiver might talk about the frustration of interrupting the child's enjoyment of a toy in order to do it and the pleasure of playing with it again soon. There might be predictions of which item of clothing will come next and descriptions of how it feels when it is being put on, the softness and colour of the fabric, the warmth or coolness that the child is feeling and so on. The routine may be accompanied by gentle play, distraction, songs or touch and ended with compliments and a clear resumption of the preferred activity. In this way, the baby is provided with supportive *scaffolding* which helps her both to predict the stages of getting dressed and to understand that the discomforts will not be great. Trusting, over time, that this will be the case, she can gradually regulate her feelings accordingly.

The scaffolding can also be non-verbal. The caregiver's tone of voice and facial expression can reflect back to the child a moderated version of her heightened emotions. This acknowledges and affirms the emotions, but at the same time demonstrates that they can be contained and managed by the caregiver. Although this process is referred to as *mirroring*, the infant's negative feelings are not reinforced but are moderated and made safe. The angry face in the infant, with the furrowed brow, raised eyebrows and open mouth will be reflected by raised eyebrows and open mouth in the mother. But the mother's eyes and mouth will then dissolve into a smile. For an infant who is comfortably established in a closely attuned relationship with a caregiver, there will be a brief pause in which he can reflect, recognise the caregiver's moderated affect and bring his own into line with it. In the course of this small, yet significant interaction, his feelings have been recognised, coped with and made safe. The infant learns that his feelings will not become unmanageable and he can move confidently into a more playful mode (see also discussion on mirroring in Chapter 2).

Infants who have not experienced this sort of verbal and non-verbal scaffolding may be harder to soothe or shift towards a playful stance. Although in most mother–infant pairs this mirroring is an entirely unconscious interaction, it may be necessary for foster carers and adopters to be consciously aware that they are leading the baby through a therapeutic process. This will result in a heightened awareness of the need to engage with the baby's face when he is angry and distressed and an emphasis on the process of reflection and then containment. The baby is then provided with proactive assistance and support with feelings, and a clear message that they *make sense* and can be calmed and managed.

Building on these approaches, giving names to feelings and connecting them to their causes can begin even with young babies, as can various interactions that promote synchrony of action and expression of feelings, such as simple action rhymes and songs, clapping games and so on. Opportunities to experience shared, pleasurable experiences are important, especially when accompanied by a commentary on the feelings experienced by both the caregiver and the child. Although in many ways, much of the above can be seen as "ordinary parenting", the therapeutic significance of this type of caregiving is heightened for children whose earlier experiences have been unfavourable. Foster carers and adopters, therefore, may need to parent with a keen emphasis and focus on these areas, conscious of the gaps they may be filling or the negative expectations they may be correcting. It may also be that they will need to hold on (with the support of their social worker) to the theoretical basis for engaging children in this way when things don't work out at first or if there is scepticism in the family about the need for detailed conversations with a four-month-old or for not allowing an eight-month-old to cry for more than a few moments.

Early childhood (18 months–4 years)

This is a crucial period of development in relation to managing feelings and behaviour and developing social understanding. Processes begun in infancy come to fruition and by the age of four, secure children are more likely to be able to take the perspective of another person than insecure children are. For looked after children who enter foster care at this stage, or for those who have come into care in infancy but have struggled to make up lost ground, this is a particularly important period in which to learn about the workings of their own minds and the minds of other people.

During the early childhood years, sensitive caregivers may continue to use parenting strategies suited to infants, adapting and fine tuning them in line with the developmental needs of each child. For example, action games and rhymes that most three–four-year-olds may have grown out of can still be new and serve an important function for children who lack social understanding. Taking turns in games, coping with winning and losing and knowing that when you are the winner, your play partner is feeling the disappointment of losing, are all experiences that can be learned from. It may be tempting to avoid such games if they cause upset, but once the child has begun to settle it is important to build competence in these situations that reflect real life. Pretend play and games are possible with this age group and provide an important opportunity for caregivers to provide scaffolding that enables the child to explore and learn about feelings, relationships and roles. Whether the game is about mummies, daddies and children or doctors and nurses or about fictional figures of good and evil from popular culture, there are many opportunities to expand on the "why" of behaviour, people's motivations, goals and desires and how they solve problems, cope with setbacks and achieve.

As children's language and comprehension develop, there are increasing opportunities to help them to *make sense* of their needs and feelings and to find ways of approaching adults to get help. Caregivers who have taken time to observe and made efforts to stand in the shoes of the child and think about what he or she is thinking and feeling will be best placed to provide these opportunities, as illustrated in the following case example.

Case example – Chantelle

Chantelle (4) was in a bridge foster placement and deeply troubled by her birth mother's mixed approaches of both love and rejection. The plan for Chantelle's future was uncertain. Chantelle's foster mother, Linda, noted that Chantelle had spells when she looked flushed and tired and her eyes flitted around the room. She became "whiny" at these times and lost concentration. Friends who did not know Chantelle would say that she looked unwell, but Linda recognised that these behaviours indicated that Chantelle was in danger of being engulfed by her confused feelings. In the early months of the placement, Linda learned to be pre-emptive at these times and respond to the signals with comfort and reassurance: 'She'd come to me and say, 'I want a drink', but you could tell it's not that and I would say "Do you think a cuddle might help?" and she'd accept that and she might cry and let herself be comforted.' Over time, however, Chantelle began to recognise that she could take action herself to relieve her distress and make herself feel better. 'She started coming to me and I might be peeling the potatoes or whatever and she'd say 'Linda, I need a cuddle' and I'd say 'Come on then', and dry my hands and we'd have one and then she'd go off again.

This example demonstrates that Chantelle has learned an appropriate way of finding relief from her difficult feelings and thus taken the first steps in managing them herself. An important next stage in this process is for the child to be helped to make sense of *why* they feel the way they do. Sensitive caregivers will have the capacity not only to name feelings for the child and to acknowledge mixed feelings but also to help the child to make connections between events and feelings and to recognise repeating patterns. In the above situation, for instance, having reflected on the origins of Chantelle's behaviour, Linda went on to share her "theory" with Chantelle by talking about her mother while they were having a cuddle. She named Chantelle's feelings of anger and longing and also helped her to make a connection between her muddled feelings about her mother and her tired and restless behaviour.

This is a good example of the *"availability plus"* nature of therapeutic caregiving. If Chantelle were merely to learn that her foster mother was there for her when she was upset, this would not be enough to prepare her to express and manage her feelings appropriately, particularly in situations when her foster mother was not there. In her future adoptive family, for instance, Chantelle has to be able to understand the source of her feelings of anxiety and her physical responses to those feelings in order to be able to take a deep breath and make sense of why she sometimes feels sad or angry when she is living in a caring environment. This is a tall order for a four-year-old, but the seeds of understanding and successful careseeking strategies have been sown in the bridge foster home and can be reinforced by her adoptive parents as Chantelle moves through middle childhood.

An important stage in helping pre-school children to manage their feelings and behaviour, therefore, is to work on the *explicit recognition of emotions*, naming them and connecting them to the events that have caused them. As the example of Chantelle shows, once language has developed, caregivers can use conversation with the child to identify or speculate on feelings and think about *why* they might be occurring. Sensitive caregivers will be alert to any approach that produces feelings of discomfort or feels intrusive to the child, but within these limits, some gentle therapeutic exercises might be introduced. Cartoons or graphics of facial expressions representing simple emotions can be used, with the caregiver exploring alongside the child what the emotions might be called and why they might occur. When self-esteem is good enough and the child is comfortable with some eye contact, a mirror might be used to explore the facial expressions of both the child and the caregiver ('this is what our faces look like when we are happy. Look how our eyes change and our mouths!'). Books, stories and videos are readily acceptable to virtually all children and can be used to identify and name a whole range of feelings. Most importantly, at this age children can begin to understand that others have thoughts and feelings that are different to their own, and any story that involves animals or people having adventures, experiences or interacting with each other can be used to help the child to speculate on the feelings of others.

Many young fostered and adopted children have lacked opportunities to *order* and *sequence* their thinking in ways that can help them to recall events correctly or understand *cause and effect* and may need specific help to achieve this. They may benefit from games and toys that require sequencing skills or enjoy constructing a story from a series of drawings or pictures that denote a clear sequence of events with a beginning, middle and end. Caregivers might help a child to make an "experiences book" which records simple events like buying a new pair of shoes or visiting the swimming pool and includes pictures, tickets and so on. This can be used to help the child to remember and sequence his experiences, order his thoughts and reflect on feelings of excitement, uncertainty, pleasure, warmth, cold and so on. Time spent alongside the child in shared, enjoyable activities such as splashing in puddles, playing with sand and water or riding on a bus can also offer opportunities for shared recollection and affirmation of events and feelings.

Young children may also need help in making sense of the messages that they receive from their bodies. Sensitive caregivers can help them to recognise and name physical sensations and take steps to regulate this if necessary, as this foster carer described.

> *When Zoe (4) came to us she couldn't stop eating. We had to help her think about the normal patterns of feeling hungry, eating and feeling full. We had to explain, 'This is how your tummy feels when it is full, feel it and look at it, there is no more space for more food'. We also explained that eating when you are already full makes you feel uncomfortable. It took a while before she could leave a bit of food on the plate.*

Dolls or pets can be used to help the child to speculate on bodily sensations and how to deal with them (how will the dolly feel if we take her out on this cold day in that thin dress? How can we help her to feel warmer?). Helping children to get in touch with themselves in these ways can be a lengthy and painstaking process and caregivers may need to be prepared and willing to repeat the same messages many times. Even at this age, children's minds are powerful information processors which take in a range of sensory and verbal information, and need to make sense of it in the context of existing structures and ideas. All forms of problem-solving require small children to *pause for thought* in order to come up with or be guided towards the most effective and prosocial response.

Finally, a key role for caregivers of pre-school children is to *model* to the child *the safe expression of their own feelings*. Children newly placed for adoption or foster care cannot predict or read the feelings of their new caregivers. Even those who are well settled may continue to draw on previous unsatisfactory experiences. For the child, a minor disagreement between adoptive parents, for instance, might be associated with or seen as a precursor to domestic violence. On the other hand, if it is followed by a brief explanation that it is normal to feel cross with each other at times and a demonstration that the incident is resolved, with feelings of care for each other restored, this provides key messages. The child can begin to understand that such feelings do not have to spiral out of control, that we can love people and feel cross with them at the same time and that minor rifts in relationships are normal and can be repaired. This commentary builds *language and reflective skills,* which can then be used in other situations, for instance, to talk about anger that emerges between siblings in the family or a difficult incident in the playground.

Middle childhood (5–10 years)

As children begin to spend more time away from their secure base, they will increasingly find themselves in situations in which it is important to express their feelings appropriately, to acknowledge that other people may have different feelings and to be able to stop and think before deciding what to do in a stressful situation. Alongside this increasing social and emotional sophistication the child is developing the more psychosocial process of learning social rules, developing a sense of self and identity and learning to behave in ways that promote acceptance with peers and in the community.

Children who lack the ability to think about what other people may be thinking and feeling can become increasingly isolated. They will find it hard to take turns, to engage in co-operative play or even to follow the plot of a film or story. Caregivers may need to offer a good deal of input in order to build this capacity, taking time to read, watch television or play games alongside the child, and using these activities to help the child reflect on their own thoughts, take the perspective of others and discuss how others express and manage their feelings and behaviour. Many of the approaches described as helpful for pre-school children will continue to be therapeutic for older children, as described by Annette, adoptive mother of a 10-year-old child.

> *I think she spent so long sort of in self-defence and sort of looking after herself that she never learned to look at it from anybody else's point of view. She often can't follow a book or a film because she can't work out what's happening, so I sort of sit with her and spell it out to her and help her to think about what the characters might be thinking or what they might do next. Yes, we do a lot of that.*

Drawing on stories with imaginary and fictional characters can sometimes make these things easier to talk about, but the child needs help to make the link with their own feelings and their capacity to resolve and manage them. For some children in this age group, strong feelings of rejection, anger and hurt can be quick to erupt and intense in their expression. Children need to know that these frightening feelings can be managed, that they will not become overwhelming to themselves or to other people. The process of "mirroring and containing", described for babies and toddlers, can also help an older child to make sense of the surge of feelings he has experienced, then to reflect, place them in context and move on.

In the following passage, for instance, foster mother Valerie describes an incident in which she had to pick up Robbie (8) from football and tell him that a contact meeting with his brother had been cancelled because the social worker had not been able to set it up in time. Valerie expresses both her own feelings on his behalf and her empathy with his feelings.

> *And Robbie was angry, really angry and he was crying and hitting and kicking and he put his thumb through his new football socks and ripped them. And I just felt so disappointed and angry for him and I just said to him, 'Do you know, I'm angry too, I'm furious they didn't set your contact up in time' and he looked at me and I said, 'I'm as angry as you are' and I really was and he believed me. And I said, 'I feel sad for you as well, because I know how sad and disappointed you'll be not to see him'. And then the anger was gone and there was just the disappointment and the upset left. And then I said, 'They are really sorry and they're going to set it up again soon and hopefully it will be next week. Calm down now then and we'll do something nice when we get home.'*

Valerie has named Robbie's angry feelings and reflected them back to him verbally, but not with the same intensity. She allows a pause, the time in which he "looked at her" and introduces the idea of mixed feelings (anger and sadness). Robbie's feelings then moderate to "disappointment and upset" and Valerie is able to offer comfort with the promise of "something nice" when they get home. The intensity of his feelings will be exacerbated by the history of losses that he has experienced. But within the few moments of this interaction, Robbie has been enabled to manage his feelings, regulate his behaviour, and feel supported and comforted by his foster mother.

For some children, particularly avoidant children, feelings are suppressed or denied. Pleasure and excitement, anger or sadness seem to be absent, leaving the child remote and set apart from the emotional life of the family. The aim of therapeutic caregiving will be to help the child to find a means of expressing feelings and a comfortable level at which to do so. The caregiver can then provide affirmation, comfort and relief to the child, helping her to make sense of difficult feelings and move on from them. The subtlety here is to find approaches that feel easy and unobtrusive to the child, to "start where the child is" and to look for signs of progress on the child's terms rather than that of the adults.

Case example – Sophie

Sophie moved to her foster family at the age of seven. She was a guarded and emotionally contained child, who showed little reaction to being separated from her mother, rarely cried and never seemed enthusiastic or excited. Sometimes she would take herself to bed without telling anyone that she was doing so. Sophie appeared isolated in her noisy, emotionally open foster family, but her foster mother, Monica, tried hard to find ways of connecting with her. Just before a family holiday about which Sophie had shown no excitement or anticipation, Monica discovered that Sophie had been making lists of what she should take and whom she should send postcards to. Monica recognised and accepted this as Sophie's way of expressing her excitement and encouraged her to make lists of other feelings when different situations arose. Different ways of expressing feelings were openly discussed in the family and there was a comfortable acknowledgement that 'the Sophie way' was valid and acceptable.

Three years later, Sophie was much more able to signal her needs, but also retained her tendency to do so indirectly. Sophie's much-loved rabbit died suddenly. Very unexpectedly from Monica's point of view, Sophie rushed up to her and flung her arms around her. This was out of character and had perhaps shocked and surprised Sophie too. Monica observed the appropriate rituals with Sophie around the funeral of the rabbit, and had taken a photograph of the rabbit and the grave. The significance for their relationship of this shared loss and their responses to it became apparent over time. It was a turning point after which Sophie began to use the photograph of the rabbit as a way of giving herself permission to get upset about other things, such as the loss of her birth mother, and to seek comfort from the foster carer.

As Monica described: 'It's still something that when Sophie's feeling sad will come back up. She'll relate it to the rabbit and she'll always come and find me or show me the picture. "Do you remember when we took this, Monica? You took this picture for me, didn't you?" That's the difference now – I know if she's up in her bedroom and she's upset about something she'll come and find me.'

In her excellent series, *Helping children with feelings*, Margot Sunderland (2003) provides simple story and work books, which point us to a helpful variety of practical ways of enabling children to speak of and process strong and difficult feelings, that are either spilling out in the form of rage or suppressed and bottled up within the child. She recommends the use of paint, clay, water, paper and pens to help children to release and describe their feelings, and to provide adults with a means of understanding the meaning of the feeling for the child (for example, is the child frightened by his anger, or does he rather enjoy the power that is associated with it?). When talking about feelings with children, Sunderland suggests using words and particularly questions as little as possible as children can easily feel "interrogated" and withdraw under pressure. Instead, she recommends exercises that ask the child to put a simple tick in a box or the choosing of a word or image, in order to reduce the pressure on the child.

Adolescence (11–18 years)

Many teenagers in foster or adoptive care have great difficulty in regulating their feelings and behaviour. This may be a continuing problem from earlier stages or may emerge as a particular difficulty in adolescence. In either case, it can feel increasingly alarming, both to those on the receiving end and to the young person him or herself. Toddler-like rages can erupt at what might appear to be the slightest provocation or teenagers might deny having any feelings, even in the most painful of situations. Once again, a crucial role for the caregiver is that of moderator – helping young people both to express and manage their feelings appropriately.

A caregiving environment in which thoughts and feelings are readily discussed and demonstrated and individual differences acknowledged and respected forms a backdrop against which a young person can learn important lessons. Caregivers who can reflect on their own expression of feeling ('I tend to go quiet when I'm cross about something', or 'I blow up like a volcano but as soon as I've done that, it's all over and forgotten') will help young people to do the same and then to think about alternative coping strategies if they are needed. The capacity to tune in to the young person, to pick up signals for support, comfort and reassurance are as important for this age group as for babies and toddlers and there is the same level of sensitivity required to judge the moment when a young person is ready to benefit from an intervention which will promote the appropriate expression of feelings. Such a moment was touchingly described by Maurice, a foster father who routinely gave all children in the house a hug when he returned from work. Fraser (15) had been a rather remote member of the family, seldom talking or even sitting with them and spending much of his time in his bedroom. One evening, Maurice noticed a brief eye contact from Fraser when he was hugging another child and he knew that this was the right moment. He asked Fraser, 'Do you want a hug?' Fraser willingly accepted and thereafter this became a regular part of their relationship. Previously, Maurice had felt sure that Fraser would resist if offered a hug but he was ready to respond the instant he picked up a signal of readiness. From this sensitive responding on the part of his foster father, Fraser could begin to learn that it was safe and rewarding to show his feelings of affection and he continued to move forward from this time.

The naming of feelings continues to be an important area for this age group, but there may be more capacity to reflect on their origins and think through a strategy to cope with them. Young people can be helped to recognise the moment when they need to "stop and think", especially when feelings may get out of control, and can benefit from knowing that an escape route is readily available.

Case example – Noah

Noah (13) was prone to uncontrollable rages, usually in the school playground. During these times he would shout and swear, hit out at other students and staff, go red in the face and shake. Afterwards, Noah would despair of himself for getting into these states and wish that he could stop them. Noah's foster mother, Gloria, labelled the episodes "getting hot under the collar", a phrase which was apt and yet served to reduce some of the sense of panic that was starting to surround them. She helped Noah to think about what might set them off (thinking that other pupils thought him "stupid") and to identify the physical precursors (feeling hot and shaking). When he felt these early signs, it was agreed that he could go to the head teacher's office and ask to go home. In fact, helping Noah to make sense of his feelings in this way and offering a strategy which involved having access to his secure base at times of stress, enabled him to gain better self-control. His rages became less intense and worrying to him and he had not needed to use his escape route of returning home.

In some situations with older adolescents, the "pause for thought" needed to assimilate feelings and assess a course of action may be over a much more protracted period. Some caregivers report that providing a means of safely releasing strong feelings (punching a cushion, cooling off in a bedroom), but then allowing young people to take stock of a situation in their own time and without external pressure, can be a way forward after a difficult incident.

Case example – Stuart

Elaine, a foster mother, described an incident when Stuart (15) went too far in an argument with her birth daughter, Vicky, aged 10. This resulted in a physical fight in which Stuart put his hands round Vicky's neck and squeezed to a point when she was genuinely frightened. Elaine reacted with initial anger and then suggested that Stuart went to his bedroom to give everyone a chance to cool off. Stuart remained (by his own choice) in his bedroom for the rest of the day and night. When he eventually came downstairs, he said that he expected that they would want him to leave. Elaine assured him that this was not the case and speculated that it would not really be what he wanted either. Stuart agreed and immediately talked about why he felt he had behaved in this way. His theory was that on previous occasions he had failed to express more mild irritation with Vicky and this had built up in his mind to the point where he "exploded" on the next occasion. He had also decided on a strategy for future occasions which was to say what he was feeling at an earlier point. It seemed that being offered time for thinking at his own pace had enabled Stuart to draw on lessons learned in the foster home, order his thoughts, and make sense of his reaction in a very constructive way.

Gaining sufficient access to the young person's mind to engage in constructive dialogue, however, can be very difficult. Teenagers who find it hard to express their thinking and feeling have often developed very effective strategies for keeping adults at bay and caregivers must be particularly intuitive in order to keep a line of communication open. Marie (15) was a young person who found it particularly hard to share the confused feelings of guilt, resentment and love that she felt for her birth parents. On one occasion, she faced a decision regarding contact that was especially hard for her to cope with and she withdrew to her bedroom. Her foster mother, Barbara, sensed that written rather than spoken words might be a more comfortable means of expression for Marie and she pushed a note saying 'just let me know if I can help you' under the bedroom door. Marie responded straight away and a series of notes were exchanged until Marie was eventually able to express her wishes regarding the contact meeting. Barbara suggested that in future, if Marie had something on her mind, she might begin by writing it down.

Finally, it is important to say that although adolescence can be a time of additional challenges, it can also be a time for reaping the benefits of consistent and sensitive care offered during middle childhood. Harriet had learning difficulties and a history of emotional neglect. At the age of nine, she had been explosive in her angry outbursts. She had managed her feelings and comforted herself through food, particularly sweets. At the age of 13, she had established a secure base in the foster home. As her foster mother described:

Harriet doesn't eat sweets all the time like she used to. Her life is full of other things that give her pleasure and give her comfort so she doesn't need it. She will start some sweeties and then she will put them in the fridge for another day and she knows nobody is going to take them and they'll be there and I think she learned that nobody's going to take her things from her, that they'll be there.

The combination of availability and sensitively providing alternative sources of comfort and feelings of self-efficacy had allowed Harriet to relax around food.

Conclusion

From infancy to adolescence, the underlying mechanisms by which sensitive responding to children's behaviour and the minds that lie behind that behaviour are remarkably similar. Caregivers reflect on the child's behaviour, the feelings that lie behind it in the child, and the feelings the child's behaviour produces in them, and then parent in ways that provide scaffolding and an emotional education – these processes are important for the smallest baby, the grieving child and the young adult. However, as in other aspects of caregiving, the task of offering sensitive care to fostered and adopted children has additional therapeutic challenges which arise from the fact that children's minds and behaviour have often been distorted by their experiences of maltreatment and loss. The caregiver needs to tune in to troubled minds and offer a carefully structured and shaped environment in which children feel safe enough to think about their lives and their feelings in order to manage them successfully.

Summary points

- Babies are born into a world of experiences, thoughts and feelings which they cannot understand or make sense of. It is essential that concerned and empathic adults are able to provide a *supportive scaffolding*, which helps young children to organise their thinking and regulate their feelings and behaviour. They do this through a verbal and non-verbal *commentary*, which reflects and responds to the baby's ideas and feelings and yet also provides comfort and reassurance.

- Sensitive parents also help their young children to understand that other people have feelings, ideas and intentions which are different from their own *and* need to be taken into account.

- Fostered and adopted children have often lacked consistent adults who are interested in their thoughts and feelings, can see the world from their point of view and provide comfort and reassurance. As a result, children may find it very hard to manage their feelings and behaviour.

- For foster carers and adopters, a primary task is to reflect on and make sense of their children's feelings and behaviours. They must attempt to tune in to their child, stand in the child's shoes and try to imagine 'what might this child be thinking and feeling?'

- Caring for a troubled child can elicit a range of strong feelings and it is important that caregivers feel safe and supported to acknowledge and talk about them.
- Foster carers and adopters can use a range of approaches to convey to their children that both positive and negative feelings are acceptable and understandable and that all feelings can be safely expressed and managed.
- Signs of progress in this area include indicators that the child is able to make some sense of his feelings, to contain anxiety, to have some understanding that other people have thoughts and feelings – and to take them into account.

Approaches for helping children to manage feelings and behaviour

N.B. It is important to choose only those activities that the child is likely to accept and enjoy.
- Observe child carefully – perhaps keep a diary, note patterns, the unexpected, etc; try to stand in the child's shoes.
- Anticipate what will cause confusion and distress for the child and avoid if possible.
- Read cues for support and comfort – be aware of *miscuing*.
- Express interest, at a level that is comfortable for the child, in his/her thoughts and feelings.
- Provide shared, pleasurable activity and a *commentary* on the feelings experienced by self and child.
- Find time for interactions that promote synchrony of action, experiences, expressions of feeling (simple action rhymes and songs, clapping games for younger children, ball and beanbag games, learning a dance together, building or making something together, sharing an "adventure" or new experience together, a game that involves a shared experience of both winning and losing).
- Make a "me calendar" to help a child to see and remember what is going to happen next.
- Collect tickets, pictures, leaflets, stickers, etc and make an "experiences book" to help a child to remember and reflect on positive events.
- Name and discuss feelings in everyday situations (happy, proud, sad, confused, angry, worried, peaceful, excited, guilty, lonely, pleased, etc). Also discuss mixed feelings and feelings that change over time.
- Play sensory games (involving touch, sound, smell, observation).
- Use clay, paint, crayons to express feelings.
- Use play and real examples to make sense of the world, how things work, cause and effect.
- Encourage children to stop and think before reacting.
- Help children recover/repair the situation/make things better after losing control of feelings – praise them for doing this.

- Use stories or puppets to develop empathy in the child – 'poor baby owl, how does he feel now his mummy has flown away to get food?' etc.
- Use television programmes/films to focus on why people feel different things and how they can feel different things at the same time.
- Speculate on and give names to the possible feelings of others in everyday conversations.

8 Accepting the child – building self-esteem

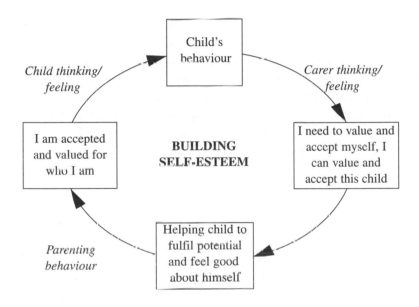

Figure 6

From the earliest interactions with their newborn infants, parents and other close caregivers begin the process of conveying a positive sense of self. A fully focused and available caregiver provides loving words, gestures and tones of voice which show the child that he or she is loved, lovable, and a subject of interest, joy, concern and value to others. Most importantly, these messages of acceptance are conveyed unconditionally. They are not withheld, for instance, if the baby is fretful or needing a nappy changed. The caregiver is able to feel and show warmth and appreciation, even at the most difficult times. It is this experience of being loved, wanted and accepted for who he is, that enables the baby to take for granted that he is *a good thing* and that others will view him in this way (see Figure 6).

As children grow and develop through early childhood and into the primary school years, parents can help them to maintain their self-esteem in the face of everyday challenges, and also generate environments in which they can feel a sense of achievement, accomplish tasks, receive praise and experience themselves as valued and special. Sensitive parents are realistic about what their children are good at or less good at, but continue to be unconditional in their acceptance of both positives and negatives. Perceptive commentary in this phase enables children to think about and make sense of a world in which everyone is different and everyone will have different skills and qualities. Discussion of the range of differences within the family or among the child's friendship groups can bring such issues comfortably into the open. Few people are equally good at sport and school and drawing and talking to babies and looking after the family pets. Thus, children can learn to feel good about what they can do and at the same time tolerate the fact that they, like everyone else, have areas where they do not shine. This will include personal characteristics, such as being more or less grumpy in the morning. Overriding this is the certain knowledge that they are loved and valued for who they are.

In middle childhood and adolescence, as young people begin to reflect on the kind of person they are and the kind of person they would like to be, their sense of self and self-esteem has to be sustained in the face of possible peer group criticism and fears of not fitting in. Even the most secure young people need support and reassurance through this period. The commentary provided in the earlier and middle years provides a foundation on which parents and adolescents can build, alongside the now established parental message, 'We love and accept you for who you are'. This can liberate young people to make choices for themselves and assert their chosen identity.

Thus, children and young people who are valued and accepted for both their strengths and difficulties can grow up with a firm sense of self-worth. They experience themselves as robust and able to deal with adversity, but also as needing to receive help and support at times. They learn to respect themselves for who they are, to enjoy their successes and to live comfortably with their short-comings. They can accept themselves and this helps them to accept others without being too jealous or judgemental. Eventually, they can transfer this level of acceptance into future relationships – with friends, partners and eventually with their own children.

What children bring to their placements

Many fostered and adopted children have a profound sense of worthlessness and low self-esteem, often complex and deep-rooted in origin. Their early parenting may have lacked warmth and acceptance – personal isolation and poverty, for instance, can make it very hard for parents to demonstrate these things when a baby is fretful or a toddler oppositional or demanding. Most significantly, parents who have themselves felt rejected and unloved will not have memories or models in their minds of parents who offer unconditional acceptance. They may have deep fears that their child will also reject them and so the typical stresses of parenting, such as dirty nappies or tantrums, can be perceived as personally threatening. Parents may come across as dissatisfied with the child when things do not go smoothly and the child receives the message, 'I am only loved and accepted when I am good'.

Low self-esteem for children may also be connected with multiple separations and losses of familiar people and, for older children, compounded by the stigma and sense of difference incurred by being fostered or placed for adoption. Fostered and adopted children, therefore, are likely to have deep-seated doubts about their fundamental goodness, whether or not they deserve loving care and whether or not they will receive it if they are naughty or needy. For some children, family life may have been frightening at times and the tendency of young children to see themselves as having a magical responsibility for negative events can lead them to experience themselves as dangerous, bad and worthy only of punishment.

Children who do not hold a mental representation of close adults as warm and accepting and themselves as loved and lovable will find it hard to face the world with confidence. They have not learned that they can be both good and bad, clever or not so clever, and yet still be accepted and valued. They often believe that if they cannot be the best then they must be the worst. Familiar defensive strategies affect the way in which children manage the stress of low self-esteem. For example, the avoidant child may tend to be boastful but then become angry or retreat into, 'I don't care anyway' when he does not succeed.

As a result, the capacity to take risks – both in learning and in forming close relationships – will be reduced. Some children may even appear to behave deliberately in ways which invite negative responses and only seem satisfied when they receive them. At least they have made the world predictable. The danger, then, is that a child becomes trapped in a negative cycle in which she expects failure or rejection and so behaves in ways that are likely to produce this outcome.

Tasks for foster carers and adopters

Foster carers and adopters are usually aware of the urgent need to help children to build a more positive sense of themselves, to experience a sense of pride or achievement. In order to work towards this goal, however, it is necessary for caregivers themselves to have good self-esteem, to feel strong and confident about themselves as individuals and as parents. People are generally motivated to foster or adopt because they feel that they have something positive to offer to children. They feel that they are, or they have the potential to be, good parents and their self-esteem in this area is generally high. But needy children may be critical, resistant or hostile towards their caregivers at times, or their progress may be uncertain or slow. They can behave in ways that invite negative responses, thus confirming their negative beliefs about themselves. These behaviours have the potential to erode the self-esteem of caregivers, leading them to feel deskilled and disappointed in themselves and trapped in negative interactions with their children.

Foster carers and adopters, therefore, must hold in mind the importance of *valuing and accepting themselves* so that, in turn, they can convey messages of acceptance to their children. This may be a key area of intervention for support workers. Caregivers who are feeling overwhelmed by their children's needs and finding it hard to parent positively may need to be reminded of their strengths and skills and that it is the child's history that is creating problems in the family, making it difficult for them to parent the child in the way they would want. They need support with their parenting, but they may also need emotional and practical encouragement to take care of themselves, to take time out as individuals or as a couple, and to pursue interests or activities that are personally rewarding and satisfying. At the same time, caregivers may also need help in achieving a realistic appraisal of their own areas of difficulty or vulnerability that are being sparked by the relationship with a particular child. By modelling parental messages of acceptance of both positives and negatives in children, support workers can convey the message to carers and adopters, 'You do not have to be perfect', alongside providing caregivers with advice, discussion and training that will help them to develop new approaches and to parent more positively. Just as caregivers need at times to understand and forgive the children, so they need to understand and forgive themselves. They may also need to understand more about the child's early experiences in order to gain a sense of *why* certain behaviours are occurring. This can help them avoid blaming the child or themselves, while accepting that both they and the child need to work together and take shared responsibility, as the problems will not only rest in the child but will have become part of the relationship. Foster carers and adopters will need to build a range of skills and strategies for dealing with difficult behaviour in ways that do not undermine their own self-esteem or that of the child, and focus on activities and interactions that both help them to regain their sense of being competent and successful parents and enable children to feel positive about themselves.

When caregivers are strengthened in these ways, it is more likely that they will feel able to *value and accept the child,* and to establish in their own minds an understanding and belief in the *whole child* – strengths as well as difficulties, positives as well as negatives. Once this mindset has been achieved, it becomes possible to convey messages of unconditional acceptance, whatever the child's mood, behaviour or achievements. This does not mean that behaviour difficulties are not challenged or that goals are not set to reduce behaviours that are upsetting or anti-social. On the contrary, it is critical for children, especially older children, to feel acceptable and accepted not only in the family, but also in their peer group and the wider community. Caregivers therefore have to manage a careful balance between accepting children as they are *and* helping them to change aspects of behaviour that threaten their acceptance by others. As children begin to believe in themselves and their fundamental goodness, they can become less preoccupied by the fear of failure and rejection and better able to make adjustments to their behaviour.

Children who feel *valued and accepted for who they are* will be more responsive to praise and encouragement, more willing to take risks and more likely to experience the good feelings of success and achievement. Sensitive caregivers can then create and support as many opportunities as possible for children and young people to learn new skills, have new experiences and feel good about themselves. Crucially for caregivers, this area of parenting builds on the dimensions of *availability* and *sensitivity.* Children need to learn to trust and to manage their feelings and behaviour in order to believe the praise of caregivers and to take up opportunities that are on offer. For some children this may always prove difficult, even with the most sensitive and accepting care, but self-esteem is so critical to healthy development that even small degrees of progress are worth working for. This chapter examines the range of enhanced parenting skills and approaches that foster carers and adopters may need to help children of different ages to develop a strong and positive sense of themselves.

Infancy (birth–18 months)

In optimal circumstances, where new parents are well supported and able to be physically and emotionally available to their babies, there is a flow of events in which the parent freely demonstrates pleasure and delight in the baby and is rewarded by the baby's positive responses. The parent's own self-esteem is raised by this success and he or she is prompted to initiate further positive interactions and also strengthened to accept that these will not always be achievable. The more negative aspects of parenting can therefore be tolerated and managed without feelings of anger or rejection towards the baby.

For foster carers and adopters, this constructive flow of interactions may be hard to achieve in the early days. They are likely to be caring for babies who have adapted their behaviour to poor care environments and may be exceptionally needy but difficult to stimulate, to soothe or to love. Such infants do not respond in a straightforward manner to gestures of concern and affection and may ignore praise and encouragement. Establishing a positive cycle of acceptance and self-esteem building, therefore, will require conscious effort and enhanced availability and sensitivity.

As in other parenting dimensions, the caregiver may be helped by having some flexible theories about why negative behaviours are occurring and a corresponding plan of action. If connections can be made between early experience and current difficulties, caregivers are less likely to take difficult behaviour personally and more able to view it as understandable in the circumstances. Their own sense of themselves as a good carer or good parent will not be diminished and they will feel more competent and motivated to work on building the child's self-esteem.

Case example – Shannon

Pauline was an experienced foster carer, but found herself bewildered and at a loss to cope with Shannon's demanding behaviour. At nine months, Shannon presented as an extremely unhappy baby – she cried almost constantly but rejected all affection and approaches, struggling and arching her back when cuddled. Pauline found herself exasperated by Shannon and wondered if she should ask for her to be moved as she was finding it hard to feel warmly towards her. A consultation with a specialist psychologist for looked after children helped Pauline to understand Shannon's behaviour in the context of her early neglect. Pauline started to realise that Shannon was expecting her to behave in the same ways as her previous caregivers and Pauline was starting to fulfil her expectation. This insight enabled Pauline to step back from the situation in order to think it through, to understand that Shannon was not reacting to her personally and that her own feelings of frustration were normal in the circumstances.

Pauline felt reassured and regained her confidence to care for and build a relationship with Shannon. A plan was devised to achieve a degree of closeness that was comfortable for Shannon and to increase this incrementally. Bottle feeds, for example, were to be given on the sofa with Pauline initially sitting beside Shannon, then gradually working towards putting an arm round her and eventually bringing her on to her lap. Carrying out the plan enabled Pauline to feel more competent as a carer. In time, she began to feel and demonstrate warmth and acceptance of Shannon, for all her difficulties.

Shannon settled considerably in the weeks that followed and she became a much more relaxed, responsive and confident baby.

This caregiver is able to combine an awareness of the need to be a *loving mother* who can promote Shannon's ability to experience her as a secure base, with the context of offering *therapeutic care* that is directed by an understanding of the child's history and specific needs. The secure base that enables a child of this age to explore more confidently can be built into small achievements, such as pressing buttons so that a toy lights up. Pleasure and satisfaction for the infant is accompanied by praise from the adult, setting up a rhythm of exploration, reward and messages of worth that promote the infant's self-esteem and strengthen the caregiver's feelings of affection, pride and commitment. Here we see in this cycle of mutual reinforcement further evidence of Donald Winnicott's famous statement, 'There is no such thing as a baby'; the baby exists, thinks, feels and grows within the context of the relationship. Both partners need to grow together.

With this age group, the accepting commentary provided around managing difficulties, such as the hungry baby's distress when waiting for the bottle or the food to get to the right temperature, can soothe both the caregiver and the child. 'I know you are hungry and I should have put it on earlier, but it won't take long now. We can just wipe the high chair down together while we're waiting and here's teddy, I expect he's hungry too.' The words acknowledge the anxieties of both the caregiver and the child, but also contain and moderate them. The tone is gentle and reassuring and the plan is a constructive, purposeful and collaborative approach to managing the situation, so that the child can be calmed enough to successfully drink or eat and then be praised for "being a good girl". The available and sensitive caregiver meets the child's needs in a way that builds trust and the capacity to manage feelings and this provides the context in which being recognised as a "good girl" becomes possible.

For very troubled and chaotic infants it is important to both create and recognise even small elements of success – the beginning of a smile greeted with 'what a lovely smile', a small achievement with a toy rewarded by eye contact, a smile and a 'well done'. For these infants, as in the example of Shannon and the incremental moves towards physical closeness, it is important that caregivers clearly signal their positive reactions, but deliver them in a gentle tone and quiet manner that will not be experienced by the child as intrusive or even scary. Over-excited praise to compensate for the child's lack of response or to get past the child's negativity may make the child shut down further. As with newborn infants, tuning in and calming the child in order for her to "hear" the messages of acceptance is essential to restoring her equilibrium and building up a more positive mental representation of the self.

Early childhood (18 months–4 years)

During this time of rapid changes, children begin to develop a more psychosocial sense of self: their gender, their ethnicity, who they are and how they fit into the family and wider social groups at playgroup and nursery. They start with a concrete and physical sense of themselves, but even by the age of three will be aware of a range of social scripts and roles, such as what toys are appropriate for a boy or a girl, how to behave when out shopping, what to do when a pet needs feeding or a baby cries. Language development means that the feelings and unconsciously received parental messages of infancy are now put into words that the child can understand. By five and often earlier, most children have quite a strong sense of what they are good at and whether they are thought to be nice or naughty, clever or stupid, helpful or difficult. The newly-developing concept of self is rarely free of an evaluative component that determines self-esteem even in this young age group.

Foster carers and adopters are commonly aware that even very young children may worry about the kind of people they are, often blaming themselves for bad things that have happened or having a sense that being loved and wanted is conditional on their good behaviour. As they become more verbal, children are often able to articulate a sense of personal failure, guilt or blame in connection with birth family difficulties.

Case example – Salina

Salina (4) had repeatedly been disappointed by her mother failing to come to visit her at her foster home. Shortly after such a disappointment, her foster mother overheard Salina saying to herself, 'If I good girl, Mummy come'. In this unguarded moment, Salina had revealed that she felt that her mother's love was, in some way, contingent upon her good behaviour and perhaps, conversely, that her "badness" was the reason for Mummy failing to come. The immediate task then for May, her foster mother, was to acknowledge that she understood that Salina was worried about being a good girl and to help Salina think differently about her mother's lack of contact. Through simple conversations, May provided Salina with some alternative reasons why Mummy did not come sometimes, emphasising that these were Mummy's difficulties and not connected with Salina's behaviour. May also worked on demonstrating to Salina, in a variety of ways, that she and other family members and pets were continuously loved, wanted and valued, whether or not they were being good.

We have already seen that in the course of day-to-day events and routines, sensitive caregivers provide a reassuring commentary which creates a *supportive scaffolding* for babies and young children. It is of significance for children in this age group that this commentary characteristically promotes the positive attributes of the child, provides frequent praise, and demonstrates admiration, pride and delight. For foster carers and adopters, these aspects of their *commentary* may need to be consciously developed and emphasised. As for infants, particular attention may need to be given to tiny steps of progress and achievement and every opportunity taken to highlight and reinforce positives in the child's appearance, talents and development.

The following adoptive mother demonstrates this aspect of caregiving when she describes helping her three-year-old child to get dressed and ready for playgroup.

> *I do her hair every day and from the beginning, I've told her how gorgeous her hair is and I say, 'We'll do your hair up and make it look pretty and we'll put this frilly T shirt on today and it'll go with these lovely trousers and don't you look lovely today' . . . I just try to reinforce it to her all the time.*

For many young children, there needs to be a subtlety of approach here, since children who lack trust and have low self-esteem often feel threatened and uncomfortable when receiving praise and admiration. Their caregivers must be attuned to this, pick up signs of discomfort and then pitch their responses at a level that the child can manage and therefore find beneficial. There may be opportunities to model the giving and receiving of praise and the parallel acknowledgement and humorous enjoyment of the fact that 'Dad is hopeless at computers' or 'Mum is useless at telling jokes'. Using story books, as with all areas of emotional education, can be a helpful way to illustrate how children and adults enjoy success, but also cope with failure.

For most young children, self-esteem can only really start to grow when the basic trust in availability has been established, but nevertheless opportunities to lay down the foundations in terms of acceptance will be important from the beginning of any placement – whether for respite care, short-term care, permanent foster care or adoption. With this age group, for example, the way children are greeted and treated with care and respect from the very first meeting is giving important messages. Similarly, helping young children to repair situations when they have gone wrong (perhaps by being naughty to test out the placement in the early days) will assist them to relax and not panic when they feel that they have failed and been bad. In parallel, physical evidence, such as photographs of the child successfully completing a task or certificates for tasks accomplished, as well as discussion and referring back to past achievements, may help the child to retain an underlying sense of being valued and competent in continuing and new placements.

Middle childhood (5–10 years)

As children move out into the world of school, peers and activities, they increasingly enter situations in which they may be compared or may compare themselves with others. Developmentally they have the task of learning the rules of the social world and their place in it, so this can mean more competition and more anxiety about getting things right. For school-aged children, the effects of experiencing the self as unworthy and unloved can begin to show themselves more clearly. Some children may verbalise their feelings, referring negatively to themselves and their capabilities – 'I am stupid/useless'. Others may demonstrate low self-esteem in counterproductive behaviour – giving up, refusing to do things, regressing when feeling under pressure and so on. The self may be blamed for the lack of success (I am bad, clumsy, ugly) and the child becomes increasingly reluctant to take the risk of failure.

Low self-esteem can become acute during middle childhood, but caregiving in this area holds great potential for positive intervention and change. For foster carers and adopters, it is of central importance to convey to the child a sense that in this family, he is accepted and valued for *who he is,* regardless of his difficulties and limitations. A first step here is to create an environment or culture within the family, in which everyone's strengths are recognised and yet at the same time, it is seen as "OK" to make mistakes and to have shortcomings – this is normal and acceptance is not withdrawn as a result.

Celine, a birth and adoptive mother of a large, multi-ethnic family had learned to value a range of skills and abilities in her children – these might be academic, emotional, spatial, practical, physical and so on. Each person's strengths – be they keeping their belongings tidy, being thoughtful to others or academic success – were highlighted, celebrated and promoted inside and outside the family. At the same time, "weak spots" were also openly acknowledged and discussed.

Jay, my son, knows that I'm useless at spelling and I'm useless at heaps of other things, so we're all very open about those kinds of things. Yeah, so we all see each other with all our strengths and difficulties.

Celine sensed that this general approach was key to enabling a very diverse family to live reasonably harmoniously together and for each family member to be instrumental in building the self-esteem of others. At the same time, however, this atmosphere of acceptance did not mean that difficult areas were not tackled.

It doesn't mean that Ruth isn't challenged for her moaning and groaning and whatever, or that Rui isn't challenged on his lack of enthusiasm in the housework department. We're like any other family, we all shout and get angry and upset and all of that, but everybody is very clear about the effort they need to make, myself included, and about what we're OK at as well and I think that's what sustains us.

For carers and adopters of children with severe learning and physical disabilities, the concept of acceptance lies at the heart of their caregiving. Where there is unconditional acceptance of the child and the realities of the child's limitations are fully embraced, then the carers can be "freed up" to value every small step, rejoice in the smallest detail of progress and reflect this unbridled pleasure and pride back to the child. The paradox here, it seems, is that a full acceptance of *disabilities* allows caregivers to become fully focussed on the child's *capabilities* and potential for development, while at the same time, setting realistic and achievable targets. Chloe (9), for instance, has severe learning disabilities and her foster mother expressed this combination of acceptance of limitation and maximising of potential.

I think everything that happens is a bonus and you just have to see it that way really. You don't sort of think, ooh, she ought to be able to do this or that. With Chloe we think well, she might be able to do such and such over time and if she does it and achieves it then it's marvellous for her and it gives us an achievement too and we are delighted. But if she doesn't manage it then it really doesn't matter a bit.

Sensitive caregivers will choose their language carefully when communicating with their children. When self-esteem is low, children are quick to pick up on words and expressions that confirm their already negative feelings about themselves. The foster mother of Jake (10) is sensitive to this pitfall.

You have to mind what you say to him if you're telling him off. You can't say 'you're silly'. You have to say 'you're acting silly', or else he'll pick up on it straight away, then he'll really get a down on himself and say 'I'm rubbish'.

As for younger children, sensitive caregivers will be alert to every opportunity to praise, highlight progress and achievement and comment on positive aspects of the child's appearance, personality and behaviour. There needs to be additional effort and creativity, however, in developing such opportunities. Productive partnerships with schools can alert teachers and classroom assistants to issues of self-esteem building. Home/school books may be used to convey positive developments in both environments and ensure praise from both directions. One adoptive mother established an arrangement whereby a classroom assistant emailed her when her son had achieved something special and she was able to greet him after school with pride and pleasure when this happened.

A poorly developed sense of self or lack of self-confidence may mean that some children miss opportunities for praise and positive reinforcement when they are outside the home environment. Caregivers may need to take a proactive approach to this and discuss with teachers and others how they might tailor their approaches and expectations to the individual child. For example, Clare (9) was highlighted as being passive and non-participative in class, even though she was an able child. Her adoptive mother sensed that low self-esteem was preventing Clare from showing her abilities and answering questions and it was agreed that the usual incentive system of stickers for good work could be used to reward her simply for putting her hand up in class. This proved a helpful strand to a general strategy of self-esteem building for Clare.

For some children, however, direct praise or expressions of pride are too uncomfortable to manage. Such approaches are rebuffed or trigger negative behaviour One adopted girl, when told her hair looked lovely, went upstairs and cut it off. One fostered boy, on receiving notification that he was to get an award for improvement in school work, tore it up in front of the teacher and refused to attend the prize-giving ceremony. Promoting positives in ways that are acceptable in these circumstances requires additional thought and sensitivity. Some carers and adopters find that an indirect approach is less threatening to the child. Telling other people (within the child's earshot) about skills and achievements, mentioning them casually in conversations between partners or on the telephone, posting a card or a note to a child or asking relatives to do this – any of these can have the desired effect but feel less intrusive and risky to the child.

The pursuit of particular interests and activities and the development of talents and aptitudes make an increasingly important contribution to self-esteem during middle childhood. Josie (10) was not a very emotionally forthcoming child, but enjoyed making things from almost any kind of material. Her foster parents kept her supplied with cardboard boxes and her foster father often worked with her on her creations. They referred to Josie proudly as their "Blue Peter" child. Sensitive caregivers will take every opportunity to support the child in following and sustaining existing interests and in trying out and developing new ones. Individual achievements will be celebrated, successful participation in group activities will be recognised, and sustained efforts explicitly mentioned to the child and in the family.

However, vulnerable children are frequently less successful in joining clubs and taking up interests than their more secure peers. They may not be ready for such risky exploration away from their secure base and they may become highly anxious when feeling under pressure to conform to the group, demonstrate their skills or take the risk of participation. Such children are likely to need additional help and support from their caregivers in order to reduce this anxiety to a manageable level and thus enable them to participate successfully. Activities may be selected on the basis that the ethos of the group is one of inclusion and self-esteem building. Caregivers may need to talk with leaders and observe some sessions to ensure that their children will feel fully accepted, supported and encouraged and that difficulties will be raised and discussed with them. Other ways of supporting activities might be taking a leadership role or pursuing an interest alongside a child, sharing the experience while still allowing the child to gain a sense of discovery and achievement. Toni's foster carers were constantly looking for ways in which to positively channel Toni's energy and headstrong behaviour. Activities which provided a focus that would reduce the tendency to flit about were important in calming children, but also gave them a sense of self-esteem and self-efficacy.

> *Since she's come, Toni's learned to swim, she's learned to ride a bike and she couldn't do any of these things when she came and she now can. And she loves swimming, she loves going out on her bike. She likes ice-skating, she likes bowling, she likes activity clubs, she goes to basketball on a Saturday.*

Toni's carers saw her impulsive behaviour in the swimming pool as an opportunity to learn a new skill and, in doing so, to gain praise rather than admonishment.

> *I wouldn't say she's a daredevil, but she's still a bit of tomboy, she's jumping off the boards at the swimming pool now and Bill (foster father) says that he'll teach her to dive properly. She's been told that she can't go on to another board unless she dives so Bill says he'll go and teach her diving because I can't do that.*

For children with disabilities, the importance of gaining self-esteem through activities is no less important, and carers and adopters often go to great lengths to enable their children to participate in age-appropriate activities, sometimes taking part alongside them. This can involve considerable time and effort and must be sustained by a strong belief in the value and significance of participation. In some cases, involving other children can support the child and help them achieve success. Foster mother, Frances, took Evie (a child with severe learning disabilities) out to be amongst other children who were playing on the green outside their house. There was also a special friend, Rachel, who came to play and prepared for her Brownie badges alongside Evie. The bond that had developed between these two children was movingly described by Frances.

> *On the day that they were enrolled, Rachel had everyone in tears because Evie started to dribble and Rachel knew it was important to get it right and Rachel got the cuff of her Brownie uniform and wiped the dribble off Evie's cheek.*

Ben (10), also a child with severe learning and physical disabilities, used to make loud and startling noises when they were in the car and in public places. Marion worked hard and succeeded in curtailing this behaviour and so they were comfortable in visiting the library and other quiet places and her friend's daughters no longer dreaded having Ben in the back of the car with them. Ben had also become a much loved and welcomed member of a church group and this provided endless opportunities for social interaction and positive feedback. Marion spoke vividly about the importance of working on disruptive behaviours in order to promote inclusion and thus enhance self-esteem.

> *So, for him to be accepted, some of his behaviour has to be modified and he will get the benefits of that. I'll give you an example. We go to quite a nice hotel and he'll walk through into the breakfast room on his walker and everyone thinks he's so wonderful and it's so great for him. They say 'Ben, you're so clever, you're marvellous, you're such a beautiful boy'. And I just think, that's part of what's building him up, not me, but the response of all these other people. And he'd never have got that, not how he was before.*

Also important in middle childhood is the idea that there are additional resources outside the family network which can play an important part in building self-esteem and resilience. Having a part to play in a variety of social roles is of great importance and children will gain enormously from feeling themselves to be valued and respected members of the wider networks of community, ethnic and cultural groups, school and neighbourhood.

A very important consideration here is that children from minority ethnic groups, children from different cultures and religions and children speaking different languages, all need to be supported in valuing their identities and celebrating difference. As one black foster mother, Dolores, commented, when black children come into foster care they experience not only the loss of family and the stigma of care, but they may also have to manage the additional challenge of racism in their wider community. Just as all children in middle childhood question how they fit and how they are valued, black children have to answer these questions in a society which, in many of its formal institutions (hospitals, schools) and informal settings (Dolores used the example of going to the supermarket and being treated differently) are racist. For black children in care, the issue of social acceptance is complicated, whether they live in a predominantly black area, where their care status may yet be undermining, or in a predominantly white environment, where either or both their ethnicity and their care status might lead to being singled out and verbally abused in their communities by both adults and peers.

Both foster carers and adopters (Massiah, 2005) talk of the need to help black children to feel good about themselves as black people and regard this as an extra and very significant part of their parenting. Dolores worked hard to give the message, both directly and indirectly, to the black children in her care, 'Be proud to be who you are! Be proud to be black!' She also described how essential it was that she acted as a role model, by being 'a strong black woman'. As a family she and her partner emphasised the importance of the close relationships, family and community values that supported the children and young people in their growth inside and outside the family boundaries. Providing role models for children and young people in transracial placements is an additional challenge, with increasing numbers of white children in black families raising related but different issues to those faced by black children in white families.

There are, of course, many kinds of difference that can affect children's sense of confidence and competence. In Wales, for example, it is often difficult to match Welsh-speaking children and Welsh-speaking foster and adoptive families. Matching asylum seeking children in families that support their identity and are not seen as threatening is always a complex matter. For children from the Traveller community, foster placement and formal schooling may take them away from the roles and identities that gave them self-esteem. These are just some of a multitude of family placement situations where children's self-esteem and identity need special attention and potentially supplementary packages of support for the child for education and for the placement (for further discussion see Chapter 12).

Adolescence (11–18 years)

Adolescents are becoming more sophisticated thinkers and one of their key tasks, alongside the general task of moving towards separation and autonomy, is to think about what kind of person they are and want to be in the future, building on the lessons from their primary school years. Some may belong to football or scouts or drama groups, where they feel accepted and relationships can develop in an activity focussed context. For others, acceptance may be about finding a niche in informal groups of friends who ring each other, go to each others' houses and who tolerate and manage the ups and downs of their peer relationships while keeping the group as a whole supportive (Beek and Schofield, 2004a).

However, the rules of the peer group are often rigid, especially in early adolescence, and young people with low self-esteem and fewer social and other skills, may struggle to find a group where they feel accepted and comfortable. For many fostered and adopted children, the gap between the kind of person they want to be or other people want them to be and the kind of person they feel themselves to be can seem insurmountable, leaving them at risk of depression or angry, acting out behaviour. Although messages of acceptance can be challenging for caregivers to provide at these times, their significance may be heightened for young people as issues of identity, genetic inheritance and future pathways emerge and the prospect of living independently becomes more of a reality.

With this in mind, accepting caregivers work to demonstrate to their adolescent children that they are whole, complete people, who have the potential to achieve self-esteem in the context of stable, productive and rewarding lives in the world of work and the world of relationships. Although many fostered and adopted young people are willing and able participants in a range of activities and interests, others may be reticent to take the risk of failure or low self-esteem may lower their motivation and drive. But both caregivers and young people need to work realistically within what is possible. This is one of the many finely balanced lines for caregivers and young people to negotiate together, but for fostered and adopted children the tendency to lose confidence in their abilities requires some particularly subtle and persistent providing of opportunities. The examples below demonstrate ways in which foster carers have enabled young people with very low self-esteem to grow in confidence through opening up and supporting activities that were particularly well suited to their needs and capacities.

Case study – Rob

Rob (13) had come into care at the age of five, but had spent much of the next five years waiting for an adoption placement that never arrived. He had been photographed on two separate occasions and invited to comment on what he would like from his adoptive family, increasing the disappointment when no suitable family came forward. Rob had learning difficulties and struggled to cope at school and in his peer group. Early on in the foster home that became his permanent placement, he had discovered the pleasure of following his foster father's enthusiasm for fish ponds. As he matured he was able to look after his foster father's fish pond and then dig his own pond alongside. This safe activity allowed him to feel responsible, competent and valued by his carers who worked hard to ensure that Rob obtained maximum benefit from the activity. As his foster father put it: 'Rob loves his fish pond. Now he's in charge of his own and he's totally reliable in that department. We encourage him all we can. We say, Rob's the top pond man ... He gave his talk at school on goldfish and got top marks.'

Case study – Sam

Sam (15) was an intelligent young man who often became restless and bored at home and his foster carers felt that he needed a channel for his abilities and energies.

Sam enjoyed and was motivated by competition but he was a "loner" who found it hard to mix with his peers and did not wish to be involved in any group activity. His foster father, James, introduced him to golf. Having learned the basics, Sam spent many hours after school and in holidays practising on the course on his own – having an available foster mother who took time to drop him off and pick him up. At weekends, James would join him for a "competition" and Sam worked hard to improve his play for this. This combination of solo and shared activity was just right for Sam – his self-esteem grew and his relationship with James was strengthened. This period of his life was probably the most relaxed and successful in Sam's long and troubled history in his birth family and in care.

This placement had been made when Sam was 14 and the goal was set as preparation for independence rather than "permanence", after a previous foster home breakdown. The sense of his role in the family and the support and space it gave him, psychologically and practically, was reshaping his sense of self and, in particular, his self-esteem.

For some young people, however, pursuing interests and activities outside the home is a step too far for them to manage and foster carers and adopters need the sensitivity to recognise when this is the case and to simply accept and value the young person for who they are at this time. Although opportunities have to be created and encouragement and support are necessary, there is a balance to be achieved since too much pressure can push a teenager into a situation that results in failure and a further blow to self-esteem. The following foster mother is a keen supporter of activities, but is also able to recognise when, for one young person, the time was not right.

Tim is 14 and has very few friends. He's tried a few things but they haven't really worked and for the last year I've more or less accepted that he hasn't done anything, not really gone anywhere or seen anyone. The entire summer holidays is a long time, but I think life has been stressful enough for him as it is. He reads and he goes for bike rides and potters about and that's OK for him and for us. But he's just beginning to emerge a bit and wanting to do a few things. So perhaps knowing when to stop pushing is important too and letting them have that space before you try again.

A further vital role for caregivers during the later stages of adolescence is to support and sustain young people's positive sense of self as they begin to move outside the family boundary and present themselves to others as potential learners, employees or partners. This may need *anticipation* and *active* intervention to increase the likelihood of success, such as not leaving the work experience allocation to chance, but working with the school to set up something specific (such as work on a fish farm for Rob who loved fish and work with a fencing company for David who was more likely to manage working flexibly and outdoors).

At these challenging times, deep fears of being dislikeable, unsuccessful or rejected that were thought to be resolved can come back to the surface, and the role for caregivers may be to provide clear feedback and evidence to the young person that this model of the self is inaccurate. Caregivers are uniquely placed to affirm the young person's strengths, skills and positive personality traits and to ensure that the young person can recognise and put them into words himself. Inevitably there will be setbacks and failures along the way and the message to the young person remains the same as through other stages of development: 'In this family, we love you and will help you to fulfil your potential, but you are valued and accepted for who you are, not what you achieve'.

Conclusion

Sensitive caregivers have the capacity to accept and value the whole child, to promote and support strengths while, at the same time, working on difficulties in ways that do not undermine messages of acceptance. This dimension of parenting is closely linked and interactive with those of being available to children and young people, responding sensitively to their needs, having a co-operative approach and including them as full members of the family. It forms a vital strand in moving children and young people towards security and is an approach which can underpin every aspect of the caregiving relationship.

Summary points

- From the moment of birth, sensitive parents and other close caregivers begin the process of helping children to feel good about themselves, whatever their gender, personality, appearance and other characteristics.

- Many fostered and adopted children have had experiences which have left them feeling unloved and unlovable or that adult care and interest in them is conditional on particular behaviour or responses.

- In order to build self-esteem in their children, it is important for foster carers and adopters to establish in their own minds a sense that whatever the child's mood, achievements or behaviour, in *himself*, he remains accepted and valued.

- Once this mindset has been established, it becomes possible to think about ways of conveying messages of unconditional acceptance that are comfortable and acceptable to the particular child.

- It is also important that caregiving families have high self-esteem as this is a model for fostered or adopted children to follow. Caregivers need to feel good about themselves, to value themselves as individuals and as caregivers and also to accept that they cannot be perfect all of the time.

- When self-esteem is improving, children show signs of being able to comfortably accept both their strengths and their limitations and value themselves for who they are.

Approaches for building self-esteem

N.B. It is important to choose only those activities that the child is likely to accept and enjoy.

- Praise the child for achieving small tasks and responsibilities.
- Provide toys and games that create a sense of achievement.
- Liaise closely with nursery and school to ensure a sense of achievement.
- Use positive language. For example – 'hold the cup tight – good, well done', rather than 'don't drop the cup'.
- Offer a brief explanation of why behaviour is not acceptable and a clear indication of what is preferred, for example: 'If you shout it's really hard for me to hear what you want to say. I want to be able to hear you, so please talk in an ordinary voice.'
- Help the child to list and think about all the things he/she has done that he/she feels proud of.
- Help the child to think about times, events, occasions when he/she felt valued and special. Use photos and other mementos to record these events.
- List alongside the child all the things that make you feel proud of him/her. This can include acceptance of limitations (e.g. a time when the child tried but did not succeed at something, was able to accept losing, etc).
- Encourage the child to draw, paint, make a clay model or play in music how it feels when she feels good about herself. Do the same for yourself.
- Suggest that the child lies on the floor, draw round the outline of the child's body. Encourage the child to make a positive statement about different parts of herself (I've got shiny brown hair, a pretty T shirt, etc) and write or draw these onto the figure. Take this at the child's pace and ensure the child feels comfortable with the statement made.
- As a family group, suggest that each person in the family writes down one good thing about all other family members, so that each child gets given a set of positive things about themselves.
- Make a poster with the child of "best achievements".
- Ask child to teach you something that he is good at – such as a computer game or a joke.

- Buy a small treat and place it in the child's bedroom as a surprise.
- Discover and support activities and interests that the child enjoys and can be successful in. They may need active support (liaison with club leader, becoming a helper at the club, etc).
- Use dolls, toys, games and books that promote a positive sense of the child's ethnic, religious and cultural background.
- Ensure that the child's ethnic, religious and cultural background is valued and celebrated within the household.
- Model the acceptance of difference in words and behaviour.
- Model a sense of pride in self and surroundings.
- Model within the family that it is OK not to be perfect, that 'no one is good at everything but everyone is good at something'.

9 Co-operative caregiving – helping children to feel effective

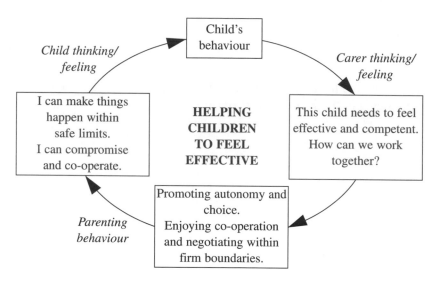

Figure 7

We have seen that sensitive parents try to ensure that they are physically and emotionally available to their babies and also that they make efforts to understand what they might be thinking and feeling. They attend to their infants' needs promptly and target their responses as accurately as possible. A further important strand of caregiving that helps the child to feel more secure is to seek co-operation whenever possible when interacting with the baby. Underpinning this approach is the belief that babies are separate, autonomous individuals who have their own ideas and goals and whose behaviours are valid and meaningful. The parent, for example, assumes that the baby is fretful *because there is something wrong,* thinks about the baby's *thoughts, feelings and goals* and does something to help. In this way, the baby gradually learns to *feel effective* (see Figure 7). His fretful noise will make a familiar person stop what they are doing, postpone their own goals and help him to feel better, by responding not only to his fretful behaviour but also to the needs and goals that lie behind it. Co-operative relationships are also developed during relaxed and *playful* activity between caregivers and infants, which promotes a collaborative approach to both fun and problem solving. Here too, the caregiver is interested in the feelings and goals of the infant and will promote solutions that suit both the adult and the child and require actions that are shared and negotiated.

However, the management of co-operative relationships is more complex than this. Frequently, there are occasions when the infant's wishes cannot be met promptly by the caregiver or his play activities have to be interrupted rather than promoted (perhaps for safety reasons or because a caregiving routine is necessary). The parent has to do things (has goals for herself or the baby) that the baby does not want or enjoy. In these situations, since the infant's autonomy is respected, sensitive parents will tend to avoid interfering abruptly or imposing their will on his. Instead, every effort will be made to achieve his *co-operation*, to bring his mood and *goals* more in line with those of the parent. This preference for avoiding intrusion and achieving a co-operative alliance with the baby will be present throughout parenting routines. For example, a sensitive parent would not interrupt an excited baby by putting her suddenly into a cot to sleep, but would play gentle games, go through a relaxing routine and reach a point where the child was ready for sleep and willing to co-operate with the goal of bedtime – albeit at a time fixed in advance by the parent, who knows how much sleep a baby needs. Harmony is valued, conflict is minimised and children's equilibrium is restored as smoothly as possible. The parent has carried out their responsibility to care for the infant, to be in charge, but in doing so has taken into account the child's feelings and capacity to manage the transition to sleep.

Beyond infancy, sensitive parents continue to enjoy and value their child's autonomy within a co-operative relationship. They promote this by offering choices, allowing the child to make decisions and by allowing him to take the lead in play and activities. At the same time, however, the approach is not laissez-faire or over-permissive. The child must be kept safe and his needs and goals balanced against those of the caregiver and an increasingly wide circle of other people. Again, such a balance will tend to be achieved through a range of tactics using a sensitive awareness of the thoughts and feelings of the child and aimed at engaging the child's co-operation. When there is a point of disagreement, caregivers may suggest alternatives, use diversion, acknowledge the feelings involved, use humour, present the preferred activity as being more interesting, etc. The caregiver *orchestrates* the situation to promote the child's effectiveness, just as caregivers orchestrate situations to promote a child's self-esteem.

As children get older, there may be greater use of explanation and reasoning which acknowledges and respects the child's perspective, while clarifying the perspective of others. The child continues to feel effective and yet also learns that it is safe to compromise, change or defer one's goals at times. In this way, the child models his behaviour on that of the parent and both are informed by an understanding of the perspective of others. As Bowlby (1969, 1982, p. 369) suggests, quoting research on *perspective taking* by Light (1979):

> *A mother who takes account of her child's perspectives and interests is likely to have a child who reciprocates by taking account of his mother's perspectives and interests.*

In Light's study, mothers whose children scored high on perspective taking were *concerned with the child's mind, his feelings and intentions*. To the question, 'What happens if you ask him to do something and he's in the middle of the game or something?', mothers of high-scoring children replied, 'I'll say "Do it when you're finished" and he will'. Mothers of low scorers were more likely to say, 'You'll do it now – I've told you to do it'. Bowlby goes on, 'Mothers of high scorers tend to make concessions and to propose bargains whereas mothers of low scorers are more likely to resort to punishment'. In this way, co-operation is very closely related to the quality of perspective taking or mind-mindedness that is promoted by sensitive, empathic caregiving. Models of parenting that focus exclusively on control by parents risk leaving children without the tools (the capacity to feel effective *and* to understand the perspectives of others) to negotiate within a co-operative relationship. This translates into relationships outside the family, since the child's capacity to cope in school will be built around the capacity not only to *accept* authority, but to understand *why* teachers need quiet in order to teach and to realise that putting their own need to speak to a friend on hold until a better opportunity arises is not only required behaviour but actually *makes sense* if they are to learn.

Through the adolescent years, sensitive parents continue to develop co-operative alliances with young people, building on the pro-social thinking and behaviour that has (with help) been developing since early childhood. They will continue to offer co-operative initiatives, but also encourage *mutuality* in which young people themselves will actively promote co-operation on the basis of a reciprocal concern for the parent. This paves the way for an adult level of independence and efficacy – success in the world of work, for instance, will only occur when a young person can enter a process of negotiation with both colleagues and strangers, in which he has an interest in meeting other people's needs as well as his own.

In summary, co-operative caregiving is based on three important principles:
• From infancy onwards, the child is viewed as a separate, autonomous

individual, who needs opportunities to explore safely but freely and to make choices, decisions and discoveries.

- The caregiver is responsible for the welfare of the child and remains in charge, but when interference or boundary setting is necessary, the caregiver prefers to seek the child's co-operation and to form an alliance based on negotiation of their different goals and compromise within reasonable and explained boundaries.
- The more appropriately effective the child becomes and feels himself to be, the more likely he is to co-operate with others, in relationships based on mutual respect for each others' perspective.

From parenting based on these principles, children are likely to become increasingly socially effective and competent and also be more likely to show resilience in the face of adversity, when assertiveness *and* negotiation with others are both likely to be required.

What children bring to their placements

In order to achieve co-operation with their child, parents must reconcile their own needs and goals with those of the child and be prepared to accept an arrangement that is reasonable and satisfactory for both parties. Parents are ultimately "in charge" and responsible for the child's welfare, but there are many areas of collaboration and negotiation through which parents build skills and resilience in children. However, foster carers and adopters are parenting children who have seldom experienced this co-operative approach to parenting as part of their early care. Birth family caregivers may have been over-involved and intrusive, denying children the opportunity to make choices, to feel competent and to be effective. They may have lacked the skills or capacity to negotiate, resulting in parenting interventions that were harsh and abrupt or weak and ineffective. Additionally, in stressed and disadvantaged households there are often fewer opportunities for play, fun and mutually enjoyable activities. Fostered and adopted children, therefore, are likely to have experienced low levels of effectiveness, autonomy and choice. They may have lacked opportunities to enjoy co-operative activities and to learn the skills of negotiation. The territory of compromise may feel unsafe to them.

For some children, feelings of powerlessness or excessive power may have been created or exacerbated by the care system itself. Many care histories involve multiple moves, often for reasons that are inexplicable to children and for which they are unprepared and unwilling. On the other hand, children whose difficult behaviour has been too much for birth families, foster carers or adopters to manage may feel dangerously powerful. Although care planning includes seeking and listening to the views of children and young people, this, in itself is not always empowering. Their wishes and feelings may not be, or may not appear to be, taken into account, and feelings on some questions (for instance, contact with a birth parent who appears both loving and rejecting) may be mixed and difficult for them to accurately process and express. (See also section in Chapter 12 on social work practice with children.)

For a range of reasons, therefore, fostered and adopted children may not have developed a sense of themselves as competent individuals, nor of adults as co-operative partners, either in exploration and play or in managing difficulties. As a result, they may become passive and over-compliant in their relationships with adults or they may seek excessive control and influence over them.

Tasks for foster carers and adopters

Most foster carers and adopters would agree that all children need to feel effective and competent and they will know that most (securely attached) children enjoy and benefit from opportunities to act on their environment, make choices and take gradual steps towards independence. But children who feel ineffective and who have lacked appropriate control and influence in their lives can behave in ways that trigger difficult feelings and painful associations in their caregivers, making it harder for them to work towards these goals. Children who are highly anxious about separation, for instance, may transfer their anxiety, making it hard for worried caregivers to spot situations in which the child might take some small steps towards greater independence. Other children are excessively challenging and strive to gain the upper hand, to be in charge of every situation. This very power-ful behaviour can make some caregivers feel out of control and overwhelmed by the child. Far from thinking, 'I must help this child feel more effective', there is the feeling, 'He is too powerful already!' For others the child's powerful behaviour triggers desperate attempts to regain control, resulting in battles that cannot be won and an escalation of conflict between caregiver and child.

In some cases, therefore, caregivers may need help in taking a step back and thinking: *how is this child affecting my sense of effectiveness and competence?* Understanding oneself and the extent to which one needs to be in control or is finding it hard to take control can be an important first step in co-operative caregiving. Discussion with an experienced and trusted professional can help the caregiver to think through his or her own earlier experiences, both of feeling effective and also of feeling powerless and unable to take control of a situation. Reflection of this nature can help the caregiver to think both about why the child is having a particular personal impact and how this might be managed. Shared thinking about the child's earlier experiences of caregiving and the ways in which issues of autonomy and control might have been handled with the child in the past can also be helpful for the caregiver. Such reflection and discussion can provide clues to the origins of children's over-compliant or controlling behaviours and indicators of the sort of messages and experiences that might begin to change these patterns. Making sense of the child's difficult behaviours in this way increases the caregiver's sense of effectiveness and competence as a parent and reduces the sense of being engaged in a personal battle. This leads to a stronger position from which to address the question: *how can I help this child to feel more effective and competent?* The caregiver is better able to take a step back, pause for thought and then think in terms of forming a co-operative partnership with the child in order to achieve their shared and separate goals.

For foster carers and adopters who are offering co-operative caregiving, therefore, there are two important areas of additional parenting activity. The first is to help children to learn that it can be safe and rewarding to act autonomously. To achieve this, caregivers will need to actively structure an environment which provides opportunities for their children to feel genuinely effective and competent. This may require extra support for children who feel helpless and afraid to take the risk of acting on their world. Or it may involve helping children to relinquish some of their desires to be over-controlling of people and events, while at the same time enabling them to feel effective in safe and appropriate ways. At all times, sensitive caregivers must be mindful of the delicate balance between facilitating appropriate dependency and promoting appropriate independence. Many fostered and adopted children still need to learn earlier lessons of trust and dependency. They need additional nurture and protection, often pitched at a level beneath their chronological age. However, they also have to learn self-efficacy and, in particular, to function and fit in at school, with their peers and in social settings outside the family. This will require age-appropriate levels of independence and self-reliance. For caregivers, an awareness of this inherent tension is vital and with it, a flexibility of approach which can allow older children and teenagers to have their baby or toddler needs met in ways that are both acceptable and beneficial to them, promoting rather than limiting the striving for autonomy.

The second task for caregivers is to help children to experience co-operative relationships in which each player contributes to the other's goals: fun can be shared, reasonable limits are set and comfortable compromises can be reached when necessary. When children have previously experienced co-operative caregiving, the principles of compromise will be familiar to them, but the particular nuances of negotiation in *this* family and in *this* relationship will be different and caregivers need to be explicit in helping children to understand family and personal norms. In many cases, however, children have experienced very little in the way of co-operative relationships from an early age and their carers must fill in the gaps in their experience, gradually building the necessary skills and helping the child to understand the principles and benefits of negotiation and compromise.

Caregivers will need enhanced skills to help children who carry deep-seated beliefs and expectations of themselves and adults that are at odds with the notions of compromise or alliance. The caregiver cannot simply impose a new set of beliefs into the child's mind – working models will only change gradually and through different experiences. The way forward is to provide alternative possible experiences and ideas (in this family, you can be influential, you do not have to be in control in order to be safe and so on) and then help the child to explore and reflect on them. Over time, the child will come to understand that he *can make things happen,* but at the same time, his influence will be kept *within safe limits* by caregiving adults. He will gain a sense that he can *compromise,* that he will not lose everything by relinquishing a little ground in a disagreement and that adults are also willing to relinquish ground for his benefit. Reflection on this process will help him to see that working together in this way has enabled him to achieve his goals as well as experiencing the rewards of closer relationships. The caregiver must bear in mind that the child will need to have a developing sense of a secure base through sensitive availability and appropriate scaffolding before he can feel safe enough to explore these alternative possibilities. Only when the foundations of trust are in place will he be able to take the risk of thinking and behaving differently. From this point, the child's mind is likely to be more flexible and receptive and the sensitive caregiver can begin to help him to reflect and absorb new ideas about himself and others.

This chapter explores ways in which sensitive caregivers can promote co-operation and help children of different ages to feel effective and competent.

Infancy (birth–18 months)

Young babies entering the care system may have lacked opportunities to learn that their *own actions* can and will be effective in achieving their goals. It may not be clear to them, for instance, that a certain movement will activate a toy, a particular gesture or vocalisation will produce a desired response, or up-stretched arms will achieve a cuddle. Even if babies have experienced some consistent care and started to feel effective in previous relationships, their new caregivers will not be picking up and responding to their signals in quite the same way and previous expectations will no longer hold good.

Foster carers and adopters, therefore, must help their babies to gain or regain a sense that they can be influential players in the caregiving relationship and that they can affect their surroundings and achieve a desired outcome. Caregivers who are intent on establishing or rebuilding this sense of effectiveness will be alert to opportunities to do this as part of a baby's daily routines. Tuning in to an infant's suck–pause–suck timing during feeding not only signals availability, but also offers the child a comfortable sense of influence over the timing of his feed. In supporting exploration, toys may be provided that enable the baby to feel competent and successful and care taken to avoid those that result in failure or frustration. Crucially, however, the caregiver will allow the baby to explore a toy in his own way so that he comes to realise, for instance, that the satisfying sound it makes is contingent on him shaking it. It is a much more powerful lesson and experience if the baby discovers the connection between shaking the rattle and getting the noise himself, rather than having it pointed out to him by an enthusiastic caregiver. The surprising new discovery can then be acknowledged and celebrated with the child.

A living environment where hazards are minimised and there are no forbidden items will offer a mobile baby freedom to explore safely and comfortably and with minimal interference. There might be additional emphasis on encouraging the baby to make choices – using everyday opportunities such as which yoghurt is preferred for lunch, which toy to play with next or which book or activity to share – all can build a sense, for the infant, that she can make things happen and that it is safe and rewarding to do so. Physical evidence in the form of first paintings and hand and foot prints can be exhibited in the kitchen for general admiration. In these contexts, self-esteem and self-efficacy are closely linked and complementary, but are different in the developmental benefits they bring to the infant's thinking and behaviour.

Building a co-operative relationship starts with positive experiences. So, for example, simple turn-taking games in which the caregiver and baby mirror each other's facial expressions, babbling or hand movements are often sources of shared joy and excitement – and if the caregiver takes care to follow the baby's lead through the game and also where possible allow the baby to decide when the game should finish, there are messages to the infant that she can be effective and influential. Where the adult has to end the game to start a bath routine or attend to another child, notice is given to the baby, 'Just one more time!'. Basic routines such as feeding, bathing and nappy changing can be seen as opportunities to share fun and relax together as well as a process of overcoming a challenge together.

Such enriched experiences of practical care may be new to older as well as younger infants and are so important and therapeutic that they are worth a good deal of focused attention and time. Where more fragile babies are unsettled by close contact with a caregiver, the starting point of comfortable interaction may have to be very low key. A foster carer who specialised in caring for vulnerable infants, for instance, described spending time simply lying on the floor beside a baby on a play mat, speaking very softly to him and allowing him just to feel comfortable in her presence. It is very important for all babies, but for anxious babies in particular, to avoid repeatedly touching a baby's cheek, calling his name, ruffling his hair or looming into his face to get a reaction. 'Waking the baby up' to the world needs to be much more subtle, much more patient and much less intrusive.

Since even in infancy children will have to do things that are not of their choosing, or be prevented from doing things they want to do, these events too must become opportunities for learning. Babies who have just learned to crawl or walk present frequent challenges as they are often particularly intrigued by what they are not permitted to do (such as pulling the cat's tail) and the reactions of others. In the new environment of a foster or adoptive home, the normal wish to explore may lead the infant into unfamiliar dangers. Although strategies such as diversion are useful, establishing the idea of boundaries is also important. The sensitive caregiver's scaffolding commentary provides the opportunity to frame each boundary-setting event in terms of protecting the infant or the environment and can be reinforced by protective non-verbal communication, such as tone of voice, touch, facial expression and so on. For infants who have not experienced consistent limits, making boundary-setting into a game is tempting but may be confusing and counterproductive. Thus, laughing while saying for the umpteenth time, 'No, don't touch the cat!' needs to be resisted. Instead, a firm, clear statement, along with an attempt to engage whatever level of understanding and co-operation the infant can manage, will help to lay the foundation for future understanding of both boundaries and compromise.

Early childhood (18 months – 4 years)

Children in this age group are required to be increasingly independent as they progress through playgroup and nursery towards the major separation of school. Their capacity (and desire) to make their own choices and to act autonomously increases dramatically during this period and their developing skills and abilities provide plentiful opportunities for them to feel competent and effective. However, it is also a period when some degree of conflict and negotiation of boundaries is part of healthy development – even if parents do worry about the "terrible twos".

For children who enter foster care past infancy, however, earlier experiences may have interrupted this progression significantly. They may have become excessively powerful in their world or they may have been in situations where they felt fearful and powerless to change things. The task for foster carers and adopters, then, is to provide experiences in which young children can feel *appropriately* influential and in control, to promote *appropriate* choice and self-efficacy. This vital process becomes increasingly possible with the development of language and comprehension. The caregiver can help the child to reflect on the experiences of efficacy and co-operation, to put them into words and to recall them after the event. In this way, important messages can become embedded in the child's mind and be used to challenge previous experiences and expectations.

As in infancy, daily routines and events for toddlers and pre-school children can be important ways of promoting self-efficacy. A trip to the supermarket, for instance, can offer a young child the opportunity to choose from a (probably pre-selected) range of breakfast cereals and a personal choice from the selection can be made each day at home. The process of choosing can be highlighted each day and can provide the basis for the discussion and following through of other preferences and choices. Games, too, may be chosen for their potential to promote self-efficacy in a way that is playful and non-threatening. Important, here, however, is the capacity of the caregiver to tailor their approach to the particular needs and perspective of their child. Some children, such as Leah, below, may feel overwhelmed by being faced directly with even simple choices and may do better with a more indirect approach.

> *Leah (3) had recently been placed for adoption. In her new family, she seemed fearful of asserting herself and became tense when asked to make simple choices, such as which sort of ice cream she would like. Rita, her adoptive mother, was reluctant to put pressure on Leah but she noted a session at a child development unit in which a large puppet (Molly) was being used to pour water into containers and the children were instructed to call out "stop" when the containers were full. She tried a similar game with Leah on a warm day when Leah seemed relaxed and they could be in the garden. It proved very successful and Rita was delighted to see Leah giggling and shouting her commands. Afterwards, Rita was able to refer back to the game to remind Leah that she could say what she wanted to happen, 'like you did with Molly'.*

As important as the Molly game itself is the opportunity afterwards to recall the event with the child and to use it as an example of when it was fun to be assertive and effective. A photograph of the child playing the game might be placed in an "experiences book" to help with this recall and variations on the game might be used in other household situations, to reinforce the message *I can make things happen* and, in particular, *I can make good things happen*.

The process of collaboration with toddlers and pre-school children builds on the fun and pleasure there is to be had for children and caregivers in shared play, humour and learning. Fostered and adopted children in this age range are likely to have missed out on shared experiences, even the shared enjoyment of a family meal, and they may have a great deal to learn and catch up on. This age period is therefore a great opportunity to actively engage the child in a wide range of activities which adults and older children will enjoy for their own sake and also enjoy for the pleasure of spending time with the child. This not only builds self-esteem, as discussed in the previous chapter, but provides numerous opportunities for self-efficacy and co-operation. There is nothing young children enjoy more than both influencing adult behaviour (making them run for a ball) and making adults laugh (with physical or verbal jokes). Although attachment theory is sometimes accused of undervaluing the role of humour, shared jokes are a key part of the synchrony and attunement that bring young children close to other people and involve them in rewarding relationships in which they can be active and effective participants. This provides the potential for warm, collaborative memories and feelings, a basis from which the inevitable conflicts between child and caregiver can be more positively managed.

It is because children in this age group become more active and assertive in seeking their own goals, that caregivers are more frequently and actively required to moderate or change them. In doing so, caregivers will also moderate and change some of their own plans, thus demonstrating to the child the skills and benefits of negotiation. Bowlby (1982, p. 355) summarises this process:

> *In the case of attachment demands, it is evident that during the course of an ordinary day the mother of a two-year-old is likely many times to attempt to change the set-goals of his behaviour. In a complementary fashion a child is intermittently striving to change his mother's behaviour and her proximity to him, and in doing so is almost certain to adopt some, at least, of the methods she herself employs. Therein lies both the hope and the warning.*

For adopters and foster carers, then, the hope lies in modelling for the child a range of constructive skills and strategies aimed at achieving the child's co-operation when there is a clash of wills or a change of activity is required. The warning is that if, for example, caregivers rely on raised voices or rigid discipline styles, then children may also raise their voices and resist rigidly.

It is normal, for example, for a young child to protest when a game has to be ended in order to meet an older sibling from school. Sensitive caregivers will have a range of tactics to deal with such a situation in a way that achieves the parental goal (sibling met on time) without a harsh or abrupt imposition of the adult's will on the child. These might include giving prior warning and helping to wind up the game, talking about how the sibling might feel if he was not met, reminding the child of something positive that will happen on the way, acknowledging that it is a shame, agreeing to resume the game on return and so on. Of importance here, though, is the confidence of the caregiver that the game will stop and the little party will set off in good time to the school. Thus the underlying message is a matter of fact, firm but respectful, 'We are going to the school to meet your brother and let's together find ways of making it a positive experience for us all', rather than a more tentative, 'Please can we go to get your brother from school?', which encourages the child to reverse roles and make the decision. This clarity of the parental goal is important, but so also is respecting the child and recognising how best to manage the achievement of compromises with the child's goals.

Young children who are unfamiliar with co-operative approaches may have been accustomed to forceful interruption or restraint and have no experience of a mutually satisfying partnership in which their own needs and those of the caregiver can both be acknowledged and accommodated. They may resist alliance formation, be constantly adversarial and resistant to diversionary or explanatory and co-operative techniques. The risk is that the need to keep a child safe and the apparent impossibility of forming a productive partnership results in new caregivers also becoming increasingly directive and allowing few opportunities for choice and autonomy. The paradox here, however, is that the more opportunities the child has to feel effective and influential, the more likely he will be to relinquish some of that influence when required to do so. The skill for foster carers and adopters is in seeking ways of structuring and organising an environment in which minimum interference is necessary and the child can take the lead safely. From such experiences, more co-operative relationships are likely to develop.

Myra, an experienced foster mother, described the behaviour of three-year-old George, who came to her having been shut in a bedroom or restrained in a push chair for up to 24 hours at a time.

He was just wild, he just ran everywhere, he just didn't seem to have any understanding of his world at all, he didn't engage with it or with anyone, he just ran around madly.

Although it was winter time, Myra discovered that the garden was one area in which George could explore safely and in which he could become more engaged with activities and relationships. He would become absorbed in tipping water, digging, collecting stones, etc. Sensing an opening for relationship building, Myra seized this opportunity, dressed him warmly and joined him in the garden, at first allowing him to take the lead and then working towards a more co-operative experience.

He would potter about, looking at stuff and I would follow him sometimes and talk occasionally and he would stop and he'd look at a bug, or whatever it was he'd found. I pretty much let him lead I think, but sometimes I'd draw his attention to things.

This was a lengthy and gradual process and Myra showed remarkable per-severance and commitment to George, spending lengthy periods outside during the winter months and also temporarily sacrificing her own plans for George's benefit.

Yes, he pulled everything out and I just decided that I wasn't going to have a garden that year and I didn't do any planting in the spring, I just thought – I can have a garden next year.

However, after several months, the results were noticeable. George started to engage with his foster mother in other activities such as table play. He also acquired some language which enhanced his self-efficacy.

So once he could say a few things, he was much more powerful because he could actually get me to do what he wanted me to and that was good for him.

Language comprehension also meant that he could benefit from Myra's commentary on what they were both thinking, about each other and about the various joint tasks they were engaged in. But George also became much more co-operative and compliant when limits were set, for example, around staying at the table during mealtimes.

Attachment theory has most to offer in sustaining foster carers and adopters in a belief in the power of simple and ordinary everyday experiences to change minds and shape behaviour and relationships In this example, giving positive choices, supporting exploration, being co-operative and negotiating within boundaries were all significant. It was very important to start where the child was most comfortable – which was in the freedom of the sensory world, where the caregiver was allowed to join him, and where co-operation eventually shifted to the world of mental representations. Myra helped George to see himself as effective and influential and herself as a person with whom he could enjoy the benefits of co-operation. He gradually came to transfer this experience into other settings.

Middle childhood (5–10 years)

Middle childhood provides increasing opportunities for children to feel competent and effective. Managing the separation and independence of school, learning new skills, taking small responsibilities at home and having preferences respected all contribute to a child's sense that he is an active player in the world and that he can have appropriate levels of influence and choice. Feelings of competence may be promoted by giving children small tasks and responsibilities around the house, such as caring for a pet, laying the table or making cakes for tea. Choices may become more varied and significant for this age group, who are developing a sense of self, and there are many opportunities, such as choosing a favourite TV or film character for a bed cover or lunch box.

Parenting children in this age group also offers many opportunities for enjoyable joint activity. Adopters and foster carers report how this can range from the fun of kicking a football around together to working together to build models or prepare meals or going shopping and having fish and chips together afterwards. When the pleasures and benefits of co-operation have been demonstrated in this way, there is a firmer basis from which to promote negotiation and compromise.

Promoting choice and self-efficacy is an area in which many foster carers and adopters find that they must adjust their approaches and expectations towards those that would be appropriate for a younger age group. Opportunities for making choices and decisions may have been limited in the past or unmet dependency needs may lead children to feel overwhelmed by the level of autonomy and responsibility that their peers may enjoy. Sensitive adjustments are needed here, in which the caregiver finds a level of effectiveness that is comfortable for the individual child. In this way, the child can feel the pleasure of successful independence appropriate for their age, for example, in the school setting, while still retaining a strong sense that the secure base is available for nurture and dependence.

Foster carers and adopters of children with disabilities are often acutely aware of the frustrations that their children feel as a result of their physical and cognitive limitations. It is particularly important, therefore, that children in this group are helped to feel as influential and effective as possible. Even children with very high dependency needs can be given opportunities for independent choice, but their carers will need to pay attention to the minutiae of their behaviour in order to identify these areas of potential and to support them.

Carers of four children with severe disabilities were interviewed as part of a research project following the progress of long-term fostered children (Beek and Schofield, 2004c). All of these carers were quick to spot opportunities for even the smallest steps of autonomy and choice, as illustrated by Frances and her foster daughter, Evie (9). Frances had gone to great lengths and expense to find touch toys that Evie could operate herself, to produce displays of sound, colour and light. Frances was delighted to have found a means of enabling Evie to act on her environment in this way.

Other carers in the study mentioned the child being encouraged to hold on to the ropes of a swing, rather than having to use the "baby" seat; children floating freely in the swimming pool; occasionally going round to the next door neighbour's to play after school; or simply being able to watch a video on their own. These were all seen as beneficial experiences which contributed to reduced frustration and general calming. Although independence was not a realistic goal for these children, it was nevertheless important for them to feel that they could achieve things for themselves and rely, even momentarily, on their own resources.

Michaela (aged 10) could take the lead when her foster father took her for walks around their housing estate, choose a correct route and find their way home. Brian and Petra were delighted with these small signs of greater autonomy in Michaela and they felt that an enhanced sense of self-efficacy had contributed significantly to the reduction of her frustration and the general calming of her behaviour.

Most carers of children with or without disabilities agreed that boundaries are a vital element in helping children to feel safe and contained. The following foster mother summarises this view:

I think if children have boundaries they know where they stand. If you have a child that has no boundaries, they're always pushing and pushing and I don't think they feel loved, whereas if you have a boundary and that child will always push it, but they know they can't go past it and they feel safe. I think a child feels safe when it has boundaries.

For primary school-aged children, as for younger age groups, caregivers must set limits around what is safe and acceptable behaviour. Children who are struggling for control, however, may be especially resistant to the normal boundaries that are required in family life, appearing threatened and even panicked by parental requests or necessary routines. Sharad and Jocelyn's adopted son, Miles (8), for instance, was very controlling and oppositional. He seemed to perceive even a friendly request to do a minor task as inherently threatening and some days there were constant confrontations. Sharad and Jocelyn attended parenting sessions specifically geared to the needs of adopters and learned three simple techniques which helped Miles firstly to build trust in his new parents and then to retain a sense of effectiveness when parenting interventions were required. The first principle was to reduce to a minimum the number of things to take issue over, thus reducing tension all round and leaving space for the "good things" – simple, pleasurable, shared activities that helped Miles to learn that it could be safe and enjoyable to be a child in this family. The second approach was to use games and play which would allow Miles both to take the lead and to allow others to take the lead. These provided opportunities to learn that both roles could be experienced within safe limits. For example, play acting scenarios in which all family members took it in turns to be the "king" and the "subjects" was a popular game for a time. Thirdly, Sharad and Jocelyn found it helpful to avoid instructions to do things wherever possible. Instead, they tried to take an approach that offered Miles a sense of choice in the matter, along with the motivator of a reward for positive response.

> We try, actually, never to ask or tell him to do anything. It's a matter of phrasing it differently really, so that you are not triggering his feelings of threat. So, instead of saying 'Please wash your hands before you have a sandwich' we might just say 'Would you like to come and have a sandwich after you've washed your hands?'

Although none of the techniques were effective all the time, each of them could be helpful in avoiding battles with Miles and helping him to feel effective while still achieving necessary parenting goals.

Adolescence (11–18 years)

Adolescence is a time when an increasing range of choices becomes available outside the family and beyond parental control. At the same time, as teenagers move towards greater independence from the secure base, they are increasingly involved in relationships with peers and other adults which require skills of *negotiation* and an acceptance of *compromise* if they are to be successful. But living together in families also requires ongoing degrees of co-operation in order to achieve some harmony, as teenagers develop their preferences in music, food, clothes, lifestyle and so on. Although freedom increases, firm boundaries for behaviour, such as expectations for family and school life, expected times to return home and so on, continue to be necessary and protective for young people. Although some points of disagreement, confrontation and conflict are inevitable, forming a co-operative alliance and working towards negotiated outcomes within firm but realistic boundaries will be the best bet in terms of preparing a teenager for adult life and adult relationships.

Not surprisingly, there are often special issues around separation for adopted and fostered adolescents. Those placed recently in their new families may only just have begun to experience safe dependency and be reluctant to move away from a recently acquired secure base. Some may find that difficult feelings and memories from their early years are triggered by the pressures both of closeness and of approaching separation. The chaotic behaviour that can ensue is all the more alarming as young people become older, physically stronger and more able to challenge or simply ignore the limits that are set around them.

As for earlier stages of development, shared activities and opportunities to relax and enjoy time together set the scene for negotiation and conflict resolution. Opportunities may be more limited for this age group, suggestions that involve "family togetherness" may be met with resistance or activities planned to be enjoyable may unexpectedly become conflict situations. It is important to take the young person's lead rather than impose unwanted activity, but it is also important for the caregiver to give a clear message that a shared activity would be welcomed and valued, since low self-esteem and anxiety can drive some young people to deny themselves good experiences. Such is the therapeutic value, however, of any activity that provides mutual enjoyment and a harmonious experience for caregiver and young person that it is worth persisting and building on the smallest of opportunities to achieve this goal. A game of pool, watching a TV programme together, painting nails or drying hair – all can build or restore a sense that co-operation can be safe and enjoyable in this family.

Many carers and adopters of adolescents wish to offer increasing levels of autonomy and independence, but find that their young person has still to fill in the gaps or simply to feel the comfort of nurture and dependency usually associated with an earlier stage of development. In these situations, there is skill in finding approaches that help the young person to experience age-appropriate independence while at the same time having their younger child's needs met. Bedrooms may be seen as both symbols of autonomy and of dependency. They are the arenas in which young people can express their individuality and yet they can also be safe havens for comfort and regression. Marie's adoptive mother, Helen, succinctly captured this dual function as she described Marie's new attic bedroom.

> *We've given her the whole attic to herself. Her room is right up on the top floor, it's a terrible mess. She doesn't take anybody up there, but up there it's her own, like, den and she's got her music and her teenage things but she can also play act that she's a little girl and do the dolly things and nobody's minding, you know.*

Helen had planned and discussed the '"teenage" aspect of the new room with Marie (14) and Marie had chosen the décor accordingly. However, Helen had also acknowledged with Marie that everyone sometimes needs a space in which they can do whatever they like without interference and she had ensured that Marie's toys, games and dolls were accommodated in the room. This combination of recognising Marie's underlying needs while at the same time respecting her stage of development gave Marie powerful messages of acceptance and understanding, as well as a manageable sense of effectiveness and autonomy.

Young people may also need additional support to enable them to be appropriately influential and effective in the more independent relationships that they start to form outside the family. They may be drawn to relationships that replicate earlier experiences of powerlessness and caregivers often need to teach and model strategies for self-assertiveness. Equipping a young person with some realistic choices about what he might do or say in difficult situations, or perhaps using techniques such as role playing a potentially difficult telephone conversation or an encounter with a teacher, can reduce anxiety and make it less likely that he will become confrontational or try to avoid the problem altogether.

There may be situations when advice and guidance are not enough and teenagers need their caregivers to actively demonstrate to them how to be appropriately effective and assertive. Sensitive caregivers are able to judge when it is appropriate to intervene and then to help the young person to reflect on the intervention and think of it in terms of a model which they might use for themselves at another time.

Case example – Emma

Sheila found that Emma (16) was feeling harassed by her boyfriend. He was repeatedly turning up at the house unannounced and asking her to come outside to see him. Sheila noted that Emma did as her boyfriend asked, but afterwards appeared distressed and was unable to settle back into what she had been doing. Sheila pointed out this sequence of events to Emma, who said that she did not know how to deal with her boyfriend's insistence. Sheila proposed that next time he came to the door, she would answer it herself and tell him politely that this was unacceptable and that in future, Emma would let him know when it was convenient for him to come. Emma readily agreed to this and was pleased to have help in regaining control of the situation in this way. Sheila and Emma were then able to talk about different situations in which Emma felt unable to assert herself and think together about how to handle them, with the goal that Emma could take the first step herself next time.

Sensitive caregivers have the capacity to stay in touch with the young person's goals and agenda even if they are very different from those of themselves or other family members. This approach is likely to lead to shared endeavour and an alliance with the young person, rather than a clash of wills and a sense of conflict. Additionally, with this age group, it becomes possible to be more explicit about the need for both parties in a conflict to relinquish some of their goals and ideas in order to achieve a positive outcome. Miriam, for instance, was always willing to provide Sherri, her teenage daughter, with lifts into town, but Sherri liked to remain in control and she would ask for a lift and then refuse to say what time she would like to go. Miriam explained to Sherri that she knew it was hard for her to be specific but she needed to plan her day too. She then gave Sherri the choice of a lift at any time between two fixed points in the day. Sometimes Sherri chose not to go at all, rather than to co-operate in this way, but at other times, she chose a time within the limits. Miriam then took care to show her appreciation and to ensure that the time spent in the car was relaxed and enjoyable.

The following story provides a clear example of negotiation within a boundary, in which vital messages are conveyed to the child and his autonomy is promoted throughout. It highlights many common issues and dilemmas for foster carers who are seeking both to protect their teenage children from harm and also to promote their sociable interests and autonomy. Greg's foster mother, Pam, banned him from using his scooter for three days as a neighbour had reported that he was using it irresponsibly on the road. Greg (14) had an angry outburst at this, but accepted the restriction. The following day, he came and apologised for his temper. That evening he was going to an activity where having his scooter was part of the fun. Pam described her response:

And I explained why we made the rules, because we care about him and that we definitely don't want him to have another bad accident as he'd had before. But then I sort of said to him, 'Well, as you've been man enough to come and admit that you were wrong with tantrums and that you do understand that we made the rule because we care about you, you can use the scooter this evening because you've come to me and we've discussed it'. So I let him have it. That was my way of, I suppose, being friendly to him and also being fair, because I didn't want to be the big taskmaster.

Pam recognised the genuine nature of Greg's apology and responded initially by reinforcing the message of caring about him and then by reinforcing her respect for his autonomy in the phrase 'because you've been man enough to apologise'. She repeated the "rules" and because she felt that he had absorbed the important messages from the incident, and she wanted to encourage him to face up to things through talking, as he had done on this occasion, rather than acting out, she was happy to compromise and allow him to use the scooter again. She saw that it was more important for him to have the autonomy of his scooter (safely) and to benefit from being with his peer group, than for her to win a battle over the punishment. For a young man of 14 years who was immature, but needed to learn to become both more independent and more co-operative, this seemed entirely appropriate.

From this brief incident, Greg would have received many vital messages. His foster mother made it clear that his safety was paramount because he was loved and valued, therefore he is a lovable person, worthy of care and protection. His apology indicated that he felt guilty for upsetting the person who cared about him – but also that he could contain his guilt and take action to put things right. The ensuing discussion allowed Pam to convey her thoughts to Greg and he was receptive to them. Sensing this, Pam felt able to negotiate the use of the scooter. From this attuned exchange, there was a positive outcome for both parties. Greg felt loved, understood and autonomous and Pam felt herself to be a good parent – "fair" and "friendly".

Safe boundaries remain important for adolescents, but the setting of limits, especially at the older end of this age group, becomes more a question of providing clear and honest feedback to a young person, both about the consequences of their actions and about the position of the carers. As with younger age groups, but often in more risky situations, making mistakes and being able to find the way back from or to repair damage to the self, to others and to relationships is of central importance in promoting young people's capacity to manage their freedom of choice. The principle of avoiding the message that any act is somehow unforgivable or any situation is irretrievable is vital in calming anxiety and preventing young people spiralling out of control and even out of the family. Involvement in aggression, experimenting with drugs, getting pregnant – these are some of the testing behaviours that adolescents may appear to have "chosen", but may still need help to extricate themselves from or manage the consequences. Young people will only accept help – or want to be extricated from trouble – if they can believe that they are not hopeless or helpless and that at least one person cares enough about them to understand and support them. This process thus builds on all three previous parenting dimensions – availability, sensitivity and acceptance.

Conclusion

Caregiving that promotes choice and autonomy and allows for a degree of negotiation within firm boundaries can help children and young people of all ages to feel more effective, to make positive choices and, when necessary, to compromise and accommodate the goals of others. These important capacities and skills will enable them to assert appropriate control and influence in their close relationships and also in the wider circles of school, peer group and, eventually, work and independent living.

Summary points

- From soon after birth, sensitive parents view their babies as separate individuals who have free will and valid thoughts, feelings and intentions of their own. They react promptly and predictably to the infant's signals of need and the infant learns that it is his own smile, cry, action or noise that can bring about a response that meets his need. In this way, he begins to feel effective and influential.

- Because they are respectful of the infant as a separate individual, parents will tend to follow her lead and avoid situations in which they interfere abruptly or impose their will on hers. Beyond infancy, sensitive parents continue to enjoy and value their child's autonomy and aim for a co-operative alliance wherever possible, within the safe boundaries provided by the responsible parent.

- Fostered and adopted children are often unfamiliar with the satisfying sense of effectiveness and the benefits of compromise that result from co-operative parenting. They may have little sense of themselves as competent individuals, or of adults as co-operative partners. Some children may find it hard to act with any degree of autonomy or be unable to make choices or be unable to assert themselves. Other children may want excessive control and influence over adults, their peers, themselves or their environments.

- In order to provide a safe and predictable environment, caregivers must accept responsibility for their children and set firm boundaries around them. Within these boundaries, an underlying sense of the child as an individual with his or her own thoughts and feelings, which are valid and understandable in the circumstances, will help the caregiver to think in terms of working together in order to achieve their shared and separate goals.

• When children are feeling more effective, they gain a sense that they can make things happen within safe limits and show a greater capacity to co-operate and compromise.

Approaches for helping children to feel effective and be co-operative

N.B. It is important to choose only those activities that the child is likely to accept and enjoy.

- Find individual activities that the child enjoys and that produce a clear result. For example, give the child a disposable camera to use on holiday or on a day out, help him to get the photos developed and give him a small album for the results.
- Within the house and garden, minimise hazards and things that child cannot touch, and keep "out of bounds" areas secure so that the child can explore without adult "interference" when he is ready to do so.
- Suggest small tasks and responsibilities within the child's capabilities. Ensure recognition and praise when achieved. If they become an issue, do them alongside the child – a chance to show availability.
- Introduce toys where the action of the child achieves a rewarding result. For example, pushing a button, touching or shaking something.
- Make opportunities for choices. For example, allow child to choose the cereal at the supermarket, a pudding for a family meal, or what to wear for a certain activity.
- Ensure that daily routines include time to relax together and share a pleasurable activity.
- Respond promptly to child's signals for support or comfort or reassure an older child that you will respond as soon as possible. For example, 'I must quickly finish what I am doing and then I will come and help you straight away'.
- Do not try to tackle several problem areas at any one time. Set one or two priorities and work on them gradually until there are sustained signs of progress. Ensure that these are acknowledged and appreciated.
- Use co-operative language wherever possible. For example, 'Would you like to come and have a sandwich after you've washed your hands?' rather than 'Wash your hands before you eat your sandwich'.
- Find shared activities that the child enjoys, for example, baking cakes, swimming, playing card games.

- Introduce games and activities in which the child takes the lead and the adult follows, and vice versa. Respond promptly when the child has had enough. Comment clearly when you have had enough and suggest an alternative activity.
- Seek opportunities for the child to co-operate with other children – you may need to be present so that this is managed successfully.
- Help the child to identify a target that they would like to achieve, do, change, etc. Settle on one where something done now will make a difference. Discuss what the young person can do and negotiate simple, relevant and achievable steps that they can take. When agreed, draw a simple staircase and write one task in each of the bottom steps of the staircase. For example, if the target is 'go to see Manchester United play at home', steps might be – use internet to find out dates of home games this season, settle on suitable date and put on calendar, find out train times, etc. Set a time to review progress and think about further steps needed. This brings both satisfaction for the child and a sense of shared endeavour.

10 Promoting family membership – helping children to belong

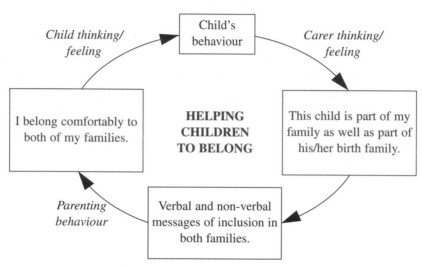

Child thinking/
feeling

Child's
behaviour

Carer thinking/
feeling

I belong comfortably to
both of my families.

**HELPING
CHILDREN
TO BELONG**

This child is part of my
family as well as part of
his/her birth family.

Parenting
behaviour

Verbal and non-verbal
messages of inclusion in
both families.

Figure 8

Family membership is conferred on children by their parents and other relatives from the moment of birth and is a vital strand of healthy emotional and psychosocial development (see Figure 8). Initiation into the family culture begins from an early age and is affirmed by the extended family and wider community. Family membership offers feelings of solidarity, unconditional acceptance and shared identity, often reinforced by shared jokes, activities and family rituals around mealtimes or celebrations. Families establish certain mutual rights, duties and responsibilities which operate between parents and children, brothers and sisters and wider family members, but families also provide a set of expectations, norms and values for living in society (Allan, 1996).

Growing children have a strong sense of themselves as members of a family group and, as diverse family patterns become more common, this can be extended to several households. Moreover, individuals may consider themselves to be members of family groups to which they are not connected by biological or legal ties, provided there is a mutual commitment to inclusion. Family membership becomes an inherent part of a person's identity, and it is recognised and affirmed

248

by individuals and groups outside the family. In a family-based society, a child who has no close family relationships will carry feelings of psychological and social dislocation. In contrast, the certainty of unconditional family membership can provide anchorage and the reassurance of practical and emotional support throughout life, acting as a psychosocial secure base for exploration and personal development.

What children bring to their placements

Each child entering foster care or being placed for adoption will bring a unique set of experiences of family life and each of these experiences will have shaped their expectations of the new family and their sense of themselves as a family member. It is important to remember that, for most children, there will have been good times as well as difficult ones, positive memories as well as sad or frightening ones. There may also have been several different families or a lengthy period in a loved and trusted foster family. For all children, the challenges of adapting to a new family life are enormous and, depending on their age and understanding, all will be grappling with different degrees of loss (of people, places, pets and friends), uncertainty (How long will I stay? Do they really want me?) and anxiety (Will I be safe? Will I fit in?). The simple tasks of getting up in the morning and having breakfast in an unfamiliar setting can be mountains to climb for a child and it is hard to overestimate the potential stresses and strains that are involved in making the move into a new family.

Many fostered and adopted children have strong feelings of loyalty and connectedness to their birth families. It is important for social workers, foster carers and adopters to bear in mind the difference between these feelings and the quality of attachment relationships. It is not unreasonable, and is in fact to be expected, for children to feel an ongoing sense of *belonging* to a birth family where they have *insecure* attachments and in which it would not be safe to grow up because of the risk of abuse or neglect.

Similarly, children can be offered and begin to accept inclusion and full membership of a long-term foster or adoptive family *before* their emotional responses and attachment relationships are secure. For some children, feeling part of a safe foster or adoptive family and taking on their collaborative norms and prosocial values may be easier to accept and build on than letting new parents come emotionally close. This may feel disappointing for caregivers who yearn to provide and experience emotional closeness with their children. Yet a sense of family belonging accompanied by an ability to fit into society are benefits that must not be underestimated and when taken into adult life are often experienced as a key source of strength, support and resilience (Schofield, 2003).

Tasks for foster carers and adopters

For foster carers and adopters, the primary task is to provide a model of family life that is emotionally warm, physically comfortable, accepting, supportive of its members and which sets clear but reasonable expectations for their shared living environment. The variations on this model are enormous and span the full range of culture, class, language, social norms and religious practice. What is important in all cases, however, is the capacity of the foster or adoptive family system to absorb new members, often children whose backgrounds and experiences are very different to their own, and to show what Brodzinsky (2005) has termed "communicative openness", the capacity to be thoughtful, reflective and open towards the child and the birth family.

There must be physical and emotional space for the new child in the family and consideration must be given to the needs of all family members before another child can be included. When the new child has been taken in to the family, existing children may need additional time and support to help them to cope with their changed position and the additional pressures that the fostered or adopted child may create. Extended family members too need to be engaged and need to understand the child and the role they can play in the child's life, as well as in supporting other members of the family who care for and live with the child. Caregivers, therefore, must be alert to the needs of the whole family system if they are to create an environment in which the fostered or adopted child can feel truly welcomed and included.

If caregiving families are to offer a sense of family membership to children and young people who are not related to them by blood, the family boundary must have a degree of permeability and flexibility. Both fostered and adopted children will need to pass in and out of the family boundary at times. This might range from physical transitions to and from the birth family, to occasional emotional transitions as children and young people explore their birth family history. The family script must allow for non-relatives to be regarded as "family", whilst at the same time recognising and accepting the varying significance of birth family membership for each child.

In her study of adolescent fostering, Downes (1992) describes the limitations of foster families where boundaries are fixed and impenetrable, suggesting that such families may perceive the outside world as unfriendly or even hostile. The "script" in such a family is likely to result in a rather closed and isolated system, proud, perhaps, of its strong identity, but reluctant to accept difference and to enable a child to manage a comfortable sense of belonging to more than one family. In contrast, a family with permeable boundaries is likely to have flexible attitudes and may be involved with a variety of other systems and groups – social and community groups, friends, neighbours and extended family. Although retaining a sense of safety and support within the immediate family, family members will feel at ease in moving in and out of the family boundary, open to different ideas and ways of life and receptive to thinking about different family cultures. The sense that *this child is part of my family as well as part of his or her birth family* can thus be more readily managed within the family group.

The various expectations of family life that children bring into their placements might be likened to "internal working models" and a challenge for sensitive caregivers is to use their reflective skills to think about the meaning of family and family membership from the child's point of view. At the same time, caregivers will need to think carefully about their own family's assumptions, norms and culture and how these might be perceived by a child who has no prior knowledge of them. The capacity to take these dual perspectives, both of what the child is bringing in terms of expectations of family life and of how the child is perceiving the new family, requires great skill and empathy on the part of the caregiver. It is here that we see a clear link to attachment theory, since sensitive foster carers and adopters provide a secure family base and also have the capacity to be reflective in relation to both their own and the child's thoughts and feelings about family membership. The combination of these two elements can enhance the child's felt security – 'I am safe and secure in this family, but I can also think and talk about how it feels to be a member of another family'. The supporting social worker may play a helpful role in providing information about the child's previous experiences of family life, assisting caregivers in taking the child's perspective in relation to the past and discussing ways of conveying messages of inclusion in the new family that are comfortable for this particular child to manage.

The balance between the two family memberships, their different meanings and roles in the child's life, will vary according to the nature of the *plan* for the child and the *quality* of relationships in both the birth family and the foster or adoptive family. In respite care arrangements, for instance, the primary source of family membership will remain in the birth family, with the respite family acknowledging and supporting this, but nevertheless including the child fully in their family culture and activities during their stay. Task-centred placements for assessment, which may be brief or lengthy, involve a delicate balance of inclusion in both families until and even after the plan is formed. Foster children, even in short placements, very much value being treated the same as carers' birth, adopted or long-term fostered children, but it may also be important for them to be included in birth family events, where their role as son or daughter, brother or sister, grandson or granddaughter is recognised and reinforced. Bridge foster carers in particular have a complex role. They must help the child to grieve the loss of the birth family, but understand that birth family membership will continue in some form; promote inclusion in the foster family during the placement but, at the same time, prepare the child psychologically for membership of a new family. At the other end of the continuum, long-term fostering and adoption confer full membership of the new family, with support provided into adulthood. However, long-term fostered and adopted children need also to achieve a sense of belonging to their birth families, at a level that feels compatible with their particular circumstances, wishes and feelings.

A further important element of helping children to be comfortable in their dual family memberships is the recognition that this is an *ongoing* process, the significance and meaning of which will be unique to the individual and will vary over time. The issue will surface at intervals in children's minds as different memories are triggered or as they come across references to families and family relationships in books, television or conversation. Children vary in the intensity of their responses to these family scenarios played out in front of them and there may be long periods, especially in permanent placements, when they will not question their place in the foster or adoptive family and birth family membership may not be a pressing concern for them. But for all children and young people, the management of dual family membership is a dynamic process which changes and develops over time, requiring caregivers to be alert to opportunities to share and facilitate that process, without being intrusive. Chapter 14 on contact will look in more detail at how contact can contribute positively to this process if it is appropriate, well-planned and supported. But it is important to remember that *birth family membership is dealt with as much in the interactions and communications within the foster or adoptive family as in ongoing interactions with birth family members themselves.*

Fostered and adopted children cover the full range of ages, personalities, physical and emotional needs and background histories. Nevertheless, they are all, to a greater or lesser extent, members of two very distinct and often very different families. This chapter explores some ways in which caregivers can provide children with *verbal and non-verbal messages of inclusion* that help them to feel a comfortable sense of belonging to both.

Infancy (birth – 18 months)

At this pre-verbal stage, messages of inclusion in the foster or adoptive family are largely symbolic, but they are no less important for that. In Mary Dozier's research on fostering infants (Dozier *et al*, 2005), she emphasises the importance of what she terms "*commitment*". This includes physical and emotional availability, but also suggests the need to see foster care as a full parenting role, rather than as an impersonal "job" of meeting the child's physical needs. This notion of commitment may seem to exclude the birth parents and be inappropriate in assessment or bridge placements, but this is far from the case. Clarity about the plan is important, but foster carers and adoptive parents who are wholeheartedly "parental" in their care for the child are often particularly good at facilitating relationships with birth families or moving children to new placements. Both tasks require sensitivity or empathy around loss, mixed feelings and building relationships and sensitive caregivers are likely to be able to apply their skills and capacities in either situation (Beek and Schofield, 2004a; Neil, 2004).

Promoting foster or adoptive family membership for young babies, therefore, will involve keeping the infant in the heart of family life: including him in the full range of family events, activities, fun, relationships, hierarchies and turn taking. In one sense, the child's experience will simply be of both familiar and novel people and events to be stored in the memory, but at a deeper level, this sort of inclusion will be giving the child a sense of security, a range of possible and varied relationships, diverse sources of self-esteem, an enjoyment of exploration and a model of family life, all of which form a foundation for the future. Conceptualising family membership in this way encourages caregivers to draw on their deep-rooted sense of what parenting and family are about and what brought them into fostering or adoption. The message is one of *investment* in the child, so that this child, this family and, in bridge placements, a future family, will reap the benefits of their purposeful and loving care.

In this age range, a continuing sense of belonging to the birth family is likely to be offered symbolically and may include photographs of birth family members, toys, bedding or equipment from home, depending on the placement plan and what is felt to be helpful to each child. Face-to-face contact has an important part to play in most care plans in foster care, but for all babies, a degree of continuity is important and can be supported by concrete reminders of the continuing existence of their families of origin.

For all children, including this pre-verbal age group, helping to manage two families is best understood in terms of a) enabling the child to feel comfortable in both and b) managing any points of contact between families in ways that are free of stress and anxiety for the child. For infants, this may be around managing the event of contact itself, but how caregivers think about, feel about, talk about, anticipate or review birth family contact will also give positive or negative messages to the child in relation to birth family members. Even the caregivers' tone of voice in talking about birth family members and contact will act as a form of *social referencing* for the infant, signalling whether to treat birth family members as a source of pleasure or anxiety. Very young children must not be "fought over" and confident foster carers and adopters can signal their commitment and availability to the child without seeming to undermine or compete with the birth parents. If contact is a part of the plan, it is essential that caregivers are able to fulfil their role in reducing the child's anxiety about where she is safe and where she belongs (see also Chapter 14). Where placements are temporary, this may mean helping the infant to feel safe and secure in both families, perhaps supporting the birth parents to achieve this when they are visiting or caring for the child. Where placements are permanent, the priority is given to building secure attachment and family membership in the new family, while also identifying and valuing elements of birth family membership which might be helpful and productive for the child now and in the future.

Early childhood (18 months–4 years)

Children in this age group are beginning to have in their minds a set of conceptions about family life – what happens in families, the way in which family members relate to each other and what they do together. They will not, however, have a clearly developed sense that things can be done in different ways in different settings and they will assume that their previous ideas will hold good in their new environment.

Sensitive caregivers who can project themselves into the mind of a child who is unfamiliar with the family will recognise that he has no way of understanding what is normal in this setting and what might be expected of him. They must, therefore, give the child *clear messages* that he will be safe and well-cared for in this family and helped to manage within the family's way of doing things. They may provide a simple outline of forthcoming routines or events, with the child's place in them clearly defined. They will need to explain and demonstrate such important matters as who will help with bathing and dressing, who is going to enter the child's bedroom and when, and family norms about nudity, night clothes, showing affection and so on. In the simplest terms, they will need to convey to the child what he might expect from daily or regular events, such as getting up in the morning, bedtimes, mealtimes, days out or weekends. But they also need to suggest that they will try to accommodate the child's sense of what is normal and necessary – the family may like a Sunday lie in, but the child may need a bit of company, even if watching a favourite Disney video.

At the same time, caregivers will need to demonstrate in *concrete terms* that the child is welcomed and wanted as a family member, whether on a temporary or a permanent basis. The physical space – the bed, wardrobe, chair, place at the table – are all important in conveying the idea that the child has a special place in the family group. Different families choose different ways of demonstrating the inclusion of a child, often using symbols that are shared by all children in the family, such as a photograph or drawing on the wall, a mug with a special picture or the child's name on it, a special hook for their coat and so on. Where children are living with uncertainty about the future, such messages of belonging are particularly important, although caregivers will need to hold in their minds that they may return home or to a new permanent family at some stage and also to plant these seeds in the mind of the child. This is not easy, but one route for experienced foster families may be a discussion of previous children who have stayed in this home for whom there are two photos on the wall – one with this family and one with their birth family/new family. Storybooks that describe the process of moving successfully into new families can also help to reassure a child.

Reassurance of safety and welcome form the foundations of family membership. Beyond this, however, the inclusion of the particular child into the particular family placement becomes a matter of enhanced skill and sensitivity. Caregivers must hold in mind other factors as they make judgements about how best to promote family membership for a particular child. There is the extent, for example, to which the circumstances and cultural norms of the foster or adoptive family overlap with the previous experiences of the child. A young child who has spent most of her life with a single, isolated parent could easily feel overwhelmed by a bustling, noisy foster family environment and may need extra help to manage. Similarly, a child who came from that busy foster family may find it strange and need time to adapt as the only child in her new adoptive family.

The plan may also make a difference; for example, thought would need to be given to whether or not attendance at a big extended family celebration was an appropriate form of inclusion for a child who was having a one-off respite stay in a foster family. On the other hand, for those children who are likely to or planned to remain in a foster family and need to be able to cope with the big family event, anxiety may be diminished by a sense of the foster carer as a secure base and by a gradual preparation, perhaps meeting some of the relatives beforehand, becoming familiar with some of the children, visiting the venue in advance and so on. Even with careful preparation, some big occasions, such as a wedding service when everyone is completely silent and then bursts into song is unnerving for most young children who are unfamiliar with the experience of communal singing – so having a family member available to take the child for a walk needs to be part of the plan. In such situations, the normal preparedness of family life simply needs to be enhanced by a sense of some extra challenges that this particular child will find and need help with.

Of course, some children will bring specific negative experiences of previous family membership and family life which will influence expectations and assumptions in the new family. For instance, young children will have a set of ideas about how adult family members relate to each other and what this might mean. In their new families, they will make inferences based on these previous experiences. There may be occasions, such as in the example below, when caregivers have to interpret family interactions to the child so that the child has a clearer understanding of their meaning and family membership does not appear threatening or anxiety provoking.

Case example – Amy

Viv noted that Amy (4) became quiet and anxious one day when Viv and her husband were having a minor disagreement. Viv realised that Amy had previously witnessed disagreements escalating into domestic violence and that she could not predict that this would not happen in her foster family. Viv therefore took care to explain to Amy that it was OK to disagree sometimes, that the disagreement was now over and that she and her husband still loved each other. After this incident, Viv felt it important to give Amy clear and explicit messages about how disagreements were handled generally in the family. This involved simple statements such as 'In this family, when children feel cross with each other, they come and tell a grown up'. Also sensing that raised voices that were comfortable for her own family created anxiety for Amy, Viv worked on generally trying to lower the volume of family interactions and creating a quieter, calmer atmosphere.

Perhaps the most complex challenge for caregivers in promoting family membership is that of taking into account the degree of closeness and inclusion that feels comfortable for their particular child. This will be affected by the child's previous experiences of family norms and culture, by the association of closeness in family life with traumatic events, by feelings of loss and grief and by the defensive strategies children have developed. Caregivers must be sensitive to each of these things and prepared to go at the child's pace in changing behaviour and promoting inclusion in the family. The family norms and culture must be flexible enough to take the child's starting point into account and to meet the child half way, at times.

Case example – Alex

In Heather's family, an important aspect of family culture was for everyone to sit at the table and share a meal and news of the day's events in the early evening. Alex (3) was highly resistant to this and wanted only to take food from the table and run around with it. Heather recognised that Alex could not be expected to take on this aspect of the family culture immediately, but she took various steps to make the table an attractive place for Alex and to give him messages of inclusion that encouraged his co-operation. For instance, she provided a high-level chair, placed very close to her own so that he could receive her full attention. She also allocated Alex his own special cutlery and crockery and ensured that she told the rest of the family positive things that he had done during the day, even if he was not sitting at the table. Alex was allowed to come and go from the table as he wished, but a simple rule was established that he could only have food when he was sitting in his chair. Gradually, Alex learned that sitting at the table was enjoyable and rewarding and he became less inclined to get down. By the end of his bridge placement, he was a willing participant in this aspect of the family culture. Heather took care to pass on the detail of his progress to his new adoptive parents, so that they could understand and build on the expectations and experiences of mealtimes that he was bringing with him.

In this example, it is possible to see how Heather is combining all five of the different parenting dimensions in promoting Alex's development. She is *sensitive* to his specific way of thinking and helps him to manage his feelings; she offers her *availability* to build trust; she *accepts* him and builds his self-esteem and she uses a *co-operative* approach within certain boundaries – all in the context of *including* him in the foster family. The communication with his adoptive family was particularly important, as Alex may have tested out the new environment and continuity of expectations would calm and reassure him.

There are often concerns, in this age group, about the names that children use for their caregivers. We would part company with an emphasis on the value of "claiming" in terms of using different names in different types of placement. If a three-year-old calls a bridge foster carer "Daddy" rather than "Paul" or an adoptive father "Paul" rather than "Daddy", this need not be seen as a challenge to the plan or as reflecting anything about the quality of the relationship. In the child's mind, "Paul" may represent either a greater or lesser sense of a secure base and family membership than "Daddy" (depending on age, experience of daddies, etc.), so the use of the words is not in itself a helpful indicator of attitude or feelings. The meaning attached to such words are fluctuating and developing for some children and there may be familiar or difficult associations with certain terms, particularly "Mummy" and "Daddy". It is not unusual for children to refer to carers or adopters as "My Mum" or "My Dad" when talking to other children, but use first names to their face. In all placements, the use of such labels can be the basis of discussion about the various mummies and daddies, but caregivers and other adults (including social workers) need to be thoughtful and patient about the child's choice of terminology and avoid "banning" terms that the child uses more naturally. The most important thing is that the child can use names that help her to feel safer and more comfortably part of the new family, while building an understanding of the different short-term and longer term roles that these parents may play in her future.

Helping the young child to maintain *relationships with birth relatives* and/or feel comfortable about their *origins in the birth family* while building relationships in the foster or adoptive family requires a great deal of care and subtlety. By the age of four, many children will be competent users of language. Nevertheless, they continue to use non-verbal communication both to convey their ideas and feelings and to gain a lot of their clues about the world. If children are aware that when their birth relatives are mentioned or contact is imminent, the foster carer or adopter seems relaxed and says something reassuring, then they can have some confidence in the situation. But if caregivers are tense, reluctant or angry regarding these issues, then children's anxieties will obviously be raised. The role of the support worker may be critical here in helping caregivers to express and trace the origins of their feelings, listening and responding when they feel that particular arrangements are stressful for a child, and ensuring that caregivers are active participants in a purposeful process of helping the child to manage the membership of two families. As emphasised in Chapter 14, there can be no assumptions that contact with birth families is beneficial – this has to be assessed in each case. There should, however, be an expectation that carers will strive to find a sympathetic but realistic approach to the child's birth family membership and that they will communicate this directly and indirectly.

Middle childhood (5–10 years)

Children in this age group have a developing understanding of family relationships and the capacity to discuss and think about different family norms and cultures. This builds on their general developmental goal at this stage of understanding how the world works and where they fit. Such understanding is built on questions, however, and around six or seven is a common age at which fostered and adoptive children, even those who have always had their situation carefully explained, may start to ask questions about the circumstances of their birth, their history and placement (Brodzinsky and Schechter, 1990).

During this age range, therefore, children's ideas and expectations of family membership will become more firmly established and they will have a growing ability to make choices about aspects of foster or adoptive family membership and to demonstrate their willingness or unwillingness to belong.

Correspondingly, the tasks for caregivers become rather more complex. They will need to give clear messages about the norms and values of their family, but be sensitive to the child's view of how families work and the level of inclusion in their family group that feels comfortable to the child. At the same time, they will need to be similarly alert to the child's feelings of closeness or distance from his or her birth family and to ensure that a comfortable and appropriate sense of birth family membership is developing.

Everyday life in foster and adoptive families provides constant opportunities to demonstrate and discuss *family norms and culture*. An expectation, for instance, that family members speak respectfully to each other can be established in all family interactions and reminders given when this does not happen. Mealtimes, shopping trips, time spent watching television together and so on can all provide opportunities to talk about family norms and what might be different in other families. Including the child in preparations for family events, helping out with tasks or projects around the house or making plans for weekends, outings or holidays can help to promote both a sense of inclusion and also an understanding of how families can work together to achieve a shared goal.

Helping the child feel that they are welcome and *at home* is important for this age group, as for younger children. Symbols of inclusion such as decorating the child's bedroom in a personal style can be very powerful, as described by Marion, the foster mother of Ben (10), a boy with severe learning and physical disabilities.

> And then from the time Ben moved into his room, he went on in leaps and bounds, he really did. Something that was his, it was his for sure because we made it his, we put a stamp on it, it was his. We put the Tweenies up on the wall. I think he knew then that he was permanent. I really did think that he thought 'this is my home'.

Clear messages of welcome and inclusion are important, but also an element of choice that enables a child to opt in and out at a comfortable level. This issue of compatibility has particular importance for matching children and placements, so that the potential for slipping easily into the family routines and, even better, finding routines and rituals that are already familiar, is increased.

With increasing verbal skills, there is potential for more sophisticated discussion and reflection on such aspects of family membership. Different family norms and cultures can be explored and the particular norms of the foster or adoptive family outlined and considered in the broader context of community, religion or ethnicity. A crucial factor in each of these areas, however, is the capacity of the caregivers to communicate openly, to help the child to reflect on

259

the nature of the foster or adoptive family and their place within it. Thinking and talking about family membership in this way will help children to move towards a sense of belonging that feels secure and comfortable to them. The example below is given by Janice, long-term foster mother of Rosie (10). It demonstrates both the way in which Janice talks with Rosie about family norms and the pride and pleasure that Rosie takes in sharing in the family culture.

> *Rosie likes it when it's somebody's birthday and when she says about secrets I say, 'Well we don't have secrets in this house except Christmas and birthdays you know'. And she goes, 'And Mothering Sunday and Father's Day' and she brings in all the other occasions. She loves them all!*

Special occasions, however, can also be difficult for children who are separated from their birth families. Certain occasions may have negative associations from the past or they may be especially poignant in triggering memories or provoking feelings of loss. The celebration of religious or cultural festivals will vary from one family to the next and there is the potential for a newly arrived child to feel isolated and bewildered by the new family's culture and rituals. One adopted child (age 6) was mystified by the family bringing a large, real tree into the house in early December. Preparation for a child's first Christmas in the family needs to include hints that a few well-chosen presents are the norm if a child may be used to a mountain of presents, or the child used to receiving a more modest number of presents may need preparation for a mountain. In some cases, asking enthusiastic extended family members to stagger their gifts a little to the new child in the family might be helpful. Care also needs to be taken about the type and amount of presents from the birth family and how this will be positively managed alongside the foster or adoptive family's celebration.

It is important to remember, though, that family life is not only about celebrations, but also about weathering storms together. Often when families face sickness or bereavement, children in placement are "protected" from the stress, sometimes going to stay with relatives or other families. For children placed in short-term foster placements, this may be entirely appropriate, but in permanent placements, inclusion in the ups and downs of family life can provide powerful opportunities for closer relationships, family solidarity and mutual support. In the following example, Sean's long-term foster mother describes how including Sean (10) in some aspects of his foster grandfather's illness and death was beneficial in just these ways.

> *Sean's been different since my dad died. He'd lost part of his family as well. It*

brought home to him that he is part of the family. We're more like mother and son now. Since Dad died I think he feels for me actually because I've lost my dad and he's never had that sort of dad. He's had foster dads before but Dave's a dad to him now.

Non-verbal messages of inclusion remain powerful for children in this age range and they will be alert to ways in which they are treated "as family" and given the same material and emotional benefits as other children in the family group. Extended family can play an important part here. Inclusive gestures on their part, such as sending cards, gifts and messages on the same basis as they would to other children in the family can help children to feel confident in their membership of a wider network of supportive relationships and offer them different roles (as grandchild, younger sibling, niece, nephew, etc) in which to feel valued and successful.

For some children, however, there remains a deep resistance to certain aspects of family membership, even when they are well established in long-term fostering or adoptive families. They may feel unworthy of inclusion or unable to trust and believe that they are fully welcome. They may also have picked up on some actual uncertainty in the family about commitment to the child as a full member, especially any sign that other children are treated differently. Alternatively, or additionally, children may feel such loyalty to the birth family or are so emotionally entangled or unresolved about birth family members that they are not free to commit themselves. When this is translated into hostile or negative behaviour and attitudes towards the family norms and culture, caregivers can feel hurt and rejected and/or it may confirm fears that the child was not "right" for their family. Negative spirals can then develop in which other family members draw more closely together, setting the "outsider" child apart and reinforcing his belief that he is not wanted or worthy of belonging.

Caregivers may need additional support in thinking about the child's perspective in these situations and in understanding the feelings that lie behind the behaviour. They will need to use their reflective capacity to find ways to protect both themselves and the child from feeling hurt and rejected. Jean, foster mother of Owen (10), demonstrates this reflective capacity and the way in which it helped her to manage Owen's difficult behaviour in respect of family membership.

Case example – Owen

Owen often behaved so badly on family occasions that they would be spoiled for everyone concerned. He also found it hard to receive gifts and would reject them rudely. Jean thought hard about why this might be happening and looked back at Owen's early history for some clues. She discovered that he had often been excluded from treats, outings and celebrations in his birth family and this gave an indicator as to why he found them difficult to cope with in his foster family. However, Jean also noted that Owen took great care to choose appropriate birthday and Christmas gifts for everyone in the family and had even been known to buy her a favourite chocolate bar as a surprise. It was important for Jean to note these small steps forward. Making sense of Owen's behaviour in this way enabled Jean to talk through with Owen why certain aspects of family membership might be so hard for him, but at the same time, to tell him how much the family appreciated his care and thought in giving things to them.

Where children find it hard to believe they are worthy of family membership or they do not trust the family's commitment, one of the most helpful experiences is to hear about or see models of how it has worked in the past. Children of this age in short-term placements like to see photos of other children who have been in the family previously to show that they have not been forgotten. If this is a bridge placement, it may be helpful to hear about, see pictures of or even to meet with children who have successfully gone home or moved to become members of new families and settled well. This gives an opportunity to talk through, normalise and anticipate the point at which the child may become a member of a new family – but not be forgotten. Children in permanent placements can benefit from knowing older, adult children of the family. Neil (10), for instance, was permanently fostered and had a helpful model of what this meant in his older foster brother, Tony, for whom the family had become a family for life. Tony was placed in the family at 10, was now 36, and, with his wife and children, was still a frequent visitor to the household.

Helping primary school-aged children to feel a continuing sense of belonging to their birth families will require a difference in emphasis depending on the planned length of the placement and whether the child came into care recently or in infancy. In all cases, an important role for foster carers and adopters is to help children to explore their growing sense of self and identity and the role that birth family membership plays in that identity. At this age children still need a symbolic and practical approach in terms of the use of photographs, family trees and family diagrams, but they also need to put their feelings into words and to know that mixed feelings about their birth family are an acceptable topic for discussion, as is the child's message, 'I love you but wish that I didn't need to be fostered or adopted and that my parents had been different so I could have stayed with them'. A stronger sense of all that has been lost may start to emerge at this stage and during the transition to adolescence. If these ideas and the associated feelings can be brought out into the open by the child and discussed in the context of a balanced but realistic view of the birth family, it is less likely that questions will smoulder away in the child's mind and hold back their comfortable inclusion in both families.

For most children, the process of orientating themselves towards membership in the foster or adoptive family and accommodating continuing loyalty and love for the birth family is gradual. What can emerge though is the most important lesson of all, as illustrated by the following foster mother of 10-year-old Tina.

> *Her cards have moved on from 'from Tina' and now they're 'love from Tina'. I know it's a silly thing, but it was very difficult for her to write 'love' in a card. Her (birth) mum always got that and now the girls (foster carer's birth children) get it and Mike (foster father) gets it and I get it. I think it's accepting that you can love lots of people, you know, it's a big step.'*

It cannot be denied, however, that for some children, the questions of middle childhood have answers that are very difficult to think about. Adam (7) had received a serious physical injury in his early years that had left a deep scar. Sue, his adoptive mother, described how, quite unexpectedly, at bedtime he had said, 'Mum, how did I get this on my tummy?' Adam got out his life story book and she had to explain that either his mother or her boyfriend had hurt him. He had said, 'I feel really sad' and 'I feel like crying'. She had suggested that he could cry if he wanted to and they had a cuddle. He then went off to bed, but the adoptive mother said that she was left feeling 'shell-shocked'. She had helped Adam express and manage his feelings, but was left to manage her own feelings of sadness and, probably, anger that this had happened to him.

For all children, reaching some level of acceptance of their two families involves a long and difficult journey and caregivers need particular skill and resilience to support them along the way. Children may have mixed feelings about both families at times of stress or may test out or play on the emotions of both foster/adoptive families and birth families. Sometimes children may idealise or demonise either the past or the present family, and there may be corresponding expressions of exclusive love or extreme anger in relation to either family. This can easily generate feelings of hurt or the temptation to collude with this splitting and caregivers may need help in keeping their bearings at this point. Supporting social workers may need to help caregivers to keep in mind that the child's fundamental needs are to be reassured that their secure base remains steady and available, to develop a realistic appraisal of both the strengths and difficulties of their birth families and ultimately to gain as clear and full a picture as possible of why they cannot live with them. Caregivers may well also need additional support in untangling the child's messages and thinking about how best to convey difficult information regarding birth family members. On the other hand, caregivers will have to model a balanced approach by acknowledging that their family too has its own ups and downs, strengths and weaknesses. Foster and adoptive families can also go through some difficult times, which may include illness, bereavement, unemployment, divorce and separation, and so on. Children may at different times themselves need and benefit from the support of a social worker or therapist as they begin to explore the more painful and difficult aspects of their membership in both families.

Adolescence (11–18 years)

Adolescents face increasing demands and pressures from external sources such as school, college, work, and their peers. It is at these times that the support and solidarity of family membership can be most needed, and yet most adolescents strive to be independent and to break away from family norms and culture. Children who come into foster or adoptive families at this stage have to manage the tension of finding a place in a new family while asserting their autonomy. They may both appreciate and reject messages of inclusion and they are certainly very sensitive to being treated in the same way as other children in the family.

For fostered and adopted adolescents, the question of 'Which family do I really belong to?' can become particularly resonant and feelings of confusion and dislocation are not uncommon. The adolescent's increased capacity to think hypothetically may lead to 'What if?' questions such as, 'What if I hadn't been taken away/given away?' This is always difficult when other children have remained at home, although many teenagers realise that they have benefited from foster care or adoption but worry about young siblings still in the birth family. Adolescents may also start to feel some responsibility for birth parents whom they perceive as vulnerable. Other connected, difficult questions, when times are tricky in the foster or adoptive family, would therefore include: 'What if my mother would love me/need me more now?' or 'What if I went back to find out?' Opportunities to air and discuss these dangerous thoughts in a calm way need to be offered, but for both parents and children this can feel too risky. It is in such situations that young people may need access to a reliable and calming social worker, who is able to hear these thoughts without panicking or trying to deny their reality. The young person needs to come to their own sense, albeit with help, of their future need for support and belonging, and where this is most likely to be found.

For some young people who have been long-term members of a particular foster or adoptive family, adolescence can confirm their settled identity and future goals. They may aim for careers and lifestyles that reflect family norms, but also express their own special skills and talents. Contact with birth families can be managed flexibly and comfortably, reinforcing rather than threatening their sense of direction in the context of dual family membership. Messages of inclusion can build on these strengths and will be given explicitly. If communication is open, adolescent and family can explore different family scripts together, making sense of each other's, opening up possibilities for change and anticipating a future of independence and interdependence, as this mother describes in her wishes for her teenage foster daughter who has moderate learning disabilities.

> *I wish for her to be safely independent, for her to be part of our family forever. I mean, there will come a time when funding from social services stops. If she has been enabled to move into somewhere independently I hope it will be, like she says, round the corner and that she will invite us for tea and she'll bring her washing home. She has talked about living with her friend in a flat, living with us till she's a hundred, so she's got these things in her mind and really what we've got to do is hope that we can make successful independence a reality for her you know.*

But for some foster carers and adopters, there can be a breakdown in hard-earned trust as teenagers begin to challenge the basis of their family membership. As with troublesome toddlers, it is hard to determine what is "normal" for adolescence. A not unexpected or unusual reluctance in a 13-year-old to go for family walks may be acceptable to some families but not others – especially in the context of other behaviours that indicate a rejection of family values. The following father expresses his disappointment and sense of rejection in this context.

> *And I suppose it's typical again that Jon (13) doesn't want to do family things as such, he wants to be out and doing his own thing. He sort of has no interest at all really in being sort of a family unit, going for a walk. He's always showing his disgust at having to go out with us. It's tiring but I suppose that's typical of him really.*

Here the parents' feelings of disappointment in the closeness of their relationship with Jon and Jon's lack of respect for what his parents see as "normal" expectations of family life make it difficult for them to accept him or value his age-appropriate enjoyment of activities, such as football and being with his friends.

In cases where a comfortable sense of togetherness has not already been established in the family, adolescence is the time when close relationships with foster or adoptive parents may become very difficult. For some angry or wary and uninvolved young people, there may be an unstoppable momentum to "blast out" of the family home prematurely or to leave home to live "independently", but usually unsuccessfully, as soon as schooling has finished. Often, however, if caregivers can manage to stay connected to their children through adolescence and into early adulthood, relationships may gradually improve. Angry feelings sometimes seem to burn themselves out, young people who have previously held themselves at a distance make efforts to get closer, and foster carers and adoptive parents often find themselves pleasantly surprised by the warm involvement that they now have with their children and grandchildren (Howe, 1996; Schofield, 2003). All of the parenting dimensions come into play as caregivers work to preserve relationships sufficiently to sustain even a limited degree of acceptance and enjoyment of family membership in the young person or to prepare the ground for later improvement. These are difficult times and caregivers may need a good deal of support in thinking through ways in which they can take care of themselves and other family members while at the same time continuing to convey messages of availability, acceptance, co-operation and inclusion to their troubled adolescent.

It is at this stage of development that young people have the *potential* to incorporate two families into their sense of self in a flexible way and take the best of what is on offer from both family memberships. Helping young people to feel a continuing sense of belonging to the birth family may seem easier with verbal and more competent thinkers in adolescence. But feelings are often running high, as teenagers face identity issues that can be hard to resolve and lurking questions as to whether their birth family wants or needs them. For fostered or adopted young people who are having contact, this may be easier to resolve if contact has gone well or is manageable. But it can be that contact continues to expose young people to painful degrees of rejection or entanglement (see Chapter 14). When this is the case, foster carers and adopters require additional skill as they attempt to help their young people to achieve a *balanced but realistic* appraisal of their birth families. The capacity of the caregiver to think flexibly and empathically about why things might have happened and why birth family members might have behaved in the way they did, can release young people from a sense that they were in some way to blame and can help them to value certain aspects of their birth family membership and to reject others. Caregivers who have the ability to recognise and appreciate positive aspects of birth family membership are better positioned to also discuss less helpful connections or less positive characteristics or events.

When young people seek to increase face-to-face contact or test out a return home, doors need to be left open so that there is a way back if needed – if not into the family home full time, then at least into the feeling of family membership. It would be a positive outcome if young adults could enjoy a congratulations card from both their adoptive or foster families and their birth families on their 18th birthday, their marriage or the birth of a child, although for some young people from very difficult birth families this may not be possible or desirable. One young mother who grew up in foster care decided that contact with her birth family had become too risky for her own child as they were still involved in criminal activity, while another young mother ruled out contact with her birth family when younger siblings at home were sexually abused and taken into care (Schofield, 2003).

Conclusion

Although not traditionally a concept that has a direct connection with attachment theory, family membership is a vital strand of sensitive caregiving in fostering and adoption – it is crucial in managing separation and loss and offers many of the benefits of a secure base. Children who are separated from their birth families, even for a short time, need to know that they are welcomed and fully included members of their new families and that, for the duration of their stay, they can find a comfortable niche of belonging and acceptance. At the same time, they need to work through their feelings about birth family membership and establish a level of belonging that is compatible with their situation, wishes and feelings. To help them achieve this, caregivers must step outside the usual goals of parenting and address the defining challenge of fostering and adoption – offering loving and inclusive care to a child who is not born to the family, while at the same time, acknowledging the child's often strong and mixed feelings about genetic links and families of origin.

Summary points

- In positive circumstances, family membership provides a psychosocial, secure base for exploration and development and the reassurance of practical and emotional support through life.

- Fostered and adopted children must manage their membership of two families. The balance between the two family memberships, their different meanings and role in the child's life, will vary according to the nature of the plan for the child and the quality of relationships in both the birth family and the foster or adoptive family.

- A sense of belonging is not the same as an attachment relationship. Many children feel an ongoing sense of belonging to a birth family where they have insecure attachments and in which it would not be safe to grow up. Similarly, children can benefit from inclusion in a long-term foster or adoptive family *before* their attachment relationships are secure.

- Achieving a comfortable sense of dual family membership is an ongoing process, the significance and meaning of which will be unique to the individual and will vary over time.

- Sensitive caregivers provide verbal and non-verbal messages of inclusion in their own close and wider family network. At the same time, from infancy onwards, they are alert to opportunities to help their children to think flexibly and empathically about their background histories.

- Children need, ultimately, to be able to think and talk about membership of both families without feelings of guilt, blame or anger. They need to feel able to move easily (either physically or in their thinking) between both families and feel comfortable with the level of communication and connectedness that they have.

- Caregivers will choose different approaches to help their child to achieve an appropriate balance of birth and foster/adoptive family membership according to the individual child's needs and the placement type.

Approaches for helping children to belong

NB It is important to choose those approaches for helping children to belong that are suitable for the individual child and the placement plan, but even in short term placements children need to feel part of the family during their life together.

Belonging to the foster or adoptive family

- Explain to the child from the beginning how the family works – its routines and expectations, its choice of food and favourite television programmes – so that the child can see how to fit in.
- Adapt those routines where possible and reasonable to accommodate the child's norms and help the child feel at home e.g. meal times or bedtime.
- Have special places for the child in the home e.g. a hook for the child's coat; a place at the table; the child's name on the bedroom door or in fridge magnets on the fridge; bedding and bedroom decoration (posters, etc) that reflect the child's age and interests.
- Promote family mealtimes and family activities (e.g. going bowling) where the child can feel fully accepted as part of the family.
- Ensure extended family members and family friends welcome the child and treat the child as one of the family.
- Have photographs of the child and of the child with the foster or adoptive family on display – alongside photographs of other children who have lived in the foster or adoptive family and moved on/grown up.
- Use memory and experience books of events and feelings about events during the child's stay to build a family story, to help the child be able to reflect on the meaning of family life and, if the child moves on, to take home to the birth family or to a new placement.
- Make sure the school knows (and the child knows that the school knows) that you are the family caring for the child and need to be kept informed as parents of any concerns, but also of things to celebrate as a family.

- Plan family life and talk about plans that will include the child, even if this is just an expectation that they will all go swimming together next week or to visit grandparents.

Belonging to the birth family

- Develop or build on an existing life story book that contains information, pictures and a narrative that links the child to birth family members and birth family history. Ensure that it includes key documents e.g. copy of birth certificate, provides a full and balanced picture (see also Chapter 12) and is nicely presented, robust, valued and cared for. Even children who return to birth families benefit from making sense of complex family histories and their place in the family.
- Have photographs of the birth family where the child would most like to put them e.g. bedroom or living room.
- Ensure that conversations about the birth family happen appropriately and are carefully managed within the family, so that the child does not have to make sense of negative, contradictory or idealised ideas about the birth family.
- Where direct or indirect contact is occurring, be actively involved in planning and facilitating contact, so that the child's welfare is paramount and contact promotes security as well as roots and identity.

Managing memberships of more than one family

- Adults need to demonstrate their own flexibility about children's family memberships and what they might mean to the child.
- Both informally and in a planned way, talk with the child about the benefits and the challenges of having more than one family and help the child to understand and manage these relationships.
- Find models around the child of children who manage multiple families e.g. in friends' families, on television, in books.
- Help the child think about/talk about the inevitability of mixed feelings.
- Watch for possible pressure points e.g. Mother's Day, Father's Day, Christmas, and find ways of indicating (where appropriate) that it is OK to give cards to more than one parent or to choose one rather than the other at different times.

- If necessary and with the child's permission talk to the teacher about family issues that may disturb the child if raised in class i.e. help others outside the immediate family circle be aware of the child's task in managing their multiple loyalties/families.

Figure 9

Summary of the parenting dimensions

	Being available – helping children to trust	Responding sensitively – helping children manage feelings and behaviour	Accepting the child – building self-esteem
Caregiver thinking	What does this child need? What does this child expect from adults? Why? How can I show this child that I will not let him/her down? I need to keep the child in mind at all times, even when we are apart. I trust in my capacity to look after the child.	What might this child be thinking/feeling? Why? I need to put myself in the shoes of the child. What are the connections between the child's past and present? How does this child make me feel? How can I manage those feelings?	I value and accept myself – strengths and difficulties. I value and accept the whole child – strengths and difficulties, similarities and differences to me. I take pleasure in the child. I trust in the child's potential for good.
Caregiver behaviour	Remains alert and available, physically, emotionally and mentally to child's needs/signals. Signals availability to the child in age-appropriate verbal/non-verbal ways. Supports exploration.	Tunes in to the child. Observes and listens to child closely/responds flexibly and empathically. Helps child to understand/ express and manage feelings appropriately. Provides scaffolding and helps child make sense of experience, past and present.	Helps the child to fulfil potential and feel good about himself. Promotes positives and enables child to be and feel successful. Tackles difficulties/enables child to repair damage. Promotes child's acceptance by others.
Child thinking	I matter. I am safe. I can explore and return. I can trust and rely on my carer. Other people can be trusted.	My feelings and behaviour (past and present) make sense – I am understood. I can manage my feelings. Other people have thoughts and feelings that need to be taken into account.	I am accepted and valued for who I am. All people have some good and bad parts, including me. Repair/forgiveness is possible.
Child behaviour	Uses carer as a secure base when anxious – can tolerate waiting. Trusts in the goodwill of others. Exploration, learning and activity.	Reflects on feelings of self and others, is empathic. Can pause for thought before acting. Expresses/regulates feelings. Has a coherent life narrative.	Approaches and enjoys activities/relationships with confidence. Enjoys success/copes with failure. Shows realistic but positive appraisal of self.

Co-operative caregiving – helping children to feel effective	Promoting family membership – helping children to belong
I recognise this child as a separate person. I am responsible/I accept, value and promote the child's need to be assertive. How can I help this child to feel more effective and competent? How can we work together? I trust in the child's potential to be active/make decisions.	I value family life/family membership. Family boundaries can be flexible and permeable. Neither blood nor legal ties are necessary. Children can belong to more than one family. This child is part of my family as well as part of his/her birth family.
Promotes autonomy and choice, respects and promotes child's assertiveness. Accepts even defiance as healthy/normal. Sets safe boundaries. Seeks an alliance – uses negotiation and co-operative discipline.	Helps child to belong in own family-relationships, culture, norms and values. Gives verbal and non-verbal messages of child's inclusion in both families. Helps child manage membership of foster/adoptive/birth families.
I can make things happen (choices/decisions) within safe limits. My views are important. I can compromise and co-operate.	I have rights and responsibilities as a member of this family. I can love/belong to more than one family.
Is appropriately assertive/self-reliant. Accepts limits. Is proactive rather than only reactive. Negotiates and co-operates.	Incorporates the foster/adoptive family into a public and personal identity. Shows a commitment to the family culture. Manages role in the birth family/contact.

273

Part III **Theory and practice**

11 Attachment and common behaviour problems

In using attachment theory to understand the origins of children's behavioural problems, it is essential to take the developmental and transactional approach which we have followed through the book. The likelihood of young children developing difficulties in their relationships with other children, for example, may arise from a number of interacting factors to do with their temperament, their experience in attachment relationships and whether the nursery or playgroup they attend provides an environment that supports children's pro-social behaviour. For fostered and adopted children of all ages, many factors will have intervened in their development that add risk, ranging from abuse and neglect in the birth family through to placement moves. But other factors may have been protective, such as a caring grandparent, early placement in a particularly sensitive foster or adoptive family or a football coach at school who channelled a child's restless energy and built self-esteem.

In this chapter we explore how attachment theory might help to explain *why* certain behaviour problems arise, what those behaviours might *mean* to the child, how those behaviours might *impact on caregivers* and how the secure base parenting dimensions could combine *to help the child manage their behaviour more successfully*. Notice that although caregivers need ideas about how to understand and manage children's behaviour, the goal is always to enable children to manage their own behaviour. From infancy, secure children are learning to regulate their feelings and manage their behaviour, waiting patiently for a feed for example, and it is building the child's capacity to manage feelings and behaviour that needs to be the focus of therapeutic caregiving.

The emphasis here will be on using attachment theory and the parenting framework, outlined in Chapters 6–10, to focus on specific problems that children and families find difficult and to identify helpful ways of responding. Although the chapter is "problem" focused, it is important to think at the same time of ways in which children, through changes in their behaviour, can begin to fulfil their potential. The task is not just about managing or eliminating difficult behaviours, but about building children's strengths, hopefulness, resilience and pleasure in their world.

What children bring to their placements

There are a number of underlying features, such as anxiety caused by separation and loss, lack of trust, low self-esteem, anger and a need to be in control, that are common among fostered and adopted children, especially in the early stages of placement. Yet children express their need to be loved, their anxieties about getting close and their anger in a variety of behaviours. In particular, there will often be a gap between children's chronological age and their emotional age, which can make behaviour more difficult to understand (What does the behaviour mean to the child? What does it tell us about the child's thoughts and feelings?) and to respond helpfully. The driving force behind most problem behaviours, however, is unbearable levels of anxiety and a lack of constructive means for resolving difficulties and reducing that anxiety. This can leave children of all ages and backgrounds with similar core anxieties – Am I lovable? Whom can I turn to? How can I avoid getting hurt? – but a range of completely contrasting behaviours for expressing them: approaching everybody for a cuddle/approaching nobody for a cuddle; sleeping constantly/hardly sleeping at all; eating very fussily/eating everything in sight; talking constantly/rarely speaking; clinging to family pets/being cruel to family pets.

The parenting task needs to be focused on reducing anxiety, while setting boundaries, building hope and limiting the damage the child may do to themselves, to others and to the family home, until the child gets to the point of being able to express feelings more appropriately and manage behaviour for themselves. Children's sadness and anger, in particular, can be extreme, often having been suppressed in previous frightening or neglectful family situations, but such emotions do need to be expressed and managed. Children need to know that when *they* are overwhelmed emotionally, their caregivers are not, and that they have a secure base to rely on (Cairns, 2002; Cairns, 2004). In this containing context, more positive and pro-social behaviours can begin to replace destructive behaviours.

For caregivers to achieve this capacity to contain the child's strong feelings, they need to be able to separate out what they are feeling from what the child is feeling when children are behaving in extreme ways. Caregivers may come to carry unbearable feelings for the child and worry that this is what they feel themselves. These feelings may then start to overwhelm the caregivers so that, in some cases, they may act on them. 'This child is full of hatred and anger' may come to be experienced (when the child is verbally abusive or harms the family pet) as, 'I fear I may be overwhelmed with anger at this child' and then 'My anger is justified because this child is hateful' and even, 'I am starting to hate this child'. If caregivers become overwhelmed by guilt and shame about these feelings, while the child is also struggling with their guilt and shame about their behaviour, a mutually reinforcing and negative cycle can develop.

Professionals need to help the family reflect on and make sense of who is feeling what and why. This is rarely simple and caregivers need to know that it is OK not to know, OK to feel uncertain and OK to feel anxious or angry, but that it is essential to share those feelings with a supportive person without a sense of failure. This kind of support needs to be offered at an early stage, while there is a fresh commitment to making the relationship work, caregivers can be empowered to remain therapeutic, repairs in the relationship are still possible and anxiety and pessimism can be replaced by hopefulness. Too often support is asked for and offered when the relationship is almost beyond repair and both child and parents feel overwhelmed.

Applying attachment theory

Whatever the behaviour, it is important when applying attachment theory to assessment and intervention to observe and record behaviours and talk with the child, the caregivers and others in contact with the child in some detail (see following chapter for further discussion of assessment practice). The aim is to establish clearly what is happening (the core characteristics of the behaviour – now and in the past – and its context), to track and make some sense of the interactions between the child and other people, and to be able to reflect on the roots of the behaviour in the child's history and current thinking and feeling – all in a developmental framework.

These are some of the areas on which caregivers and practitioners can usefully focus:

- The *timing and history* of the behaviour and its impact on the child's relationships. When did it start? What currently seems to precede it? What are the consequences?
- The underlying *function* of the behaviour for the child. What does the behaviour allow the child to do? What does it allow them to avoid doing?
- What may be the *underlying anxiety?* Or is the behaviour now just a habit?
- What is the *meaning* of the behaviour for the child? Does the child break nice things when angry or because of feeling unworthy to have them or both?
- Does the child show signs of *magical thinking* e.g. believing that by breaking things he/she has made the caregiver ill?
- The *balance between attachment and exploration* for the child. How does the child react to feelings of upset/stress and manage distance/closeness? Is she able to learn, show interest in and explore/enjoy the environment? Is there any sign of a capacity to use caregivers as a secure base?

- The age-appropriate balance between *care by others / care for others / care for the self*.
- The nature of the *child's internal working models* of self, others and relationships. Does the child have multiple and conflicting models of the self and others, for example, victim, persecutor, rescuer (Liotti, 1999)?
- The child's *relationship with their body*, for example, can the child recognise and enjoy sensory experiences of taste, sight, sound, touch and smell? Does the child have a relaxed relationship with food? Is their body an appropriate source of pleasure or an object of control or attack?

The range of behaviour problems

There is a wide range of behaviours that caregivers and children find difficult and distressing. For the purposes of this chapter we have divided them into a number of broad categories, from aggression and hyperactive behaviours through to indiscriminate affection / attention seeking with a final focus on issues that affect the body, such as sleeping, eating and self-harm.

- Aggression, oppositional and defiant behaviours
- Hyperactivity, poor concentration and risk taking
- Lying, stealing and manipulative behaviours
- Compulsive caregiving, compliance and self-reliance
- Indiscriminate approaches to adults and children
- Social withdrawal
- Dissociation
- Sexualised behaviour
- Sleeping problems
- Eating problems
- Wetting and soiling
- Self-harm

This is not an exhaustive list, but it captures some of the main areas of concern for caregivers and the wider range of professionals – social workers, teachers, psychologists, psychiatrists and therapists. The approaches discussed here can be adapted to other behaviours, since they focus always on the core principles of *reflecting on the meaning of behaviour, containing the child's anxiety and behaviour* and *building the child's capacity to think and to manage their feelings* in the context of a secure relationship.

For each area of behaviour we consider the possible roots of the behaviour and how the primary goals of nurturing the child and promoting security and resilience, while setting limits to protect the child and others, can be addressed in foster and adoptive families. Throughout, an awareness of what is going on in the child's mind will be a focus, since the parenting dimensions rely on the notion of changing how the child thinks and feels in order to change the way they behave.

This core idea is compatible with a wide range of parenting approaches that draw on cognitive-behavioural as well as attachment-based theories. Here the emphasis will be on building in responses that are helpful to the child through the ordinary and everyday parenting tasks that can, with some additional thought and targeted parenting behaviour, become in themselves therapeutic. For fostered and adopted children the therapeutic process will always be a matter of unlearning previous lessons about how to survive and manage themselves in the world, alongside learning new ways to think about, value and trust themselves, others and relationships. Children may continue to use some familiar strategies if they can become more constructive (e.g. retreating to a bedroom, if this is to think things through, can be helpful at times), but they need to build in new and more flexible ways of thinking and pro-social approaches to problem solving. It is only in the context of *mind-mindedness*, being aware of their own thoughts and feelings and the thoughts and feelings of others, that children will be able to learn how to regulate strong emotions and manage their behaviour.

Aggressive, oppositional and defiant behaviours

What are often referred to as "conduct problems" include a range of behaviours that indicate the child's inability 'to observe the formal and informal rules of close relationships, family life, school or community' (Greenberg and Speltz, 1988, p. 177). These are some of the behaviours that are most likely to threaten a placement. Driven most often by some combination of need, anxiety, anger and lack of internalised boundaries, oppositional behaviours can range from extreme tantrums in pre-school children through to open aggression, defiance and, for some older children, delinquency. Especially troubling can be apparently gratuitous violence targeted at small children, elderly people or animals, where the vulnerability that would make a secure child react with concern will make some particularly disturbed, maltreated children overwhelmingly anxious and aggressive. The repressed anger, fear of rejection, need to be in control and dismissive attitude to the feelings of self and others, so common especially in disorganised/avoidant children who have been maltreated, can be a powerful combination.

Cognitive-behavioural models suggest that conduct problems result from children's faulty learning of the rules and parental responses to bad behaviour that actually reinforce it by giving it additional attention. That aggressive and oppositional behaviour is *learned* behaviour is likely to be at least part of the story for many fostered and adopted children, given what we know of their birth family histories. But attachment theory offers a rather different and complementary formulation of what may be going on, suggesting that the origins of this behaviour in the toddler and pre-school years can be linked with the failure of certain social and developmental processes in attachment relationships at that stage.

First, it is anticipated that young children who have experienced sensitive parenting in the first year to 18 months will have internalised mental representations of a self that is valued and an attachment figure who provides an available, sensitive and secure base. Anxiety and strong feelings can be managed within this relationship, so that communication is open, the parent and child co-operate, pro-social behaviour is increased, and the likelihood of violent outbursts and oppositional behaviour is reduced. In contrast, insensitive and maltreating parenting increases the likelihood that infants will be overwhelmed by anxiety that they need to defend against, will not be able to manage their feelings or behaviour and may become impulsive and aggressive.

As described in earlier chapters, the shift towards a goal-corrected partnership at around three years of age relies on the child's and the parent's ability to recognise and think about what each other feels and wants to do. The next step is to be able to develop negotiated and co-operative plans for being close or being apart, for sociability and for exploration, for safety and for risk-taking and for enjoying new experiences separately and together. For example, a four-year-old child can feel comfortable playing in the garden before lunch with a friend, while the parent is in the house. If disputes arise over who gets to go on the slide first or a child falls off the slide and the problem cannot be resolved by the children, help is at hand. Parents can get on with surfing the internet or cooking the lunch while confident that the child is safely occupied in the garden and will call them if needed.

If we now think of this scenario for fostered and adopted children of different ages who were not in the past offered this scaffolding and do not now have the ability to negotiate goals, it is possible to see how every step of the way there is potential for tantrums and angry outbursts. A controlling, anxious pre-school child might try to insist on lunch immediately or demand the parent's presence in the garden or cling to the parent at the computer or in the kitchen so that the parent's activity becomes impossible and the friend asks to be taken home. The thought that the parent may need or wish to do something other than pay attention to the child is unacceptable. Negotiation offered by the parent such as, 'I'll play in the garden for ten minutes with you and your friend and then I really must get the lunch', is not possible when the child suspects indifference or fears rejection or simply needs to stay in control. The presence of the visiting child may fuel the child's anxiety and/or may be used to embarrass and pressurise the parent. If asked to play and wait for lunch, a child of any age might start to be aggressive with the friend or destructive in the garden or the house in order to stay in control. Overwhelmed with anxiety and anger and lacking other strategies, the child can only act impulsively on their feelings. There is no capacity to "pause for thought" and reflect on which option might cause least harm/actually make them feel better. Anger easily spills into oppositional and destructive behaviour. But lack of the capacity to take into account the perspective and feelings of others is one of the key to their difficulties. As Weinfield *et al* (1999, p. 78) put it, 'In many ways, aggression is dependent upon a lack of empathy or emotional identification with others'.

The displays of aggression and the frenzy of destruction that foster carers and adoptive parents sometimes describe in children who have no way of managing their feelings and behaviour is often exacerbated by children's sense of their own dangerousness and fear that their world is falling apart. Children know when outbursts occur that this is a very bad thing to do and through the angry/anxious blur may even realise that the consequences will be to feel even less loved and lovable than before. How can they be forgiven? Will this friend ever come round again? Although it can seem that children are unable to think of the consequences of their extreme behaviour – why would they act this way if they did? – even the most out of control child is aware at some level that smashing furniture and hurting another child is a major breach of the rules (for some children, this is why they express their extreme feelings this way). But this is a juggernaut with a momentum that cannot easily be stopped, a catastrophe unfolding. As the child looks at the broken chair or the hurt friend and feels at once that this situation is so serious that it is beyond repair, it can drive them to the despair that results in a broken window as well.

The broken furniture and windows can be thought of as external representations of internal damage in the child, with each breakage recalling the numerous other breakages that the child has both caused and experienced. Although this is hard for a distressed and angry caregiver to bear in mind at the time, subsequent reflection needs to take into account that the child's shame and guilt, however much it is concealed and denied, has a long history.

Parenting strategies

It is important to recognise that foster and adoptive caregivers will have to manage their own feelings of disappointment and anger when a situation that they were trying to resolve in a reasonable way gets so out of hand. Empathy with the child is important, but may not be easy when the child can be smiling and laughing contemptuously while behaving in a threatening manner. On the other hand, the escalation in the child should not be too hard for a parent to empathise with. When in sheer exasperation a parent shouts at a persistently defiant child louder than they know they should, guilt can often increase the parent's distress and make the shouting even louder. As a parent, too, it is impossible to turn back the clock, to take back that initial yell. Hopefully, the parent will be able to acknowledge to themselves and even the child that they overstepped the mark, forgive and calm themselves and the child – while trying to find ways to help the child learn from what has just happened and to make it less likely to happen next time the child (and the parent?) is overwhelmed by anxiety or anger. A thoughtful, secure base for the caregiver in the form of a partner, friend or supportive social worker is a necessity in these circumstances, to enable the caregiver to face and explore their thoughts and feelings and those of the child.

When responding to any one incident, it is important to put it in the context of what has been learned about this child's behaviour pattern. Are there times of day when this behaviour is more likely to happen? Aggressive or defiant outbursts could be associated with the fear of separation and the bad dreams that occur at bedtime or leave a residue when waking in the morning. It could be that a pattern develops around meal times or when other children or adults come to the house. It may be that after school is a time when the child's pent up feelings from the day need to burst out or the child needs extra attention and calming reassurance. *Anticipation* of the child's vulnerable times can sometimes help to reduce anxiety, so that mealtimes, getting up or coming home from school can be carefully orchestrated to give the child a comfortable transition, in which the offer of a secure base through the availability of the parent is critical. Avoiding trivial confrontations, picking only the battles that need to be fought, as experienced carers often describe, can be helpful. Identifying such times of potential stress and responding in this way may be the best route to building security, since it is often when children feel most needy (for example, when unwell) that they can be most difficult, but may be most ready to relinquish control/accept care. A powerful attachment story of illness gets stored by the child as an episodic memory of, 'The day I was ill and mum made me that special soup and tucked me up', to be returned to when next the child is ill or even in adult life when the family reflects together on childhood illnesses or mum's soup.

Many carers report that children react with a whirlwind of aggression and defiance just at times when something good is about to happen – such as a birthday treat. As one carer put it, 'He knows he does it, but he can't help himself'. Children are often unable to believe in good things, so that a treat in store becomes an expectation of being disappointed – a rather cruel trick. Spoiling good things and remaining in control are better than the risk of being tantalised and let down. Somewhere in this dynamic also is the fear that they are not worthy of good things. They are not lovable or worthy and the shame of the last disastrous event or wrecked family outing (or the many other times when they were themselves rejected) reappears when the next event looms. It also seems likely that, because children's feelings of being overwhelmed and the destructive behaviours that result make no sense to them, they experience a frightening lack of control and corresponding dissociation. It is as if something inside them and beyond their control was what actually pulled the tablecloth off or made the baby cry. Thus when asked, 'But why did you do it?' they genuinely have no answer and cannot take responsibility.

As in the account described earlier of the child's play with a friend in the garden going disastrously wrong, we can see that developmentally there are a number of major areas that can be a focus for intervention, which are equally relevant to thinking about what might be helpful for the big occasion outbursts. First, children need to be enabled to express feelings, including anger, in a way that allows for the possibility of sharing and containing anxiety in advance e.g. they could be given an underlying or more explicit message that 'we don't know what your friend will like to play with or have for lunch but I will be here to help you!'

Secondly, children need to learn the core skills of perspective taking and open communication so that co-operative joint planning and negotiation are possible. Again, perspective taking needs to be a lesson learned when anxiety levels are low. Saying to the child when the friend is upset and the situation is already on the downward slope, 'Now look what you've done – he's really upset. He won't want to be your friend now', is a recipe for total panic in the child. The response at the time needs to be to normalise the situation, 'I guess we're all a bit hungry and need our lunch', and hope that the visiting child will respond to a co-operative and nurturing signal. For some children, a later discussion about the friend's experience of the visit may be possible, but for other children this will be too hard to think about. It may be more useful to note the need to address the issue at one remove, and use a story book that focuses on how difficult it is to have a friend round or how difficult it is to be the friend in a strange house. For older children who have grown up finding it difficult to distinguish between anger and hunger, let alone anger and sadness, it may be necessary to go through a slow process of developing an awareness of and a language for a range of feelings.

Thirdly, we need to find ways of helping children *pause for thought* at any stage of an incident and step back from initiating destructive behaviour or, once it has started, find a way to stop. This too can be discussed in real situations or using stories of boys and girls or princes or princesses or animals in the jungle. The goal is to build the child's skills and protect the child's sense of self by enabling the child to think through and communicate feelings more appropriately, thus saving the chair from getting smashed, but if the chair's fate is sealed then perhaps preserving the window and if both are done for, finding a way of repairing the relationship and learning lessons that may protect the child and future chairs, windows – and relationships.

Fourthly, the child's growing ability to manage their feelings and behaviour results from being safe enough to *test out the boundaries*, *make "mistakes"* and *repair the damage*. There will be times when anger, envy or despair can overwhelm any child and get expressed in broken toys, spilled meals and torn up pictures that were just not good enough. Although children from backgrounds of abuse and neglect may do such things at a more dramatic level – breaking their expensive new toy deliberately, throwing rather than spilling meals and tearing up other people's pictures as well as their own, they still need to be helped to repair the damage, to understand that "losing it" to a greater or lesser extent is part of the "normal" human condition and that in relationships we all need to give and receive forgiveness.

Fifthly, working *co-operatively* but safely with a child can be hard when the child is out of control, but this nevertheless has to be the goal. Children can be invited to make choices, but those choices are between options that are laid down by the parent. Although "time out" following behaviour that is deemed unacceptable is a commonly-used part of behavioural approaches, it needs to be used with care where children are so anxious about separation and rejection and find it difficult to think in terms of cause and effect. Traumatised children who lack internalised sources of security may be retraumatised by being shut away from their external source of security. On the other hand, "time out" to sit quietly with the caregiver, think and calm down is invaluable.

In this area there are plenty of opportunities to combine approaches that value *learning* new ways of doing things, alongside an attachment-based model which suggests that the learning is within a secure base relationship in which the caregiver promotes constructive solutions within firm boundaries – solutions that rely on the child's understanding of their feelings and those of other people.

Hyperactivity, poor concentration and risk taking

Problems with concentration, attention, hyperactivity and risk taking are common among fostered and adopted children, especially those who have experienced abuse and neglect (Rushton *et al*, 2003; Howe, 2005). Dysregulated children may be unable to sustain focus or concentration or to screen out internal, interpersonal and other distractions in order to sit quietly or to complete tasks at home or school. These behaviours are often, but not always, seen alongside oppositional behaviours and can be particularly troublesome because of the way in which they intrude into every aspect of family and school life, from getting up in the morning, getting to school, coping in the classroom to sitting in front of the television as a family in the evening. High activity levels and impulsivity often bring children into conflict with both families and schools, who are trying to socialise them into a range of acceptable behaviours. As Magai (1999, p. 796) suggests, in this context, 'the combination of negative reactions from others and poor academic performance often leads to anxiety and negative self-esteem (Barkley *et al*, 1983; Campbell, 1973, 1975).'

Also challenging for caregivers and practitioners are the competing and possibly interacting explanations or causes of such behaviour. In particular, conclusively ruling in or ruling out *attention-deficit hyperactivity disorder* (ADHD) or *attention deficit disorder* (ADD) as a diagnosis for children who have experienced significant maltreatment and losses in their lives is extremely difficult, even for experienced medical practitioners. Maltreated children may show a range of chaotic and dissociative behaviour and attachment research suggests that avoidant and disorganised children tend to be more restless and hyperactive (Grossman *et al*, 1999, p. 772). Some of these behaviours are also characteristic of children who suffer from epilepsy and other neurological conditions, so attachment history will always need to be just one part of the multi-disciplinary assessment of these behaviours.

Parenting strategies

Where the diagnosis of ADHD or ADD is made, it is often hard for children and families to manage both the diagnosis and difficult behaviours which may continue, even where medication has been prescribed. On the one hand, the diagnosis and treatment can offer great relief to children and families if it reduces very disruptive behaviour. It also offers a "no blame" solution, which can restore confidence for all parties; because this is a medical condition, the child is no longer "naughty" and the parents and teachers are no longer "failing". On the other hand, as many families (birth, foster and adoptive) find, it can become difficult to manage the child's behaviour and appeal to the child's reason and potential for co-operation in the normal way when the child has a medical reason for still, at times, behaving chaotically and even dangerously. Where medication has been prescribed and has been successful, it needs to be seen as a window of opportunity, while the child is calmer, to establish more constructive relationships in the family.

Does attachment theory have anything to offer here? Undoubtedly, there will be children for whom a medical diagnosis and medication is useful and necessary. But because such behaviour to some degree is so common among fostered and adopted children, it seems sensible to at least start by thinking about and responding to the behaviour as meaningful and reasonable in the circumstances. This means using understandings from attachment theory and the wider research on the impact of unresolved trauma and anxiety on children's minds and behaviour. As the chapter on disorganisation suggested, disorganisation, disorientation and dissociation are all possible responses to overwhelming anxiety and fear. Thus chaotic, restless, risk-taking behaviour *and* lack of concentration, absences and trance-like states can be understood in terms of a *defensive response to the child's previous exposure to fear* in the context of the lack of an available, attuned, safe and anxiety-containing caregiver's mind.

Parenting strategies, as for aggressive and defiant behaviours, have to apply the core dimensions of availability, sensitive care, acceptance and co-operation, whether or not the child is on medication. This kind of parenting means going back to the basics of attunement and relationship building, while also setting age-appropriate limits. This is far easier said than done when children seem completely out of control, and it requires the carers to hold onto a belief in the power of their relationship with the child to provide a source of healing and change. It also requires a considerable amount of skilled and containing support for foster carers and adopters in order to provide safe boundaries, but remain sensitive to the child. Whether or not diagnosed as having a disorder, these children will be testing.

Accepting the restless, chaotic child, finding something to love in a child who may not make eye contact or focus on what you are saying, can often be the hardest thing to do. Accounts from experienced foster carers and adopters suggest that every opportunity must be tried to find times in the day and the week when the child and the caregiver can be comfortable together and enjoy an activity, whether it be reading a story at night or going swimming or just racing freely round the park, so that control – by the child or the caregiver – is not the only agenda. It is important to bear in mind that the child's activity and behaviour generally is not just an external problem but reflects an intolerable internal mental state of restlessness and confusion. The inability to think and focus is itself a source of anxiety for the child, just as risk-taking behaviours are a source of anxiety to the parents.

Lying, stealing and manipulative behaviours

Fostered and adopted children may arrive in placement with a number of related behaviours that involve deceit, such as lying, stealing and manipulating. Such patterns have evolved as survival strategies in birth families and sometimes they persist or increase through moves of placement or even cause placement breakdown. Very often foster carers and adopters find children who behave in these ways especially challenging and hard to "accept". The thought that children are being devious and deceitful, saying what is plainly untrue, and in particular blaming other children or getting them into trouble, seems to indicate for some carers a child who is almost beyond redemption. In some cases, the last straw is when children start to set the parents against each other. It is not unusual for foster carers and adoptive parents to say, 'I can put up with anything but lying'.

The most important starting point for caregivers here is that lying is universal among children generally, not just those in foster care and adoption. Indeed children's first successful lie, probably at the age of about two or three, is a key positive development in their understanding; not everything in your mind is known to other people. Other people do not know if you really took that chocolate when you say, 'It wasn't me!' At that age most families treat these early attempts at lying as a big joke, 'But I saw you eat that last chocolate – and anyway what's that all round your mouth?!' Concealment or tricking other people is built into many traditional children's games, such as hunt the thimble or hide and seek, games where concealment leads to resolution and reunions. Sneaking up on someone and tricking them is the whole point of 'What's the time Mr Wolf?' and is the source of all the anxiety (will I be spotted and be out of the game?), the giggles and excitement.

These examples may seem a very long way from the behaviours that exasperate and worry carers and adopters, such as children who say that it was not them who broke the window or who hit a small child or claim that killing the family rabbit was only an "accident". It is true that "stealing" a chocolate and lying about it by a young child is not the same as a 15-year-old boy stealing the last money from the purse of a foster carer's sister, a single mother on benefits who had kindly agreed to look after him for the day (Beek and Schofield, 2004a). The layers of betrayal, hurt, anger and disappointment in this last case example were compounded by the fact that the foster family had looked after this boy for four years, were committed to the placement as permanent and had expected some level of trust.

Very often, as in this case, the deepest hurt is when the betrayal affects someone close to but other than the caregivers themselves. Harm coming to a relative or friend who let the child into their family is hard to manage, as carers and adopters feel responsible. This sense of responsibility and guilt fuels greater anger at the child, which in turn leads to greater denial and shutting down in the child: 'I didn't steal it'; 'My brother did it'; 'She wouldn't mind if I had the money, she's not mean like you'; 'She doesn't need it – they've just got a new telly'; 'I don't care what you think'. Sometimes such a theft is impulsive and simply in pursuit of money, but it may also have meaning and the victim may not have been targeted randomly. This teenage boy was struggling with feelings of failure in the foster family (he had recently been suspended from school) and may not have been able to cope with the fact that the foster mother was protective and loving towards her sister.

Although there is a big gap between acceptable and unacceptable lies, there are similarities that are essential for carers to hold on to if they are going to find it in their heart and minds to forgive and help children learn from such incidents. Lying and even stealing, taking something to which you have no right, *make sense* and although these behaviours breach normal moral codes and must be addressed, they should not be seen as a sign of something intrinsically wrong with the child. Lying of all kinds is a very common way in which all children (and, of course, adults) try to *protect their self-esteem, preserve the image* that other people have of them and *avoid punishment*. If children/adults think they can get away with explaining their late homework/late arrival at work by saying they were sick or the computer crashed, then very often they will. "Lying" to control other people is also common, just as adults often control others by controlling who has what information, both at work and in the family. Stealing from schools, places of work, hotels and restaurants is also common – often justified by the attitude that 'they won't miss them', the very excuse that children no doubt use to themselves when shoplifting or helping themselves to food from the fridge – or money from the purse.

The fact that different kinds of dishonesty are common does not minimise the seriousness of lying and stealing for families, and, indeed, the fear that if stealing persists it can lead to criminality is alive in the mind of the parent of any 15-year-old who has been found stealing. But it is important to understand why some families find behaviour such as lying, let alone stealing, so upsetting that they terminate a placement. As suggested throughout this book, trust is a key building block in families, not only for the individual child's development but also for feelings of family belonging. Children who lack trust and need to control may use forms of dishonesty to manipulate the family and it is often not so much the lying itself but the sense that the child has taken over the family that is hard to cope with. When a seven-year-old boy dishonestly tells his adoptive father, 'Mum said I could have extra pocket money (stay up late, go out to play football, eat the rest of the cake,' etc), it sets the parents at loggerheads: 'What? And you believed him?'

Sometimes what has to be managed is the fact that it is the carers' very acts of kindness or assuming the best of the child that are being taken advantage of which hurts most. Thus, believing that the child could not possibly have vandalised the neighbour's shed by painting abusive words on it, and forming an alliance with the child to deny this "unfair" allegation, can build a castle of unity that collapses in rubble when the truth comes out – because there is red paint on the child's trousers put out to wash. And the child still denies it. Children often get to the point where they appear to believe that they are telling the truth and even become indignant that other people do not believe them. This may simply be driven by a not unreasonable wish not to be found out, but for some children who are in dissociative states (see chapter on disorganisation and section on dissociation below), the capacity to "forget" or to "depersonalise" experiences and events as if they were happening to someone else, may mean that at some level they have shut off from awareness of their own responsibility for certain acts. This is far from straightforward, but whatever the source or nature of the "lie", the child can only begin to develop constructive and trusting relationships if they can be helped to live with and face up to the truth. But this is a very gradual process.

Parenting strategies

Parenting strategies that are particularly relevant for tackling dishonesty and manipulation come from all of the caregiving dimensions. Building trust in the caregiver's commitment to the child can reduce anxiety – not only in ways that might diminish the child's need to be controlling and impulsive, but also in ways that might enable the child to admit that they have done something wrong, in the knowledge that the consequences might be serious but not disastrous.

In the example of the vandalised shed, loss of pocket money to pay for paint for the shed to be repainted and an expectation that the child will do it is appropriate and not catastrophic for the child. Here, as in all management of behaviour problems, being clear about the issue, making it an opportunity for learning, but also taking the heat out of the situation is helpful – thus showing appropriate anger and disappointment (it's always important to model open communication of feelings and to share and name what is in the caregiver's mind), but remaining calm. If a shouting match results, the child is still in control. It is also essential to avoid saying things like, 'This is the worst thing any child in my care has ever done' (even if it is true), as the notion that the child is the very worst risks either making the child feel hopeless about change or glamorises their position as champion of the naughty kids – or both, since grandiose behaviour is a key defence for children who otherwise feel hopeless and worthless.

The best solution may well be open communication about the problem and practical co-operation. If repainting the shed is a big job, then the caregiver might go to the DIY store with the child to get the paint and offer to work with the child to do the repainting – or at the very least bring a nice snack and a cup of tea to refresh the worker. A strict behavioural approach might suggest that this attention is rewarding the child's bad behaviour, but the benefits of supporting and co-operatively working towards *a repair* out of concern for the child and the neighbour (as fully explained to the child) can be helpful in itself. The episode will undoubtedly pass into the family history, perhaps assisted by a photo of the mother and son painting the shed.

This straightforward open and trusting approach should not minimise the original offence, but reinforce concepts of straightforwardness, concern, repair, support, family and community solidarity. These in turn should help the child reflect on the benefits of belonging in this family and obeying its norms, including honesty and mutual concern, as well as lowering anxiety that he is irredeemably bad. Any or all of these may help the child's trust in the carer's response to bad behaviour, reduce the child's need to control, and reinforce the model of the self as flawed but worthy of love and the model of adults as available, accepting and loving – and also flawed, since that is the human condition and true for all of us. The goal is to build for the future as well as deal with what has just happened; to give the child the message that, although this behaviour *and* the lie about it were unacceptable, the caregiver has faith in the child's inherent value and potential for good. What you hope is that next time the child would own up to vandalising the shed, then become able to express regret spontaneously and genuinely for such incidents – and finally be able to resist the impulse to do them in the first place, in part because he understands the impact on others, in part because he wants to keep the love and respect of his carers, and in part because he is now able to make friends and is too busy playing football with his mates.

Compulsive caregiving, compliance and self-reliance

In describing the characteristics of disorganised patterns in children (Chapter 6), it was explained that one of the role-reversing ways of adapting to a frightening birth family environment was to behave nicely and in fact look after the frightening and/or frightened caregiver. This is, in a way, another kind of "manipulation" of relationships in order to avoid trouble and survive, physically and psychologically. Though it may not even be seen initially as a behaviour "problem", it can become so when imported into a foster or adoptive family.

The child's attentiveness to the birth parent is often accompanied by compulsive self-reliance, so that the child looks after themselves as well as the parent. In many birth families, the child has also taken on the role of looking after and protecting younger siblings – a role that is prosocial and rewarding, but has the additional benefit of taking stress from the parent and reducing the threat to all the children, including the child who is taking over the caregiving role. Typical scenarios would be older children taking younger children out of the way to play. Neil (15) told how in his birth family when he was about seven or eight, he and his younger brother Pete (then 6) would take their three even younger siblings up into the loft where they felt safe and could play when their mother, who had mental health problems, left them alone in the house (Beek and Schofield, 2004a). This was reported by Neil as a fond memory, although he had been ejected from the family at the age of 10, while Pete was left to care for the little ones without him.

Parenting strategies

In such contexts it is not surprising that, when these children come into foster care or adoption and continue to suppress their need to be cared for and determinedly care for themselves and others, there is still a deep well of unmet need, sadness and anger. Although their behaviour creates distance in the new family, the roles that they have taken on are their source of security; self-reliance, for example, has been built on the notion that the caregiver is simply not safe enough to trust. Thus, starting where the child feels safest may mean allowing the child initially to employ their familiar strategies. Sometimes practitioners advocate that 'you should start the way you mean to go on' but it seems more helpful in reducing anxiety to start where the child is.

A new adoptive mother was told that Jenna (9) would want to look after her and make her cups of tea, as she had done for her own mother. But she was advised that this would not be a good idea and that from the outset she must insist on Jenna being looked after, treat her as a nine-year-old and give her back her childhood. The adoptive mother was not happy about this advice and decided that if making her a cup of tea was important to Jenna and made her feel safe – even if this was because it meant that she felt in control – then this was a good enough place to start their new relationship. There was plenty of time to make cups of tea together and for Jenna to learn to receive as well as to give.

As with all defensive strategies, caregiving and self-reliance have their uses, even in new family environments and the aim must be to encourage the child sensitively to develop some other strategies, such as care-seeking, as trust develops, without needing to let go entirely of what makes them feel safe. The child can respond more flexibly and use the care that is offered, since it is flexibility – in this case giving and receiving – that is the goal. Jenna's adoptive mother had the confidence to go at the child's pace.

As with more blatantly controlling aggressive behaviours, children's caregiving behaviours and self-reliance make sense and are reasonable under the circumstances. However, where fostered and adopted children behave "nicely" and do not appear to challenge carers and adopters, it requires extra effort to see behind a relationship that seems inexplicably slow to develop and to ensure that the parenting dimensions are all operating to help the child relax, trust and become her own person, while accepting the value of relationships.

Indiscriminate approaches to adults and children

It is common to find that children who have not experienced a secure base provided by a sensitive, responsive and available caregiver will be less discriminating in their approach to both adults and children. The child may treat their foster carers or adoptive parents the same as stranger adults or, indeed, may appear to show more interest in or affection for unfamiliar adults than for the familiar caregiver. Even when children with a history of this kind of disinhibited behaviour have developed secure attachments in new families, they may still be inclined to be less discriminating than other secure children. It is encouraging to note that the behaviour does not in itself mean that children have not formed a secure selective attachment, but it leaves some questions unanswered about why such behaviour persists and, of course, leaves some concerns about possible consequent risks.

In order to make some sense of this behaviour and respond appropriately, we need to make an attempt to understand what is going on in the mind of the child. Lieberman and Pawl (1988, p. 343) describe the case of Sarah, a 21-month-old child, who had experienced five changes of carer before she was 12 months old. Some of this early care had been neglectful, but immediately prior to the move to the current family she had experienced sensitive caregiving and thrived. Her new foster family hoped to adopt Sarah, but were troubled by the child's indiscriminate behaviour patterns persisting, even after nine months with them.

Sarah demonstrated this behaviour vividly when a video recording of family interaction was being made as part of the assessment and she focused her attention primarily on the camera man. Curiosity and interest in a stranger is developmentally appropriate, but a degree of wariness accompanied by some increased proximity to the caregiver would be expected from secure children. Sarah displayed a mixture of approach and anxiety, but was unable to return to the foster carer and use her as a secure base, spinning round in the middle of the space between the cameraman and the carer. The therapists concluded in their overall assessment that Sarah had formed an attachment to her current foster carers, but that her expectation of loss and the associated feelings of pain and anxiety had led to her attempting 'to experience a sense of effectiveness rather than helplessness by actively seeking contact with the stranger and offering herself rather than being passively taken away'. This approach behaviour followed by disorganisation was interpreted as a direct response to her experiences of moves and her anxiety about having to leave the placement. The clinicians in this case reported that, by the age of 30 months, Sarah related more positively towards the foster carers. She still approached strangers, but with what they call a "brave swagger" as if defying the stranger to take her away.

Even children of Sarah's age, and certainly older children, discover that their advances to strangers are regularly greeted with signals of pleasure and delight, even when those strangers may feel a little uncomfortable with the inappropriateness of the approach. Positive comments are likely to be made and children learn that they are pleasing the adults. Many children in all kinds of families are encouraged to be sociable and speak to strangers, such as shop assistants. Although new families are appropriately concerned, for children there can be a fine line between expected sociable friendliness, with the benefits this brings, and inappropriate approaches to strangers that *may* suggest a lack of selective attachment to the carer or that will put them at risk. Where the child is clearly unable to use the primary caregiver as a secure base, it does raise some concerns about the child's internal models of relationships. It may be that previous internal working models of caregivers who reject or abandon persist, and the target for the caregivers is to offer a more consistently available and reliable secure model. The previous model will not entirely go away, but the child needs to acquire some flexibility in thinking about caregivers who disappear and caregivers who stay and can be trusted.

Parenting strategies

What is important in such situations is for caregivers to understand that the child who approaches others indiscriminately is unlikely to be indifferent to the primary carers. The child may be demonstrating the constant need for attention of the ambivalent child, inappropriate learned behaviour towards strangers or a more deep-rooted struggle with the fear that the new parents will be lost, as in the case example of Sarah – or a combination of all three. Where it seems the child is likely to be primarily anxious about loss following a series of other losses, it is important for the caregivers to understand the child's internal battle. The child is attempting to defend herself against yet another loss by remaining in charge – even in charge to the extent of almost prompting the move. Although it may seem strange to think of a 21-month-old having such complex thought processes (i.e. being so needy and yet trying to stay in control of the situation) this is not uncommon in children whose will to survive has been tested so drastically first in the birth family and then by the continuing uncertainty about how she can make herself feel safe in new families. Understanding that this is so may help to make it less painful for new carers that a child appears not to be responding to committed and sensitive care and may even seem to "prefer" strangers. Such understanding may also make it more likely that carers will remain physically and psychologically available and accepting of the child. But it is undeniably hard, specially for adoptive parents who have waited a long time to care for a child, to find that even a very young child can bring so much emotional trauma from the past, can put up so many barriers to their care and cannot see in them the good parents they are trying so hard to be. It is also the case that the child, during introductions to prospective adopters, may have greeted them with rewarding smiles, but then the adopters are disappointed to find that she may do that for everyone.

This behaviour does have implications for how moves are managed and particularly how children are given messages when placements (and attachment relationships) are to be short-term or permanent. Where the child's placement is a bridge placement and a further move is expected, the quality of caregiving and trust building will need to be the same as in permanent placement. In most cases, therefore, there will be arguments for building in initial contact with bridge carers after the move, so that the loss will not be total and there is evidence that people's lives can carry on and children can be thought about by previous carers even when separated. The new family's concern for the child's safety and need to keep her close, while also facilitating exploration, can be emphasised. Where the placement is intended to be permanent, as in Sarah's case, she would need very clear messages of ongoing availability from the new family within all the dimensions, including the family membership dimension. As she is pre-verbal, this may need to be done by photographs and drawings with the family and simple signs such as 'Sarah's Room' accompanied by a drawing and a photograph. Communicating reassuringly about future time is a big challenge with young children, but a large colourful calendar can be used to indicate family events which are days, weeks or months into the future, and which can be discussed. For children of all ages, the calendar offers a reassuring visual message, in this case about the shape of the child's future in the family.

Working towards selective attachment, with some associated degree of "stranger anxiety" or appropriate wariness, means replicating, but in an adapted form, the process by which sensitive care produces secure attachment in infants. It needs very *focused availability*, so that sharing the care of the child beyond perhaps one or two caregivers may not give the right signal at this stage. It will also be particularly helpful to build a link to the foster/adoptive mother for when they are apart. As one story suggested earlier in relation to contact, holding on, when separated, to something like a cardigan or a cushion that belongs to the caregiver, a *transitional object* that may be returned to the caregiver at reunion, can help the child retain trust in the secure base. All children benefit from this type of concrete symbol, as verbal messages often become a blur in the mind of an anxious child. In the example of the child who took the cushion to contact, he was able to rush back into the house afterwards and replace it on the settee, saying, 'I brought it back for you' – having not only felt comfort but a sense of achievement for looking after the foster carer's cushion.

For older children, concerns about indiscriminate approaches to other adults are often focused on the need to keep children safe when they are of an age to socialise more freely, walk themselves to school and be beyond the protective eye of a parent. As one foster carer said of her 11-year-old long-term foster daughter, Helen, who had been part of her family for five years, 'We've become very close, but I still think she might go off with anyone who offered her a bag of sweets' (Beek and Schofield, 2004a). Helen had been singled out for rejection and abuse during her early years. She also had moderate learning difficulties, could be explosively angry and had been diagnosed with ADHD during a court assessment when she was seven. It is not unusual for fostered and adopted children like Helen to have a number of factors that could in different ways explain or combine to produce certain problem behaviours. Because of Helen's learning and behavioural difficulties, she had led a rather protected life since being in foster care, placed in a small special unit attached to a mainstream primary school, collected for school each day and not yet trusted to go to the local shops on her own. Although the social worker and the foster carer felt confident in the quality of the close relationship between Helen and her foster carer, managing her move to a mainstream secondary school represented a significant degree of risk. Yet she needed to be helped to manage risk in the playground and going to and from school and to learn to identify who it was appropriate to turn to when in difficulties. So setting up a key person at school was a necessity, but so also was a hierarchy of other people (e.g. playground supervisors) who could be alerted when necessary. A variety of secure bases were needed to form a network around the child.

Social withdrawal

In contrast to children who appear to approach others too easily and without discrimination, some children appear to be permanently shut up in their own worlds. Socially withdrawn children are characterised by anxiety and insecurity in a range of settings. Their tendency to isolate themselves and failure to be appropriately assertive or sociable leads to a degree of peer rejection and isolation which reinforces their negative self-image. They are often submissive, defer to adults and peers and feel negatively about their own competencies (Furman *et al*, 1979). Typically they come from a background of neglect and unavailable or unpredictable caregiving, which has left them unsure of their own value. Children who have also experienced abuse of a physical, emotional or sexual kind can often feel and be more helpless than angry or aggressive.

This is an only too common problem for children who have experienced family adversity, maltreatment, separations and moves prior to entering a foster or adoptive family. For these children, too, there can be a lack of discrimination, in that they may not discriminate between primary caregivers and strangers – although some children who are withdrawn generally may be so clingy with particular carers that they find it hard to let them out of their sight. Dependent, clingy children may nevertheless be socially withdrawn in the sense of not only lacking social skills, but being unable to establish a rewarding, open and mutual relationship.

We can see fostered and adopted children who are shut off in this way at all ages from infancy to adolescence: babies who lack interest in their world and do not react with the usual infant delight at bright colours and noisy rattles, but instead sleep a lot and maintain a flat facial expression, empty eyes and an unnatural physical stillness; toddlers and pre-schoolers who may raise a very tentative smile when this is expected, but often lack spontaneity, energy or engagement in the world of play; primary school-age children for whom hiding at the back of the class is possible, but who hover anxiously in the playground, where the free flow of other children's play passes them by and for whom avoiding being a victim of bullying is their priority; teenagers who may find it possible to retreat without too many questions into their bedrooms, but once there find it hard to occupy themselves comfortably. These children's social development is blighted not only by their lack of ability to approach others for warmth and sharing of ideas and feelings, but also by their lack of pleasure in activity, which itself often offers a chance to share experiences and be companionable. As Beek and Schofield (2004a) found, some boys and girls who find it hard to communicate feelings in family relationships and are anxious and even fearful about social interactions, begin to enjoy an activity such as football and can enjoy the companionship of the team, and then the shared triumphs and disasters of each match which become a chance to express and share safely the range of feelings. Children who cannot achieve closeness in their family relationships *and* also lack such outlets are doubly troubled.

Where children see themselves as lacking in social skills or when their attempts to bring about contact with others are unsuccessful, they will experience raised anxiety and confirmation of a negative model of self and others. Withdrawn pre-school children may go on to have significant problems in the primary and adolescent years, when extreme social withdrawal will be very different from the active sociability norms for the age group and can lead to them experiencing not just isolation, but more active rejection and even bullying. As Rubin and Lollis (1988) suggest, the combination of anxiety, low self-esteem and peer rejection may contribute to the development of anxiety disorders or depression.

Parenting strategies

Socially withdrawn children and young people need *to build trust with carers* but also *to have confidence-boosting social experiences,* which can often be of a relatively simple kind. Rubin and Lollis (1988) describe an intervention in which isolated children who were paired with younger children for some "treatment" play sessions became more sociable subsequently than those paired with children of their own age. It is not surprising that children who are given the opportunity to play in a situation where they feel more competent can become more assertive and, indeed, can feel themselves to be actively helping a less competent child. It is very common, in fact, for fostered and adopted children to be drawn to younger children, both in the family setting and at school, but it may be that carers should accept this as an appropriate starting point and only gradually work towards age-appropriate peers. Children often select playmates and companions with whom they feel comfortable, and the research suggests that these experiences can be more than a passing phase while they catch up to their chronological age – they can offer opportunities for a more therapeutic process in terms of reshaping the child's experience of themselves and ultimately the child's mental representation of himself, his internal working model. There are many additional secondary gains in terms of teacher or parent approval when children are helpful to younger children, but it seems that the benefit to the child can be more significant in terms of helping to reshape how they see themselves and aiding their self-esteem and social skills. On the other hand, there should, over time, be a progression to age-appropriate peer relationships and this may need to be engineered through providing and supporting activity-based opportunities for the child or young person.

The root of the social withdrawal lies in anxiety, with the lack of social skills having its origin in the child's low self-esteem and inability to feel effective. Parenting that builds trust, self-esteem and self-efficacy will therefore be particularly important for socially withdrawn children and needs to be offered in a thoughtful and focused way. It is not enough to wait for opportunities to emerge – a planned approach to building self-confidence and social skills is necessary. In this area a therapeutic approach can be built sensitively and at the child's pace into every aspect of parenting, from greeting the child in the morning, through daytime activities, to settling them down at bedtime – and then giving clear signals of care and availability for when the child is asleep. The aim is not to enable the child to be the life and soul of the party, but simply to feel comfortable with herself and with other people, so that she can fulfil her potential both for relationship building and for exploration, fun and learning.

Dissociation

Children who have experienced *fear without solution* (as described in Chapter 5 on disorganisation) may have had to cope by a process of dissociation, which is a form of withdrawal but will be more profound, taking the form of behavioural and mental "freezing" or "absences" to avoid being overwhelmed by fear. Children who have begun to experience dissociative states in infancy and early childhood may become sensitised, so that even relatively minor fears and stresses may subsequently trigger a dissociative reaction (Greenberg, 1999). Even in adult life, such reactions may occur and the triggers may be obviously negative, such as a violent partner, or potentially positive but profoundly anxiety provoking, such as trying to parent a crying baby.

Children's freezing and distancing from the reality of their present or past worlds can prove hard for carers and adopters to manage. Behaviours which suggest that the parent and the child are operating in separate realities can be alarming. For example, caregivers can start to feel rather disorientated as well as angry when it appears that, as discussed above, children appear to believe their own lies. As with other defensive strategies developed in order to manage overwhelming anxiety or fear in the birth family, when dissociative reactions persist in the foster or adoptive family, they can become a barrier to even the most sensitive caregiving. It is hard to tune into the mind of the child when the child is attempting to keep that mind empty of significant thoughts, feelings and memories.

Crystal (5) had a birth mother with significant learning difficulties and a father who was violent (he carried a gun), frightening and had sexually abused her. Although in foster care she showed none of the difficult, aggressive or oppositional or manipulative behaviours that have been described above – indeed she was like a little doll – her foster carers found it impossible to love or even like her. Crystal was present in body but absent as a person. She would at times go into a dissociative, trance-like state for long periods, sitting on her bed with her tights half on and half off.

It requires tremendous attention to detail, to observe the child for signals of feeling and need that can be responded to in order to set up the arousal–relaxation cycle (Fahlberg, 1994). Often this will not be easy because signals are so slight or so misleading.

Parenting strategies

For children who react at times in this way, caregivers will almost certainly need advice and guidance, initially from social work support services but most probably from mental health services. This is where mental health professionals who specialise in understanding and working with formerly maltreated fostered and adopted children have a great deal to contribute, as these children will present with a range of problem behaviours.

Traumatised children in dissociative states may present with withdrawn trance-like behaviours, but they may also present with dangerously aggressive behaviour. Child psychotherapy may be helpful and necessary and children may initially be reached through art or play therapy or through their senses rather than through words. The models of direct work advocated by Nessie Bailey and the group of workers, particularly Judith Morris, who contributed to the original BAAF *In Touch with Children* project in the 1980s, emphasise the use of sensory materials to enable children to get back in touch with touch, taste, smell, sight and sound. Some sessions use clay and water while other sessions are given over to each sense; for example, *smell* can be explored through a range of different everyday items from herbs to perfume and *taste* experiences can include tasting lemon juice and jam, or involve shared cooking. Children who are disconnected from their senses and their bodies through neglect or trauma need help to feel and think about who they are again, physically as well as psychologically, before they can get in touch with other people or allow others to get in touch with them. Developmental and attachment goals are the same for all children in terms of building trust, regulation of feelings, self-esteem and self-efficacy, but for these children the starting point may need to be at a very basic level to launch the process of awakening the child's capacity to participate as a whole person in an attuned relationship with an attachment figure.

Sexualised behaviour

There is a wide range of behaviours that are described as sexualised. For some children, the inappropriate and indiscriminate seeking of proximity to stranger adults takes the form of a sexualised approach, an approach that may also occur with familiar caregivers. Children may have learned to associate any kind of affection with a sexual relationship. There may also be problems with sexualised drawings, masturbation in public or excessive masturbation that causes injury and amounts to self-harm. There can also be problems with self-exposure, premature sexual activity or, at the extreme, sexual assaults on other children which may or may not be associated with violence. These behaviours can all happen separately or in combination, often but not always where there has been a recorded history of sexual abuse. These behaviours may be as a result of recorded or unrecorded sexual abuse, but may also be due to other forms of maltreatment, such as extreme neglect or fear of physical abuse, where children turn to their bodies for comfort, to express anger or to take control. Thus, in addition to those children with a known history of sexual abuse, there will be other children who present similar problems.

Sexualised behaviours rarely occur independently of a range of other relationship and behavioural difficulties. Children are likely to be anxious and insecure, sometimes using caregiving or compliant strategies to control adults in ways that were designed in a sexually abusive relationship to ensure some predictability and to avoid any possible threat of violence associated with the abuse. Other children may be anxious and aggressive, if for them aggression is associated with sexuality.

Parenting strategies

Such behaviours need to be tackled directly, particularly where the child is a danger to himself or to others, is becoming stigmatised and isolated or is causing so much difficulty that a normal family life becomes impossible. The challenge is to reduce the behaviour without inducing shame and disgust (Cairns, 2002; Cairns, 2004), while also offering a relationship experience and physical care that can revise children's sense of themselves and their bodies. Younger children need to be socialised and educated within the family's norms, while being offered more appropriate forms of physical contact and affection. With older children and adolescents, for whom concerns may be about premature, promiscuous and risky sexual activity, parents need to set boundaries in terms of expected times for coming in and so on in the context of open communication about the reasons and the risks (Farmer and Pollock, 1998). In more extreme cases of sexual aggression, placements need to be very carefully chosen to avoid putting other children at risk.

The children's use of their bodies in relationships, whether for comfort, for control or to feel accepted, is only likely to change once they start to feel respect and liking for themselves and their bodies, can build relationships in more appropriate ways and are motivated to accept the norms and values of the foster or adoptive family. Where sexualised behaviour is in the context of dissociative states, 'learning how to behave appropriately' will rarely be simple, as the child is excluding so much from conscious awareness. As in other areas, tackling difficult behaviour needs to be done thoughtfully and in the context of building a supportive relationship – but here there must be an expectation that expert advice and external support will be available from child and adolescent mental health services.

There has been much concern about appropriate care for children who have been sexually abused and present symptoms in the form of sexualised behaviour, especially in the context of potential false allegations of sexual abuse against carers. There has been guidance and training on what is described as "safe care", designed to establish clear boundaries that protect children and carers. Some boundaries are obviously necessary, such as not sharing baths with children, but others suggested by some fostering agencies are more contentious, such as not allowing a child to sit on the carer's lap, and seem to prohibit the kind of normal, everyday affectionate physical contact with children that is part of family life. For children who have often had frightening experiences of physical contact and have a troubled relationship with their bodies, the implications of such restrictions on attempts to make family life both "normal" and therapeutic need to be carefully considered.

From the point of view of attachment theory and relationship building, and indeed from the point of view of many foster carers and adopters, there is a major problem with offering a loving family environment that does not allow or minimises physical contact, even for children with a history of sexual abuse. Non-intrusive, non-sexual but affectionate or concerned and caring physical contact is at the heart of most family relationships. The cuddle for the infant becomes the bedtime story and then the simple arm around the shoulder for the adolescent, but the physical contact is valuable. It is an important contrast to the aggressive or sexual contact or simply the lack of warm contact that children may have experienced before. It is understood that physical contact is not a comfortable or straightforward area for many children, but the goal is that it should become so.

Avoidant children, for example, will be reluctant to allow cuddles or even an arm round the shoulder in the early days of a placement, but the usual parenting goal would be to move to a point when the child would feel more trusting and comfortable with physical contact. Equally, it is understood that ambivalent/resistant children may demand to sit on anybody's lap and throw themselves into the arms of family members, but the goal would be to moderate this behaviour and make it appropriate and selective – not eliminate it or ban it.

Discussions with carers suggest that agencies vary greatly in how the boundaries of "safe care" are defined and how the legitimate anxiety about false allegations is managed. However, child-centred and therapeutic care must also manage the issue of children's need for physical contact and comfort without further damaging the child's development and sense of an integrated psychological and physical self.

Sleeping problems

The quality of sleep – the experience of going to sleep, sleeping, dreaming, and waking up to face the day – can be an indicator of the degree to which children are comfortable with their bodies, their selves, their thoughts and memories and their daily life. In infancy, the regulation of sleep as part of the arousal–relaxation cycle, the way in which babies settle to sleep after eating or playing or a toddler calms visibly and nods off after a bedtime tantrum, is a physical process, but reflects a psychological cycle of achieving a sense of ease with the self in the world. For neglected or frightened infants and children, sleep can become a retreat or a shutting down or a frightening loss of control in an untrustworthy environment.

Going to sleep and waking up are not unlike a separation and reunion for children. Most parents instinctively manage the separation very carefully, with warm baths and bedtime stories and a kiss good-night, with a reassuring 'Sleep well, see you in the morning'. Reunion in the morning is accompanied by a warm greeting, using familiar language, 'Hello lovely girl!', 'Morning sweet boy!' with gentle signals that the day needs to begin. Children have the parent's support – clean clothes are ready, breakfast is on the table and so on. Ritual and availability are at the heart of the predictability that allows children to manage the transitions of physical and mental states that occur either side of sleep.

For children from birth family environments that are chaotic, neglectful or abusive, there may have been a range of negative experiences associated with sleep. Bedtimes may have been unmarked or going to the bedroom may have been a punishment – with some children being locked into bedrooms for long periods. Beds themselves may be far from welcoming, wet, soiled, with inadequate covers and shared with too many other children or even with abusive adults. Children may also have been punished for wetting the bed.

Joe's experience was of being singled out for rejection in his family. At the age of five he was sent straight to his bedroom when he returned home from school and had meals separate to the rest of the family. When he wet and soiled the bed he was smacked and put in a cold shower.

For children in families where domestic violence has occurred, and many fostered children and children adopted from care will have had this experience, lying in bed may be associated with extreme anxiety, feelings of fear and responsibility for their mother and an alert, hypervigilant state. For some children, bedtimes and night times are when physical or sexual abuse took place. One young woman who grew up in foster care described memories of her birth family, when she would take a knife to bed and put it under the pillow to protect her younger brother from her mother's violent partners – she was eight years old at the time. Other children recall the fear of footsteps on the stairs. In contrast, for some children in violent or neglectful families, bedtime with brothers or sisters may have been a time to feel safer and to be able to play or relax and support each other.

Parenting strategies

Children of all ages coming into foster or adoptive homes will bring with them a wide range of experiences of sleep, bedtimes and getting up, so their behaviours need to be very sensitively observed and understood. It should not be assumed that children have had negative experiences, but even for children with some positive elements in their histories, bedtimes are quite likely to put them back in touch with both the good and the bad feelings about the birth family and to summon up feelings of loss. Even going to sleep in a strange bed is like a "giving in", a loss of control and an apparent acceptance of the move which may be resisted.

Where children seem to struggle with the separation of going to their bedroom and falling asleep, or have recurrent nightmares or wake in the morning feeling completely unable to start the day, a great deal of time and attention needs to be devoted to making sense of what is going on for the child and to creating a practical and relationship environment that helps the child regulate and enjoy both their sleeping and their waking up.

The five parenting dimensions all have a part to play. Having defined the situation as one of separation, availability is a critical message to give if trust is to enable falling asleep to be accepted and pleasurable. Signalling when bedtime is approaching and allowing calming down time can help. The ritual of bedtime stories is an opportunity to devote special time to the child, but can also be a way of associating trust and exploration, as stories feed the imagination and are a source of learning. Having the choice of stories encourages the child to feel effective as well as valued. Some families take turns to choose stories. One foster mother found that, having battled with a child to go upstairs, the problem resolved simply when she went upstairs first – and he made the choice to follow her to hear the story. When it later became a problem again, they started a game of whoever got to the bedroom first could choose the story. Both were co-operative routes which achieved the carers' goal of bedtime without the child feeling he had "given in". This child had been through several previous placement breakdowns.

Messages of availability at bedtime may be crucial even for older children. One adoptive mother reported how her 14-year-old always settled to sleep well, but needed to say goodnight and so, if she was out for the evening, her daughter would contact her on her mobile. Messages of availability through the night may be helped by open bedroom doors, lights on in the hallway, popping in to check the child before going to bed – and *making sure the child knows* that this happens reliably e.g. saying directly in the morning, 'You seemed a bit restless last night when I popped in to check you,' or 'You looked very peaceful last night, you must have been having nice dreams.' Even using a baby monitor may help anxious children who need to feel they have instant access to the caregiver or just to keep in touch.

Waking up in the morning needs to be carefully thought through in similar ways. As in every aspect of parenting, each small aspect of caregiving behaviour (the tone of voice, the right temperature of hot chocolate) gives messages to the child about what is going on in the mind of the caregiver (i.e. the importance to the caregiver of the child's physical and emotional needs) and offers security. Often this kind of parenting is carried out quite unconsciously, but the process may need to become explicit and talked through with the child, so that the child can begin to name both their anxieties and their feelings of comfort and to ask more openly for what they need.

Accepting the child may mean allowing the child initially to do what makes them feel comfortable around sleep. One carer talked of allowing a very distressed child, who panicked and refused to undress, to go to sleep in his clothes when he first came and gradually encouraging him to choose and then enjoy wearing some nice pyjamas. The practical environment will obviously depend on age, but it too needs to build self-esteem as well as reassurance. Comfortable and age-appropriate bedrooms are a good start. Some children like to bring a duvet from a previous home – and even if it is tatty or the colour clashes with the newly-decorated bedroom, this may be the best way forward for that child in the beginning. In contrast, some children welcome the new duvet and the new room as a sign of a new and safer start. Sensory messages of continuity and comfort, sight, smell and touch, will need to be specific to the needs of each child – and close communication with previous caregivers (birth, foster, adoptive, residential) is therefore essential to establish what might represent a threat and what might be a source of comfort for a particular child.

Even the dimension of *family membership* has a part to play, as children can be gradually inducted into family rituals (such as bedtime stories, or cuddles all round, or putting out the next day's school clothes before bed) that they can see working for other family members and can help them to belong. As one young man who grew up in foster care commented, his new family sat him down on his first day and explained how the household worked, and once he knew what was expected, he felt more relaxed and comfortable.

One concern (also raised above in relation to children with sexualised behaviour) that arises from current foster care policies is that "safe care" rules to avoid false allegations are being applied so strictly in some areas that carers are not allowed to sit on a child's bed to read a bedtime story, and in some cases foster fathers are not allowed in the child's room at all. Even having a child on your lap to read a bedtime story in the living room may be seen as too risky and not permitted. Although some safe care rules around bedtime are appropriate where children have been abused (e.g. not taking the child into the parents' bed), it seems to be very unfortunate if foster care perpetuates the idea that bedtimes are in fact danger times in which there can be no trust. Quite apart from the fact that carers' birth children or adopted children can have bedtime stories on a lap or in bed, thus making the foster child feel significantly different and even contaminated, cuddles and gentle physical contact are a major part of restoring the child's ability to relax mentally and physically at bedtime.

Eating problems

Eating problems range from the relatively minor, such as a child who tends to be rather fussy about food or eats rather too much, to the child who has bizarre eating habits, severe obesity, anorexia or bulimia. We need to think about the full range, in the knowledge that fostered and adopted children often have difficulties in managing a comfortable and straightforward relationship with food and with their bodies.

Although Bowlby emphasised that proximity seeking rather than feeding was the key motivator for infants in their attachment relationships, the role of food and the nature of the feeding relationship between infants and their mothers and fathers are powerful factors in the way in which feelings are expressed and relationships develop. The parent's ability to tune in to the child and build the synchrony that is part of the development of an attachment relationship, is often at its most vivid around the sensitivity, timing, pace and mood in the feeding relationship. The build up of strong feelings in the infant when hunger is experienced, and the resolution of that tension when the feed is successfully completed, creates a rhythm that often defines children's daily lives – as indeed mealtimes mark out and give structure to our days throughout our lives. Food remains a means by which we show our care, concern and affection for those we love or feel responsible for, but is also an area in which we express our feelings about our bodies and ourselves and can become the focus of battles if family relationships are in difficulties.

As discussed in the chapter on disorganisation and in relation to other behaviour problems such as sexualised behaviour, very often children who have been maltreated have a disturbed relationship with their bodies. From infancy through childhood, the experience of not having your body cared about, respected and loved is matched by feelings of uncertainty about how needs will ever be met. Bodily sensations such as hunger and the satisfaction of hunger are not clearly identified and a troubled physical self contributes to the child's emotionally disturbed sense of self.

Insensitive parenting in the birth family may mean that the timing of responses to the child's needs has been unpredictable and the child may have regularly been left hungry too long until overwhelmed and in despair or may have been expected to feed when not hungry and faced angry and intrusive expectations to eat, with food being forced on the child. The rhythm of hunger and satisfaction may never have been properly established, so that the child becomes out of tune with their own bodily sensations. In these circumstances, children do not experience or respond straightforwardly to bodily signals of hunger and food becomes a focus for other needs. They may eat to excess, eat compulsively, "steal" food or go for long periods of not eating adequately or find little that tempts them. Eating a very limited range of foods is not uncommon, and may, at least, in part be due simply to a family history of poverty and using limited or cheap food options, but can also be yet another sign that children who need control do not trust novelty – trying a new taste involves taking a risk and trusting the person providing it.

Parenting strategies

Just as food is an important part of children's early experiences in relationships, so it continues to be significant in new families in foster care and adoption. Knowing where the next meal is coming from is of critical importance for children, but similarly the caregiver's wish to give children food that they will enjoy and will nourish their bodies is a very powerful feeling and reflects a basic and primary parenting goal. For many caregivers and children, meeting physical needs can be an easier starting point in the early days of placement than meeting emotional needs or achieving psychological closeness. Indeed, if food is a more comfortable area for the child, mealtimes can build the foundations for other aspects of the relationship, such as shared pleasure, reciprocity and developing trust. However, for some children the lack of comfort with their bodies, distorted attitudes to food, combined with the need to stay in control of any relationship, may mean that food which is offered may be seen as "never enough" or rejected or treated with contempt. Food can rapidly become the currency of love and control, of giving and withholding.

Because the giving and receiving, the making and the consuming of food are both necessary for physical survival and so emotionally charged from infancy to adolescence, food is one of the most common battlegrounds in foster and adoptive family life. Control over what is eaten, when and where, can become central in the overall issue of who is in charge – and whether the caregivers can ever really be trusted to care enough. Children who need to feel in control are experienced at monitoring others, but it is not hard for any child to see how important it is for caregivers who have bought, cooked and put food on the table for the benefit of the child, to have that food eaten, and preferably eaten with signs of pleasure. It is therefore an area in which caregivers need to be particularly aware of ways of managing their feelings (i.e. not feeling as if their entire status as a parent is on the line here), so that they can find ways of taking the heat out of the situation and not become drawn into battles.

This is one occasion when "picking your battles" seems to be wise. As one foster carer reported, her three-year-old found it impossible to sit at the table throughout the meal. So she allowed him to get down at intervals, but only allowed him to eat when at the table, where she made his time especially enjoyable, talking with him and talking about him positively to others and so on. Gradually he spent more and more time with the family at the table until he could last the whole meal and it became part of the daily ritual that he too enjoyed. Mealtime was important in this foster family, not only for food but also for open communication (What did you do today? How did that feel?), self-esteem building (Well done! or Oh dear – better luck next time) and family solidarity (How can we help?). Just as the child resisted involvement with both the shared food and the shared relationship (as well as finding it hard just to sit still), so the caregiver used the attraction of both the food and the relationship to win him over. She built in some boundaries, but also wanted him to choose to eat and to choose to be with them, thus building self-efficacy and co-operation. The association between food, emotion and a sense of self cannot be ignored and so must become part of the work with the child. Eating is never only about getting the right number of calories into children's bodies.

It is also possible to help convert the child's need to control what is eaten into a positive development of self-efficacy in other ways, for example, by encouraging the child to shop and choose food, to choose which cereal to eat each day, or to be involved in cooking food for themselves and others. Children will vary in terms of what they find helpful, but for most children some combination of reassurance that food will be there when they want and need it, taking the pressure out of the situation, a degree of choice at some stage in the process and a sense of secondary gains e.g. teatime is a good time to chat and be part of the family, can help.

Where the child is overweight or obese, the success of caregiving that builds trust, self-esteem and self-efficacy is likely to precede success in helping the child to not just reduce their food intake but also to eat more healthily. The fact that carers and even older children know that food is not just about food does not make it a straightforward task to change what are often quite fixed patterns of thinking and behaviour. The other key caregiving dimension, thinking about and managing feelings, is also a pre-requisite, because without the capacity to pause for thought and find other ways of thinking about, for example, feelings of abandonment by the birth family or an experience of rejection in the playground, it will not be easy to stop the child from managing feelings through food. Excessive and comfort eating becomes a very powerful habit, and bingeing on anything and everything can become a powerfully driven compulsion. Moderating and relinquishing that behaviour will require going back to basics in emotional terms, accompanied of course by some practical measures, such as making sure the kitchen cupboard is not full of crisps and chocolate. If the rest of the family are eating high calorie/high fat food, it is difficult to imagine how the child will be able to move to a healthy eating choice. The family membership dimension, accepting the norms and values of the family, makes it likely that children will want to fit in.

Less commonly, fostered and adopted children may develop eating disorders such as anorexia and bulimia. These children, the majority of whom are likely to be girls, engage in food restriction and/or binge eating and use vomiting, laxatives or excessive exercise to control their weight. The physical impact of such disorders on the body can be extreme, whether as a result of achieving very low weights, depriving the body and major organs of adequate nutrition, or as a result of physical damage through vomiting. The disruption to children's social and educational development can also be very serious indeed. Where such disorders occur, the entire life of the child and young person (and often their families) can revolve around anxiety and anger-driven battles over food.

There are many different ways of understanding and thinking about the origins and consequences of these eating disorders, but research suggests that such eating disorders are often associated with insecure attachment and are linked with attempts to establish control through their eating behaviour. According to Greenberg (1999, p. 509 citing the work of Cole-Detke and Kobak, 1996), 'This type of control is chosen because women with eating disorders do not have the ability to examine their own psychological states, and cope instead by diverting distress to a focus on their own bodies'. This allows them to move attention 'away from attachment-related concerns and towards the more external and more attainable goal of body change'.

Control over the body has links to control in relationships in ways which we can see connect with other kinds of controlling behaviours. The behaviour represents the girl asserting a rigid control over her body as if asserting autonomy, but the effect is to bring mother and daughter closer and girls with eating disorders regularly report that they have become closer to their mothers since the eating disorder became a problem. This is not surprising since the level of concern raised by such behaviours means that mothers are forced to monitor the child closely, perhaps follow the child around to try to ensure adequate food intake, and to reduce the opportunities to eliminate food. Cole-Detke and Kobak (1996) suggest that eating disorders can be seen as a distorted form of proximity seeking, with the caregiver having to follow the adolescent anorexic child in order to be protective rather as the parent of a toddler maintains a close eye to prevent danger.

For these children in foster and adoptive families, medical advice is required as is, almost certainly, some therapeutic input for the child. Eating disorders of this kind seem particularly resistant to change, rather like a kind of addiction, and the centrality of food to everyone's day-to-day life and indeed survival makes it a particularly challenging kind of behaviour to manage and change.

Wetting and soiling

For some fostered and adopted children, wetting and soiling have been a problem from the time that it would have been normal to become clean and dry in the toddler years. For other children, these behaviours have occurred as a form of regression, when they were traumatised by abuse as older children or stressed by later moves and losses. Wetting and soiling sometimes appear to be reactive and specific, e.g. bedwetting when anxious before contact, but sometimes can seem more like an active communication, especially when children urinate in particular places in the house or leave faeces or soiled pants behind the settee or in an adoptive mother's bedroom drawer.

The picture is a complex one in terms of what feeling is being communicated (e.g. anger or longing or both) and each child's pattern needs to be understood in terms of what has prompted it in the past, what may be sustaining it as behaviour in the present – and what it may mean to the child.

> *Christine (14) had been sexually and physically abused by her father from infancy until the age of nine. In her foster placement it was a while before the soiling reduced and then gradually the bedwetting stopped. But, perhaps paradoxically, even at the age of 14, daytime wetting continued, with Christine being described as wetting herself while watching the television and only feet from the nearest toilet. She was in mainstream school, but this was one of the various symptoms that contributed to her isolation in her peer group.*

It was not easy to know what Christine made of this problem – except that it was not clear that she saw it as a problem in the way that other people obviously did and would. A smell that was offensive to others may have become a comforting and familiar way of being able to keep herself to herself, and being sent to her room to change seemed to be a way of retreating from the pressures of the family to her dolls, books and vivid fantasy life. For such children who have experienced multiple traumas and, as Christine did, seem to retreat into a separate world of their own, it may be that they are not consciously aware of these behaviours and certainly could not respond coherently to the question "why?". Christine showed some signs of dissociation in her glazed presentation and tendency to block out both her own problem behaviours and their consequences.

Although attachment theory may not seem to have a direct role in explaining or treating such behaviour, it is not hard to see how, as with other bodily symptoms, feelings about the self and others in relationships have been part of the problem, and therefore can potentially become part of the solution.

Parenting strategies

Bedwetting beyond the pre-school years in foster children new to placement is common and even adopted children may regress when they move into their new family. Many children respond to very simple routines, once in a stable and non-frightening environment, where bed is a clean, safe and comfortable place to be and "accidents" are treated calmly and supportively. Taking a low-key approach, reassuring the child that such behaviour is understandable in the circumstances, avoiding any humiliation for the child, building other strengths in the relationship, these simple and traditional sensitive parenting strategies will be sufficient for many children. Where symptoms persist, behavioural strategies of rewards (through star charts or treats) are commonly suggested and will work for some children. But other children will find this hard to respond to, since such strategies require a degree of impulse control, negotiation and co-operation. A degree of trust and relinquishing of control to the caregiver/manager of the star chart is necessary.

For Christine, traumatic experiences in the past and muddled and incoherent thinking in the present, made it unclear what she would respond to by way of rewards or sanctions. This behaviour was not, of course, her only symptom. She seemed to lack a sense of self, adopted the identities of other children and said she did not want to be Christine. She lied persistently and pointlessly – which also contributed to her isolation at school and at home. In children with more extreme histories of abuse such as Christine's, it may still be that behaviourist methods can help. But it seems likely that, until she became more coherent in her thinking or until she felt able to see some benefits in giving up this behaviour, these physical symptoms would persist. Although Christine was having therapy, it may also be that, until she could fully make sense of and resolve her feelings about her extremely traumatic bodily experiences as a young child and until she felt totally loved and safe, the social niceties of keeping clean would continue to seem an irrelevance to her.

As with other symptoms, the advice of mental health practitioners is likely to be necessary to distinguish between children for whom gentle persistence with the usual range of strategies while building self-esteem and self-efficacy might work and those children for whom this behaviour is more deeply rooted in a range of traumatic experiences and who require more specialist help.

Self-harm

Self-harm, in the form of cutting, scratching, burning the skin for example, is the ultimate attack on the body. It does occur in the general population, with men and women leading ordinary lives, holding down responsible jobs, while concealing this secret under long sleeves. But it is particularly common among disturbed populations of young people and adults, especially in secure psychiatric institutions and prisons. It also seems to be 'associated with the use of dissociation as a central defence mechanism and is strongly linked with sexual abuse' (Howe, 2005, p. 212).

The origin, pattern and function of self-harming behaviour for the individual child or young person, like other forms of problem behaviours, are varied. Self-harming behaviour may begin or increase in adolescence, but it by no means always starts then and can be seen from infancy through middle childhood. Pre-school children who have been maltreated may scratch away at exposed parts of their bodies or at their nipples and genitals (Schofield *et al*, 2000). Often the child may have a history of being left in cots or strapped in buggies or locked in bedrooms for long periods. One fostered girl aged 10, who had been emotionally and possibly sexually abused, already needed to wear trousers to hide the scars on her legs (Schofield *et al*, 2000).

Self-harm seems to be related to the child's attempt to manage unbearable emotions, with physical pain substituting for emotional pain. It may also be accompanied for children by some sense of relief and resolution of the kind that adults who self-harm describe, an undesirable but necessary "solution" to problems rather than the problem itself – a point of view often expressed by those who self-medicate with drugs. This parallel is not surprising, as it does seem that the experience of physical pain releases morphine-like chemicals in the brain that numb the emotional pain (Howe, 2005).

An important link between self-harm and other problem behaviours that characterise troubled children is that self-harm is not only a form of attack, it is a form of control. If the child feels that there has been little that they are able to control in their life, then control of their own body is what they have left.

Parenting strategies

How can foster carers and adoptive parents manage the signs or symptoms of self-harm? Since there are very real risks to the physical as well as the mental health of the child, it would be expected that guidance is sought from a paediatrician and a mental health team as soon as there is a suggestion that a child may be hurting themselves deliberately. However, although therapeutic help might be offered to the child, the parenting of the child within the family would still have a very important contribution to make in restoring the child's capacity to manage their emotions without attacking their body.

If we start from the premise that this behaviour in fostered and adopted children has its origins in some form of traumatic abuse, then building trust and confidence in the safety, both physical and psychological, provided by the caregiver has to be the starting point. The caregiver needs to be able to accept the full extent of the child's history of abuse, without themselves feeling overwhelmed by it. Since both traumatic histories of abuse, especially sexual abuse, and self-harming behaviour are very anxiety provoking, these need to be talked through with a support worker in order to enable the foster carer or adopter to find a way of containing their own anxiety and then containing the child's.

As with more extreme eating disorders, the issue of control in the relationship combined with the risk to the health of the child from self-harm needs to be managed without providing the only focus of daily life. This can only be possible where carers and adopters feel that the health risks are being managed by a professional team and that they have "permission" to focus on other areas, such as building self-esteem. Primarily, the child will need access to a containing relationship with the caregiver but may also benefit from a secure base relationship with a therapist.

Summary points

- *There are some key questions to ask/points to consider when assessing children with behaviour problems:*
  - the *timing and history* of the behaviour and its impact on the child's relationships;
  - the underlying *function* of the behaviour for the child;
  - what is the *meaning* of the behaviour for the child?
  - the *balance between attachment and exploration* for the child. Is there any sign of a capacity to use caregivers as a secure base?
  - the age-appropriate balance between *care by others/care for others/care for the self*;
  - the nature of the *child's internal working models* of self, others and relationships;
  - the child's *relationship with their body.*

- *There is a wide range of behaviours that caregivers and children find difficult and distressing:*
  - aggressive, oppositional and defiant behaviours;
  - hyperactivity, poor concentration and risk taking;
  - lying, stealing and manipulative behaviours;
  - compulsive caregiving, compliance and self-reliance;
  - indiscriminate approaches to adults and children;
  - social withdrawal;
  - dissociation;
  - sexualised behaviour;
  - sleeping problems;
  - eating problems;
  - wetting and soiling;
  - self-harm.

The approaches discussed here focus on the core principles of:
  – reflecting on the meaning of behaviour;
  – containing the child's anxiety and behaviour; and
  – building the child's capacity to think and to manage their own feelings and behaviour – in the context of a secure relationship.

• *Although sensitive and responsive parenting can make a difference, it is necessary for there to be multi-agency assessment and support in many cases where behaviour problems are severe and persistent.*

12 **Keeping attachment in mind – the role of the child's social worker**

There are many ways in which attachment theory can be applied to social work practice with and on behalf of fostered and adopted children. Understanding the impact of caregiving experiences in attachment relationships, separation and loss is essential whenever practitioners, carers and parents need to make better sense of how children feel, think and behave. It is at the heart of the matter when practitioners need to make decisions about what in the current or a potential new placement will help children move towards security, resilience and the fulfilment of their potential.

One of the key principles that is explored in this chapter is that social workers who work with and on behalf of children will be making their own contribution to the children's ability *to trust, to manage their feelings and behaviour, to accept and value themselves, to feel effective and be co-operative* and to *experience a comfortable and secure sense of family membership and belonging*. In other words, these core attachment-related developmental goals of carers/adopters are shared by practitioners, and practitioners will be guided by the same principle of *providing a secure base* for children that underpins the attachment caregiving dimensions.

A second key principle that is explored here, and that underlies both social work practice and the caregiving dimensions, is the need for social workers to be *thoughtful and reflective – about the child and about key people in the child's life*. Sensitive practitioners, like sensitive parents, need to be interested in and thoughtful not only about the child's *behaviour* at home, at school and with their peers, but also about what the child might be *thinking and feeling*. This may seem obvious but even when the question is asked, 'How does the child *feel* about these carers or that move of placement?' the parallel questions are not always asked, 'What does the child *think* is the reason for the carers' behaviour or the placement move?' 'What does the child *think* will happen in the new placement?' Trying to establish directly the child's *wishes*, as required by legislation, may bypass the important issue of what sense the child makes of their experiences and their options. What is going on in the child's mind needs to be thought about most carefully and this will require an understanding of the differences between the mind of the infant, the toddler, the school-age child and the adolescent.

The third and closely-related principle that underlies both social work practice and the caregiving dimensions is that social workers need to be able to be *reflective* about *their own thoughts and feelings*. Decisions to place a child in one family or another, to move a child or to separate siblings are never made lightly and will provoke powerful feelings in social workers. As with any stress that affects our most basic beliefs about ourselves as professionals and as people – in this case the belief that we are acting with the best interests of the child in mind – there is always a possibility that powerful emotions will be denied and defended against, especially when the anxiety surfaces that our actions may actually do harm. A defensive response to this anxiety will limit the worker's capacity to remain available and sensitive, thoughtful and reflective. Attachment theory can be used to think about the different ways in which workers manage their high risk/high gain responsibilities to the child, *and* their need for a secure base for "exploration" (in terms of flexible thinking and activity) in the form of sensitive supervision and support from the agency.

In this chapter, core aspects of foster care and adoption practice with children in placement that can benefit from drawing on attachment theory are explored. Models and concepts from earlier in the book are applied here to some selected areas of practice with and on behalf of children, but it is hoped that the approach will inform the full range of practice. Attachment theory does not provide a manual for working with children, but it does offer some very important principles and ideas that can provide a theoretical framework that enriches that work. A companion chapter (Chapter 13) on assessing and supporting foster carers and adopters follows.

Assessment and planning for children

Messages relating to the assessment of children are threaded through all previous chapters, but here we focus specifically on the practice itself. Assessment as discussed here may be in relation to a child at home who is to be taken into care, a child who is being assessed for a planned move to a permanent new family, a child whose placement and support needs are being reviewed or for whom difficulties are emerging, or an adolescent who has had numerous placements but for whom it is still hoped that a family for life will be possible.

Attachment in context: ecological and transactional models
It is important to stress at the outset that attachment as a way of understanding a child's mind, behaviour and relationships must be placed within the total picture

of the child's development, and this in turn must be put in an *ecological* framework that includes reference to the influences of outer worlds such as community, poverty, culture, ethnicity, religion, law and policy (Bronfenbrenner, 1979; Jack, 2001). Children's inner and outer worlds are interacting all the time, so the model for assessment must be *transactional* (Howe, 2005; Schofield, 1998a). For example, an event such as a change of school may not in itself make or break a placement, but can interact with strengths or vulnerabilities in the child and the placement and the birth family to start or accelerate an upward or a downward spiral. Security or insecurity of attachment has widespread implications for many areas of the child's functioning inside and outside the family, as we have seen, but it is not the whole story and needs to be put in context.

Social work practitioners and other experts are often asked by agencies and courts to 'assess the attachment between' a child and his or her parent or a child and a sibling. Such a request is reasonable and indeed necessary as part of a wider assessment, but attempts to isolate the attachment issue are generally unhelpful. Attachment-based information about the child's ability to trust in a selective attachment figure, the capacity to regulate affect and the defensive behaviour that results when the child is stressed, for example, needs to be firmly integrated into a range of other important information, such as the child's physical and mental health, education, past and present experiences of abuse and neglect, experiences of racism and much more. Children's experiences of trauma in close relationships, for example, will often be expressed through their bodies and physical symptoms; while health problems in turn will impact on their sense of self and may affect their peer relationships. For all children, achieving a comfortable and healthy relationship with their body will be one of the most important relationships in their lives and is inseparable from achieving self-esteem, self-efficacy and other benefits of attachment security.

The links and complex connections between these various areas of development and aspects of functioning need to be constantly taken into account. Education, in particular, is a key area where attachment-related issues interact with other factors to affect progress. A child's own sense of pleasure in achievements, whether building a tall tower as a toddler or doing well in a maths test as an older child, accompanied by the wish to please important other people such as carers and parents, are key motivating factors that promote task persistence and problem solving. In parallel, being able to think through and resolve feelings leads to the kind of regulation of emotions that facilitates concentration and learning, at home and in the classroom. In contrast, the poor social skills, lack of impulse control, preoccupation with anxieties about rejection and confused thinking that results from all kinds of abuse, particularly the emotional component of abuse (Howe, 2005), reduces the capacity to focus and problem solve. The lack of a secure base limits the insecure child's capacity to explore in ways that may lead to a persistent lack of pleasure and enjoyment as well as lack of success. It needs to be recognised, however, that children from very similar histories of abuse and loss can take very different routes through school – and contributory factors that shape these varied pathways will include attachment patterns, but will also include factors ranging from the genetic characteristics of the child to experiences of discrimination and racism to the role of the very committed head teacher who leads her staff in giving the best possible support to even the most difficult and disruptive children.

To assess attachment in particular relationships without taking into account the way the child's mind and behaviour interact with a range of identities, environments and activities would be omitting important sources of information. The quality of a specific attachment relationship can and should be reported to a planning meeting or court, but should never be treated in isolation or be used on its own as a basis for planning. The aim should not be to separate attachment entirely, but, on the contrary, to integrate an understanding of attachment as part of a holistic approach to children's psychosocial development.

Practicalities: gathering and making sense of information

In order to assess children's needs within this transactional and dynamic developmental framework, and how they will or can be met in a current or future placement, it is necessary to gather information about the past and the present: children's development, behaviour, relationships, achievements, safety, quality of caregiving, the impact of past therapeutic interventions and so on. This is a familiar list and yet very often assessments get hung up on particular areas of obvious difficulty and do not go far enough in identifying the full picture of strengths and difficulties. Both apparently minor areas of risk and glimmers of hope need to be carefully noted. Often assessments, even expert assessments, become geared to achieving particular outcomes, especially when court proceedings are in progress. This needs to be borne in mind if such assessment reports become the basis for subsequent decision making.

A full assessment needs to be based on a thorough *reading* of files, *interviewing* former and present caregivers, teachers, health visitors, *direct observation* of the child and the caregivers and *direct work* with the child (Brandon *et al*, 1996; Howe *et al*, 1999). If there is one important message here it is that such gathering of attachment-relevant information cannot take place at a planning or review meeting in the first instance. It often requires, for example, a visit to the school and a meeting with the teacher to get the full story of how the child relates to others, manages feelings, handles authority or peer relationships. Speaking personally to a previous foster carer is far preferable to relying on a file report alone. Interprofessional meetings may helpfully then pull together the whole picture. In one case a health visitor reported to the social worker on her three visits to a toddler at home prior to the child's admission to care. On each occasion the child had been strapped in a high chair. With everyone present it was possible to establish that none of the professionals who visited the home had *ever* observed the child out of the high chair – thus giving a much more powerful picture of just why the child was so developmentally delayed and was so unable to handle the freedom and choice of simply being able to explore in the foster home.

Assessments at key stages and regular intervals are now rightly a cornerstone of practice, and in family placement the careful recording of this material is particularly critical. Once a child is in placement it can be assumed that the history is "known" and it is the present that simply needs to be reviewed. The image of a child's early experience of being continuously in a high chair or shut in a bedroom, or indeed enjoying Sunday lunch each week with grandparents, needs to be held in the mind of professionals, since the experience will certainly be affecting the mind of the child.

The task is then to place this information about children's development and relationships in its theoretical context in order to make sense of the links between the past and the present, and then *predict the future*. Although this may seem again to be stating the obvious, there is a tendency in some assessment frameworks to focus on the assessment of *current* developmental status and caregiving experiences without paying sufficient attention to the child's *developmental trajectory*, for which knowledge of the past, the present *and* a theoretical basis for thinking about implications for the future are all required.

Attachment theory is not the only theory that social workers should be knowledgeable about, but all developmental theories (whether, for example, of cognitive or moral development) by definition are about developments across time and through different stages, which lead to more or to less healthy outcomes. Social workers and other professionals need to know the *likelihood* of a range of developmental needs being met by each of a range of options – return home, residential care, foster care, adoption and so on. Assessments should include a description and evaluation of the child's present development and circumstances and "needs"; but without the capacity to *predict* the likelihood of certain future developmental outcomes (the trajectory or developmental pathway) appropriate and evidence-based decisions (the purpose of the assessment) cannot be made.

Key to the application of attachment theory will be information gathering that draws on the range of *behaviours* (from secure base behaviour and co-operative relationships to aggression and other behavioural problems) which can tell us about the child's state of mind and which collectively provide a full developmental attachment picture (see also Howe *et al*, 1999; Howe, 2005). Chapter 11 (this volume) provides a framework for addressing attachment-related issues in assessing behaviour problems, which needs also to be taken into account here.

The earlier chapters on attachment patterns (Chapters 1–5) provide an insight into *patterns of behaviour* that are associated with different *strategies* for achieving proximity or for coping with insensitive care and maltreatment. It is these patterns of behaviour and strategies that should form the heart of an attachment-based assessment of children's family and social relationships. But it is preferable for social workers to talk in detail about *how* and *why* a child manages stress, for example, by shutting down on their feelings or provoking anger from an adoptive parent in order to stay in control, rather than saying that this *is* an avoidant or disorganised child. A degree of tentativeness is appropriate, perhaps saying, 'This child's behaviour is consistent with an avoidant strategy'. In other words, accurate *descriptions* and *explanations* of the *meaning* of behaviour in different circumstances across time can be presented by the assessing social worker to other professionals and to families and placed in a theoretical context that makes sense to everybody. There is no advantage in using attachment terminology to "trump" other professionals who have not been on the same attachment training courses or read the same books – the challenge is to help everyone (including birth relatives, foster carers and adoptive parents) to make the link between *behaviours*, including apparently irrational behaviours, and the child's *history, thoughts and feelings* – and to set out the *attachment-related mechanisms* that could help to explain these links.

Constructing a chronology is central to all assessment. But within this chronology, alongside the identification of events for the child and the family and the professional interventions, it is important with an attachment focus to note the points in time or periods in time when children experienced particular kinds of caregiving – periods of sensitive or insensitive care when physical and emotional needs were met or not met; major separations e.g. when the child or caregiver was in hospital; events that built self-esteem or in contrast acts of rejection; the experience of fear; evidence from the child's behaviour as noted over the years of upward or downward developmental spirals. Note needs to be taken of strengths as well as difficulties – periods of time when perhaps a child was stable at play-group/school or was known to have friends, read for pleasure, enjoyed looking after animals or played football for a team. The history should take careful note of the child's experiences in both birth family histories and all foster and adoptive family histories. It may be that a child has experienced periods of satisfactory or unsatisfactory care in any one or all, so no assumptions should be made.

Assessing and making sense of attachment-related strengths and difficulties

Given these principles, the developmental dimensions identified earlier in relation to parenting can be used to provide a focus for the kind of attachment-relevant information that could usefully be recorded: the capacity to trust and to use a secure base for exploration; the capacity to manage feelings and behaviour; self-esteem and children's capacity to accept and value themselves as they are; the capacity to feel effective and be co-operative; having a comfortable and secure sense of family membership and belonging.

- **The capacity to trust and to use a secure base for exploration**

Assessment of children of any age needs to include an indication of the child's capacity to trust in the availability of others. This has been a starting point for applying attachment theory to understanding children's states of mind and behaviour throughout the book. Although the concepts are closely linked, it can be helpful to separate out (as Marvin *et al*, 2002, do in their Circle of Security intervention) evidence of the child's use of a caregiver as a *haven of safety* when they are anxious, upset or fearful of danger and evidence of the child's use of the caregiver as a *secure base for exploration*. For secure children, caregivers provide both, and indeed it is trust in the fact that the haven of safety is available that can sustain the child while they play, learn and explore.

However, the picture is not always straightforward. Assessment observations of insecure-anxious dependent children who have been seriously neglected may find that they retreat to the caregiver when they are upset, indeed may be clinging to the caregiver much of the time, but without being able to explore, play and learn. This relationship is therefore not providing a secure base for the child, although the relationship may be described by other professionals as a "strong attachment" and may form the basis for planning e.g. this child may be said to have 'too strong an attachment to the birth mother to accept a new permanent family in adoption'. Such assessment errors are very common and may even be made by quite experienced professionals from a range of disciplines, who lack an in-depth understanding of attachment theory. As mentioned elsewhere in the book, it is preferable to avoid the term "strong" attachment altogether as it tends to imply a healthy relationship when this may be far from the case.

In contrast, an insecure avoidant child who seems to bury himself in playing or activities may appear to be confident to explore, but does not acknowledge feelings or seek comfort. This child is unable to use the adult as a haven of safety and often plays in ways that will be less rich than secure children whose anxieties are allayed by available parenting. Such children may be seen as "resilient", another common assessment error, or said to have no attachment.

In assessing capacity to trust, it is useful to gain some sense of the child's *internal working model* to help explain the child's behaviour. The child's beliefs and expectations about the availability of others may be apparent through consistently wary or consistently clingy behaviours. However, the range of behaviours that are role-reversing and controlling, more characteristic of disorganised children, can make it difficult to interpret what the child is thinking and feeling. If, for example, a child behaves contemptuously and dismissively towards a parent or carer, attachment theory would suggest that, paradoxically, one factor to be considered is that the child may be actually anxious about or frightened by the caregiver.

The assessment should address the question of what adaptations the insecure child has made to past and present experiences, for which a careful reading of the earlier chapters on secure and insecure attachment patterns, behaviours and strategies would be helpful. In particular, it is always important to identify where *fear* may have played a part in the child's experience, since fear contributes to disorganisation and can produce particularly persistent difficulties in learning to trust. Fear may be as powerfully present in histories of neglect as in histories of abuse, but may yet be overlooked. Tiny infants who are left for long periods in their cots or toddlers and older children who are left alone in bedrooms for long periods experience neglect and think, 'There is nobody there for me,' which is frightening enough – but they also experience existential fear – 'If I'm forgotten and abandoned and nobody is there to respond to me, do I really exist?' The development of destructive behaviours, soiling, compulsive masturbation and self-harm often emerge in such contexts.

Any assessment of the presence or absence of secure base behaviour and trust needs to focus on describing the *evidence* from a *range of sources* (i.e. not just a single observation of a family meal or play or contact) of the child's capacity to explore and to use a selective attachment figure as a secure base. The task then is to make sense of the evidence and communicate it in ways that other professionals can understand or that help the caregivers make sense of what may be going on. As suggested above, applying the label "avoidant" is less helpful than describing the behaviour in detail and explaining how that strategy may have emerged in response to certain kinds of caregiving and, for example, *why* rejected children who deny and devalue feelings may go on to bully other children or act in a grandiose way. Thus a behaviour like bullying needs to be investigated in terms of the context, the characteristics of the victims and what might be in the mind of the child. *Although lists of behaviours attached to attachment patterns are a helpful and convenient shorthand, they are not a substitute for using a theoretically-based knowledge of how each strategy works, formulated in a way that can be easily and usefully communicated to caregivers and practitioners from other disciplines.*

Where children do not trust and are reluctant to accept the care of any caregiver, it will be important for *the plan* to identify the ways in which this behaviour may affect a particular type of placement or a particular match and what would be needed to make the plan work for the child and the existing or new family. The caregiving chapter on providing availability (Chapter 6) offers some indications of the level of time and commitment that children of all ages require in order to build trust. This may seem more obvious when caring for infants, but many carers of teenagers find themselves having to focus intensely on tuning in to what will help young people learn to trust. The levels of anxiety of adolescents can be intense and their need for a secure port in the storm requires at least the same degree of availability, even if availability is in terms of keeping each other in mind (and keeping mobile phones on) when apart. The teenagers who move into "independent" living need far more support than is often available, and leaving care assessments for teenagers can be as important as matching assessments for young children in adoption. The goal is the same – stability and security in relationships for the longer term and into adult life.

- **The capacity to manage feelings and behaviour**

Critical to children's ability to engage comfortably with the world will be their ability to manage or regulate their feelings and behaviour. In their play or school work, as well as in their relationships with family and friends, being overwhelmed by feelings such as anxiety, shame or anger makes it almost impossible for children to achieve their goals. It is necessary for the social worker to bear in mind that the child's capacity to express and manage the full range of feelings appropriately in relationships relies on *mind-mindedness*. In infancy it is the mind-mindedness of the caregiver which contains and regulates the child's feelings, but as the child grows there is a period of co-regulation, followed by the child's increasing competence, in the absence of the caregiver, to think about their own mind and the mind of others in order to regulate their feelings. This in turn allows children to think rather than just react, to *pause for thought* and then to choose between pro-social options for behaviour that will achieve their goals.

In the assessment, this issue can thus be looked at in two ways. First, it is helpful to gather information about if and how a child expresses a range of feelings and any signs that feelings are being comfortably managed, or suppressed, or are coming out explosively and excessively. As discussed in Chapter 11, both *aggression and oppositional behaviour* or *social withdrawal* can be seen as indicative of a failure to manage feelings appropriately. Both verbal and non-verbal, direct and indirect communication of feelings are relevant; thus the assessment will include reports of tantrums as well as headaches or tummy aches at times of stress (Cairns, 2002). Secondly, it will be useful to assess the extent to which the child seems able to understand and take into account the feelings of others when they have strong feelings of their own. Can the child manage a goal-corrected partnership with an adult or another child in which perspective taking and "a pause for thought" about the goals of the other, in the context of one's own goals, before acting facilitates mutually rewarding relationships? Here both the *chronological* and the *emotional* age of the child will need to be taken into account.

Of concern here is the need to identify and understand patterns of behaviour that would indicate the coping or defensive strategies adopted when strong feelings surface – or the lack of strategy and dysregulation that lead to extreme aggressive behaviours or to denial and dissociation. As with other detailed information about the child, this information contributes to the *assessment, planning* and *placement* process, not only in helping practitioners to think about placements and families who could provide the therapeutic level of care needed by a child, but also in being able to give caregivers a better understanding of what they might need to expect. In the case of children who easily become dysregulated, this requires a particularly high level of care – and the availability of therapeutic advice and support. In most cases, the therapeutic plan would need to include paying attention both to the fundamental need for children to learn *to think* about their own feelings and the feelings of other people, while also helping them to develop more appropriate and constructive strategies for *expressing and managing their feelings* and for *responding empathically* to the feelings of others.

- **Self-esteem and children's capacity to accept and value themselves**

Fostered and adopted children may have a number of problems in accepting and valuing themselves. Early experiences in stressed, preoccupied, rejecting or frightening birth families lead children to question their lovability and worth. Such feelings are compounded by separation and loss when children move into or between placements, although if they find a family who fully accepts and values them, these moves will be a positive turning point. For many children, failures in school, both academically and socially, are especially hard to manage and affect self-esteem. Feeling *different* from people around you, whether because of religion, culture or ethnicity, can compound children's anxieties. Just feeling different from children who grow up in their birth families, with additional pressure from feeling stigmatised as a fostered or adopted person, can make children ask the most difficult questions: 'Why me? What's wrong with me?' Internal working models of the self as not worthy of love or attention can become established for some children and lead to distress and despair that may come out as anger.

Although the experience of low self-esteem is common, the exact nature of this difficulty for each child needs careful attention within any assessment. The obvious starting point is the child's history, to see where there may have been at least some opportunities for the child to feel loved and valued or where particularly harsh forms of rejection or scapegoating may have occurred. Children's experiences in their sibling groups may have provided a sense of value, whether in receiving or giving affection, but one of the hardest messages to recover from is the message that your parents loved your brother or sister, but did not love you.

Because children with low self-esteem have to defend against the feelings that this induces, assessment on the basis of behaviour or on the basis of what the child says openly is not likely to give you a straightforward or accurate picture. Smiles and reassurance or boastfulness in children may be confusing and it is likely that different children's anxieties will focus on different areas of esteem. Thus, for some children, their physical appearance may be the source of their main anxiety, while for other children it will be feelings about their school work, their sporting ability or, a core concern, whether they are a good or a bad person. Commonly, the source of anxiety is not clear; for example, the child may apparently be worried about his appearance, but at a deeper level is most concerned about whether he is good enough to be part of the family.

Accepting the self is not just about self-esteem in terms of personal qualities or perceived success, but can be seen as linked to the *developing self-concept and identity*. In this broader context, children's ability to accept and value their gender, ethnicity, community, culture and religion are important parts of the picture. In the minds of children who experience various degrees of disruption and discontinuity, being lovable or unlovable or being a good or a bad person may get linked to being a girl, being black or having a disability. Placements where children are of different ethnic origin to their carers need to take special steps to ensure that the child understands and values their own as well as the family's characteristics. Accepting our varied strengths and difficulties means accepting that we are all different. But feelings of *difference* of all kinds, including the difference of being fostered and adopted, can become muddled together in the child's mind. The assessment needs to sort through where these factors interact or accentuate each other in order to make plans, arrive at a good placement match and provide carers and adopters with a foundation of knowledge on which to build.

Multiple sources of information and observation relating to self-esteem are important in assessment, planning and supporting placements, whether to confirm a pattern or to show some very different aspects of the child's sense of self. School and home may see two very different children. Children who can manage friendships without too much anxiety about the self may see hostility and rejection in the caregivers. Other children may trust the carers but find it almost impossible to cope at school. Children vary in whether they find the wider peer group less or more intrusive or persecutory than the family group.

Similarly, children may struggle with some dimensions of self-esteem, for example, academic achievement or ethnicity, but not others. Such differences will emanate not only from the child, but also from the environments they find themselves in and what is valued in those environments. Actual performance in different settings will be an important part of any assessment, but children's *perceptions* will be an indication of their own sense of what matters as well as their sense of what is valued by adults and peers. With children who seem more or less confident in different settings or on different dimensions, it will be important that the whole picture is passed on to caregivers in order to establish which areas may be celebrated and which areas may need help to improve from a low base. Children often have different working models of themselves and they need help to integrate them into a coherent sense of self, rather than leaving bits split off. They need to accept themselves as one person who has strengths and weaknesses, as all children and adults have, rather than as different people, some of whom are unacceptable and to be denied.

Plans need to ensure that in existing or new placements this child can be accepted and valued for who she is, including ethnicity, gender, class, disability, but also in terms of a whole range of strengths and difficulties, from personal qualities to academic achievement. At the same time, the placement needs to offer opportunities to have experiences that maximise sources of self-esteem and quite consciously give positive messages to the child, 'Be proud to be black' and 'We love you for being yourself'. Although agencies can rarely match the football mad or the studious child with carers or adopters who value exactly the same things in their own lives or in their children, openness and enjoyment of difference of all kinds and the capacity to find something not just to accept but to love in this child is a basic necessity, whatever the child's source or level of self-esteem.

- **The capacity to feel effective and be co-operative**

Asking the question, 'How effective does this child feel?' is even less straightforward than asking about a child's self-esteem. As the chapter on co-operative caregiving points out, there are a series of paradoxes here. First, although some children who feel powerless behave in a dependent and passive way, other children become so frightened by their caregiver and their own powerlessness that they can only feel comfortable when they are in total control of others – and so seem very powerful. A second paradox is that being undemanding and self-reliant can actually be quite controlling, since the message to the parent is, 'I won't let you look after me'. Even dependent and clingy children can be controlling, with the message, 'I won't let you get on with your life – I need you'.

A third paradox is that the more *appropriately* effective (in some senses more powerful) a child is helped to be, the more likely it is that the child will co-operate and compromise. Such a child has learned that assertiveness *combined* with being prepared to make some concessions and co-operate with others is most likely to achieve their goals. In each of these apparent paradoxes, the child's behaviour can be explained and does make psychological sense – but without this kind of understanding, the assessment might not be reading the child correctly.

Because of the nature and complex links between effectiveness and co-operation, the assessment needs to look at them separately and together. Thus, questions about the child's capacity to make choices or confidence that they can complete a task, can be asked alongside questions about occasions when the child is able to compromise and co-operate as opposed to feeling in a panic about loss of control, digging their heels in and saying "no".

As with managing feelings, the ability to be mind-minded and see the other person's point of view is critical to children's co-operation and compromise, as is trust. Co-operative children trust that if they do back down, for example, in terms of relinquishing their turn at a computer game to another child, their turn will come round again soon. Children will find it easier to co-operate in some relationships and environments than others. They are most likely to feel effective and co-operate when they are least anxious and best able to take the perspective of the other person – and for some children that will be with caregivers, while for others it may be with foster carers' birth children, with grandparents, with friends, with the basketball team or with teachers. This is all valuable information for an assessment, as the child's capacity to be appropriately assertive but co-operative in even one of these areas suggests that they have some of the necessary skills and qualities to build relationships.

Just as this is a complex area for assessment, it becomes a complex area to include in a *plan* that defines the child's needs for the future. Balancing freedom and control is quite a sticky and challenging issue to negotiate in most families, but in foster and adoptive families, children from backgrounds of abuse and loss are likely to be controlling in some way (see Chapters 3, 4 and 5 on insecure patterns) and find any compromise hard. A child needs a clear message that parents are taking responsibility for the child's welfare and want what's best for them, but this requires the child to trust that this can be the case. There is no shared history of co-operation from earlier years for carers/adopters to build on and the feeling that they or the child are out of control can be scary. Falling back on the exclusive need to control a child who is unco-operative is a risk for most caregivers who feel under pressure, and a range of strategies (as described in Chapter 9) is needed. But the way in which issues of self-efficacy, control and co-operation are discussed in an assessment can help foster and adoptive families – and indeed children themselves – to see the behaviour in a more complex and sympathetic light, in order to remain more empathic, thoughtful and constructive. New carers need help to understand that the child's learning will take time and that it will be important to be consistent in setting and negotiating within boundaries.

- **Having a comfortable and secure sense of family membership and belonging**

In family placements, a sense of belonging and being part of the family contributes to the child's confidence in caregivers as a haven of safety and a secure base that supports enjoyment and satisfaction in play and school. For some children, it is often initially the relationships with and a sense of *belonging to the whole family,* rather than the particular attachment relationships with individual caregivers, that form the safe haven and the secure base, especially for teenagers or for children suspicious of "mums" or "dads" in the early days of placement. Grandparents, family friends and older children in the family are often the first to be able to help the child relax and the first to receive the child's confidences.

Assessment of family membership becomes relevant in a wide range of circumstances; when return to the birth family is an option, when kinship carers or foster carers are being assessed as long-term carers or adoptive parents for a child in their care or when placements are in difficulty and family commitment by carers or children is felt to be an area of concern. It is also an important part of an assessment of contact or at the stage of leaving care. However, all children of all ages and stages need to be living in a family to which they feel they belong, so that difficult as it is to assess, family membership does need to be thought about in the same way as the more obviously attachment-related issues such as trust and self-esteem.

Assessing the nature and significance of a child's family memberships requires a great deal of sensitivity to the child's experiences and views, and the way in which the child is treated, talked to and talked about in the families to which he may be said to belong. It also requires the worker to tune in to the use of language, metaphor and ritual that characterises different families. Families define their boundaries and develop very different ways of signalling to each other and the outside world: 'We belong together'. These differences may be based on culture, class or ethnicity or simply ways of talking that need to be listened to with care. A child who says of an adopter or foster carer, 'She's not my real mum,' may be stating a biological and socially recognised fact. This does not in itself mean a lack of commitment to the family – she may love her adoptive or foster mum very much – any more than an adopter or foster carer who says, 'I'm not trying to replace her real mum' suggests a lack of love or commitment to parenting a child into adult life as part of the family. Similarly, the use of birthday cards with 'To Mum' or 'To Daughter' on the front mean a great deal in some families, but would not be traditional or valued in others. Practitioners need to acknowledge their own views of such things as well as the meanings and experiences of different families, in order to be sure that they do not draw the wrong conclusions.

Assessing the extent to which the child has need of particular kind of contact to reflect their membership of the birth family will also mean awareness of the significance and subtlety of roles, relationships and family communications. As the chapter on contact will explore in more detail (see Chapter 14), contact needs to be thought about in terms of its impact on all the dimensions discussed here, for example, not only "roots and identity" but also self-esteem. But it is an area in which social workers' own assumptions and those of other professionals need to be questioned. It may be difficult for some social workers (or doctors or judges) to imagine that a child can feel fully part of a permanent foster family and yet have weekly contact with a birth father. And of course this can only be possible where the father is not just fully accepting of the placement, but actively supporting of it and in close communication with the carers. Similarly, it may seem impossible for a teenage girl to feel that a brief meeting three times a year is all that she needs to feel part of the birth family. Both these cases (from Beek and Schofield, 2004a) demonstrate that a child-centred definition of how much contact is needed and under what circumstances for it to be meaningful or not disruptive is very diverse and specific to the child.

In the area of family membership, the developmental benefit of achieving a comfortable sense of dual or multiple family memberships is clear. But the way in which this is to be achieved for a child will rely on an understanding of the needs of this particular child, the availability of families and the formal and informal arrangements that can support it. In writing the plan, as in writing the assessment, it will be important to clarify the principles on which family membership as a source of security is based and the way in which it interacts with attachment security on the one hand and permanence on the other. Many children struggle with these complex issues – as indeed do families and practitioners. Flexibility is essential since many children placed for permanence in foster care or adoption will, for example, perhaps need contact with former carers in the early days, but this need may fade over time to infrequent or indirect contact. Likewise, contact with certain siblings may be more or less important and frequent at different stages. As the chapter on contact (Chapter 14) stresses, there can be no rules of thumb – but all children do need to feel fully and safely part of the family in which they grow up and from which they will move into adult life, so any contact plan must take this into account. But many children will also wish to keep or make contact with birth families into adult life, and need to be prepared for this eventuality.

Identifying age-related strengths and difficulties

Here it seems helpful in the context of an attachment-related assessment to provide a cumulative list of questions that could be asked within each age group. We have drawn on the child development and attachment literature, but we acknowledge also the contribution of a range of authors who have developed similar questions (Fahlberg, 1994 and Cairns, 2002) and also practitioners (such as Rachel Agnew, social worker with Norfolk Adoption and Family Finding Unit) whose assessment questions we found helpful.

By "cumulative" we mean that, even for older children, it is important to start with the questions for 0–6 months and work forward to see how far the child has reached in relation to the appropriate developmental level for their chronological age. It may seem strange to think about whether a teenager discriminates between smells and tastes, for example, but this infancy stage may never have been properly negotiated.

Where problems are identified in this list, links need to be made both to the attachment pattern chapters, in terms of, for example, thinking about why a child may not be showing their feelings at a particular age, *and* the parenting chapters, to consider ways of helping in relation to certain difficulties. In tackling any one difficulty, such as an infant's lack of interest and pleasure in the environment or an older child's difficulty in managing their anger, it is necessary to address the *quality of caregiving across all the dimensions*. In both these cases the consistent availability and sensitivity of the caregiving will help, but so also will parallel actions to raise the child's self-esteem and build co-operativeness. Even family membership will have a part to play, as signals to the child that they fully belong may reduce anxiety and free the child up both to enjoy exploration and to manage their behaviour.

Making sense of the pattern of the individual child's development in the context of their age and stage will help focus attention on which of the parenting strategies described in Chapters 6–10 may be most helpful. Of course, within each age range there will be differences between children at the younger and the older end of the range and this needs to be taken into account.

0–6 months

- Does the child react appropriately (i.e. show interest/react but not panic or freeze) to light, sound, smell, touch, taste?
- Does the child show interest and pleasure in the environment?
- Does the child's face show a full range of emotions? Does the child frown, smile, laugh, rage, cry?
- Does/how does the child communicate their needs? For proximity? For food? For play?
- Does the child use a range of attachment behaviours to attract the caregiver's attention? Examples?
- Does the child accept affection/comfort? Can the child be soothed when upset/aroused?
- Is the child beginning to use the caregiver as a secure base for exploration?
- Does the child turn to/show interest in particular voices, faces, cuddles? If so, in whom e.g. primary caregiver and/or older sister?
- Does the child vocalise?
- Can the child take turns with/converse with adults – initiating and responding to vocalising, facial movements?
- Does the child make choices/assert themselves?

- Is the child physically thriving and appropriately active?
- Is the child comfortable in their body – able to relax and also be active?
- Is the child sleeping regularly and in a relaxed way?
- Can the child wait – with help e.g. voice of caregiver?
- Is the child co-operating at least some of the time with nappy changes, feeding, going to sleep?
- What does the child do when stressed?
- What might be the child's internal working model of self, others and relationships? (Start with 'I' statements – I am . . . Other people are . . .)

With such questions, the answers need to be accompanied by a reflection on the "why?" – why is this baby not reacting to light or sound? – and also by a plan for capitalising on the strengths and repairing the difficulties. In this age group the therapeutic parenting focus is on awakening or reawakening the child's drive/capacity for attachment building *and* exploration. This is best understood in the context of enabling the child to experience a rhythm to the day, in which equilibrium is restored after both routine (feeds, nappy changes) and unexpected disruptions (a dog barking, fireworks). As these questions indicate, the child's use of their senses and comfort in their *body* often provides a route to make contact with and soothe the young infant, but in asking these questions we are requiring caregivers to be *mind-minded* and tuned in to the infant so that the child begins to feel understood and to trust in the availability of a secure base.

6 months–18 months
- Does the child show a clear preference for one or more attachment figure/s?
- Does the child target attachment behaviours at this/these attachment figures?
- Can the child use at least one attachment figure as a secure base for exploration?
- Can the child play independently and constructively?
- Does the child protest at separation from attachment figures?
- If so, how does the child protest at separation from attachment figures?
- Does this behaviour vary between attachment figures?
- Does the child settle to play at reunion?
- Is the child less keen on/wary of/frightened of being approached or held by a stranger?
- Does the child show a full range of feelings, both positive and negative?
- Does the arousal–relaxation cycle seem to be working i.e. does the child express needs, and can the caregiver restore the child's equilibrium?
- Is the child's vocalising becoming more recognisable as language/

conversation? (e.g. some limited vocabulary, tone, intonation)
- Is the child comfortable in their body – able to relax or be active? More regular in feeding and sleeping?
- What does the child do when stressed?
- What might be the child's internal working model of self, others and relationships?

From the early part of this period we are expecting to see evidence of some form of selective attachment and to be able to identify whether the attachment is more or less secure and more or less organised, using the patterns described earlier. The child's functioning and relationships need also to be understood in the context of the very first moves towards self-efficacy and autonomy, so play and exploration, and the early signs of communication and language readiness are important.

18 months–3 years
- Can the child tolerate some gaps in caregiver availability?
- Does the child gain comfort from people (specific attachment figures?) or from things (toys, objects) or both?
- Is the child beginning to show empathy (older end of this age range)?
- Can the child express a range of feelings but not be overwhelmed by them?
- Does the child use their mobility – to explore, to have fun, to approach, to avoid, to control?
- Does the child have the capacity for symbolic and imaginative play?
- Can/does the child use language to communicate needs, feelings, ideas and goals openly and accurately? To ask questions, listen to the answers and learn? To manipulate?
- Can the child play let's pretend/play symbolically? Engage in parallel play?
- Does the child ever pretend to feel what they are not feeling – seem false?
- How is the child managing increased independence? Appropriate or excessive assertiveness or tantrums?
- Is the child comfortable in her body – able to enjoy/manage sleeping, eating, toileting appropriate to her age?
- What does the child do when stressed/anxious? Approach caregiver for help; shut down on feelings; cling, demand and resist comfort; control others?
- What might be the child's internal working model of self, others and relationships?

At this age, autonomy and dependency issues are particularly important and children will be learning to manage separations and the availability or otherwise of their attachment figures as they become more competent walkers and talkers. The family and the cultural environment will be making a big difference, with some children being expected still to be babies, while in other families much more self-reliance will be expected. The development of symbolic play and language are the triggers for a leap forward in the sophistication of play and relationships. For new carers, children of this age need not only to find the secure base experience that is so important from infancy but also to have the opportunity to lead. Parents who simply sit and gently comment on a child's play, following their lead, give powerful messages to the child both of their own competence and the parent's availability and interest in whatever they do. This following of the child's lead is a useful strategy also for older children, but at this beginning stage, for actively shared play a good basic principle is to follow when the child is confident and to offer support and sanctuary when anxiety strikes.

3–4 years

- Can the child take the perspective of others? Understand that others have feelings, goals that differ from their own? Can the child negotiate a goal-corrected partnership?
- Can the child name simple feelings?
- Can the child co-operate?
- Can the child successfully keep a secret? Tell a lie but accept being found out?
- How is the child managing peer group relationships? Balanced, pro-social, increasingly co-operative? Making and keeping friends?
- Can the child cope with not winning sometimes?
- Is the child rather too bossy – at home, at school, with friends?
- What does the child do when stressed/anxious? Approach caregiver for help; shut down on feelings; cry, cling, demand but resist comfort; control others?
- What might be the child's internal working model of self, others and relationships?

If availability and the development of a secure base is a core task of infancy, it is mind-mindedness that is key to this crucial turning point developmentally and suggests the focus of therapeutic parenting. The child's capacity or lack of capacity at this age to reflect, to be empathic, to take the perspective of others, builds on the child's early experiences of being thought about in an attuned relationship and will be shaping the child's emergence into the world of peer relationships.

All insecure children will suffer to some extent with difficulties in making sense of the thoughts and feelings of others, but for disorganised children this lack of social or emotional intelligence will be accompanied by more deep-rooted fears that lead to the formation of controlling strategies at this age. The assessment needs to note the ways in which children are acknowledging or defending against painful feelings, which may then emerge as aggression or withdrawal. Parenting can be actively focused on a combination of promoting reflection and perspective taking and helping children to manage their feelings and behaviour in the light of this social and emotional education.

5–6 years

- How is the child managing the opportunities/pressures of school? Learning? Social relationships? Authority of teachers?
- Does the child have a conscience – show an understanding of and wish to abide by rules and expectations? Show shame, guilt, wish to make reparation?
- How does the child cope with being told off?
- Can the child say sorry and mean it?
- What is the child's self-esteem like? Does the child think she is "good" or seek constant reassurance?
- How effective does the child feel themselves to be?
- Does the child look after things? Are they ever destructive?
- Does the child ask for help appropriately (sometimes but not excessively)?
- How does the child respond to praise? At home? At school?
- Does the child respect appropriate physical boundaries? With family members? With friends? With strangers?
- What might be the child's internal working model of self, others and relationships?

Assessment of children during this transition period from home to school provides rich data which can indicate the likely nature of early years experiences and also provide some hopeful or more worrying indicators of what is in store developmentally through the rest of middle childhood, depending on what kind of caregiving is available. The ways in which parent–child attachment relationships have shaped the mind and behaviour of the child will now emerge in the relationships with authority figures and peers. The expectation that children will be ready to learn may not be in keeping with the child's capacity to concentrate and manage the stress of relationships and of success and failure, academically and socially, without direct support. It is particularly challenging for a child who has not been reliably held in mind to cope with the demands of school, where a general lack of trust in the self or other people makes meeting a big group of children and adults an overwhelming experience. Therapeutic caregiving must be targeted towards helping the child manage this tricky combination of stresses at home and school. This may need to include not only a focus on direct support for the child, but also advocacy by the caregiver for the child with key people in a range of environments. A thoughtful and developmentally sensitive assessment can help predict what active help may be needed for each child to negotiate this transition successfully – enjoying the new school life rather than just surviving it.

7–11 years
- Does the child like/feel proud of certain aspects of himself?
- Does the child understand and accept the rules at home? At school? Have strategies for managing their behaviour?
- Is the child happy to get involved in activities – organised activities or hobbies?
- Does the child have a balanced approach to friends – values friendship but can be true to himself?
- How does the child manage the stresses of competing with others, academically and socially?
- What might be the child's internal working model of self, others and relationships?

The tasks of this age period focus on managing the developing sense of self in the context of learning and following the social rules. Thus, acceptance/self-esteem building and co-operation take centre stage in terms of parenting, though as ever within the context of an available secure base to which a child can retreat when the pressures of the playground or the classroom get too much. Assessing children of this age will require a degree of sensitivity to the real world pressures as well as the inner-world meanings or difficulties for the particular child. A child of different ethnicity to the rest of the school community or a child with a physical or intellectual disability may find themselves under a range of pressures from adults and peers which would make even the most secure child angry or withdrawn. But it is likely to be necessary to recognise that the child's most usual defensive strategy – such as shutting down on their feelings when stressed – will be interacting with the pressures within and outside the family. The necessary caregiving qualities will again be a mixture of sensitive availability to the child in the home and advocacy outside of it in order to ensure that external pressures are not preventing the child from becoming confident, competent and happy.

11–15 years

- How flexible is the child's thinking?
- How competent is the child in managing difficult feelings?
- How is the child feeling about/managing a changing body?
- How is the child feeling about/managing the changing expectations of school?
- How is the child feeling about/managing the changing expectations of the peer group?
- General level of self-estccm?
- Can the child co-operate with parents and other authority figures?
- How much can/does the child enjoy learning and/or activities?
- Is the child able to be assertively his own person, or is he more inclined to be preoccupied with/go along with whatever other people want from him?

Throughout the book we have tended to group all adolescents together, but in assessment terms it is helpful to at least disaggregate early and middle from late adolescents. In many ways, the transition from 11 to 15 is as critical as the transitions of the early years and this parallel is often noted by researchers and parents, given the shared tendency for young teenagers to, at times, be over-whelmed by strong feelings and to have outbursts which may be similar to toddler tantrums. Assessment with attachment in mind should focus on the extent to which the child is secure and psychologically robust enough to weather this big step forward towards adulthood without loss of self-esteem – a special risk at around 12–13 years old – and without being drawn into negative behaviour patterns that may in some cases start to write the child's future life script e.g. via suspension from school, offending behaviour or early teenage parenthood. Children in this age group may still be looking for a supportive permanent family, so assessments need to look very carefully at the child's relationships and needs. Whether children have been through multiple placements or have just arrived in care, a new attachment relationship in a new family should still be considered as an important opportunity, even where birth family ties are strong. The two are not mutually exclusive.

16–18 years

- Does the young person have at least one supportive family to belong to?
- Does the young person have a secure base – preferably an attachment relationship within a network of resources?
- Does the young person have a close confiding relationship with peers/friends? Any relationship with friends?

- Is the young person engaged in purposeful activity that could offer identity and self-esteem – e.g. in education or at work?
- Does the young person feel competent e.g. to assert themselves appropriately, to try new things?
- Can the young person think about self and others, manage her own feelings and behaviour?
- Is the young person hopeful for the future?

A great deal of attention has been drawn in this book to the child's need for a secure base that will last into adult life. In this adolescent age group, the expression "secure base" is used very deliberately to include both the emotional support and availability of attachment figures *and* family membership. The transition to adulthood will need a whole range of personal skills and resources as well as external supports and resources that families, friends and, where necessary, agencies will provide. Practitioners involved in assessment and planning need to be thinking about *interdependence* rather than independence, so that children are not given the message that they should and could be "independent" at 16 or 17 years old. Both fostered and adopted children who may leave school at 16 can still be quite immature and find it very difficult to establish themselves either in post-16 education and training or in employment. Without the structure provided by school, young people's lives may seem to drift and, with excess time on their hands, their risk and stress and the family's stress may increase – just when carers and parents were looking forward to family life becoming more settled as children move closer to adulthood. Leaving care teams need to be alert to these concerns in foster families, but adopted young people and their families may need similar levels of support specific to their needs

In summary, *for all these assessment questions and for all ages* there will be follow-up questions that lead to action – if a young person has a secure base in the current family, how can this be preserved in the Leaving Care Plan? If the child does not trust the caregiver enough to build a secure base relationship, how can this be tackled by focusing on caregiver availability? If a child has no supportive family to belong to, how can this be provided – even if this means a foster family getting to know and supporting a 17-year-old in residential care? If a child or young person is too anxious and reluctant to try new things, how can he be introduced to a new activity? If a foster or adoptive family member is not able to offer this special help, perhaps a befriender or mentor might.

Not all the answers to these questions will be in the parenting chapters (5–10), but there will be ideas that can be adapted and talked though. The key here is that if the child is not achieving developmental goals, at whatever age, then action needs to be taken. For no child should it be said that they are beyond help and hope.

Planning and matching

Security, stability and permanence, whether in birth, foster or adoptive families, are the ultimate goals of all planning for children. Decisions about matching are being made at all stages: which is the best emergency placement available for this child? Which foster family might best support this child to return home or move into adoption? Which foster or adoptive family is most likely to be able to offer a successful family for life? Matching the child to the family who can best meet their current and future needs requires the best possible assessment of the child's wishes, strengths, difficulties and needs for the future; the new family's wishes, needs and parenting capacity; and the inter-agency resources for supporting the match. The matching process draws on often unspoken assumptions or beliefs about the priorities among children's needs and the most important elements in family characteristics and quality of caregiving. Knowledge of attachment theory has a contribution to make in helping practitioners from a range of professions involved think about the way in which children and families might fit together.

Several issues must be borne in mind here. First, as stressed above, any planning or matching decision must take into account the full range of health, education, identity and other needs alongside the child's attachment-related needs. Attachment questions must be threaded through the linking and matching process as they are in the assessment itself and not seen in isolation.

Secondly, the assessment of children in relation to the core attachment issues described above can be looked at alongside the assessment of the associated caregiving capacities in foster carers and adopters (see Chapter 13). Both similar and different patterns in caregivers and children can work; foster carers or adopters and children who do not demonstrate their emotions and are happy quietly reading their books side by side may get on well, but so also can carers and children with very different patterns; more effusive carers may be intrigued and appreciative of rather contained children or more contained carers may warm to more outgoing children and adapt their caregiving accordingly. On the other hand, a carer and a child who are both anticipating rejection and both withdraw if they suspect they are not loved may get into a negative cycle of distance from each other (Beek and Schofield, 2004a; see also Steele *et al*, 2003).

Thirdly, just as there is no guarantee of success in any plan, however well founded in good assessment, there is no such thing as a perfect match. Matching children to families is always a process of drawing up a list of areas where some wishes/resources/needs of children and adopters or foster carers seem to be a pretty good fit, while acknowledging the areas where the fit may not be so good or the implications of the placement (e.g. change of school, geographical distance from siblings) may have an impact on an otherwise good match. In both planning and matching, the quality of the original decision needs to be as good as professional expertise and theoretically based knowledge can achieve – but in placing many more troubled children it will also be high-quality social work practice and the availability of interagency resources for support post placement which will give the match the best possible chance of success.

Different models of matching in adoption and permanent fostering have been emerging around the country, although there has been little research on outcomes (Hadley Briefing Paper, 2002). All adoption panels follow required procedures to make the final matching decision, but current models of linking children to families are very diverse. They include those that are more agency or professional judgement-led and those innovative models that are more prospective adopter-led (for example, the use of child appreciation days), with each model offering a very different sense of who is "choosing" and on what basis (Cousins, 2004). But in all agencies, whatever the route to the match, the final decision needs to be supported by the kind of comprehensive and yet subtle assessment of children and foster carers or adopters which is being advocated in this chapter.

There are many planning and matching dilemmas and here we highlight just two of the most difficult to illustrate the role that an understanding of attachment can play.

1) Can/should children be moved from existing stable short-term placements where carers wish to keep the child to new permanent families in foster care or adoption?

This is one of the most vexed questions in family placement work. For practitioners, the question of moving a child often hinges on how the child will cope with separation and loss, whether the child is likely to form a new attachment to new caregivers following a separation – and the possible change of legal status if adoption is to be the new placement of choice. The impact on children of separation and the loss of attachment figures was the starting point for Bowlby's development of attachment theory and social workers are always painfully aware of many children's struggle to manage their experience of separation and loss.

On the other hand, the reality of any placement service is that one or more moves are inevitable in almost every case. Children who come into care as an emergency, or even with some short-term planning, are unlikely to be placed initially in a family who could, should or would want to become that child's family for life. The role of bridge carers in settling children and resolving developmental problems before they are prepared and placed for adoption or long-term foster care is a skilled and critical part of family placement work but it assumes a move. So, the goal must always be to plan *necessary* moves very carefully and to avoid *unnecessary* moves, with an emphasis on developing good practice that helps children to *manage any move more successfully* (see section on helping children when they move later in this chapter). The key question here though is – what is a necessary or unnecessary move? This can only be defined in terms of a placement plan that is *most likely* to achieve a permanent placement that meets the child's needs and leads to a family for life – which may mean supporting the child and family in the present placement or may mean a move.

The attachment-related language that is often used in this area of practice can be rather unhelpful. As mentioned in Chapter 3, it is probably not helpful to think of attachments being *"transferred"* – a secure attachment relationship cannot be gifted, it has to be earned by the sensitive care provided by the new parents and will depend on the child's readiness to accept that care. This process can certainly be facilitated or made more difficult by existing caregivers in the way that the move is managed for the child, but the decision to move the child or the belief that the move will be straightforward on the basis that there is an existing secure attachment are not well founded in attachment theory. The positive influence of the child's capacity to think and to trust may well be outweighed by their need to grieve in a family that might find this difficult to accept. Similarly, the term *"reattaching"* has some limitations. It implies that the child has become *unattached* or *detached* from previous caregivers prior to forming a new attachment relationship. Although the child does lose the availability and care of the previous caregiver, it is almost certainly more helpful to think of the child as having multiple attachments which will change in significance as a child settles into a new permanent family, and the new caregivers become primary attachment figures.

First, and most obviously, when making the decision for a child to stay or to move in order to achieve permanence, it is important to assess in great detail the quality of the child's experience, relationships and psychosocial functioning in the current placement. The fact that a placement has been stable is rightly seen as in itself valuable, but stability does not on its own promote development. We have to allow for the full range of possibilities in terms of the *quality* of the caregiving and the child's current and potential future development and well-being in order to think about the potential benefits and risks of a move.

Where children are thriving across the full range of developmental areas and appear to have a selective attachment to the foster carers, a secure base for exploration, show some evidence of affect-regulation, self-esteem, self-efficacy and becoming part of the family, then the current placement is likely to be meeting the child's attachment and other needs. Most children in placement will be struggling with some if not all of these areas, but at the very least the child should be able to use the caregiver as a secure base to some degree and the caregiver should be providing care that reflects the five parenting dimensions in promoting these core developmental processes. Where the placement not only meets the child's current developmental needs, but the family is also willing and judged to be suitable to offer a family for life, then moving the child is almost certainly adding an unnecessary risk to the child's development. If this decision means, as it sometimes does, that a child will remain in foster care rather than be moved to adoption, very great care must be taken to ensure that the principle of permanence is planned into the foster placement. Agencies vary in the way in which they mark the special nature of such a planned foster family for life, but it will be important to protect both the attachment relationships and family membership when thinking, for example, about parental roles and contact (see Chapter 14).

During an assessment of a child's development and the quality of caregiving in the existing placement, it is important to recognise that there will be stable placements where children are not making the progress that was hoped for. This may happen even in the context of sensitive care, most often where children have had traumatic histories of abuse and loss or even where events in the birth family or in the foster or adoptive family (e.g. the birth or placement of another child or a bereavement) have unsettled the child. It is often not easy to be clear whether, for example, an apparent lack of warmth in the parent–child relationship is a result of the foster carer or adoptive parent's inherent limitations or is a consequence of the level of stress imported by the child – so in all cases the first response must be to help and support the caregivers.

However, where the child is not thriving and the quality of care is not good, even with all possible support, the child may need to be moved. There is a general anxiety about moving children, which is appropriate, but one of the main barriers to a full assessment that picks up unsatisfactory placements and leads to a necessary move is that the child's difficult behaviour and failure to thrive may be explained *only* in terms of the disturbance in the child or the child's history. Although the child's history will of course be a major factor, the possibility must be acknowledged that caregivers may either not be responding sensitively enough or may even be causing the child's disturbed behaviour. In the current climate, there is a risk that a wish to avoid moves and to achieve stability generally (reinforced by performance indicators) will combine with a misuse of attachment theory to leave children in placements that do not meet their needs and may actually contribute to poor outcomes and future psychopathology. These are the most difficult cases, but do need to be thought about in a child-centred way.

In relation to misuse of attachment theory, the problems can arise when practitioners from a range of disciplines (e.g. social work, psychology, psychiatry, the judiciary) fix on the idea that attachment relationships (even insecure relationships) are so significant, and the loss of them so traumatic, that children cannot then form a new attachment relationship. It is obviously the case that early or long-standing secure and insecure caregiver–child relationships are significant and that their loss is not easy for the child to manage. This has been the focus of much of the discussion in this book. But, as with the removal of children from troubled, neglectful or frightening birth families, the removal of children from troubled, neglectful or frightening foster or adoptive families may be necessary. The whole system of family placement is built on the premise that new attachment relationships can be made at any age and that the management of loss and separation is preferable to leaving a child in a family where the child's needs cannot be met or the child is being harmed. It is important to apply this belief system to the prospect of moving children from foster or adoptive families, where unsatisfactory or harmful care has been identified. Attachment theory and research need to be used not only to emphasise the impact of loss, but also to recognise the possibility that throughout life it is possible to form attachment relationships that can become secure and that for some children this may mean a move.

There are, of course, no moves that are risk free – but also few decisions to leave a child in an existing placement that do not acknowledge that there may be some element of risk of the placement not meeting the child's needs or of it breaking down. In practice, placements are rarely fully meeting or not meeting a child's needs. They are more likely to be meeting some but not all of the child's needs – just as any future placement to which the child may move is likely to meet some but not all of the child's needs. Full and detailed written assessments that are based on good evidence, research and developmental theory and then reviewed by a multi-disciplinary group of professionals are the only way of increasing the likelihood that security will be promoted and risk minimised.

The attachment-related parenting and developmental dimensions outlined in this book should help practitioners to clarify what it is they should be looking for and prioritising. Availability and sensitivity, the capacity to see and reflect on the world from the child's perspective, are the foundation stones of caregiving, with the child's capacity to trust, use the caregiver as a secure base for exploration and manage their feelings and behaviour as useful indicators of progress. But the evidence of the successfulness or limitations of any placement in these terms – and the assessment of the merits of a current placement and the impact of a move – will be found not only through close understanding of the quality of the attachment relationship, but in areas such as the child's social presentation, health, education and peer-group relationships.

One final factor that should be informing all placement decisions, but particularly these very difficult and finely balanced decisions, is the life-span perspective. The ultimate goal for even the newborn infant is a healthy, stable and socially well-integrated adult life. True permanence means a family who meets the child's needs and will be there for the child through childhood, adolescence, young adulthood and parenthood.

2) Placing siblings together or apart?

As with the previous dilemma, decisions about the significance of sibling relationships relative to other factors in an assessment of a child's needs when planning for permanence draw on a range of different assumptions, theories and research. But the general principle of keeping or placing siblings together, unless there is a good reason not to, is established in legal and practice guidance (Children Act 1989 Guidance, Vol 3; Lord and Borthwick, 2001). Research reviews suggest that 'being placed with a brother or sister will usually be protective' (Sellick *et al*, 2004, p. 81), but assessments in individual cases must always address the needs of each child separately as well as together (Rushton *et al*, 2001). Many children in care have very complex sibling groups of full-, step- and half-siblings – and indeed "siblings" who were in the birth family, who may have no biological or legal connection but may be important figures in their lives. The significance of these relationships, which may be presented as an argument for placing siblings together, can relate to a range of factors to do with shared genealogy and identity, shared history and experiences and/or closeness through providing or receiving support in adversity. Where siblings are separated or not placed together following a separation, it is often in order to avoid sibling conflict, to enable a younger and less damaged child to be adopted or to separate out the oldest and most disruptive child from the rest of a sibling group – although too often it is because no joint placement is available. The quality of sibling relationships and whether they have shared or non-shared previous environments of abuse and neglect in the birth family are complex issues. Assessment is particularly difficult once children have been even temporarily separated and the aim is to predict the impact on each other or on potential new families of bringing them back together.

Children can report completely opposite experiences of separation from siblings. Lisa (17) described how separation from her more disruptive older sibling at the age of 10 (to give her a chance to "settle" and make progress) had, as she saw it, blighted her childhood, led to a series of broken placements and left her unable to trust anyone. In contrast, Brenda (17) reported that she had said that she wanted to be placed with her older sister when she was 10, but later regretted this decision as she established close relationships with their new carers and a successful school and social life, while her sister did not commit herself to the carers (indeed, hankered after her previous carers) and distressed their foster parents by stealing and drug taking.

Although a decision about sibling placement is not obviously a question that hinges on attachment to each other, it is not unusual for children to be described as "attached" to one or more of their siblings. The notion of attachment to siblings needs to be examined by going back to basics and thinking about the role of attachment figures as able to provide a haven of safety and a secure base for exploration. Although this sounds like the description of an adult–child relationship, in some birth families, and especially where care was unpredictable or not available from parent figures, older siblings often do provide care and protection for younger brothers and sisters. This ranges from organising breakfast to protecting younger children from violence. The concept of a secure base may also apply, as young children often find it more difficult to play in the absence of older siblings who make them feel less anxious. Although even a close sibling relationship lacks many of the characteristics of child–caregiver attachment relationships (for example, the older child is less likely to be able to provide scaffolding for learning or to promote perspective taking and mind-mindedness than a parent), there will be aspects of the relationship that have *some* of the characteristics of an attachment relationship (reducing anxiety, supporting play and exploration), as well as a shared identity and history, and loss of that relationship is likely to lead to a profound sense of loss and grief.

Where one sibling provides and the other receives nurture and protection, there are often some difficult issues to resolve about the "parental" child when placement plans are made. In some cases, separating the siblings in order to "allow" the older child to be a child again is recommended. It is to be hoped that dealing with this issue by physically separating siblings would only be done where there was absolutely no prospect of carers being able to work to change the nature of the relationship within a placement in which both children can find security. As we have seen, caregiving as opposed to careseeking behaviours are not in themselves a bad thing – many cultures would advocate such roles for older children. Clearly, where older children have a history of sexually abusing or traumatising or overwhelming younger children, there might be good reasons for a separation in the interests of both children, but where the relationship is actually experienced by both children as largely positive, using a plan for separation rather than therapeutic caregiving to promote each child's development seems to create unnecessary losses.

Particularly difficult, but also quite common, are the cases where separating siblings is recommended because potential rivalry and hostility between siblings are especially bitter and may continue into placements. Here the challenge is to draw a line between a rather extreme form of normal sibling rivalry, which may be manageable, and something that is so deep-rooted and pathological that it is unlikely to be resolvable in an ordinary placement and may reduce the chances for both children of achieving stability and security in a placement. It would be hoped that contact arrangements may then be used to keep the links – though here too there will be tensions in maintaining a contact-based relationship.

Another point at which attachment becomes highly relevant to this area of decision making is where a child's secure attachment to a current carer may conflict with plans to place a child with siblings. Here, the risk of disrupting the attachment may outweigh the benefits of bringing siblings together.

Raymond (3) had been placed separately from his two older siblings when he first came into care at the age of 18 months. He became a much loved child in his foster home and was very well settled. His older brother and sister were also doing well in their foster home, although his sister had some behaviour problems. It was decided to move Raymond to live with his siblings as a permanent placement. From the outset he withdrew emotionally and would not engage with the foster carers. At the same time, his sister's behaviour started to become more difficult and within two years she had to leave this family. Although gradually Raymond settled in the family and started to accept the foster mother as a mother, he developed significant behaviour problems and it was not clear that what he had gained in terms of sibling relationships compensated for the loss of the original family.

All of these situations regarding sibling placements can overlap with the question of whether younger children should be separated from older siblings in order to be adopted. This suggestion may arise because younger children are less damaged, because it is easier to find adopters for younger children and/or because the older child may express a clear wish not to be adopted. As with all of these very difficult decisions, the needs of each child must be considered separately (including their need for a relationship with each other) and, very importantly, practice in long-term foster care and adoption must be able to accommodate these situations. Where young children who might have been adopted are placed with older siblings in foster placements that are designed to be *as permanent as adoption*, agencies must ensure that the new placement is offered every possible safeguard to ensure that the special status of the placement is recognised – on files, at reviews, in terms of the parenting decisions to be made by the foster carers, contact arrangements and so on. Similarly, where the younger child is separated, it is not enough simply to make a plan for contact. Social workers need to actively recruit adopters who can enable the relationship to flourish – both through face-to-face contact but also through acknowledging this relationship in the photos on the child's bedside table, sending postcards from holiday or including siblings and their changing worlds in conversation. What Brodzinsky (2005) refers to as 'psychological and communicative openness' in placements and agencies will be needed to support separated siblings in what may well be placements that emerge from compromises designed to ensure the best interests of each child.

Social workers' relationships and work with children

It would be surprising in a book that explores and highlights the importance of relationships as a source of security and resilience, for there not to be a section on the social worker's relationship with the child. Here we focus on attachment-related principles of social workers' relationships with and support for fostered and adopted children – and then focus on three linked areas where attachment issues and understandings are particularly relevant: listening to children and ascertaining their wishes and feelings; life story work; and helping children when they move.

Social workers acknowledge the importance of building trusting and reliable relationships with children and children value relationships with social workers who support them through thick and thin. For most children, relationships with social workers will be one of a range of potential sources of support, but they can be of great significance for the child. Social workers who offer consistent, well-informed, thoughtful, respectful, non-judgemental and containing care and concern, are willing to listen *and* are active on behalf of children and their families, provide a thread across and within placements which can contain children's anxieties and help to hold children and families together.

There are, in practice, many potential barriers to successful relationships. At its most basic, where social workers move between jobs or are moved as a result of agency reorganisation or are only temporary, there can be a sense that getting close to children is neither possible nor desirable – it will mean yet another loss for the child. Some foster carers protest that, without a longer-term commitment by workers, a relationship should not be expected nor confidences asked for from the child. Even for social workers who are stable in their post and work in structures that promote continuity, it can still seem that competing demands to write reports, organise and attend meetings or court hearings, deal with emergencies and so on make it impossible to find the time to make a steady commitment to a child.

But in some situations, the difficulties may run deeper than agency constraints. Social workers who are having to face up to a child's needs and the problems in meeting them, might find it hard to visit a child who is behaving badly, whether in an excellent or a less than ideal placement; or a child who has been suspended from what was an appropriate or inappropriate school placement, or a child who has been waiting for too long for an adoptive or long-term foster placement, or an adopted child in a fragile placement who has significant behaviour problems and shows few signs of recovery from previous trauma even after several years in placement. Although none of these problems are caused by or likely to be easily resolvable by the social worker, when combined with problems of time and resources, it may become simpler at times to minimise the importance of a social worker in a child's life than to engage with a child's anxiety, sadness and disappointment, which they feel powerless to relieve. Social workers want to do their best for the child for whom they have responsibility, and it is hard when outcomes can seem as much beyond their control as they are beyond the control of the child. However, painful though it is for the social worker, this is a pain that the child and the carer may also be finding unbearable. The social worker needs support from colleagues and supervisors to stay in touch with the stresses and uncertainties and to provide, wherever possible, some measure of emotional containment for the child.

These challenges of an organisational, professional and personal kind should not mean that we do not aspire to gain some understanding of and maximise the contribution that a social worker can make to the child's secure base. In particular, it is helpful to think about what the social worker may be able to offer that is unique to their role. Clare Winnicott (1964, p. 45) offered this account of the distinctive nature of the social worker's relationship to the child.

The social worker starts off as a real person concerned with the external events and people in the child's life. In the course of her work with the child she will attempt to bridge the gap between the external world and his feelings about it and in doing so she will enter his inner world too. As a person who can move from one world to another, the social worker can have a special value all her own for the child and a special kind of relationship to him.

Children's social workers have the responsibility for *holding all aspects of the child's life together* and this has some powerful resonances in terms of the anxiety-containing, reflective and caregiving functions of a secure base. Social workers will be familiar with the child's history, know the birth family (parents, grandparents, siblings) and the foster or adoptive families and understand the child's physical health, mental health, educational and identity needs. They will appreciate the impact of the child protection and court processes on the child and the families and may have been involved with the child during these stressful times. Once the child is in placement, social workers will retain the primary role in the professional network, ensuring the child's well-being, advocating for the child at school, and providing continuity when children return home or move on to foster care or adoptive placements. The social worker is the immediate face of the local authority's corporate parental responsibility and this professional/ personal role brings many of the same rewards and challenges of any parenting.

One further challenge is that social workers have to become concerned and focused on the child's needs, but then delegate the parenting role to a foster carer or adopter. The worker's feelings here may be along a dimension from a wish to relinquish all responsibility to the new family ('They're the experts/the real parents') through to finding it difficult to relinquish responsibility at all ('I'm the only one who really knows what this child needs'). Managing shared parenting responsibilities requires a great deal of support from supervisors, who can help social workers clarify where and why they are finding themselves at particular points on this dimension in relation to particular children. With the growing role of adoption support, it is likely that in adoption too a range of professionals will be working alongside adoptive parents beyond the adoption order being made and will need to negotiate their own role and responsibilities just as carefully.

These are features of managing the child's "external world" (their circumstances, their moves, their day-to-day care), but for the social worker this role crosses inevitably into some appreciation of what has been going on in the child's "internal world", which can then be built on through direct work with the child. Entering the child's internal world means listening to the child. This includes ascertaining their *wishes* and *feelings*, as required by legislation (Children Act 1989 and Children (Scotland) Act 1995), but also ascertaining the *meanings* that the child has attached to people and experiences. It will include an awareness of the sense the child has made of all the external events on the child's file with which the social worker is familiar – and to appreciate all the many experiences and memories which the child has stored away that will not be known to the social worker. The social worker can, though, try to see the world through the child's eyes in order both to understand what the child is thinking and to help the

351

child make sense of the external world. The social worker can share both the sadness and the joys of the child's life. If the social worker can help to bring together and make sense of the external and internal worlds of the child in this way *and* in themselves offer predictability and continuity, it will help the child to feel more secure and more competent.

The nature of the relationship between social worker and child must be viewed within the range of functions and goals that the relationship might have. This is not a relationship as between family members (although parent-like feelings and certainly parent-like activities on behalf of the child are often required, and "going the extra mile" like a parent is much valued by children) or as between friends (although carers and children sometimes say of a reliable and constant social worker – he or she is more like a friend.). Whatever the interconnectedness that may emerge in the context of contributing to a secure base, for a child, the basis of the relationship is that between a professional and a child, a relationship for which there are responsibilities that are laid down within law, procedure and practice. It is therefore useful to think about the relationship and the work with the child as threaded through the range of practice, from first assessment prior to placement through to supporting permanent placement at home, with relatives, with foster carers or with adopters. But the personal and professional boundaries in this, as in other areas of social work with children, need care. The social worker's empathy for and relationship with the child must be sustained in order to fulfil their professional role effectively, and the purposes and boundaries of the professional role will guide the extent to which social workers engage emotionally with and make commitments to the child.

Listening to children: ascertaining wishes and feelings

Ascertaining children's wishes and feelings and taking them into account is not only a requirement of law and procedure (Children Act 1989 and Children (Scotland) Act 1995), but is also an important part of applying a developmental attachment model to the assessment and planning process. How can social workers begin to undertake accurate assessments of children's past, present and likely futures without taking into account what children think and feel about their experiences and what they might think about future options? The *meanings* the child attributes to events are as important as the events themselves in terms of shaping behaviour. Apart from the benefits to the decision-making process of more accurate information about the child's thinking and feeling, facilitating the child's participation will offer an opportunity to build the child's sense of self-efficacy and reduce feelings of powerlessness.

The twin tasks of ascertaining children wishes and feelings and taking them into account both need to be considered in the light of children's developmental history (Schofield, 1998b, 2005). Given our attachment-based understanding of the complex patterns of children's thinking and the impact of abuse, neglect and separation on children's minds, it can be helpful to separate out these different areas of development and think about how they contribute to listening to the voice of the child (see Figure 10, adapted from Schofield, 2005).

Figure 10

The voice of the child: a developmental model

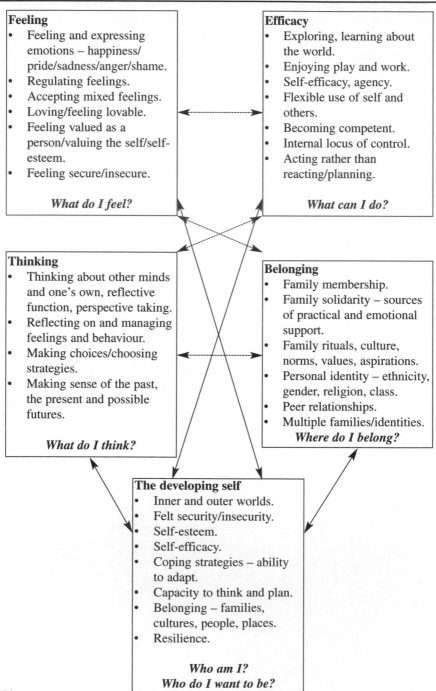

Feeling
- Feeling and expressing emotions – happiness/ pride/sadness/anger/shame.
- Regulating feelings.
- Accepting mixed feelings.
- Loving/feeling lovable.
- Feeling valued as a person/valuing the self/self-esteem.
- Feeling secure/insecure.

What do I feel?

Efficacy
- Exploring, learning about the world.
- Enjoying play and work.
- Self-efficacy, agency.
- Flexible use of self and others.
- Becoming competent.
- Internal locus of control.
- Acting rather than reacting/planning.

What can I do?

Thinking
- Thinking about other minds and one's own, reflective function, perspective taking.
- Reflecting on and managing feelings and behaviour.
- Making choices/choosing strategies.
- Making sense of the past, the present and possible futures.

What do I think?

Belonging
- Family membership.
- Family solidarity – sources of practical and emotional support.
- Family rituals, culture, norms, values, aspirations.
- Personal identity – ethnicity, gender, religion, class.
- Peer relationships.
- Multiple families/identities.

Where do I belong?

The developing self
- Inner and outer worlds.
- Felt security/insecurity.
- Self-esteem.
- Self-efficacy.
- Coping strategies – ability to adapt.
- Capacity to think and plan.
- Belonging – families, cultures, people, places.
- Resilience.

Who am I?
Who do I want to be?

Even where practitioners are sensitive to this range of interacting developmental factors, children who have been subjected to fear or uncertainty and do not believe that there is anyone they can trust are unlikely to engage easily in sharing their feelings. In part, this is because children who have been traumatised may find it difficult to process information about experiences and options in an organised way or let themselves think about, let alone communicate about, what they *really* think and feel. Children will, in most cases, of course, have very mixed feelings about parents and other family members, who may at times have offered them care but at other times hurt or neglected them. Similarly, children may have mixed feelings about foster carers and adopters when they still have loyalties to the birth family or are wary because they mentally represent all caregivers as dangerous. In addition, all children, even older children and teenagers, will find it hard to think through the advantages and disadvantages of moves to hypothetical families or changes of legal status. It is likely also that, to some degree, children, quite appropriately, find it hard to speak to strangers and authority figures. Most fostered and adopted children have had a series of people asking them about what they *really* want – social workers, psychologists and solicitors as well as family members – so such hesitation to confide would seem very reasonable. The question of trust has therefore to be considered alongside the extent to which a child is able to reflect on and talk about their past, their current circumstances and their fears and hopes for the future.

Both trust and the difficulty in formulating a view that may touch on divided loyalties or uncertain futures will be very relevant in thinking about children who express mixed feelings, and for whom saying, for example, that they may want less contact with one parent than another is too anxiety provoking. In such circumstances, children cannot communicate openly and often act out their views, sabotaging one parent's contact, for example. At other times, the child may want his wishes to be kept a secret, saying, 'If I say I don't want to go home or have contact, does my dad need to know I've said it?' or 'I want more contact with my dad but I don't want to say so and upset my carers'.

Attachment theory provides a helpful framework for making sense of children's anxieties where they have lacked or lack a secure base and have no history of trust and open communication. But there are also specific benefits in having an attachment-based understanding of insecure children's different strategies for managing anxiety when social workers are ascertaining and making sense of children's thoughts, wishes and feelings (Schofield, 1998b). Understanding the difference, for example, between a child with an avoidant strategy for coping with anxiety and a child with an ambivalent/resistant strategy will enable the social worker to make better sense of why a child may show little emotion and be dismissing of the importance of contact or may be intensely preoccupied with and show extremes of emotion during and when discussing contact. Contact may be equally important to both children. In particular, it will help explain why a maltreated child with a disorganised pattern may communicate their need to control others in words and behaviour, while actually experiencing feelings of helplessness and despair. Such observations of behaviour may be much more powerful than direct enquiry, but they do need careful interpretation with the help of a colleague or supervisor.

Because attachment theory proposes that these defensive strategies are associated with the need to reduce anxiety, and particularly anxiety around proximity to and separation from attachment figures, it is likely that children who are separated from attachment figures, for example, when they come into foster care, will intensify these ways of expressing or avoiding the expression of emotion, achieving or denying the need for proximity, controlling others or being quietly compliant. For many maltreated children, such heightened anxiety will have been cumulative in the context of fears of separation and loss generated by domestic violence, parental drug and alcohol misuse or direct threats to the child that the parent will commit suicide or abandon the child in other ways. Once in foster care, children may smile as if nothing has happened, but will be monitoring the carers' faces and behaviours in anticipation of danger.

How and what children communicate will be closely related to how they think and manage difficult ideas and feelings. Many children who have to manage the idea that they may not be lovable or have to cope with the prospect of separation from siblings will be drawing on a whole history of defending against the pain of feelings and fear of the outcome of moves. From infancy to adulthood, the fear of being left entirely alone is universal, for example, but it is important to make sense of how differently children and young people communicate such fundamental anxieties when they are included in discussions about their future. Theory can help workers to tune in to how children's minds may be working and how this may affect what is communicated, directly and indirectly.

It is essential when emphasising the complexity of children's thinking, and the impact of abuse, neglect and separation on how children communicate, not to give the impression that children cannot be trusted to tell adults the truth about their experience. Understanding psychological complexity is about facilitating that communication. When, for example, children report events in the birth, foster or adoptive family that provoke child protection concerns or their behaviour suggests that there may be some problem with their care, it is very important that children are heard, taken seriously and offered whatever help they might need – just as birth parents, foster carers and adopters need to be heard and offered whatever help *they* need in the context of allegations. In such circumstances, it is especially important to sort out whether reported abuse is current or whether feelings have been stirred up that bring back memories of abuse in earlier families. Sometimes a child's chance remark in anger can lead to placements being ended unnecessarily. On the other hand, some children have continued to be exposed to neglect and abuse in birth, foster and adoptive families, in spite of their expressed concerns, because it was assumed, by social workers, that the child's behaviour just demonstrated a reaction to the move.

Children need to be listened to at all stages of family placement work and by all professionals with whom they come into contact. But this is within the context of ensuring that responsible adults take responsibility for children's welfare and that fostered and adopted children are not burdened with the full weight of making important decisions – any more than are children who grow up within birth families.

> *Children should feel that they have been properly consulted, that their views have been properly considered and that they have participated as partners in the decision making process. However, they should not be made to feel that the burden of decision making has fallen totally upon them.* (Children Act, 1989 Vol. 3: Para. 5.35)

If we consider one of the key points procedurally when children will be asked for their views – the six-monthly looked after children review – it is apparent that practice varies considerably (Thomas, 2005). Here, there is a high expectation that children participate in a range of ways, including a combination of completing a form, talking with the social worker prior to the meeting and attending the meeting itself. This needs to be conducted sensitively. One story from research into long-term fostered children's experiences highlights how taking the child's wishes and feelings into account is about more than just including the child in the review.

> *Cherilyn (14) was in a very successful long-term placement and had regular contact with her birth mother, who was still a heroin user. Cherilyn was also very successful at school and hoping to go to university to read law. A very emotionally contained girl, she kept her care identity and her school identity quite separate. When she arrived home from school one day to attend her review, she found the school Head of Year sitting in her living room with her foster carer and her mother. Cherilyn had not been consulted by the social worker about the invitation to the school to send a representative and was very upset.*

Rules of thumb based on good interdisciplinary principles, such as inviting educational professionals to a review, may make a great deal of sense in many cases, but Cherilyn's circumstances were such that this felt like a crossing over of her two worlds and an intrusion into her family and her home. She was very close to her birth mother (as well as her foster mother), but would not have wanted the school to think of her as associated with her mother's world.

What can happen is that reviews may take the place of social work practice, as a convenient way of getting the views of a range of people rather than making time-consuming separate contacts with school, birth parents, etc. But in a period where interagency collaboration is emphasised more than ever, the child as a person and her experience of such processes need to be taken into account if the system is to be truly child-centred.

Life story work: developing a coherent narrative

A major theme of the book has been the critical importance for children of being able to give shape and meaning to their lives; to find some way of explaining *why* things have happened in the way that they have, *why* parents, carers and professionals have acted in the way that they did – and indeed *why* they themselves may have developed particular strengths and difficulties. *Life story work* is often a key focus for making sense of the events that have occurred in a child's life and there are a number of very helpful texts that offer guidance on the process and the product of life story work (e.g. Ryan and Walker, 1999; Camis, 2001; Fahlberg, 1994). But life story work, often undertaken at critical points of change and commonly in anticipation of permanent placement, can never be isolated as a one-off event, when life story work is actually life-long for all of us. Even in adulthood or old age we review the meaning of our life, its various peaks and troughs – and what it all might say about who we are as people. For fostered and adopted children, who take rather particular routes through childhood and into adult life, this process will have rather specific elements that lead them to think hard about their answers to such questions as 'Why was I so unlucky?' and/or 'Why was I so lucky?' about their diverse family experiences.

An attachment theory-informed approach to life story work would take as a starting point the child's need to have *information* that enables them to put together *a coherent story*, one that has *meaning* for the child, has a beginning, a middle, a here and now – and a sense of what the future might hold. In this formulation, as elsewhere in attachment theory, the emphasis is on the crucial links between cognition and emotion, thinking and feeling. Processing this life story information at an intellectual or emotional level is rarely straightforward for the child and the social worker's role will be central in working alongside the child, taking into account the child's appraisal of events, what they thought happened and why, and what kind of little girl or boy they remember themselves to be, before offering ideas that might help the child to have a more accurate and balanced picture.

The use of ecomaps and other practical and visual ways of representing the child's pathway or journey is extremely helpful for children of all ages (Fahlberg, 1994; Ryan and Walker, 1999; Camis, 2001). It is generally accepted now that, whatever approach is taken, the process of life story work is as important as the product and the task needs to be integrated into a holistic approach that enables a child to have some capacity to think about and revisit their story and its meaning throughout their life. Apart from placements made at birth, fostered and adopted children are not able to draw on a continuous and shared family memory that carries their story from birth onwards, so this gap must be filled by books, pictures, tapes – and by significant people, such as the foster carers, adopters and social workers who know about the early days, helping the child to build a *constructive memory of the present*, perhaps in an "Experiences Book", for the future. For children placed in new families at birth, there may be some preoccupation with the birth parents' feelings and circumstances during the pregnancy and what happened even during the hours or days in the hospital that may have elapsed between birth and placement. This shows the child trying to grasp the meaning of the losses and gains that the move to a new family has for them, primarily in terms of core questions such as 'Was I a lovable baby?' Perhaps this is why for all children, not only those adopted as infants, the original birth certificate is a particularly poignant part of their life story.

Attachment theory would emphasise that what children need above all if they are to be able to reflect on themselves and present themselves to and communicate openly with others, is a *coherent narrative* that makes sense and which leaves them with a view of themselves and their history that can be reflected on without being overwhelmed or having to defend against thinking about the past. If children have to work so hard to exclude the past from conscious thought, it can limit their capacity to engage with and experience the world differently in the present.

This focus on helping children find meaning and shape in their lives is a task for social workers, foster carers and adopters, and can not just inform life story work itself but also support the commentary on how the child's current life is unfolding. Above all, listening to children needs to be based on such developmental understandings but it also needs to be an active process (Schofield, 2005). Children in foster care and adoption are on a journey and many parts of it are difficult. They need to feel that someone is with them on that journey and they need a framework to help them think about it and feel safe. This is a child describing how his adoptive mother gave him help to manage a particularly difficult part of his journey – the court processes and delays leading up to the making of an adoption order.

> *Mum referred to it as like a train. And then we started, and then we were going along, and we had to stop at a station, and we go along again and we break down and then we got stuck up a hill. Stuff like that.* (Thomas, adopted child, aged 9, in Thomas and Beckford *et al*, 1999, p. 73)

There are three important and connected messages for practice in life story work that link to attachment theory. First, the role of the practitioner or carer undertaking life story work, as in other potentially therapeutic relationships with children, is to offer a *secure base for exploration* – in this case *exploration of the past, the present and the future.* It will only be if availability, sensitivity, acceptance and co-operation are present in the relationship that the task of thinking and reflecting on the past becomes safe enough from the child's point of view.

Secondly, the child will bring their characteristic strategy for managing stress and anxiety to this relationship and this stressful and potentially anxiety-provoking piece of work. So it is helpful again to be aware of these different strategies and the reasons behind them. For example, the child may be open to a secure, balanced, undefended and straightforward discussion about the past that allows for complexity and difficult feelings ('I know my mother wanted to look after me when she first had me, but she started taking drugs and she didn't look after me properly and then her boyfriend hurt me. That upset me a lot.'); or the child may shut down on and deny feelings, dismissing the value of relationships ('I don't mind/don't care about my mum; it's best not to think about memories'); or the child may be preoccupied with and angry about relationships and defensively split them into wholly good and wholly bad ('My mother was the best/worst mother ever and I love her to bits/will never speak to her again; my foster carer never cared about me at all, she just did it for the money and that's not fair, but my residential worker really, really loved me and never said an angry word); or the child may have a range of controlling strategies for not engaging with difficult questions ('You can't make me do life story work'; 'I'm going to do it my way'; 'I can't remember the past and don't care about it anyway'; 'I'm not listening').

Thirdly, some types of information about the past can be managed more productively by children at different developmental stages and at different stages in their recovery. Children become better able to think and to allow confusing negative and positive feelings to be accessed and processed once they feel more secure. But most young children will find it very difficult if not impossible to integrate two different ideas into their mind ('A mummy is supposed to look after a baby, but my mummy hurt me'; 'I long to see my mummy, but she scares me'.). Even in adolescence and adulthood, it is difficult to manage or reconcile these apparent paradoxes. When doing life story work, children and young people often pick up a summary message, 'I know my Mummy and Daddy loved me really', which gives them an apparently comforting story to tell to themselves and to others. But if this story does not fit with their memories or with other stories they've heard, it cannot help them resolve the dilemma of why they were injured by Mummy or why Daddy left. There is a risk that they are left with the alternative story: 'Then it must have been my fault'. The ongoing nature of the caregivers' and workers' task here cannot be overemphasised, and it is necessary to check back to the child weeks and months after issues have been raised to see how the child is storing that piece of information *now* and the meanings it *now* has.

Most practitioners, foster carers and adopters work hard to help children reach as realistic and balanced an account of their history as is possible – finding positives, facing up to negatives and accepting that some things will never be known for certain – especially the answers to the "why" questions. The *facts* of domestic violence, moves in the birth family or in care, the splitting of siblings in the birth family or for adoption may be known, but in explaining *why* – which is what the child may ask or need to know – the social worker often has to construct a range of possible explanations for the child to consider. The child may be told that the mother had learning difficulties and didn't know how to feed babies properly, the father took drugs, the child's older sister got hurt, and so on. In all this complexity, children can often arrive at their own simple but contrasting explanations – that they were *taken away* by social workers, *given away* by parents or *caused the separation* by their bad behaviour. Each, as Fahlberg (1994) suggests, leads to different kinds of anxieties about whether they were protected enough or loved enough or are bad children who will break up the next family too.

In the course of constructing a life story, the "why" question may require the child to imagine what key people were thinking and feeling in order to explain why a parent or carer or social worker did what they did. There is no doubt that the doing of life story work can in this way be an opportunity to draw on and build the child's capacity for empathy and perspective taking. But it is never easy to manage the range of challenging stories that must be made to make sense for the child without leaving the child more fearful or lowering their self-esteem. Sometimes the story of hurt and loss is very difficult to bear, but just about understandable or manageable; for example, 'My mum was only 14 when she had me and her mum didn't help her look after me, so she left me in my cot too much and I didn't grow very well and had to come into foster care'; 'My previous foster carer loved me, but when her husband got ill she stopped fostering, so I had to leave'; 'My adoptive parents wanted to look after a child but they didn't understand that I would break things when I got upset, and they said they couldn't look after me.' The fact of a child's legitimate upset and anger at these experiences of rejection needs to be acknowledged, discussed and recorded, and, as the story is revisited at different ages from early childhood to adolescence, the capacity to empathise with these significant people and the balance of anger, sadness and resolution is likely to change.

But for children with histories of more extreme abuse and neglect, putting themselves in the mind of the abusive or neglectful parent, foster carer or adopter in order to begin to think about why they might hurt children – and why hurt them in particular – may be almost too overwhelming. It can be difficult for workers to make understandable or bearable actions and motivations that are confusing and frightening to the child. It can be hard to find redeeming parts of the story on which the child might build. 'My birth mother did not protect me from physical abuse by my father because she was frightened of him too' may help, but leaves the child feeling anxious about the safety of the mother. 'My mother and father both neglected me' is very difficult to cope with – 'Surely one of them would have noticed I was hungry?' Although some children are able to develop some empathy if their parents' history includes them being victims of their own parents, this story then risks creating fears that as parents they too will inevitably abuse or neglect their children – a common concern for looked after and adopted children. But however difficult it is to find a balanced way of thinking about some birth relatives, it is essential not to demonise the child's birth family. A way of telling the story must be found that avoids the sense that any human being is bad beyond explanation or forgiveness, since the child themselves, their siblings, their peers – and their foster carers or adopters – will all do bad things sometimes and need to be understood and forgiven.

The concept of *resolution* as part of life story work is therefore difficult but important to think about for many reasons. In contrasting "unresolved" adolescents and adults who have had adverse caregiving experiences with those who have had similar early experiences but are classified as "earned/secure", there is an explicit notion that bad experiences in relationships can be processed or resolved, most commonly through subsequent experiences also in relationships. Although in childhood this is most obviously through the provision of sensitive caregiving, therapeutic work with children, including life story work, can also be part of the package which helps children to come to terms with or resolve their difficulties. This does not mean reaching a point of being able to scrub the experiences from the mind. On the contrary, it means developing the capacity to 'stay open to the pain of a difficult past', which Cassidy (2005) suggests is an essential part of achieving security. This does not mean being constantly aware of or thinking about the past – far from it – but it does mean that when feelings or ideas that relate to painful memories of the past inevitably surface and risk interfering with life and relationships in the present, then it is necessary to be able to have a way of managing those feelings or actual memories without being overwhelmed and without suppressing or denying them.

This young woman (24) who grew up in foster care was able to think about what happened in her life and put a framework around it that helped her to make sense of it.

> *I was given an opportunity when I was taken into care to have a normal, decent life. To go to school, to go to college, the works. I wouldn't have had that when I was with my mum. But it also gave me the insight to see how she is and that it's not her fault. I think she's probably ill.*

Even where circumstances are extreme and the "resolution" cannot be an easy one, some way of accepting the past still has to be found. This 28 year old woman had been neglected by her birth mother and had been present when her younger brother was killed by her mother's boyfriend – a very clear memory from when she was four years old that she was able to talk about in a research interview. She had then been in a very stable foster family placement, married, bought a house and had children. When she looked back, she still blamed her mother for not caring enough about her, but she had let go of some of the longing, anger and bitterness towards her mother that she had felt as a child.

> *I wish I'd been given the right start in life and I wish that . . . and I just came to the conclusion recently that it is just pure luck who you are born and how your life is going to be . . . I think that's the only way to look at it, I really do. I think if you are lucky enough to be born to parents who are able to look after you and love you . . . but unfortunately I wasn't.*

This woman had remained in contact with her birth mother through childhood and adulthood. She had felt rather detached emotionally in her foster placement, but was still very much a member of her foster family in adult life (Schofield, 2003).

What such stories suggest is that the seeds of acceptance and resolution can be sown in childhood in life story work and in all the many ways that the child is enabled to think about and reflect on their feelings about a difficult past. But that living with the memories and accepting the reality of their childhood is a life-long task, which for these two women was aided by the fact that they also had some positive memories to incorporate into their narrative and a foster family to belong to currently. This gave them the capacity to live with but not be dominated by their histories.

Helping a child move to a new placement

The process of moving a child from the birth family into a new placement or from one placement to another, goes to the heart of attachment-sensitive practice. It links with many of the other issues dealt with in this chapter, but particularly the question of the social worker's relationship with the child, the importance of listening to children and the role of life story work in helping children develop a coherent narrative, a story that makes sense. Moving placements has been touched on in various parts of the book so far, primarily in relation to the role of the new carers in responding to the child sensitively, understanding the impact of loss and meeting the challenge of developing the child's trust in the new family. Here we focus on the role of the child's social worker, who has the task not only of making the plans and arrangements for a move of placement, but also working directly with the child through the process.

No one model for practice can fit all the varied situations where children must move, yet some core principles apply, whether a young infant is moving into an adoption placement or a teenager is moving into supported lodgings. Even in emergency placements, the same principles are relevant, as work needs to be done retrospectively to pick up the pieces. A full appreciation of the impact of loss and separation needs to be at the heart of the practice, but also the hope for growth and fulfilment of potential in the new family. The social worker and the carers need to sustain this dual position and help the child to grieve for the loss or the rejection but build hope for the future.

1) Open communication

From the early stages of the development of the plan for the move, the child needs to have accurate information in a form that, as far as possible, makes sense to the child – even if it is accurate about the fact that the future is uncertain. Reasons for the move need to be clarified as far as possible, although as the section on life story work suggested, it is not easy for the child to sort through the often myriad reasons why a move may happen and rarely easy to soften the blow of a rejection.

Practical strategies are needed when working with the child (Fahlberg, 1994; Sunderland, 2003). Putting ideas and feelings down on paper, doing flow charts, drawings and lists together – any way in which the buzzing confusion of possibilities can start to take shape and make sense should be tried. Keeping the work in a special folder between sessions helps the child know that the worker is thinking about them between sessions and looking after their work, and allows them to go back and revise or re-think. This care also gives the message that they and their ideas really matter. Once a family is identified, information needs to be as detailed and concrete as possible. The family profile, photographs, video – and the opportunity to meet the new family prior to the move – all have a role to play in easing the process, both building in continuity and explaining what will be new and different. Such things are taken for granted in making adoption placements, but in foster care (although it may not always be possible) it is important that it is also seen as good practice. It is more helpful, though, in all cases to present the new life in a calm, moderate and balanced way, avoiding the temptation to get the child too excited about a fairy tale ending of smart cars or big houses or perfect new parents, perhaps unconsciously as a way of making the move more welcome or avoiding the pain of the loss and separation.

At the point of the move, openness may take the form of a toddler taking a photograph of herself with the bridge foster carer to the adoption placement. The adopters can talk in simple terms about the child missing "Jane" and feeling a bit sad, with reassurance that Jane is still thinking about the child and has the child's picture up on her kitchen wall, but confirming that the child's bedroom and place are now in her new home. Older children should be given the chance to introduce themselves to the new family, not feel on that first visit that they are being talked about as if they were not there.

2) Secure base availability

The child cannot be free to think constructively and flexibly about the move unless anxiety is reduced. When children are moving, it is to be hoped that the existing carer will be supportive to the child, but it may be that the social worker is the one most able to offer a secure base through their continuous role in the old and the new placement. The core principle here is that a secure base for exploration allows the child to feel safe enough to explore their feelings and thoughts about the move.

The social worker needs, therefore, to be accessible to the child, whether through regular visits that the child knows about – for example, on a calendar that the child can understand and at a level on the kitchen wall that a younger child can see – or for older children through telephone and email. These routes for communication need to be clarified with the current carers.

Foster carers describe creating a supportive circle of people around the child at this time, not only the carers themselves but teachers, head teachers, birth family members, new family members as well as the social worker, to increase the options available to the child in terms of finding a secure base. These key people need to be helped to be as consistent as possible in their telling of the story about the move, as the child needs reassurance and may test out any weak links to see if someone will give a different version of why they are moving.

Because trust is at the heart of things here, the plan for the move should take advantage of whatever continuities are available. Perhaps the bridge carer may be invited to hear about or to visit the child's new school with the adoptive parents as well as visit the child's new home, so that the message to the child is that their former secure base caregiver is working with their new secure base caregivers to ensure their comfort and happiness.

3) Helping the child to regulate their feelings

The principles that link sensitivity, mind-mindedness and managing feelings are important here in relation to helping children move. The practitioner needs to work hard to gain as accurate a picture as possible of what is in the child's mind – much of which will be inferred rather than directly communicated. This includes the child's *appraisal of events* (e.g. being rescued, taken away or given away). Tuning in to the child's primary hopes and fears, beliefs and expectations may help the practitioner to see where anxieties can be allayed. The balance here to be achieved is between validating the child's feelings and anxieties, while reassuring them that these feelings are "normal" and can be managed.

4) Protecting the child's self-esteem

When children change placement, it may mean that they feel "chosen" when going to a new placement and that the move builds their self-esteem. But any move is likely to make children anxious about how loved and valued they have been and will be. Even where moves are well-planned and children have been waiting impatiently for a permanent family, children may still feel what seems like an irrational sense of anger at the foster parents who have let them go. Where placements end acrimoniously, rejected children will need support to manage the blow to their self-esteem. Agencies have become more sensitive to the ritual of the move and the importance for children's self-esteem of, for example, having smart suitcases and not bin bags for their things, but there are many ways in which children need signals that they are valued.

5) Co-operating/working with the child to feel effective

One of the major difficulties for children who move placements is that they can feel like a parcel being moved around by others. Feelings of powerlessness need to be countered by active attempts to involve the child in all discussions about the plan and the move itself. Wherever it is possible for the child to be included in making choices about the arrangements for the move, this can be important – although children reluctant to move may take the opportunity to protest by not being involved. Some children fear that they have been too powerful and have brought an unplanned move about.

It may be painful to involve the child in packing their suitcase, but it can prove a valuable opportunity for the child to begin to think about preparing themselves for their new life, to express feelings and to ask questions. Choosing small items to take with them, jointly taking photographs of the family pets – these may provoke strong feelings in the children, but if the foster carers who know the child can explore those feelings and allow sad feelings to be mixed with a degree of anticipation and hope, this may help the child feel neither too powerless nor too powerful and be open to the possibilities in the new family.

6) Family membership

The move from one family to another sees changes in so many aspects of the child's life. The care and time taken in bridging a child into an adoptive placement is less likely to be available for planned or unplanned moves in foster care, but the principles of clarifying what it means to belong to a new family need to be explored in any placement move.

Fitting into an unfamiliar family requires the child to grasp both their daily rituals, norms and values, but also the many assumptions that make up their everyday life. If the family assumption that dirty clothes are put in the washing basket is not communicated, then the child may hide her dirty clothes under the settee – and be dismayed, as one foster child reported, when this is viewed by the family as somehow a moral fault (a "dirty girl") or a problem behaviour. The bigger picture of "belonging" to the family can only develop if the child is helped in a very intensive and active way to make sense of the way this family does apparently minor things. That process needs to be built into the way in which the move is managed.

There are many ways in which children's experiences of moves can be more helpfully managed and the task is to apply such principles and ideas across the range of moves. Where children are in a placement planned to be a bridge placement, for example, the move to a new placement can be managed constructively and co-operatively between the two sets of parents, with the support of both the children's social worker and the family placement worker. There is always some risk, some consequence of the loss for the child, but skilled and sensitive bridge carers, whether for infants or for older children, are able to help the new parents to become familiar with the child's routines and needs, prepare the child for the move, accept strong feelings of anger and sadness as legitimate, and celebrate rather than resent the point at which the child seems to be increasingly able to see the new caregivers in the parenting role.

Where placement moves happen as an emergency, or are unplanned or follow long periods of uncertainty or unsettled behaviour, the feelings can be extremely powerful, as children and carers attempt to hang on to their own self-esteem and sense of self, with mutual blame and recrimination a risk. Here, the social worker's role is critical in helping all parties to deal with the emotional fall out –

and indeed it is important for the child's social worker and the family placement social worker to work together to avoid the splitting and blaming being reinforced by the practitioners.

Moving children between families in any circumstances is a challenging task, in which attachment theory has a useful role to play both in understanding the impact of the separation on all concerned, including practitioners, and in thinking through how resources in the child, the family and the professional network can best be mobilised to manage the feelings of those involved and help them to be positive about the future.

Summary points

- Social work practice with children utilises many of the principles of parenting, especially availability, sensitivity, acceptance, co-operation and helping to provide a secure base.

- Assessment of children should integrate attachment issues, internal working models and so on within a wide developmental range of functioning in friendships, activities and schools as well as physical and emotional health.

- Relationships between social workers and fostered and adopted children are challenging to build and sustain through difficult times, but are extremely valuable in bringing together inner and outer worlds and as a source of potential continuity.

- Working with children must involve listening to children. This requires a number of skills and resources, but also requires a developmental perspective to both facilitate and understand communication.

- Children should feel empowered but they should also feel understood and know that "parents", those adults with responsibility for them, will take responsibility for their welfare.

- Life story work has value at many different levels and across time, so that identity and achieving a narrative coherence become possible i.e. 'Because my life makes sense, I can start to make sense to myself'.

- Moving children at some stage is an almost inevitable part of the process of achieving permanence, but the decision making, planning and practice of moving children can usefully draw on the developmental principles which are now well established by attachment theory.

13 Keeping attachment in mind – the role of the family placement social worker

If children are to settle and make progress in their foster or adoptive homes, they must experience close, nurturing and supportive relationships with their caregivers. They need not only to be kept safe and well, but also to receive the care that helps them to build trust and achieve their full potential. Family placement social workers play a pivotal role in achieving these good outcomes. Firstly, they must assess whether or not prospective caregivers have the capacity to provide this sort of environment and to sustain it when under pressure. Then, they must support caregivers in meeting children's physical, educational, emotional and other needs on a short-, medium- or long-term basis. Short-term caregivers may need additional input when children move on, long-term carers and adopters may need sustaining as the years pass and different issues emerge for their children.

Social workers in family placement teams make complicated judgements as they recruit new caregivers, assess who is and is not suitable to foster or adopt a child, and match children with new families. They must establish a positive working partnership when placements are running smoothly and, in the most difficult cases, they must help caregivers who are locked into angry and negative cycles and feeling hurt, angry or overwhelmed by their children. Attachment theory does not offer ready solutions to these intricate problems, but it can provide us with a helpful framework for thinking about practice across the broad spectrum of family placement social work.

The assessment of foster carers and adopters

The assessment of potential foster carers and adopters is a central task of family placement social work. In attachment terms, the process of assessment and preparation can be seen as an assessment of the capacity of the prospective caregiver to provide a *secure base* for a child. This will involve the social worker in various lines of enquiry. The couple or individual must be able to provide good physical care, promote the child's education and health and encourage pro-social

369

values. At the same time, the social worker must assess their capacity to provide a safe, warm and nurturing environment in which children can sustain or rebuild their trust in adults and their belief in themselves and also be supported to explore the wider world and develop their potential. A further important area to identify and develop is the capacity of the prospective caregivers to *adjust* their parenting approaches so that they take into account the particular history, level of emotional maturity, coping strategies and personality of each child *as an individual.* As social workers pursue each of these strands of the assessment, they must take into account the full range of cultural, ethnic, class, regional and individual differences in styles and approaches to parenting.

What, then, are the core qualities that we are looking for in prospective caregivers and how do we know if people possess them? How can we be sure, not only that they can provide high-quality physical care, but also that they possess the necessary skills and resilience to offer the therapeutic caregiving that the majority of looked after children will need? We suggest that, from an attachment perspective, exploring the applicant's strengths and difficulties within the structure of the five dimensions of parenting already proposed (see Chapters 6–10) can make a helpful contribution to the assessment process. The parenting dimensions highlight the capacities that are necessary if caregivers are to help children become more secure and resilient. Strengths in each dimension can be identified, but also areas of difficulty or uncertainty that might provide pointers for additional social work support or intervention in the future. The parenting dimensions may also be used to generate key questions which will help applicants to think realistically and systematically about the additional needs of looked after children and how they might meet them.

The capacity to be physically and emotionally available

The core question here is whether or not the applicants will be able to maintain an "open door" in terms of allowing and enabling children both to *move towards* them to receive comfort and nurture when they need it and also to *move away* when they are ready to explore. In order to be physically and emotionally available in this way, caregivers will need to be alert and responsive to the child's signals, both for closeness and for distance. It is also important that they can stay in touch with children's underlying needs and signal their availability, especially when children are giving confusing or contradictory messages. Even young infants may have learned not to expect and not to seek comfort (Stovall and Dozier, 1998). For children of all ages, caregivers need the capacity to persist in offering care and comfort, and to be flexible and adjust their parenting to the needs of the individual child.

The assessing social worker might begin by considering the extent to which a couple can demonstrate these capacities for openness and availability within their own relationship or with their existing children. For instance, at times of stress, are partners able to be physically and emotionally available for each other? Do they make time to talk and think together, can they offer comfort and nurture to each other, or does one or both tend to immerse themselves in a hobby or a friendship group to the exclusion of family life? Equally, in the normal course of life, can partners support each other to explore the world outside their relationship, to pursue their working lives effectively or perhaps to enjoy separate hobbies, interests and friendships? The same questions might apply to a single applicant. Who, for instance, is the person or range of people that will be physically and emotionally available at times of need and also be encouraging and supportive of their endeavours? How will these supportive others demonstrate their availability and how will the applicant demonstrate their need? Equally, to what extent does the applicant currently fulfil these secure base functions for other adults or children?

Of central interest in assessing the capacity of applicants to be physically and emotionally available to a child is their own experiences of secure base availability, particularly in childhood. It is widely accepted that an account of a person's early life is a necessary and important aspect of the assessment, but it can be difficult to know exactly what to make of this account and whether or not it bodes well for future therapeutic caregiving. If a person's mind is *pre-occupied* with painful experiences from the past, it is likely that he or she will find it harder to be emotionally available to pick up the child's signals, particularly if these are signals of distress. Similarly, if painful experiences have been *suppressed* rather than thought about and resolved, it is possible that they may be awakened by close contact with a troubled child and, again, become barriers to connecting and helping.

How can we know, therefore, whether an applicant with a particular family history (whether positive or negative) will be able to use his or her experiences constructively to help a child? It is important to recognise that the *way in which a person talks about* their history of attachment, separation and loss is significant, as well as *the events* themselves. Thus, the assessment needs to focus on the *sense* that people have made of their experiences, the extent to which, for instance, they can understand *why* their parents behaved in the way they did (whether this was more or less nurturing and loving), as well as what it was that happened. Also important is the extent to which the individual has been able to build trusting and confiding relationships in adult life, whether these have continued their positive childhood experiences or have been new experiences that have helped them to make sense of a difficult past and, to some extent, move on from it.

When secure adults talk about their early histories, they tend to give a fairly concise, coherent account and they can recall both positive and negative aspects of their upbringing (Main and Goldwyn, 1984). They can support their descriptions of their relationships with parents with relevant examples and they show an ability to collaborate and engage with the interviewer. They also have the capacity to understand other people's perspectives. The assessing social worker might, therefore, look for evidence that a person can do the following.

- Talk about their childhood reasonably concisely and coherently – their story makes sense.
- Make a realistic evaluation of childhood experiences and accommodate the fact that there were both positive and negative aspects to this. For example, 'My father was loving and devoted, but I remember feeling rather angry sometimes that he spent so much time at work and not with us'.
- Provide convincing examples to support their general descriptions. For instance, 'My mother was a very committed parent. She attended every school event even though it meant catching three buses to be there.' Or even more specifically, 'My father was a very loving parent. For example, I remember when I was ten years old and I was really ill when we were on holiday in Scarborough, and everyone else went to the beach and he sat with me and brought me all my favourite drinks and he read books to me and made me feel better.'
- Demonstrate the ability to "stand in the shoes" of the other person. For example, 'When I look back, my mother must have been quite lonely and isolated when we were young, it can't have been easy for her'.

When adults reflect on difficult experiences, including loss, trauma or abandonment, the key question is to what extent these events have been *processed and resolved*. Has the individual been able to put them into context and made sense of them in ways that do not involve excessive guilt, anger or blame? If they have not, the risk is that they may not have ways of managing their difficult feelings and find it hard to connect with those of a child. Or, in the presence of a troubled child, their own attachment needs may be activated to a point where they *override* their capacity for caregiving. Evidence of satisfactory processing of negative events, then, might be that a person can:

- Think flexibly about the reasons why difficult experiences may have occurred, place them in a wider context and view them as "understandable in the circumstances". For example, 'My father was remote and a bit harsh but then, he had had a lonely and isolated childhood, feeling unwanted and being brought up by his grandparents'. For some people, there may realistically be no explanation that entirely removes blame, 'My mother never really wanted children. She always gave priority to her boyfriends and we were rather in the way', but it should still be possible as an adult to remember, talk calmly about and accept the anger, sadness and disappointment that this had entailed.

- Provide some account of the significant "turning points" during childhood, adolescence or early adulthood, times when a different and more nurturing type of relationship was experienced that had increased felt security. These relationships might be offered by grandparents or other relatives, teachers or other adults who were particularly interested and supportive or by friends and partners. An example of this sort of turning point might be a statement such as, 'When I met my wife, I realised what I had been missing all those years and she and her parents taught me how to be close and to trust'. Turning points might also have occured in therapy, when a therapist has offered a secure base relationship that enabled the person to explore the past safely and move on.

When this sort of evidence is present in a person's accounts, they can be said to have adequately overcome the negative effects of harmful relationships in their early lives through the support of other adults in childhood or through having opportunities to form close and trusting relationships later on. This will increase the likelihood that they can offer this kind of availability and trust to children.

Although an assessment of this kind will contribute to a decision to approve or not approve prospective foster carers or adoptive parents, the most useful application of our understandings of attachment in the assessment of potential caregivers will be to think of it in terms of providing *indicators for preparation, training and support*. Such an assessment can help identify strengths to be built on and any difficulties that may need extra support. An adult, for example, who does not express many feelings but idealises his relationships with his parents will be thinking about parenting in a rather limited way. He or she may have a set of ideas about parenting being always happy, rewarding, fun, enjoyable and so on. Notions of parenting as at times difficult, stressful, mundane and isolating will not be present. It may prove difficult, therefore, for this person to anticipate the rollercoaster of highs and lows of parenting that frequently characterise the early months, or which may occur later on in a placement. The parent may be overwhelmed with unexpected feelings and the child may then be blamed for being "difficult". At the other end of the spectrum, a person who is preoccupied with relationships displays emotions rather impulsively and excessively, who "wears their heart on their sleeve" in close relationships, may need additional support in understanding and being available for a child who has learned to close down their emotions and who appears cool and detached.

Highlighting areas such as these during the assessment phase can alert both applicants and future family placement social workers to potential strengths and difficulties in placements. There will be applicants who will not be suitable for approval and need to be counselled out or turned down by the fostering or adoption panel, but where there is potential for change and difficulties are accepted and recognised, interventions can be targeted accordingly and effective support, supervision and training provided.

On a practical note, it is important to bear in mind the *additional thought, time and energy* that is needed to remain physically and emotionally available to a troubled child (see Chapter 6 for examples of this). Family life inevitably involves important commitments to a range of other family members, to work, to friends and community, but assessing social workers will need to feel confident that these things are not at a level where they will consistently divert energy away from the needs of a troubled child. Support networks are also an important consideration here – are they robust enough to share some of the family's responsibilities when additional time is needed for the child or to provide relief when caregivers need to re-charge their batteries in order to sustain higher levels of availability? Will the family need to receive additional support in these areas?

The capacity to respond sensitively to the child

We have seen that the capacity to tune in to the child, *to see the world from the child's point of view*, is key to helping the child to manage difficult feelings and behaviour (see Chapter 7). Caregivers need to be able to understand and make sense of the child's feelings and behaviour in order to communicate that understanding to the child and help him to "make sense" of himself. Caregivers must also support the child in experiencing the full range of emotions, but help him to manage and regulate them so they do not become overwhelming. There are important issues here to which social workers need to be sensitive. For example, where couples are being assessed, it may be that one partner comple-ments the other in terms of the ability to think about, express and manage their own feelings and potentially help the child to do the same. There may also be gender, class and cultural differences that need to be taken into account when making sense of the way in which feelings are communicated and managed and the quality of parenting that may be available for a fostered or adopted child.

Again, indicators of these capacities need to be picked up by the assessing social worker in the interview. In particular, social workers need to see if caregivers have the quality of *mind-mindedness* in order to tune in to the child's thoughts and feelings and to help the child also to develop mind-mindedness. This capacity in potential caregivers can be thought about and discussed in respect of a range of relationships. Is the applicant able, for instance, to take the perspective of a parent or other close person when reflecting on childhood experiences? For example, a comment such as 'My older brother was mean to me when I was young, but it must have been hard for him because he'd been the centre of the household for 10 years before I came along' indicates the capacity to empathise with the brother's thoughts and feelings and make sense of sibling rivalry in a balanced way. A sense of the extent to which an individual can stand in the shoes of another can be elicited by simple questions, such as 'How do you think he/she felt about that?' or 'Why do you think he behaved or felt that way?' When exploring the capacity to see the world through the eyes of a child, a short case study which invites the question 'How do you think the child might have felt and thought in that situation?' can also provide a helpful indication.

There are many variations in the degree to which people can comfortably think about and discuss a range of feelings and emotions and this must be taken into account in an assessment. However, the two extremes of this continuum might raise legitimate concerns. A person who shows a marked resistance to thinking and talking about their own feelings is likely to find it difficult to understand a child's strong feelings or to permit their expression. Opportunities to help the child to make sense of his feelings and manage them appropriately may therefore be more limited. Equally, a person who appears pre-occupied by their feelings may lack the capacity to pause for thought at times of heightened emotion, particularly when caring for a troubled child. When, for instance, a child is demanding or difficult, the adult may not be able to take a step back, see the situation from the child's point of view, and think about why the behaviour might be occurring and how best to deal with it. Instead, their feelings of anger or disappointment are likely to overflow into the situation and they will be unable to deal constructively with the child. 'Adults who have unresolved trauma from their own childhood may be overwhelmed by the emotional needs of traumatised children and, at certain times, be unable to think about their own or their child's feelings' (Steele *et al*, 2003).

In ascertaining the capacity of an applicant to manage their own feelings and behaviours, therefore, the assessing social worker might look for evidence of the way in which difficult situations have been successfully negotiated and resolved. How, for instance, do people view and deal with differences of opinion in their partnerships, close relationships or with the authorities? Can they express their point of view calmly, show their feelings at an appropriate level, reach a resolution, move on and *reflect* on the incident in a balanced way afterwards? Is it safe to be angry in this family? Considering the prospective adoptive or foster family as a whole, further useful evidence might be sought in terms of the ability of all family members to communicate openly with each other, to show feelings appropriately and to manage and contain them in the interests of the rest of the group. Do parents, for instance, manage their personal disagreements so that they do not adversely affect the children in the family? The quality and quantity of exchange between different systems of the family (adult–adult, child–child, adult–child) might be observed and considered and evidence gathered that there is a moderately positive "flow" within and between all groups and an absence of notable barriers or obstructions.

The capacity for acceptance

In order to sustain, restore or develop their self-esteem, children need caregivers who can accept them unconditionally for who they are, for both their strengths and their difficulties and regardless of their differences, interests or personalities. Indeed, differences and diversity need to be seen as something to be celebrated. If caregivers are to build a child's self-esteem in this way, they must first be able to accept themselves, to feel comfortable with the people they are and to reflect this model of self-acceptance back to the child.

Indicators of good self-esteem in prospective caregivers can often be found in their general demeanour and presentation. Applicants who present themselves positively, take pride in themselves and their appearance, appear comfortable with themselves and their surroundings and are reasonably satisfied with their achievements and accomplishments are likely to have good self-esteem and to be able to model this for a child. Assessing social workers might look for indicators that applicants can describe their skills, talents and abilities, but also acknowledge and accept their weak spots and limitations. They might also look for similar appraisals of other close family members. Humour and warmth are often part of the way in which families enjoy and accept each others' qualities and short-comings. There should be evidence that the individual can respect and take care of himself as well as others, ensure that his own needs are met and not set unrealistic or impossibly high goals and targets for himself. A family ethos of "nobody is good at everything but everyone is good at something" conveys an easily recognisable message of acceptance to the newcomer.

It is important to remember that most people have experienced low self-esteem at different periods of their lives, especially at times of loss or disappointment. If applicants can reflect on these times, recall how they felt and behaved and think about what helped or hindered the process of recovery, then they are more likely to be able to be empathic and supportive to a child who has low self-esteem and a poor sense of self. Awareness of children's need to have their confidence built may be acknowledged at a cognitive and verbal level, but the potential as caregivers to support children and actively build their self-esteem will depend also on the capacity for empathy, tolerance and patience.

Running through this model of acceptance in family placement is the notion that an important element to be assessed is the capacity to accept difference. It is essential that prospective foster carers and adoptive parents are able to accept not only a child's strengths and difficulties, but also any differences in culture, class, religion and ethnicity. Effective matching procedures should achieve some degree of compatibility between the child and the family, but the *fit* is rarely perfect. Applicants should therefore demonstrate that they are genuinely open-minded and adaptable, so that differences are not just accepted, but are positively embraced.

The capacity for co-operative caregiving

Children who have lacked opportunities to feel effective and competent will need caregivers who are comfortable in facilitating this. Children will need to accept parental limits and boundaries, but within these, to learn that co-operation and compromise can be enjoyable and rewarding. Caregivers, therefore, must have the capacity to promote autonomy and effectiveness, and to act authoritatively as responsible parents but to do this in a way that emphasises co-operation rather than control and forms co-operative alliances with others.

Reflections on childhood can provide examples of applicants' own early experiences of feeling effective and competent. Did their parents or caregivers promote and enjoy their children's assertiveness or did they tend to be controlling, disempowering or repressive? Can they give examples of co-operation, compromise and negotiation of difficulties in their childhood? With family? Among friends? At school? For some people, these skills and capacities have had to be learned in adult life, perhaps in the context of a close relationship or a work environment. In the following statement, for instance, the speaker pinpoints experiences in his working life which (along with a trusting relationship with his wife) taught him the value of co-operation: 'My father was very Victorian and controlling. It wasn't until I joined the police force that I learned that it's much easier to defuse a situation by meeting the person half way than by coming down heavy on them.'

In the applicants' current lives, the assessing social worker might look for evidence of co-operative relationships, perhaps within the relationship between a couple or with neighbours or community groups. Does the individual have the capacity to relinquish some of his own wishes and goals at times and take into account the wishes and goals of another person? If there are situations of potential conflict (perhaps a difficult neighbour or family member), is there evidence of appropriate assertiveness and the capacity to reach a solution that feels to some extent acceptable to all parties? Long-standing feuds and battles, situations where individuals cannot relinquish any of their ground for the sake of more harmonious relationships, or a strong sense of helplessness and an inability to be appropriately assertive might be areas of concern to be addressed and explored within the assessment.

Although levels of anxiety will always be understandably high when assessment to become a foster carer or adopter is the agenda, often the way in which applicants respond to aspects of the assessment process itself can demonstrate their capacity to be collaborative and co-operative. Social workers need to reflect with a supervisor on how they have experienced the interviews, since if they have felt comfortable and relaxed or, in contrast, controlled or intimidated, this may offer some insight into how the applicants can co-operate when under some stress-and how potentially a child may feel in that family. Thus, the views expressed by applicants on how children need to be brought up provide one source of information about parenting style, but the interview process itself may offer additional insights into attitudes to control and co-operation, if carefully reflected on in supervision.

The capacity to offer family membership

When children are removed from their families of origin, even for a short time, they need to be placed in an environment in which they feel welcomed and gain a full sense of belonging. At the same time, children need to sustain or develop a comfortable and appropriate sense of belonging to their birth families.

In order to provide this sort of environment, foster and adoptive families must have the capacity both to admit new members, but also to be flexible enough to allow those members to pass to and fro (physically and/or emotionally) across the family boundary as needed. In some families, indicators of this sort of permeability of boundaries can be found in examples of including non-family members or extended family members into the group. They may have a family history of sharing the family home or their family life with older relatives or of taking in children or adults who need additional support. There are many individual and cultural differences in the extent to which this happens, however, and some people may have had little opportunity to test out the flexibility of their family boundary in this way. In this case, evidence can be sought about the extent to which the family connects and communicates with other systems – schools, community groups, special interest groups, friends and neighbours. But also at the level of attitudes – do they view the world outside the family boundary as essentially safe and trustworthy or as threatening, hostile and unsafe? Is there reason to believe that they would be able to support a child or young person to move across the family boundary and establish positive relationships in the outside world, while at the same time offering a supportive sense of family membership? Are they open and flexible in the way they talk about the meaning of family membership and the need of children to feel part of their family as well as their birth family?

A further area of enquiry might be the extent to which the family system is able to tolerate *differences* in terms of beliefs, values, expectations, etc. Whilst a sense of family solidarity and identity is reassuring and supportive to a fostered or adopted child or young person, the sense that family membership is *dependent* on adhering to the value system, traditions or interests of the family (for instance, a love of animals or a sporting ability) can feel excluding and rejecting to a child or young person who has not been born into the family and may not share this value or interest. It is important to consider, therefore, the degree to which the family can accept and tolerate differences, respect and value the individual while at the same time promoting his inclusion into the group.

The willingness to open the family to a newcomer does not necessarily guarantee that, in reality, individual members or the system as a whole are flexible enough to accommodate the changes and pressures involved. Downes (1992, p. 39) makes the following comment in relation to her study of adolescent foster care, but it is equally applicable to all types of foster care and adoption and to all age groups of children.

> *When an adolescent joins the family, each family member needs to be able to shift their position to some extent in response to the adolescent, rather than the family prescribing a slot into which the adolescent must fit.*

In this area, the assessing social worker will need to be alert to the expectations of all family members regarding the new child and the extent to which they have anticipated change and adjustment. Evidence of flexible thinking is important here. For example, an expectation, from all family members, that a new child will become a "playmate" for an existing child would indicate a worrying level of inflexibility in the system. However, if the parents were able to anticipate that this may or may not be the case, they are likely to be able to prepare the existing child accordingly and enjoy the new sibling relationship, if it emerges, or support her through any subsequent disappointment if it does not.

Supporting foster carers and adopters

The availability of a secure base, both as a source of support and comfort and as a safe haven from which to explore, is as significant for adults as it is for children. In the words of Bowlby (1973, p. 407):

> *For not only young children, it is now clear, but human beings of all ages are found to be at their happiest and to be able to deploy their talents to best advantage when they are confident that, standing behind them, there are one or more trusted adults who will come to their aid should difficulties arise. The person trusted provides a secure base from which his (or her) companion can operate.*

Many new caregivers are parenting for the first time and for most, it will be their first encounter with children who are separated from their familiar environments, distressed or traumatised. Caring for troubled children is a heady mixture of joys and rewards, anxieties, puzzles and, at times, despair. There will be times of significant strides forward in the child's development or relationships and times when progress is very slow or there is little in the way of positive response from the child. New adopters or foster carers, in particular, may be temporarily "rocked" by the impact of the child on their lives and behave uncharacteristically. A great deal of patience and support from social workers is then needed to help re-establish their personal equilibrium and restore their capacity to be constructive and in tune with the child. Successful, experienced foster carers or adopters may also find that when they take a particular new child into their family that they are similarly "rocked" and start to doubt themselves and their abilities. Both new and experienced carers need support, but the focus of that work will need to take into account such differences in starting point.

If caregivers are to continue to provide a secure base through these ups and downs, they, too, need a secure base from which to operate. They will need to feel supported and encouraged as they explore and develop their parenting role for the child and they will need the positive outcomes of their caregiving to be recognised and celebrated. At times of difficulty, they will need relationships in which they feel safe, calmed and reassured so that they can think more clearly about the needs of the child and how to address them. This can be thought of as a form of *safe exploration* at a thinking and feeling level.

The caregiver's secure base will be formed partly from close, personal relationships, but the family placement social worker also has a crucial role to play, within a relationship which draws on both professional and personal qualities in the worker. In general terms, this can be conceptualised as *reducing anxiety* through providing reliable and consistent support and, when equilibrium is restored, as *supporting exploration* through an underlying belief in the caregiver's capacity to parent the child.

Supporting caregivers to be available

It is natural and understandable that caring for someone else's child, especially when the child is distressed by separation or trauma, should generate a certain level of anxiety in the caregiver. A first step in reducing this anxiety is for the family placement social worker to ensure that he, or a reliable substitute, is *physically available* to the caregiver. Dependable message takers, unambiguous systems for responding to messages, and an efficient out-of-hours service can all contribute to the caregiver's sense of safety and protection. *Practical assistance* such as ensuring that payments and complaints are quickly processed, providing relevant information and advice and a clear referral route for additional resources are also important components of reducing anxiety.

Above all, however, caregivers need their family placement social worker to be emotionally available to them. Particularly valued are workers who show genuine interest in the whole family, take account of their needs and circumstances, listen carefully and are non-judgemental in their approach (Sellick *et al*, 2004; Sinclair *et al*, 2004). When this sort of relationship is offered consistently and reliably, caregivers feel encouraged and enabled when life is on an even keel, but also reassured that help will be at hand if it is needed.

The following foster carer captures these two strands of availability as she describes the role of her social worker.

> **Foster mother:** *She looks after me. She looks after me and she comes in and she sits down and she's very normal. We have a very, very good relationship. I'm not really one who enjoys meetings much, but she knows exactly how to get me to, you know. 'I've got to see you, now get your diary', sort of thing, but she does it in a nice way. It's not really heavy or anything and she'll come and have a natter. I can discuss anything at all with her, and her with me. She knows how to get the best out of me. You know, I know that if ever I need her, all I have to do is call. And she's on the end of the phone.*
>
> **Researcher:** And does she visit you whether or not there's a problem?
>
> **Foster mother:** *Yeah. It's fine, I like to know that she's interested and she's there if I need her, and there was a time when I needed her, and she came up trumps, she was there and she went through everything with me and she helped me. She got me back on track and you know, she was excellent.*

Most importantly, the relationship with a trusted and consistent worker can represent a "safe space" in which caregivers can take the risk of expressing difficult feelings towards the child or doubts about their own abilities to meet the child's needs. Caregivers commonly experience a number of barriers to achieving this level of openness, however, and workers must be alert to these if they are to achieve a trusting dialogue. Firstly, there is a tendency for the assessment process for both fostering and adoption to lead caregivers to feel that they have been "chosen" because they have particular skills and capabilities in caring for children. In this context, it can be hard to admit to the need for recognition and praise when things have gone well or to feelings of anger, bewilderment and despair at difficult times. They may be fearful of admitting to their true feelings in case the child is removed or they are considered to be bad parents. Additionally, some troubled children behave well at school, with the social worker or with other family members, leading caregivers to feel guilty or inadequate for failing to achieve a close relationship. In many cases, children respond differently to mother and father figures, typically expressing anger and resentment towards the mother figure and leaving her isolated and unable to share her feelings – although some children cling to the mother and marginalise or feel anxious about the father figure. Families need help to avoid splitting and be available for each other as well as the child.

It is important, therefore, for the family placement social worker to give messages of availability during good times and difficult times and even if carers are apparently resistant or not needing support. Social workers need sufficient time and emotional capacity to do this and they can signal their availability to caregivers by setting regular and adequate times for supervision, being punctual, reliable and focused. They also need to convey messages of trust to the caregivers, to work on an underlying assumption that the caregiver is the person who lives continuously with the child and is therefore the expert on the child and best placed to understand the child's capacities and limitations. Caregivers may need to explore different ways of managing their child and these may be at odds with what the social worker would recommend. Provided these are not harmful in any way, an important role of the social worker may be to support this exploration, but then to provide a sounding board and a chance afterwards to reflect on the advantages and disadvantages of the approach. There may also be times when the caregiver needs the security of receiving sound information or advice from the social worker or being referred to another resource.

Supporting caregivers to respond sensitively

Caring for a troubled child can elicit a range of strong feelings in foster carers and adopters and there is a critical role for social workers in helping them to manage these feelings so that they do not become overwhelming to the caregiver, or problematic for the child. Feelings of love, tenderness and protectiveness, for instance, are healing to children who have suffered adversity, but difficulties can arise when the caregiver cannot manage them alongside supporting the child's needs for exploration and autonomy. Equally, an expression of anger is a valid response to difficult behaviours and followed by a "repair" of the relationship may carry a valuable message to a child. If, however, anger is excessive because it is triggered by the caregiver's own earlier experiences, it can have a harmful effect on both the adult and the child and, if not reparable, prove detrimental to their relationship.

A skilful and sensitive social worker and proper reflective space are therefore needed to help an individual to talk about their feelings, to unravel their origins and meanings and to think about ways of dealing with them. Caregivers must feel safe to express feelings openly, and to know they will not be judged and are not alone in feeling the way they do. They may need to be reassured that their responses are understandable in the circumstances and that their strong feelings can be contained and managed, firstly by the worker and eventually by themselves. Only when feelings have been acknowledged and accepted in this way can the worker help the caregiver to become more reflective and address some of the underlying issues. Support groups, informal linking of caregivers and more formal "buddy" schemes can also play an important role here, but they should be seen as an additional or optional source of support, rather than as a substitute for an allocated social worker.

All practitioners will be aware of extremely sad situations in which foster carers or adopters have become locked into seemingly hopeless and destructive relationships with their children and appear overwhelmed by their negative feelings. Ironside (2004) describes this as a 'provisional existence' – a life in which caregivers lose hope for the future, lack a comfortable sense of themselves and begin to experience a form of 'inner decay'. This extreme state of mind might be understood as a form of projection, whereby the child manages to transfer to the caregiver something of the pain, associated anger and despair of his earlier experiences and the caregiver begins to re-enact some of the negative parenting that the child has suffered in the past.

*The foster carer may feel that the child has been able to penetrate their psychological defences and at this point will feel that they **have been invaded** by a poison chalice rather than that it is **as if** they have been so invaded.*
(Ironside, 2004, p. 41)

The role of the family placement social worker in these difficult cases is to help the caregiver to understand and manage this process. A shared exploration of the child's history may help the caregiver to grasp that the feelings belong to the child (rather than to the caregiver) and that they are understandable in the context of earlier experiences. The caregiver is then better placed to put the child's feelings into words, to reassure him that they are understandable and to demonstrate that they can be managed by the caregiver and will not spiral out of control.

An additional complexity which the family placement social worker will need to bear in mind is the possibility that the child's troubled behaviour elicits feelings and reactions associated with the caregiver's own earlier experiences. A caregiver's unresolved loss, for example, may be reawakened by a child who is grieving for a lost parent. Or a caregiver who has an internal model of a rejecting parent may feel personally hurt and rejected by an emotionally withholding child. Alternatively, a carer who has experienced neglect in their family of origin may find herself being overprotective of a child, because of her determination not to be neglectful – but this can limit the child's autonomy. The family placement social worker, in these circumstances, will need considerable sensitivity and skill, first of all to help the caregiver to take a more reflective stance and then to explore possible connections with the caregiver's own history. In some more difficult situations, caregivers may value some independent counselling to help them to address unresolved issues from the past. For many, however, discussion with a trusted and sensitive social worker will help them to understand and manage their personal feelings and develop strategies to cope with them alongside meeting the needs of the child.

Supporting caregivers to accept the child

We have seen that, in order to provide unconditional acceptance and thus to build the self-esteem of the children and young people in their care, foster carers and adopters must, themselves, have good self-esteem and demonstrate an acceptance of their own strengths and difficulties, both as individuals and as parents. Many children placed in foster care or for adoption make significant strides forward in their new families, especially bearing in mind the disadvantaged starting point that many will have come from. When placements are running smoothly, it can be all too easy for social workers under pressure to overlook the need to acknowledge and affirm the caregiving skills that have contributed to this and to celebrate the child's success alongside that of the caregivers. As one worker supporting a very settled long-term placement put it, 'There just never seems time to praise, reassure and say thanks'.

But needy children may be hostile, unrewarding or disparaging towards their caregivers and this can be powerfully undermining to self-esteem and detrimental to the therapeutic relationship. A key role for the family placement social worker, therefore, may be that of sustaining the caregiver's own self-esteem and the foundation stone for this lies in modelling in the supervisory relationship, the level of acceptance and empathy that might be expected of the caregiver in his or her relationship with the child. Rogers and Stevens (1976) propose empathy and unconditional positive regard as essential elements of the helping relationship and this can provide us with a useful framework. An empathic approach involves an accurate understanding of the other person's inner world:

To sense his confusion or his timidity or his anger or his feeling of being treated unfairly as if it were your own, yet without your own uncertainty or fear or anger or suspicion getting bound up in it. (Rogers and Stevens, 1976, p. 93)

This level of understanding enables the counsellor to "move about freely" in the client's inner world and communicate to the client things that he is only vaguely aware of in himself. Alongside this approach, it is important to demonstrate acceptance of the client as a whole person and without conditions being attached.

He (the counsellor) prizes his client, as a person, with somewhat the same quality of feeling that a parent feels for his child, prizing him as a person regardless of his particular behaviour at the moment. It involves an open willingness for the client to be whatever feelings are real in him at the moment – hostility or tenderness, rebellion or submissiveness, assurance or self-deprecation. (Rogers and Stevens, 1976, p. 94)

Rogers and Stevens hypothesise that an empathic relationship is the forerunner to open communication and reflection, and when this is combined with unconditional acceptance, it is more likely that constructive change and development will occur. Although we would not see foster carers or adopters as "clients", this model of a supportive relationship has valuable lessons for the family placement social worker role.

It is important, of course, that the family placement social worker holds in mind the distinction between acceptance of the person and acceptance of questionable or harmful parenting behaviour. As in the caregiver's relationship with the child, acceptance does not mean that these things are not discussed or challenged; the principle is, rather, that an accepting and empathic relationship forms the basis from which caregivers can be helped to express and explore their feelings and responses and to view them as "understandable in the circum-stances". Once distressing emotions are processed in this way, caregivers can gain access to more positive feelings about themselves and the child. They become less preoccupied by the fear of failure and rejection and more able to make adjustments to their behaviour and think more creatively about their parenting strategies.

When caregivers' self-esteem is very low, family placement social workers may need to help caregivers to restore their belief in their parenting strengths and capacities and that it is the child's history that is generating problems in the family, rather than the inadequacies of the parents themselves. At the point of approval, all foster carers and adopters will have been assessed as having the required competencies to care for troubled children and up to six referees will have spoken or written positively about their strengths as individuals and as prospective caregivers. It may be helpful to re-connect caregivers with these appraisals and convey trust that they are essentially "good" parents who are doing the best they can in difficult circumstances.

Additionally, family placement social workers may need to help caregivers to acknowledge the impact that caring for a troubled child has had on them and on their close relationships. If they are to help their children to respect and value themselves, they must be able to model this in their own lives and they may have lost sight of their own needs as they struggle to meet those of a child. At such times, social workers might have to provide emotional and practical encourage-ment (such as respite care or additional financial support) for caregivers to "take care of themselves", to take time out as individuals or as a couple and to pursue interests or activities that are personally rewarding and satisfying.

When an accepting relationship has been established and the strengths and needs of the caregivers acknowledged, the family placement social worker is better placed to help caregivers to realistically appraise their areas of weakness or vulnerability. Sensitive issues from the caregiver's own past may be explored if they seem to be intruding into the parenting relationships. A caregiver whose own painful struggles have been acknowledged and accepted may be more able to "hear" a child's painful history, feel more empathic and be more able to make connections with difficult behaviour. At the same time, a fair appraisal of a person's strengths and skills can lower their resistance to advice, discussion and training and open their minds to developing new approaches and to parenting more positively. They can be encouraged, then, to build a range of skills and strategies for dealing with difficult behaviour in ways that do not undermine their own self-esteem or that of the child, or simply to focus on activities and interactions that enable them to regain their sense of being competent and successful parents and help the child to feel like a competent and valued son or daughter.

Supporting caregivers to form a co-operative alliance

In order to form co-operative alliances with their children, foster carers and adopters need a sense of collaboration and a shared approach to problem solving within their professional network. They need to be effective and influential members of this network to feel that their opinions are valued and taken into account and that they are part of the planning process for their child. For foster carers, it is important to be able to assume parental autonomy, appropriate to the type of placement, for the children in their care. Carers, for instance, convey important messages of support and collaboration when they can work alongside children and young people in discussions with schools and health professionals, collaborate with their birth relatives or make straightforward parenting decisions. Roles and responsibilities should be clearly allocated and, particularly in long-term placements, parental autonomy promoted wherever possible.

Children who have a range of additional needs attract a range of professionals and when caregivers are under stress, there is potential for unhelpful "splitting" and the formation of co-operative alliances with some or angry feuds with others. A placing social worker, for instance, may be "blamed" for not providing sufficient information about the child (with the inference that, had the family "known" the full story, they may not have accepted the child) or a team manager who cannot authorise more spending on a particular child may be "blamed" for the child's lack of progress (with the inference, that if a particular input was available, the difficulties might be resolved). This is not to deny that all of these issues do occur and that there are occasions when indignation and anger are wholly justified. The danger, however, is that the caregiver becomes trapped in a "conspiracy" with one professional or another, that the issue (which often cannot be changed) renders the caregiver helpless and hopeless and becomes a barrier to more creative thinking. In reality, of course, there are often additional perspectives on the situation (the carer might have been given information but been unable to truly "hear" it until experiencing the child's behaviour for themselves after placement, or the team manager might feel that a relatively high level of resources have already been allocated to this child, compared to other equally needy children). The role, then, for the family placement social worker, might be to acknowledge and work through these divisions, to help all players in the situation to understand each other's perspectives, and to create a climate of co-operation which respects the role of the caregiver as the primary expert on the child within a supportive professional network.

Supporting caregivers to offer foster or adoptive family membership

The key issue for family placement social workers in this area is that of working with the whole family, systemically and individually, so that the fostered or adopted child can feel appropriately assimilated and included in the family group.

Good practice would be for whole family sessions to take place at regular but infrequent intervals when family relationships are running smoothly so that when difficulties arise, this is not seen as a heavy intervention or as a sign of failure. Open communication about family membership can help all family members to reflect on what being a member of their family means, on family norms and values, culture and routines. Children who have lived in other families can offer different contributions and mutual understandings and insights can develop. The shared construction of a family ecomap in which differences and similarities, shared and separate experiences, are charted and acknowledged can help to build a sense of family solidarity as well as recognition of the individuals within it.

The potential for splits and disruption to the family system are many and various in foster and adoptive families. Parents often find their loyalties torn between protecting younger or less troubled children from a more troubled and disruptive child and working therapeutically with that child. Couples can themselves feel a wedge driven between them by a child who favours one over the other or who needs a great deal of time and attention. Children who have loyally supported their parents' plans to adopt or foster may find it hard to admit that they have negative feelings towards an incoming child. A newcomer to the family may be vulnerable to hostility or feelings of exclusion from existing family members, or may, themselves, be a perpetrator of bullying or intimidation.

Viewed in terms of attachment, when relationships are unbalanced in these ways, the family is no longer able to act as a secure base for all of its members and insecurities may develop in the system. This might result in a family member turning to an inappropriate attachment figure, competition for a particular attachment figure, defensive behaviours or the resurfacing of past anxieties and insecurities (Byng-Hall, 1990). The role of the family placement social worker, then, is to provide a secure base for the whole family so that these family dynamics may be openly acknowledged, discussed and addressed.

Individual sessions with the social worker could be the best starting point for some family members to express their dilemmas or worries and there may be a role for ongoing individual counselling in particular circumstances. If, however, the emphasis is on working towards a stronger sense of membership and inclusion for all family members, there is an argument for a whole family approach. When difficulties have become entrenched and open communication cannot be achieved, it may be that a specialist referral for family therapy is needed. If, however, a trusted family placement social worker, is able to create a safe space within which all family members are able to express their concerns, listen to others and feel listened to themselves, there is the potential for helpful intervention. Once reasonably open communication has been established in the family, the role for the social worker might be to help all family members to "make sense" of each other's behaviours, to understand each other's "working models" of themselves and others and thus to feel more empathy and acceptance of each other. In this sort of climate all family members are likely to feel more committed to family membership and to be better motivated to say and do things that promote family unity and the enjoyment of family life.

Case example – Carrie

Carrie (13) was the birth child of Pip and Martin. She became depressed and withdrawn and appeared particularly angry with Ian (10), her long-term foster brother who at that time was having epileptic seizures and outbursts of angry behaviour at home. A family session with the family placement social worker enabled Carrie to say that she was worried that Mum and Dad might not be able to manage Ian's behaviour and the family might "fall apart". In the same session, Pip said that they could manage Ian's behaviour but they were concerned that they were not able to give Carrie as much time and attention as usual, at that time. Ian said he didn't know why he was behaving this way and he couldn't help it. The social worker suggested that Ian's behaviour was a symptom of his current health problem, which was being investigated, that it was often linked with epilepsy and that it could be helped by medication. Pip and Martin agreed to go on a course to help them to understand more about managing Ian's condition. A plan was made for a day out all together – something that had not happened for several months.

After this session, the family seemed more united and at ease. Carrie was reassured that her parents were concerned for her, that Ian's behaviour was not an intentional attack on the family and that her parents could manage it calmly and the family would survive. Ian was reassured that his behaviour could be managed and that his foster carers were actively seeking help and support for him. Pip and Martin regained their confidence and competence as parents. A more comfortable balance and feeling of family solidarity had been re-established.

Supporting caregivers to offer birth family membership

All fostered and adopted children are, in different ways, members of more than one family and we have seen that the balance between the two family memberships will vary according to the nature of the plan for the child and the quality of relationships in both the birth family and the foster or adoptive family. The goal for caregivers is to enable their child to establish a sense of birth family membership that is compatible with the placement plan and comfortable for the child to manage. The role of the family placement social worker is to support caregivers emotionally and practically, to do so, while at the same time, ensuring that they can offer a suitable level of membership of their own family to the child.

If caregivers are to promote a level of birth family membership that is compatible with the placement plan, they need to have a clear sense of what that plan is, and to be promptly updated of changes and developments within it. At the same time, they need to feel that they are active contributors to this plan, able to provide a unique perspective on the needs of the child and often also on the position of birth family members. A strong working partnership in which the caregiver feels fully informed, respected and included will form the foundation for open discussion of birth family membership and how it can be promoted in ways that make sense in the context of the plan.

The role of the family placement social worker as mediator, for example, in the adjustment of contact arrangements over time requires careful listening and a clear sense of the important issues of contact (see Chapter 14) and great subtlety on the part of the social worker – but positive outcomes can be of great long-term benefit.

Case example

A foster mother of two school-aged children found that weekly contact on a Saturday, whilst manageable in the short term, became too disruptive on a long-term basis. She found that she could never take the children out to buy clothes or shoes and foster family activities were curtailed. The family placement social worker and the children's social worker worked together to help the birth mother to understand the difficulties from the foster mother's point of view. Mutual understanding was further developed by the foster mother and the birth mother meeting informally over coffee and without the children present. A change to teatime contact during the week was agreed and the process of building trust was continued by meetings every six weeks between the foster mother and the birth mother. The arrangements proved satisfactory for all concerned and continued to evolve and be appropriately adjusted as the children got older. The role of the family placement social worker was crucial both in building empathy and understanding between the parties but also in helping the carers to recognise and promote the right balance of foster and birth family membership for the children.

In fostering situations, the importance of including carers in planning and ongoing review of contact arrangements should never be overlooked. A study of long-term placements (Schofield *et al*, 2000) found that, where foster carers were excluded from discussions about contract arrangements, they often felt an appropriate level of parental anxiety. This might be about relatively small things, such as whether the children would have a proper lunch on the long car journey to contact or whether there were suitable toys to play with when they got there, but it led to a sense of unease around the contact itself. When carers are included in the planning fully enough to be able to get this sort of thing right for the child, they become less anxious about the detail of the arrangements and more able to promote contact and a helpful sense of birth family membership.

A strong working partnership is no less important when planning post-adoption contact. If adopters are to use contact to achieve a comfortable level of birth family membership for their child, then they must feel fully engaged in the plans and included as partners in negotiating contact as early as possible. The process of engagement should begin in the pre-approval training stage and continue through the assessment process. The purpose, benefits and drawbacks of contact should be fully explained and debated and opportunities provided for applicants to express their concerns so that these do not become obstacles or sources of difficulty later on (Logan and Smith, 2004).

When contact plans for a particular child are being made, a sense of partnership is equally important. In Neil's study of young adopted children having face-to-face meetings with a birth relative, she found that 'family-friendly contact with adopters in control' was one of the keys to successful contact (Neil, 2002; Neil *et al*, 2003; Neil, 2004). When adoptive parents felt that they could plan and adjust arrangements to be more comfortable for themselves and their child, their anxiety was reduced, as was that of the child. This normally involved a "relaxing" of the arrangements, once a level of trust had been established, and birth relatives typically expressed gratitude and warmth towards the adopters and were better able to support the child's sense of adoptive family membership.

In all placements, contact is a dynamic process with the needs and wishes of all parties likely to change over time. It is also important, therefore, that the sense of adopters and foster carers as respected and active working partners is maintained. Within this working partnership, the social worker must support the caregiver in creating the right balance for the child between foster/adoptive family membership and birth family membership. There should also be support available for the birth family so that they too feel comfortable and clear about their role, whether the child is returning home or staying in care or being placed for adoption. In long-term placements, which are the primary source of security and stability for the child, foster/adoptive family membership must be respected and promoted, but at the same time, a comfortable level of birth family membership can in many cases evolve over time and, in itself, will contribute to the security and stability of the placement.

Conclusion

The foster and adoptive families who take on the exceptional task of caring for children at risk are always going to be exceptional families and they need exceptionally skilled and knowledgeable social work practitioners to be alongside them and support them. But it is not enough for social workers to be skilled and knowledgeable. What is also necessary is for social workers to share many of the qualities that we seek in foster carers and adopters: empathy for troubled children and for their families of origin; energy and commitment to work with and on behalf of children; the capacity to think about and face up to pain and difficulties, without denial or minimisation; the ability to remain steadfastly hopeful and determinedly positive that all children have the capacity to change for the better and that no child is beyond help. But at the same time as sharing the parents' *commitment to the children*, family placement social workers need the capacity to be *thoughtful, empathic, containing and reliable for the parents*. In their availability for and sensitivity to the caregivers, they are offering them commitment and a secure base which can liberate their capacity to be thoughtful about, care for, enjoy and love their children.

To provide this level of support, family placement social workers in turn need a secure base in their organisations, provided by managers and colleagues who can enable them both to continue to learn and develop their skills and knowledge and also to remain committed, energetic and tuned in to the children and families with whom they work.

Summary points

- If children are to settle and make progress in their foster or adoptive homes, they must experience close, nurturing and supportive relationships with their caregivers. They need not only to be kept safe and well, but also to receive the therapeutic care that helps them to build trust and achieve their full potential. Family placement social workers play a pivotal role in achieving these good outcomes.

- Both assessment and support of foster carers and adopters, using an attachment perspective, can draw on five parenting dimensions:
  - *the capacity to be physically and emotionally available;*

- *the capacity to respond sensitively to the child;*
- *the capacity for co-operative caregiving;*
- *the capacity for acceptance;*
- *the capacity to offer family membership.*

- At the assessment stage, family placement social workers must explore whether or not prospective caregivers have the capacity to provide this sort of parenting environment and to sustain it when under pressure.

- Family placement social workers can use theory to help foster carers and adopters to understand children's behaviour and relationship strengths and difficulties as well as understanding their own reactions to the children.

- Family placement social workers need to provide caregivers with a thoughtful, available, reliable and containing secure base, to liberate their capacity to, in turn, be thoughtful about, care for, enjoy and love the children in their care.

- In turn, family placement social workers, who have to make very difficult judgements and who, at times, monitor and support both very complex and anxiety-provoking *and* very joyful and rewarding family situations, need employing agencies who will support and value them. They too need a secure base to enable them to make the very best both of their professional skills and knowledge and of their personal capacity for empathy, for managing feelings and relationships and for energetic advocacy on behalf of foster and adoptive families.

14 **Attachment and contact**

Contact for children separated from their birth family, whether temporarily or permanently, in foster care or adoption, is one of the most significant and yet challenging areas in planning for, working with and parenting children. Managing two families, practically and psychologically, is a major task for the child and for those who wish to promote the child's well-being into adult life. The potential role of contact and the contribution of attachment theory to making sense of the impact of contact seem so significant that a specific chapter is dedicated to it. Throughout this chapter, it becomes apparent that, as Ian Sinclair has said, there can be no easy "rules of thumb" regarding contact (Sinclair, 2005). There can be no substitute for a developmentally-informed and child-centred approach to the issue, since it is the potentially positive or negative impact of contact on the particular child's progress and welfare that should be central in assessing, planning and supporting contact.

Children, in particular those who are late placed, commonly have divided loyalties between their foster carers or adopters, who are their current sources of care and protection, and their birth families, for whom they may have strong but ambivalent feelings of love and anxiety (Beek and Schofield, 2004b). They must find ways to think through and accept the membership of two families (Fahlberg, 1994; Thoburn, 1996), while also managing their personal histories in ways that do not involve excessive anxiety or blame. Contact is the point at which the two families overlap in the child's life and mind and is therefore a delicate and complex area. It holds the potential to assist children in managing their dual family identities and to develop or sustain positive relationships with their relatives, built on realistic understandings and appreciation of their strengths and difficulties. However, contact can involve difficult transitions, the arousal of painful memories and feelings, and the exploration of relationships that have been destructive in the past. The quality of contact can therefore have a positive or negative impact on the child's capacity to return to the birth family or the child's sense of permanence in the foster or adoptive family. Short-, medium- and long-term plans *and* the nature of foster carers', adopters' and children's emotional investment in the placement need to be taken into account.

The parenting qualities that have been discussed in relation to the range of children's development all have a part to play in ensuring that contact works well for children and meets their needs. In particular, what we have referred to as sensitivity (i.e. the capacity to reflect on the thoughts and feelings of self and others in an open and thoughtful way) can be seen as critical to both successful parenting but also successful contact (Beek and Schofield, 2004b; Neil *et al*, 2003). The quality of "communicative openness" in adoptive parents has been linked not only to empathy for the child and the birth parents, but also the ability to communicate an acceptance of the child's dual family identity (Brodzinsky, 2005). It is seen as the likely key to successful contact in adoption (Grotevant *et al*, 2004; Neil, 2004). This cluster of related parenting qualities is equally likely to be the key to contact in the full range of foster care, from emergency through to permanent placements. Although contact will vary in frequency and purpose in different foster and adoptive placements, making contact work for the child, for the birth family and for the foster or adoptive family will require not only an appropriate plan, but some very particular qualities of "openness" in the carers.

Attachment theory can usefully inform a number of different aspects of social work practice and parenting in relation to contact. In particular, it can assist in:

- the overall assessment of the risks and benefits of contact in individual cases;
- the assessment of the appropriateness and specific arrangements for contact for each child, including by direct observation;
- ascertaining the wishes and feelings of children with regards to contact;
- working with children to promote the benefits and minimise the risks of contact;
- providing support for foster carers, adoptive parents and birth families in thinking about and managing contact – and remaining child-centred.

Understanding secure and insecure attachment patterns and the developmental consequences of maltreatment is particularly necessary in situations where *observations* of children's behaviour at contact are used in assessing the quality of relationships with birth relatives, which, in turn, is often used as a basis for decisions by local authorities and courts about permanency planning as well as about future contact.

The premise on which this chapter is based is that contact must be defensible in each case on the grounds that it is *developmentally beneficial to the particular child* – not that contact is deemed to be an automatically required feature of any family placement. This premise of developmental benefit should not mean that contact is less likely to happen, but that in each case there should be a careful assessment of its benefits for the specific child. The presumption of reasonable contact in the Children Act 1989 operates within the overall paramountcy principle of the welfare of the child. Although there is no presumption of contact in the Adoption and Children Act 2002, contact in some form (most often indirect contact) plays a part in the majority of adoption plans for children from care and again needs to be justified in terms of benefit to the child.

Within a family placement context, the welfare and development of the child, to which contact should contribute, is broadly defined and will include the security associated with attachment, alongside safety, health, education, emotional and behavioural development and identity. As we have seen already, however, these developmental issues (which can be affected positively or negatively by the presence or absence or quality of contact) interact (see Figure 11). The experience of a secure base in attachment terms and in terms of family membership is likely to free children to be more confident in themselves, their bodies, their relationships and their play and learning. The absence of a secure base leaves children overwhelmed with anxiety that needs to be defended against and limits their self-esteem and confident, pleasurable engagement in the world. Contact can be involved in upward and downward spirals of both kinds.

Figure 11

Contact and the developing mind of the child

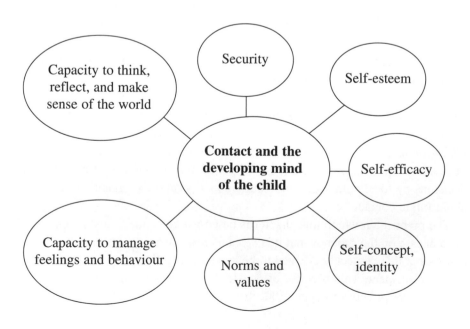

Contact, therefore, needs to be understood in terms of the contribution that it makes to each separate area of development, but with an eye to the effect on this total picture of the confidence or anxiety, comfort or fear that may be associated with the contact experience for the child and for the foster carers, adoptive parents and birth relatives.

Although the focus of planning should be on the purpose and the quality of the experience of contact for the *child*, if the *foster carer* or *adoptive parent* is made more comfortable and committed or, in contrast, more anxious by contact, then this will affect their capacity to keep the child in mind and to help the child to process the experience in a constructive and therapeutic way. This range will arise from an interaction of the appropriateness of actual contact arrangements with the caregiver's capacity (sensitivity/openness) to manage the idea of contact and the events themselves, in the context of managing their own needs and feelings.

Similarly, it will make a significant difference to the course of the placement if contact brings out the most constructive, supportive and loving behaviour in *birth relatives* or, in contrast, provides further opportunities for birth relatives to be angry, resentful or actively abusive of children. Here, too, appropriateness of arrangements will interact with the birth relatives' capacity to perform their role constructively and with sensitivity to the child, within the constraints of a contact visit and in the light of their own needs. These differences in the experience of contact will affect all aspects of children's sense of security and, in particular, will promote or diminish the possibility that children will recover from previous harm, revise their working models of the world, become less defensive, more open and more resilient.

Children's development and growth through childhood is not only about the quality of the child's internal world, a point made throughout this book. It is also important to think about the interaction of internal and external worlds and therefore bear in mind the impact of contact on the child's external social worlds (see Figure 12).

Contact arrangements should, therefore, also be tested in terms of the role they play in enhancing the *developing social world* of the child i.e. not only the quality of relationships within the foster, adoptive and birth family but also in the child's ability to engage with activities, school and friends. Thus, contact arrangements that are too rigid to allow the child to play for the school football team or go to a friend's birthday party or attend a birth family wedding, where this is appropriate, need to be thought about carefully.

The final part of the picture is to think about how the quality of contact is determined by the interaction between the major characteristics of the people and systems that include and surround the child (see Figure 13). Risk and protective

Figure 12

Contact and the developing social world of the child

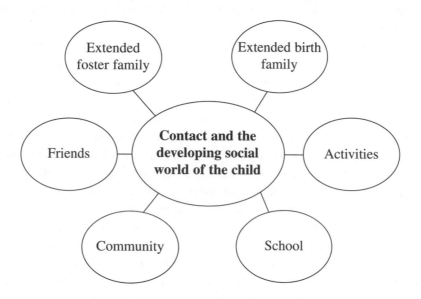

factors that can threaten or build security for the child can come from the child, the birth family, the foster or adoptive family or the professional networks that set up and support the placement. But it is most likely that it is the *interaction* between these factors that makes the difference. The contrast between contact involving birth families who can be supportive to a particular child *with help* from the social worker, adopter or carer and contact involving high-risk birth families who are *not properly supported or monitored* shows that we need to think flexibly about both potential benefit and harm for the child when key factors interact. The nature of the placement plan will always be a very significant factor in contact decisions and practice. Where a child is in a short-term foster placement and return home is a possibility, contact is the foundation on which reunification is built. As this chapter will discuss, this need not and should not constrain the depth and secure quality of a child's relationship with the foster carers, but it does mean that contact arrangements must provide both a source of continuity with the birth family and the possibility for therapeutic change to facilitate return home or perhaps to a kinship placement. Contact and the perceived quality of relationships with birth relatives invariably also contributes to the assessment of whether return home is possible or in the child's best interests as a route to security, stability and developmental well-being. This assessment is not straightforward – again, this is discussed in more detail below.

Figure 13

An interactive, dynamic model of contact

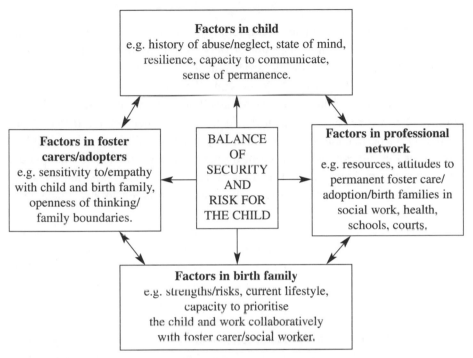

(Adapted from Beek and Schofield, 2004b)

Where a child is *placed for permanence* outside of the immediate birth family and in adoption, foster or kinship care, developing a secure attachment in the new family will be a priority and there needs to be a sense of the longer time frame in thinking about contact. For some children, emotional healing and healthy development will take many years and the primary attachment relationships in the new family will play a critical role. Where contact either facilitates this process or at the very least does not interfere with it, then contact has an important role to play. But where contact exposes children to extreme anxiety and emotional dysregulation (Howe and Steele, 2004), then contact may be too damaging to permit, because it returns the child to the defensive position they were in when taken into care and prevents growth through openness to the security of the caregiver's mind. As Neil and Howe put it (2004, p. 229).

Because a secure attachment and a sense of permanence provide the optimum

399

environment for a child's socio-emotional development, in the immediate term it has to outbid the psychosocial tasks of resolving feelings of loss and dealing with issues of identity if these involve contact with a dysregulating birth relative.

Even in short-term placements where return home is still a possibility, contact that is known to create unmanageable anxiety for the child and is dysregulating may need to be limited or special arrangements made for an alternative secure base to be present. The principle is the same. Unless the child's anxiety can be reduced and their mind and expectations of self and others can be reshaped in the context of a secure relationship in the foster family, then the child may never make it into a permanent family in which they can settle. Cases in which children may be at risk of psychological harm through contact will not be uncommon, given that the majority of looked after children will have experienced some degree of neglect or abuse, so such risks must be included in any attachment-based model of contact.

Every contact arrangement, therefore, requires careful thought and management to ensure that the child feels secure, is protected from anxiety and is supported to cope with any dilemmas and uncertainties that may arise. This practice in relation to contact will be set in the context of the overall aim of any placement plan, which is the child's developmental growth and happiness. Children at different ages and stages in their development may need and benefit from different types of contact and different types of support in managing it. This chapter follows the pattern of earlier chapters in focusing on children at each developmental stage. Within each age group, the different contexts of contact are taken into account, in particular, the distinction between placements which we call short-term or bridge placements, where the child will move on to a permanent placement (including returning home or to kinship placements) or to "independence", and placements which are planned to be permanent in long-term foster care and adoption.

Infancy (birth–18 months)

Infants who come to a foster or adoptive home straight from hospital or in the early weeks will not have formed an attachment to their birth parents and will build their first attachment with their new foster or adoptive primary caregivers. In the UK, where the placement of young infants is permanent and for adoption, there is unlikely to be face-to-face contact with the birth relatives.

Where a very young infant is in foster care and there is a likelihood, a faint possibility or almost no chance at all that the child will return to the birth family, it is probable that frequent contact will be set up by the agency or by order of a court – sometimes as often as five times a week – with the apparent intention of building an attachment relationship with the birth relative, most usually with the mother. (Where extensive contact arrangements are made *only* for legal reasons i.e. there is agreement that the child will not return home but the final order has not been made, questions need to be asked about reducing the contact in the interests of the child).

Two important issues emerge here. First, it might be thought that in this context the baby is forming its primary attachment to the birth mother, because of the frequency of contact and an often unspoken assumption about building on the biological tie. In fact, it is more likely that the infant's primary attachment, if placed at a very early stage in the foster home, will be to the primary caregiver, which in this case will be the foster mother. This does not rule out the benefit of continued exposure to the care of the birth mother through contact and the possibility of an attachment relationship with the birth mother in the event of an early return to her care. Indeed, the foster carer will be able to use the fact that the infant is relaxed and easy to feed as a result of her care to enhance the mother's success in caring for the child during contact.

However, the role of the foster carer as the primary attachment figure for the infant must not be overlooked or undervalued; neither should the contact plan and any assumptions about the child forming her primary attachment with the birth mother mean that the foster mother should pull back from immersing herself in the *maternal preoccupation* that Winnicott (1965) described and which is so critical to the healthy development of the infant through these early weeks and months. All the benefits of caregiver availability, sensitivity and attunement for the infant's confident and relaxed engagement with the world and developing mind are relevant here. A misreading of attachment theory might suggest that the foster mother should in some way stand back emotionally and cognitively from the infant – either to facilitate the attachment to the birth mother or, as discussed in previous chapters, to avoid the pain of loss when the child moves, or to facilitate the new attachment in the adoptive family. In fact, the primary gift of sensitive caregiving is *not* only in the fact that a relationship will last (and this is to be valued when it is appropriate), but to reduce anxiety, shape the baby's developing mind (and brain) and awaken the baby's potential for play and exploration and a positive sense of self. Even where the birth mother is offering good enough care during contact and the foster carer wishes to support this, the carer needs also to be responding in a wholehearted, thoughtful and "committed" way (Dozier *et al*, 2005) to the infant in all aspects of her parenting. There should be no sense that the baby is simply being looked after physically by the carer with the birth mother providing the emotional input. For the foster carer, loving and fully engaging with the mind and whole person, as well as the physical needs, of a baby can only be beneficial to the baby – grief, if there is to be a move, can be managed better by a very young mind than the prolonged absence of loving care in the sensitive early months and years of life.

Coming from the birth family at beyond 2–3 months old, there will be an expectation that there is in most cases a prior relationship with the birth mother, a developing attachment or, beyond 6–7 months, an attachment. (Exceptions can occur where mothers have effectively abandoned the care of the infant to a number of other adults and the child may have no selective attachment.) Where there are such significant concerns about the nature of the child's caregiving experiences that the child has come into care, this relationship is likely to be insecure. However, there will be some infants who may be secure, having come into care because of maternal illness or because a Schedule 1 offender (convicted of previous child abuse) has just joined the family. From this point on, foster carers will be managing their own developing relationship with the child in the context of contact with birth parents with whom the child may have a secure, organised insecure (i.e. avoidant or ambivalent) or disorganised insecure attachment and to whom the child may or may not be returning. Other birth relatives are also very likely to be part of the picture, as they may wish to keep in contact or be considered as future carers. It can also be the case that the foster carers are themselves relatives of the birth parents and need to manage both relationship building and contact in this context.

With infants to whom verbal explanations of what is going on at contact may be offered ('That sounds like your Mum/Granddad arriving to see you – isn't that lovely?'), the words will be less important than the tone of voice and the mood of the caregiver. Promoting security will mean managing the framework of the contact experience to ensure that the child has a meaningful, positive and undisruptive experience, which includes providing calming and reassuring non-verbal messages to the infant, *and* also giving calming and encouraging messages to the visiting relative. Continuity will be important as part of a message to the infant that the world is a predictable place in which it is safe to relax and this may need to be negotiated with birth relatives. Continuity from birth family home to foster home may have been respected in small ways – perhaps the child had been addressed using a particular diminutive of her name, which the foster carer has also adopted. Perhaps a particular teddy from home, a duvet or clothes were brought to the foster home to build continuity for the child. Perhaps links are built in other ways, with the birth parent continuing to be involved in choosing clothes or toys for the child, especially where return home is a possibility.

But at contact, the birth parent may need to adopt some of the ways that are now familiar to the infant in the foster home. If the child is accustomed to being bathed at a particular time or in a particular room, then this needs to continue where possible, if this is an experience being provided by the birth mother or father at contact. If the infant is used to being held closely or in a particular way for feeding, rather than held at a distance or propped in the buggy, then the birth parent needs to be encouraged to offer the child the same experience. Continuity is not the only factor here – infants at contact should be given the best possible care. It may be, of course, that caregiving at contact is part of the assessment of the parent's capacity to parent the child. The foster carer or observing social worker would need to be alert to and assessing evidence of the birth parent's capacity to be sensitive in talking to and handling the infant, but it is not helpful developmentally for the infant to experience discontinuity of care (or poor care) through lack of communication and the parent's "failure" noted, in the name of assessment.

One of the more challenging aspects of planning contact in infancy is determining the amount of time that might be deemed desirable or necessary. There is no evidence that any particular amount of time is more or less likely to be associated with preserving an existing or building a new attachment relationship with a birth relative in the context of contact. More does not mean better. It is helpful for the young infant to be familiar with the sight, voice, smell, touch and presence of the birth parent and for the older infant to be able to experience play and games with the birth parent, so that this can provide a platform for the relationship if the infant returns home. But the appropriate amount of contact time will depend on the infant's age and what is reasonable and possible. For very young infants with extended contact, the likelihood is that, out of four hours of contact time, two – three hours may be when the infant is asleep. If birth parents are sitting in the foster home during this time, it is likely to be a major problem for them, but also for the foster carer, who is unable to get on with the household routines (cooking the evening meal or doing the washing) in ways that may impact on the time she has to spend with other children or with the baby when the baby wakes later. Contact needs to be planned around the role that the parent can reasonably play in the child's life, but it should not be done arithmetically by weight of hours in an attempt to ensure that the infant preferentially attaches to the birth parent.

Even more challenging in terms of providing predictable, sensitive and available care in the foster home and building security in the mind of the infant is a contact plan that means the infant is taken to a neutral venue, such as a family centre, for frequent and/or extended periods of supervised or unsupervised contact. This arrangement gets round the problem of intrusion into the foster home and may appear to promote the freedom of the birth parent to parent the child in a more relaxed manner, away from possible competition or criticism by the foster carer. However, the key premise of attachment theory is that when anxious, as when separated from the current caregiver or when confronted with birth relatives who may have been rejecting or frightening, the infant will seek proximity to an attachment figure who offers care and protection. Since this role is likely to be filled by the foster carer, the infant is in a dilemma that is akin to that which promotes disorganisation. The infant may only have access to a caregiver who is a source of anxiety. Even infants who may be thought too young to remember have memories which can make contact distressing and disturbing. (Even a newborn baby will respond to a familiar nursery rhyme told to them during pregnancy, so infants should never be thought too young to remember.) It is not unusual to hear of infants under six months old who become very distressed when taken to contact, but not when taken to see other places and people.

What is more, and this is crucial to understanding this process, older infants who have developed defensive strategies to cope with neglectful or frightening birth family environments may have been encouraged and enabled to relinquish these in the context of the relationship with the foster carer. Thus, the older infant may have started to approach adults more openly rather than shutting down, but then at contact find themselves approaching caregivers who may frighten them or make them anxious. The context of contact often exacerbates this difficulty, as birth relatives are often being assessed and, not surprisingly, feel under pressure to demonstrate their good relationship with the child or their parenting skills. This can lead to intrusive parenting (scooping the child up, tickling them), which again makes the child highly anxious, but against which they have lowered their defences.

Where there is to be contact away from the home, for whatever reason, it is still desirable for the foster carer to be present, if at all possible, so that there is availability in times of stress, but also so that messages of availability are reinforced in the child's working model. If this is not possible then the length of time away from the foster carer should be limited and other sources of security and continuity should be built in, such as using the same supervisor each time (someone who comes into the foster home to greet the baby and returns the baby with a debrief for the foster carer), and the use of transitional objects such as teddies from the foster home. This may appear to be reinforcing the child's ties with the foster home, but in fact, if the infant's anxiety is reduced, the infant is more likely to relax and accept care or play with the birth parent and the parent is more likely to find the child rewarding. Birth relatives need support and help to understand this and to help them tune in to the infant's needs at contact.

Generally, assessment of the quality of children's relationships with a birth relative, through *observation* at contact can be very revealing, but the *interpretation* of what is observed and what it might say about past and future parenting capacity does need to take into account the full range of attachment issues. Anxiety and separation will be affecting both the mother and the child and reinforcing the use of defensive strategies. Mother or child may appear to shut down on feelings or act as if helpless. On the other hand, where the child shows distressed, disoriented, dissociated or disorganised behaviours in the presence of the birth relative, that are not evident at other times, then there should be concerns, as mentioned above, about the dysregulating effect of contact on the child.

The primary task of caregivers and supervising social workers in all their talk, behaviour, non-verbal messages and practical arrangements around contact is to reassure the infant, reduce anxiety, and make contact a positive and security-promoting experience – and avoid experiences that unsettle and frighten the infant and decrease the likelihood of a successful permanent move back home or to a new family.

Early childhood (18 months–4 years)

This age group presents particular challenges and opportunities for contact, whether contact is aimed at facilitating a return to the birth family or is in the context of a plan for permanence in foster care or adoption. Young children will be seeking meanings that give a shape to and make sense of their experience, but have a very limited capacity both to make sense of the complex circumstances of loss and separation and to handle their emotions and their behaviour. Such difficulties are exacerbated for young children who are insecure and for whom the world is full of uncertainties and dangers. Although pre-school children have gained some skills in language and perspective taking by the age of three or four, it is not surprising that they find it difficult to make sense of why their mum and siblings arrive at the strange house, smile at them but then go away leaving them behind. They struggle to understand why they go in a car to a strange place to see the parents, brothers and sisters, who used to be constant companions.

Although, over time, toddlers and pre-school children may accept the routine of these events, and adapt to the two families, some children will continue to struggle with their feelings. These feelings may, of course, be mixed and change, as young children start to settle in the foster or adoptive family. Even though they initially resist the relationship with new caregivers, over time it is hoped that young children will start to turn to them for support and treat them as a secure base. They may then start to object to separation, as an infant forming an attachment would do. On the other hand, if the foster carer or adoptive parent is neither adequately sensitive nor committed, the child may feel uncontained both at home and at contact and be distressed, defended or disorganised in both environments.

Given that it is very difficult to help a three-year-old understand that they are in foster care because, for example, they are at risk of physical or sexual abuse or neglect, the primary goal must be to build the child's developmental health and define a role for contact in that process. The focus then must be, in attachment terms, on how contact can promote the child's sense of security and not put it further at risk. It may be that, although reasons for being in care are hard to communicate (although it must be attempted even with young children), seeing birth relatives may give some helpful messages to children about who they are, about the fact that they still matter to significant people from their previous life, and about the idea that people do not disappear into thin air just because they do not live with them anymore.

As with infants, assessment through observation and interpretation of toddlers' and pre-school children's (and parents') behaviour at contact is rarely straightforward and developmental attachment theory can be brought to bear. Children in this age group have learned how to pretend to feel what they do not feel and to suppress expressions of negative feelings. This is an age when children may be struggling to manage feelings of longing, anger and/or anxiety. At contact, feelings will sometimes be suppressed (a still face or a fixed smile) and sometimes spill out (persistent crying or tantrums). Children at this stage are unlikely to be able to explain their views or experience of contact and it is only in their often ambiguous behaviour that they will express their feelings. This is not to suggest that older children in this age group should not be consulted about their wishes and feelings about seeing birth family members, but it does mean that recording and making sense of children's behaviour at times when they are not having contact and then before, during and after contact, are very important and subtle pieces of assessment work.

In some cases, though, the child's extreme difficulties are apparent.

Three-year-old Imogen was very volatile, attacking young children but clinging to her bridge foster carer. When angry or upset, she could scream for hours and was resisting all attempts to change her behaviour. At contact with her mentally ill mother at a neutral venue, roles were reversed and Imogen was very controlling and contemptuous of her mother. After contact she became very distressed and disorientated – and then aggressive.

Imogen had coped with neglectful and often frightening experiences in the birth family, but when her controlling strategies were challenged in the foster home she became overwhelmed with anxiety and rage. An assessment had unhelpfully described her as having a "strong" attachment to her birth mother and at contact she was put back in touch with her former self, both in terms of her fears and her coping strategies. In spite of her young age, Imogen had already experienced two broken placements and her current placement seemed to be at risk. Contact was not the only problem, as this very disturbed and distressed child needed the undivided attention of a therapeutic caregiver and hers was a busy foster family. However, the quality of contact needed to be taken carefully into account in trying to settle and heal Imogen and halt her downward spiral.

With this age group, scaffolding the experience of contact through language and explanation can give messages that relationships in the foster or adoptive home are offering security and that contact with birth family members will enhance security and contribute to the child's trust in the environment. In order for this to be the case, contact needs to be predictable, both in terms of the timing, the presence of the birth relative, the comfortableness of the venue and, where relevant, the presence of the foster carer or supervisor. It is also important that, where birth parents have drug or alcohol problems, they are not intoxicated at contact, even though this may mean that the contact meeting is postponed or curtailed. As with the case of Imogen, above, patterns across the range of the child's relationships need to be understood in order to offer a therapeutic package in which contact plays a constructive role and is part of the solution, not part of the problem.

Because children's feelings of disappointment and distress are so great when birth relatives do not appear as planned for contact visits or are too intoxicated to see the child, it is not unusual for foster carers and adopters to avoid giving children notice of contact arrangements. It seems likely though that, on balance, the need for communication to be open and the environment to be honest and predictable – for the child to know, for example, that there will be several days or weeks or even months before the next contact is due – is preferable to the possibility of the birth relatives arriving back in the child's life without an opportunity to talk though their feelings and help the child anticipate and enjoy the meeting. Even for young children the use of calendars can be helpful in relation to predicting the timing of contact, as for other minor and major events in the child's life. Where there are long gaps between contact meetings, family photographs are helpful in keeping the idea of birth relatives alive for the child. Throughout this process the approach should be low key and not overemphasised – noting when visits are due, offering the opportunity to discuss the birth family, but tuning in to the child's feelings, with no assumptions made (e.g. avoiding, 'Oh, you must be so excited and looking forward to seeing your mum/dad/ sister!'). Parents' possible failure to attend a contact visit needs to be anticipated and managed, perhaps by planning another activity which can take its place if necessary – although actively engaging the social worker or an assistant where possible to bring the parent to contact may be preferable to serial disappointments. This is a difficult balance, but repeated failures by birth relatives to appear should mean a closer look at the contact arrangement, rather than making contact itself a secret that excludes the child. Even with court-ordered contact, it should also be possible to vary contact arrangements where these are no longer in the child's best interests – and have a clearly-documented assessment for why this variation is necessary to take back to court.

For young children, as for infants, the presence of the foster carers, or at the very least a familiar social worker, at contact is likely to be helpful. If there is to be a point during contact when the foster carer is not in the room, then it will be important for the child to have clear communications and even evidence that they will be returning to the foster carer after the meeting, such as the foster carer discussing what they will do after the contact and holding the child's coat or the child holding the carer's scarf or a toy from the foster home.

Although face-to-face contact for young children in adoption is less common than in foster care, early evidence suggests that it can work well, it does not appear to affect children's developmental well-being or the attachment relationship and it can be reassuring to adoptive parents and birth relatives (Neil, 2004). Young children in Neil's study were meeting birth parents or grandparents with whom they had no significant previous relationship because they came into care in infancy. What appears to be helpful in these cases is the unambiguous fact in adoption that the child is permanently a member of the adoptive family and so contact is determined by the adoptive parents, who are also the child's primary attachment figures. This includes controlling the timing and the venue, as well as being present as the child's parents. This study also suggests that contact works best in situations where adoptive parents are able to be empathic towards the child and the birth relatives, and where some degree of "communicative openness"/ collaboration happens in order to maximise the success of contact for the child, but also the adopters and the birth relatives (see also Brodzinsky, 2005; Grotevant *et al*, 2004).

Although in permanent, long-term foster placements the social worker is often playing an active role in planning contact, unlike in adoption, it is also the case in foster care that contact works best where foster carers feel themselves to be key players in the decision making about contact and are also able to be sensitive or empathic to the child and the birth family (Neil *et al*, 2003). A foster carer belief system that supports the notion that children can be members of more than one family is also valuable in enabling parents and carers to work comfortably but actively together to ensure that contact is a success (see also Chapter 10 on family membership).

There are clearly many cases in which contact is a constructive force in young children's lives, facilitating a sense of security in the foster family through reducing anxiety, guilt and split loyalties, while also ensuring positive experiences with birth relatives which may lead to returning to them. But there are contact arrangements in both temporary and permanent placements in which traumatised children are re-traumatised through their contact with birth relatives. Young children are particularly at risk for a number of reasons. First, they have fewer strategies for communicating their distress accurately and behaviours that arise from anxiety before, during and after contact are not always easy to interpret as linked to contact, since young children may generally be showing difficult behaviours, such as tantrums and bed-wetting. Second, limited understanding of language and the world make it difficult to understand the explanation that 'Daddy is talking like that because he has a mental illness'. Third, because of their age and size young children are more likely at contact to be picked up, experience a nappy change or a feed, sit on a lap or be held close. Thus, the child will experience a great deal of physical proximity that should be a positive part of contact, but where there is a history of maltreatment, this may be experienced as distressing and intrusive.

Although being retraumatised by contact is a risk in some cases, young children can also be distressed by sudden cutting off of contact. It is still sometimes said that children should not have contact with birth family members for a period when they first come into care or should not have contact with bridge foster carers for a period when they move into adoption, so that they have time to "settle" or "to form a new attachment". Each case must be looked at carefully, but unless birth relatives or former foster carers are likely to create a significant problem at contact, then the benefit to be gained from reassuring the child that they have not just been abandoned and that they are wished well in their new home is likely to outweigh the possible upset. This contact may be in person or it may simply be a card. Birth families and bridge carers often hold back because they do not want to intrude or cause problems for the child. Foster carers in particular are indoctrinated with the importance of "letting children go". As none of us would want to be "let go" from our close relationships, it should not be too hard to imagine the child's experience of loss.

Children are more likely to manage these moves with less damage to their sense of self and the continuity of valued relationships, if social workers are clear about what each child needs and how to manage this constructively. For this age group and even older age groups, communication about and after the move needs to be not only verbal but also non-verbal and concrete e.g. a good luck card rather than a passed on verbal message. Taking a photo of the child and the foster carers or a small photo album of their time in the foster family into the new foster care or adoptive placement can be a help in addition to contact arrangements. This process may be separate from or part of life story work, depending on the child's circumstances, but it seems that some of the good practice that has developed around moves to adoption could usefully inform all moves. Children are more likely to turn to their new caregivers for comfort if they feel that the world still makes sense and if they are not so overwhelmed with anxiety about loss that they shut down on their feelings.

Middle childhood (5–10 years)

For this age group, carer/parent attachment figures continue to be very important, but children also develop rich lives outside the family home and can find safe havens among their friends or use a teacher as a secure base. As their thinking changes, contact can be an important part of helping children at this stage to make sense of who they are and where they fit within this range of relationships.

At an age when identity, self-concept and self-esteem are important aspects of development, contact should be playing a part in clarifying the "facts", reinforcing positives and enabling children to work though more troubling and worrying questions about their histories and themselves. As Owusu-Bempah and Howitt (1997, p. 201 cited in Neil and Howe, 2004, p. 226) put it:

> *Socio-genealogical knowledge is fundamental to our psychological integrity. It is essential to our sense of who we are, what we want to be, where we come from and where we belong in the order of things.*

But the narratives of fostered and adopted children are complex and do not easily fit culturally available frameworks. There are many truths and a number of realities to which children may have been exposed, in relation to both why they are not with their parents and the reason for their care or adoptive status. Discontinuities may have occurred not only in family environments, but in relation to ethnicity, religion, language and community. Contact can be useful in helping to make sense of the story, but most children will need active help from caregivers to process this information into a coherent narrative, especially if the child receives rather different messages from the foster carer, the social worker and the birth family at contact.

If contact arrangements in all types of placements are working well, they should be contributing to all aspects of the child's welfare in this age range (as in Figure 11), not just "roots and identity", a term commonly used in court. For example, contact should help build children's self-esteem, very important at this age, so that messages from birth relatives such as, 'Well done for your school work' or 'What a lovely new haircut' accompany the family membership/roots message, 'We still value you as our son/grandson/brother'. One difficulty is that in living apart children's lives move on and birth families may not know what matters to the child. Social workers, foster carers and adoptive parents may be keeping birth families up to date at varying (but often infrequent) intervals and where close working relationships can be established between caregivers and birth families, birth parents will receive school reports or be involved in school parents' evenings. It is clear in this context that contact needs to be facilitated and not be a test of birth parents' commitment. On the other hand, birth relatives who are negative about and to the child, in spite of information and support, must be recognised as harming the child's development.

This variety of outcomes alone highlights the range of possible "overlap" between foster/adoptive and birth families and how this will define and be defined by contact. Where families are working closely together to achieve the child's return home, birth parents may visit the foster home or foster carers may be making regular visits to the birth family's house to get the child accustomed to seeing it as home again, but also for the foster carer to be able to offer help and support to the birth family in parenting the child more effectively. Even in some long-term foster placements there can be a significant degree of overlap. For example, in long-term foster families which previously provided respite care for the children with disabilities who are now placed permanently with them, contact may be frequent, medical appointments may be shared and birth families can provide the respite care (Schofield et al, 2000). In other cases, where foster carers are able to establish a good relationship with the birth mother or father and there is no risk to the child, contact may be as frequent as once a fortnight. In these situations, the normal hierarchy of attachment relationships which children in this age range have is likely to include the birth parents or grandparents. Contact with siblings may also offer sources of self-esteem and security to children as well as shared identity.

More commonly in permanent placements for foster care or adoption, contact is quite limited, but can still demonstrate to the child the goodwill between their two sets of parents (Beek and Schofield, 2004b; Neil et al, 2003). Infrequent but regular contact becomes an opportunity to catch up on news and, if made a special occasion such as a trip to the zoo or to the seaside, it can offer a chance to enjoy time together and provide semantic and episodic memories of the kind that the child can process and revisit. One adopted child, Sue (10), commented on her contact with her birth mother in the park.

> *We go for a walk around the park and we've bought some crisps and go out to the ducks and give them cheese-and-onion flavoured crisps or something. Then mum starts to tell jokes and I, I can't tell any jokes and we'd all be drunk, feel as though we were drunk by the end of it.* (Thomas and Beckford *et al*, 1999, p. 93)

Where there are good relationships between carers and birth relatives, some spontaneity becomes possible. A spur of the moment decision to drive her three unrelated foster daughters round to their different mothers on Mother's Day to drop off cards and presents was one foster carer's way of setting up brief but informal "contact" outside normal arrangements, in a way that helped the children and their birth mothers feel special (Beek and Schofield, 2004a).

Other arrangements for these school-age children where contact may be more risky can be said to be security promoting and "safe enough" through special care being taken to ensure that supervision is appropriate, birth parents are on time and so on. Almost invariably this works best when foster carers, like adopters, are actively involved. But for the child of this age, consultation is certainly necessary to establish their views. Some arrangements include the child having staying contact with birth relatives, again even when in permanent placements. Where children have a secure relationship with carers and a sense of permanence, they can use the explanations their carers provide to help them feel secure and to reflect on their contact with birth parents. In a study of adults who grew up in foster care (Schofield, 2003), there were a number of young adults who had memories of contact with birth mothers who had said consistently over the years that they would fight to get "their" child back. But they also remembered foster carers saying calmly and sympathetically, 'Well, it's not surprising that your mum says that, as she wants you to know she loves you. But you and I and she know that you are staying here so you needn't worry.' This empathic and mind-minded approach to making sense of the birth parent's thinking and behaviour, in the context of a secure relationship in the foster home, enabled contact to continue without risk to the child's sense of permanence.

What is likely to present more risk to development and a sense of security, is where, as in infancy and early childhood, the arrangements for contact are perceived as out of the foster carers' or adopters' hands. Too often foster children in middle childhood are taken by different escorts to social services venues, where supervisors may not know the child and the foster carer then gets poor or no feedback on how the contact visit went. It is sometimes assumed that children between the ages of 8–10 can manage their own relationships with their birth families with the minimum of help and supervision. But in some cases, emotionally troubled and confused children, who have experienced extreme neglect, physical and sexual abuse in their birth family, are involved in contact of this kind. One long-term foster carer reported that, because of the low priority given to the safety of the contact arrangement, a new supervisor had not checked who was allowed to have contact with her ten-year-old foster daughter and a birth family member who had sexually abused the child was allowed to attend the contact. This carer subsequently adopted the child and insisted that as part of her adoption support package she had a consistent staff member to undertake the contact arrangements, to support her daughter and to give her feedback as a parent. It is unrealistic to expect a child to speak out against the presence of a family member, even when, or especially when, she might be frightened or when she is offered presents.

As with younger children, some signs of children's feelings are difficult to spot. Secure and insecure attachment patterns will affect the way in which children respond to contact and talk about contact, with some children concealing their feelings and being dismissive of the value of contact, while actually struggling with their fears of further rejection. On some occasions, reactions are very graphic, but reveal a complex set of feelings and attempts to cope, as this case example (a case also referred to in the chapter on disorganisation) suggests:

> *Donna (5) had been physically and sexually abused and neglected until the age of three. Her father was a frightening figure who dominated and attacked her learning disabled mother. In foster care Donna was hard to get close to. Like a little doll, she was well-behaved at home and school, but had little facial expression, showed no variation in her mood and was fixed in her behaviour, which at times included sitting in a trance-like state for up to twenty minutes at a time. She said that she wanted to go home. She was taken to contact by the same social work assistant, who over time discovered that she needed to take a plastic bag each time, since Donna was invariably physically sick on her way to and from contact with her birth parents.*

In this case, Donna's view – that she wanted to return home – was being taken seriously by the court, but this account of contact, which was consistent with what

413

was known of her history, suggested that her relationship with her parents was still dominated by fear and confusion, reinforcing her tendency to dissociate in response to even small triggers in the foster home.

Managing two families and two family identities can undoubtedly be helped through contact, but it can also be made more difficult. Similarly, the child's felt security as well as clarity about their identity can be increased, or it may be threatened. Each child, each placement and each birth family must be very carefully considered with the short-, medium- and long-term developmental goals for the child in mind when contact arrangements are made.

Adolescence (11–18 years)

Although in adolescence contact may well be more flexible and, with the advent of mobile phones, increasingly out of the control of carers and adopters, teenagers often still need support to make the most of contact and to feel secure. In fact, mobile phones can be useful in keeping the secure base in reach. Amanda (15) was in long-term foster care and had only had sporadic contact with her parents since the age of three, partly because of their prison sentences for drug-related offences. On one occasion, it was arranged for Amanda to meet her mother in the local shopping centre. When her mother did not appear, Amanda immediately telephoned her foster father as arranged and he was instantly available to pick her up.

This could have been the end of contact, but in fact after this incident Amanda went on to have several more successful contacts, when she and her mother went swimming together. The next time her mother did not turn up, Amanda had arranged a contingency plan and went shopping with her friends – though her foster father was still available by phone so she knew he was thinking of her and could collect her if need be. Amanda could explore her relationship with her birth mother through contact, accept its strengths and limitations, but with her foster family still acting as a secure base.

For young people in this age group, negotiations between carers and young people to facilitate and manage contact safely are often crucial. In the following example, a carer outlines her responses to her foster daughter's increasing confusion about contact and the entangled relationship with her birth mother and siblings, who were living at home. Zoë's previous placement had ended but she had been well settled, for over two years, with her current carers, Veronica and Larry. Veronica had done much to encourage Zoë (12) to feel part of her foster family, but she also felt strongly that Zoë needed to work through her relationships with her mother and siblings and establish a comfortable and realistic sense of her position in the family. To facilitate this and in the absence of risk to Zoë's safety, Veronica and the social worker decided to "let go of the reins" a little and agree to Zoë's persistent requests to sleep over at her mother's home, twice a month. Over time, this arrangement proved rather too much for the birth mother and Zoë to cope with and it was reduced to once a month, which seemed manageable. As a result of this freedom within safe limits, Zoë lost her sense of urgency regarding contact and instead, was able to find a comfortable "niche" in her mother's household when she visited. As Veronica put it:

> *I think if you put a block on something that someone wants to do, they want to do it even more. I think it is important for Zoë to feel part of the family, you know, to get her niche with her sisters and brother . . . and I think she has, yes, she has. I know she has.*

Where children are more vulnerable or anxious and circumstances are more uncertain, the physical presence of the carer during the contact meetings may still be needed as an explicit reminder of the availability of the secure base and as a necessary source of reassurance even for the older child. Samantha (14) had learning difficulties and she became highly stressed by her birth mother's erratic attendance at contact meetings, hosted and supervised by social services. Her foster mother decided to change the arrangements so that she could supervise them herself and the birth mother could also choose a venue in which she felt comfortable. When Samantha had easy access to her secure base in this way, she was able to relax and enjoy her contact and also to manage her loyalties to both families.

> *If we keep it like it is now and it's successful and Samantha's not unhappy, she looks forward to it and it's made pleasant and then afterwards we chat about it and it's still all nice and she doesn't wet the bed that night and she doesn't have a tantrum before we go and she doesn't keep saying 'What time is it, what time is it? and that sort of thing like we used to have, you know, then I think well, we've got the right formula, because it's Samantha's needs not (birth mother's) needs that I'm supposed to be fulfilling.*

Although the foster carer emphasised prioritising the child's needs, the contact only worked because the birth mother's needs were also taken into account.

Special gestures outside of normal contact arrangements and orchestrated by the foster mother can also enrich the relationship and enhance the role of birth relatives in this older age group. In this case, two sisters were wrapping up 30 small birthday presents for their birth mother's 30th birthday.

And, you know, Laura (14) loved wrapping them up and Emma (10) did. So they were all wrapping them up and anticipating, you know. Laura put the numbers on all of them and they had a lovely time. And that was nice. But I suppose the thing is I felt totally secure with the girls. It's not detracting from the placement at all, I don't think, the level of contact. (Foster mother)

Frequency of contact must be shaped around the child's needs and views and although Laura and Emma (and their long-term carers) were happy with fortnightly contact, this had to be negotiated to ensure that the times suited the birth mother but did not limit the foster family's life and joint activities.

Frequent contact of this kind would not work or be appropriate for all permanently placed children or all families. At the other extreme, Jenny, a 14-year-old adopted by her foster carer, had been having one-and-a-half hour supervised contact with her birth family three times a year (supervision was necessary in this case as there was a history of emotional and sexual abuse). Although this does not sound like a long meeting for such intermittent contact, her mother and grandmother had significant learning difficulties and it was not possible to sustain the conversation for long. It was thus stressful for Jenny and her family. After careful consultation with Jenny, the arrangements were renegotiated to half an hour in a café three times a year, with a consistent and familiar adoption support worker doing the transport and the supervision. This met Jenny's need, which was to make sure that her family were alright, and the family's need to see her as she grew into her teenage years, without either party feeling under pressure. For both Jenny and her family, it felt preferable that they meet in a community setting rather than a social services venue. Birthday and Christmas cards could also contribute to the continuity of relationships. When contact visits are an ordeal, attempts must be made to change them to suit the child's and the birth relatives' needs and capacities. Again, there should be no rules of thumb. In Jenny's case there was quite a long journey to get to the café for the meeting – but the brief time was still the right plan for this child and was meaningful. The child herself preferred not to have her two families together, so the continuity of social worker was important in sharing her task of thinking about the two families.

Contact can, as in this case, help to confirm the child's life story, in that it was apparent that the family could not care for her. But in other cases contact that seems as if it must be a good idea, e.g. a long-lost brother reappears, can cause its own complications when it confuses the story and even gives a harmful message.

Lottie (14) had been abandoned by her adoptive family at the age of five following emotional and physical abuse and the adopters cut off all contact with her. Later in childhood, her much older adoptive brother started to visit. Although this was welcomed by Lottie, her brother defended his parents and denied that anything very serious had ever happened to her. He also tended to undermine her position by saying that she had had it easy in her foster home and her difficult behaviour just showed she was ungrateful.

The explicit and implicit messages were that Lottie's memory of her childhood were inaccurate, that any sadness and anger were unjustified, and that she was herself more likely to be the cause of trouble.

Of course, being mature enough as an adolescent to have a choice about contact may not make it easy to "choose" between two families and two identities, particularly on special occasions. Joshua (15), for instance, was in a very successful long-term foster family, and had unusually frequent contact, spending part of most weekends with his birth father. The arrangement was flexible, and could be altered by agreement if the foster family had a commitment or the birth father had to work longer hours. The families met together and arrangements were informal. However, the comfortable arrangements did not mean that there were no complications. Joshua's loyalties could feel torn, but his carers accepted this and encouraged him to talk through his complex feelings. Using his secure base in this way, Joshua was able to reach a compromise regarding Christmas arrangements, as his foster mother described:

He now finds it difficult. Josh is like 'Oh, but I wanna be here Christmas and I wouldn't mind going there Boxing Day'. You know he finds it hard. He says, 'I wanna be in both places'. In the end he says, 'I think I should be here Christmas Day and then I'll go to my dad's Boxing Day' – something like that. He says, 'I feel as if I should be here, just part of the family at Christmas'.

Here contact and family membership issues cannot be easily resolved, but the carer helps him to make the best of what is always a difficult decision by valuing both families. Joshua knows he loves and is loved by both families and is becoming more autonomous and effective through his role in making contact decisions.

Flexibility of arrangements is usually greater in adoption than foster care, because adopters are in charge and can more readily adapt arrangements to the child's changing needs. But some adoptive families of older children can find themselves trapped by plans made at the court hearing. One adoptive mother

417

accepted the contact plan for her son when he was placed with her at the age of 11 (Euan's adoptive parents, 2004). She knew that it was important for him to have contact with both his parents (who were still drug users), but the arrangements were for unsupervised contact (four times a year with each parent) and over time she became uncomfortable at leaving him in households for several hours when drug taking was likely to be going on. She felt unable to challenge the plan as it had been part of the court case and as an adopter she felt unable to change it and access the support she needed. When she did ask for supervision for contact she was told she might be expected to pay. In these circumstances, adoptive parents can feel more isolated than foster carers and adopted children may also find it difficult to mediate between their two sets of parents.

Sometimes children in adolescence are, through contact, still struggling with destructive attachment relationships with birth parents that have not changed since early childhood. Natalie (13), for instance, appeared emotionally drained and cognitively confused by the contact with her mother (Beek and Schofield, 2004). Phone calls and unsupervised days out in the mother's home town perpetuated a relationship in which there had been a role reversal, with the mother requiring her daughter's support for her health problems, criminal convictions and depression. This pattern of role reversal and dependency, accompanied by neglect, had contributed to Natalie being looked after in the first place. The carers described mother and daughter now competing over who would end a telephone conversation and who loved who more.

> Lisa (birth mother) says, 'Oh, you put the phone down first' and Natalie says 'No, you put the phone down first' . . . Then Lisa says, 'I love you' and Natalie says, 'I love you' and Lisa says, 'I love you more than you love me'. 'No you don't, I love you more'.

In some extreme cases in adolescence, teenagers are exposed through contact to frightening relationships that have also persisted from early childhood. Patrick (13) had been physically abused by his father as a younger child and continued to be exposed to his father's violent temper towards his partner during contact. Earlier in this foster placement, from when he was about 9 or 10, Patrick's carers were extremely anxious about this and noted that he was often in a 'trance-like state' when they collected him from his father's home. It seemed that the traumatising and disorganising effect of the fear and dread that he had experienced in his father's care was repeated during contact. As an accommodated child (placed under a voluntary agreement under s20 Children Act, 1989), the local authority felt that there was little they could do. In spite of exceptionally committed, loving and sensitive carers, Patrick's anti-social and violent behaviour escalated and the local authority moved him into a residential facility, where his behaviour was continuing to deteriorate. It seemed that Patrick had, in his foster family, a window of opportunity to heal some of his early damage, but his carers had no way of protecting him from his father through contact arrangements that were out of their control.

Conclusion

In this case, as in all cases, the impact of contact on children's development and the interacting factors that determine whether contact will promote security or increase risk is clear. Contact is one of the most important aspects of any placement plan, whether in a short-term, bridge or permanent placement, and whether in infancy or adolescence. There are just no short cuts. A full assessment, followed up by careful reviews, taking into account and being reflective about all areas of development and the thoughts, feelings and behaviours of all parties to the arrangements, are necessary in order to promote the child's well-being into adulthood.

Summary points

- Contact must be defensible in each case on the grounds that it is developmentally beneficial to the particular child.

- Managing two families, practically and psychologically, is a major task for the child and for those who wish to promote the child's well-being into adult life. Contact needs to be planned and facilitated in ways that recognise this task.

- Fostered and adopted children must find ways to think through, make sense of and accept the membership of two families, while also managing their personal histories in ways that do not involve excessive anxiety or blame.

- Contact with birth relatives can help or hinder this task depending on the interaction between factors in the child, the foster or adoptive family, the birth family and the agency.

- Parenting qualities that promote children's development all have a part to play in ensuring that contact works well for children and meets their needs; in particular, sensitivity to the feelings of the child and the birth family.

- Secure and insecure attachment patterns, as well as the emotional age of the child, will affect the way in which a child responds to and talks about contact. Assessments and plans need to take this into account.

• The plan for the placement will be an important consideration in determining the contact plan (frequency and other arrangements), but for all children in all placements, feeling secure in the foster or adoptive home *and* at contact will be important.

Looking forward: providing a secure base for children, families and social workers

In attachment theory, John Bowlby offered a framework for thinking about the power of relationships, which has inspired generations of researchers, practitioners and parents to seek for the deeper meanings in children's behaviour. It has helped us to be profoundly aware both of the harm that can sometimes be caused in family relationships and also of the lifelong benefits that a sensitive, available and loving secure base can bring to children. Foster care and adoption have the potential to provide such a secure base, rebuilding children's trust in themselves and others.

Attachment theory provides a way of understanding the therapeutic process in foster and adoptive parenting. The application of this model can help carers and adopters to plan and target their caregiving effectively and to feel the deep satisfaction of helping children to develop and achieve their potential. It can equally help social workers and other professionals to organise their thinking and practice, both when assessing, training and supporting caregivers and when helping children to deal with the impact of maltreatment, separation and loss. If used accurately and flexibly and as part of a comprehensive developmental approach to the promotion of children's welfare, attachment theory has an important contribution to make to improving outcomes for children.

By providing a relationship-based and developmental framework for understanding *and* helping, attachment theory can itself provide a secure base for social workers – it can reduce anxiety and liberate the practitioner's capacity for thinking, feeling and action. Children, and the foster and adoptive families who love and care for them, will be the beneficiaries.

References

Ainsworth M D S, Bell S and Stayton D (1971) 'Individual differences in strange-situation behavior of one year olds', in Schaffer H (ed), *The Origins of Human Social Relations*, New York: Academic Press, pp. 17–52

Ainsworth M D S, Blehar M, Waters E and Wall S (1978) *Patterns of Attachment: A psychological study of the Strange Situation*, Hillsdale, NJ: Lawrence Erlbaum

Allan G (1996) *Kinship and Friendship in Modern Britain*, Oxford: Oxford University Press

Allen J P and Land D (1999) 'Attachment in Adolescence', in Cassidy J and Shaver P R (eds) *Handbook of Attachment: Theory, research and clinical applications*, London: Guilford Press

Barkley R A, Cunningham C E and Karlsson J (1983) 'The speech of hyperactive children and their mothers: comparison with normal children and stimulant drug effects', *Journal of Learning Disability*, 16, pp. 105–110

Beek M and Schofield G (2004a) *Providing a Secure Base in Long-term Foster Care*, London: BAAF

Beek M and Schofield G (2004b) 'Promoting security and managing risk: contact in long-term foster care', in Neil E and Howe D (eds) *Contact in Adoption and Permanent Foster Care*, London: BAAF, pp. 124–143

Beek M and Schofield G (2004c) 'Providing a secure base: tuning in to children with severe learning difficulties in long-term foster care', *Adoption and Fostering*, 28:2, pp. 8–19

Belsky J and Cassidy J (1994) 'Attachment, theory and evidence', in Rutter M and Hay D (eds) *Development through Life: A handbook for clinicians*, Oxford: Blackwell, pp. 373–402

Bowlby J (1944) 'Forty-four juvenile thieves: their characters and home life', *International Journal of Psychoanalysis*, 25, pp. 19–52, 102–127

Bowlby J (1951) *Maternal Care and Mental Health* (WHO Monograph No 2) Geneva: World Health Organization

Bowlby J (1953) *Child Care and the Growth of Love*, London: Pelican Books

Bowlby J (1969/82) *Attachment and Loss: Vol 1 Attachment*, London: Hogarth Press

Bowlby J (1973) *Attachment and Loss: Vol II Separation, Anxiety and Anger*, London: Hogarth Press

Bowlby J (1980) *Attachment and Loss: Vol III Loss, Sadness and Depression*, London: Hogarth Press

Bowlby J (1988) *A Secure Base: Clinical applications of attachment theory*, London: Routledge

Brandon M, Schofield G and Trinder L (1996) *Social Work with Children*, Basingstoke: Macmillan

Bretherton I, Ridgeway D and Cassidy J (1990) 'Assessing internal working models of the attachment relationship: an attachment story completion task for three year olds', in Greenberg M T, Cicchetti D and Cummings E M (eds) *Attachment in the Preschool Years: Theory, research and intervention*, pp. 273–308, Chicago: University of Chicago Press

Brodzinsky D (2005) 'Reconceptualising openness in adoption: implications for theory, research and practice', in Brodzinsky D and Palacios J (eds) *Psychological Issues in Adoption Theory, Research and Application*, New York: Praeger Publishers

Brodzinsky D M and Schechter M D (eds) (1990) *Psychology of Adoption*, New York: Oxford University Press

Bronfenbrenner U (1979) *The Ecology of Human Development: Experiments by nature and design*, Cambridge, MA: Harvard University Press

Byng-Hall J (1990) 'Attachment theory and family therapy: a clinical view', *Infant Mental Health Journal Vol 11*, no 3

Cairns K (2002) *Attachment, Trauma and Resilience*, London: BAAF

Cairns B (2004) *Fostering Attachments: Long-term outcomes in family group care*, London: BAAF

Camis J (2001) *My Life and Me*, London: BAAF

Campbell S B (1973) 'Mother–child interaction in reflective, impulsive and hyperactive children', *Developmental Psychology*, 8, pp. 341–349

Campbell S B (1975) 'Mother–child interactions: A comparison of hyperactive learning disabled and normal boys', *American Journal of Orthopsychiatry*, 48, pp. 51–57

Carlson V, Cicchetti D, Barnett D and Braunwald K (1989) 'Disorganised/disoriented attachment relationships in maltreated infants', *Developmental Psychology*, 25(94), pp. 525–31

Cassidy J (2005) 'Staying open to the pain of a difficult past', *Clinical Applications of Attachment Theory*, Conference Paper, Paris, 2005

Cassidy J and Berlin L J (1994) 'The insecure/ambivalent pattern of attachment: theory and research', *Child Development*, 65, pp. 971–991

Cassidy J and Shaver P R (eds) (1999) *Handbook of Attachment: Theory, research and clinical applications*, London: Guilford Press

Children Act 1989, Guidance (Volume 3), London: The Stationery Office

Cole-Detke H and Kobak R (1996) 'Attachment processes in eating disorder and depression', *Journal of Consulting and Clinical Psychology*, 64(92), pp. 282–290

Cousins J (2004) 'Are we missing the match? Rethinking adopter assessment and child profiling', *Adoption and Fostering*, 27(4), pp. 7–18

Crittenden P M (1995) 'Attachment and psychopathology', in Goldberg S, Muir R and Kerr J (eds) *Attachment Theory: Social, developmental and clinical perspectives*, Hillsdale, NJ: Analytical Press, pp. 367–406

Department for Education and Skills (2004) *Every Child Matters*, London: The Stationery Office

Department of Health (1999) *The Government's Objectives for Children's Services*, London: The Stationery Office

Department of Health (2000) *Assessment of Children in Need and their Families*, London: The Stationery Office

De Wolff M S and van IJzendoorn M H (1997) 'Sensitivity and attachment: a meta-analysis on parental antecedents of infant attachment', *Child Development*, 68, pp. 571–591

Diamond N and Marrone M (2003) *Attachment and Intersubjectivity*, London: Whurr Publishers

Dodge K A, Bates J E and Petit G S (1990) 'Mechanisms in the cycle of violence', *Science*, 250, pp. 167–83

Downes C (1992) *Separation Revisited: Adolescents in foster family care*, Aldershot: Ashgate

Dozier M, Stovall K C, Arbus K E and Bates B (2001) 'Attachment for infants in foster care: The role of caregiver state of mind', *Child Development*, 72, pp. 1467–1477

Dozier, M Lindhiem O, and Ackerman J P (2005) 'Attachment and biobehavioral catch-up' in Berlin L, Ziv Y, Amaya-Jackson L and Greenberg MT (eds) *Enhancing Early Attachments*, New York: Guilford

Dunn J (1988) *The Beginnings of Social Understanding*, Oxford: Blackwell

Dunn J (1993) *Young Children's Close Relationships: Beyond attachment*, London: Sage

Euan's adoptive parents (2004) 'Adoption with contact – the impact of drug use in children exposed to parental substance misuse', in Phillips R (ed) *Children Exposed to Parental Substance Misuse*, London: BAAF

Fahlberg V (1988) *Fitting the Pieces Together*, London: BAAF

Fahlberg V (1994) *A Child's Journey through Placement*, London: BAAF

Farmer E and Pollock S (1998) *Sexually Abused and Abusing Children in Substitute Care*, London: John Wiley and Sons Ltd

Fonagy P, Steele M and Steele H (1991) 'Maternal representations of attachment during pregnancy predict the organisation of infant-mother attachment at one year of age', *Child Development*, 62, pp. 891–905

Fonagy P, Steele M, Steele H, Kennedy R, Mattoon G, Target M and Gerber A (1996) 'The relation of attachment status, psychiatric classification and response to psychotherapy', *Journal of Consulting and Clinical Psychology*, 64, pp. 22–31

Fonagy P and Target M (1997) 'Attachment and reflective function: their role in self-organisation', *Development and Psychopathology*, 9, pp. 679–700

Fonagy P, Target M and Gergely G (2002) *Affect Regulation, Mentalization and the Development of the Self*, New York: Other Press

Forrester D and Harwin J (2004) 'Social work and parental substance misuse', in Phillips R (ed) *Children Exposed to Parental Substance Misuse*, London: BAAF, pp. 115–131

Furman W, Rahe D F and Hartup W W (1979) 'Rehabilitation of socially withdrawn preschool children through mixed-age and same-age socialization', *Child Development*, 50, pp. 915–922

George C (1996) 'A representational perspective of child abuse and prevention: internal working models of attachment and caregiving', *Child Abuse and Neglect*, 20(5), pp. 411–424.

George C and Solomon J (1999) 'Attachment and caregiving: the caregiving behavioral system', in Cassidy J and Shaver P R (eds) *Handbook of Attachment: Theory, research and clinical applications*, London: Guilford Press, pp. 649–670

Gilligan R (2000) 'Promoting resilience in children in foster care', in Kelly G and Gilligan R (eds) *Issues in Foster Care – Policy, Practice and Research*, London: Jessica Kingsley, pp. 107–126

Goldberg S (2000) *Attachment and Development*, London: Arnold

Goldwyn R, Green J M, Stanley C, Smith V (2000) 'The Manchester Child Attachment Story Task: relationship with parental AAI, SAT and child behaviour', *Attachment and Human Development*, 2:1, pp. 65–78

Green J M, Stanley C, Smith V and Goldwyn R (2000) 'A new method of evaluating attachment representations on young school age children – the Manchester Child Attachment Story Task', *Attachment and Human Development*, 2(1), pp. 42–64

Greenberg M T (1999) 'Attachment and psychopathology in childhood', in Cassidy J and Shaver P R (eds) (1999) *Handbook of Attachment: Theory, research and clinical applications*, London: Guilford Press, pp. 469–496

Greenberg M T and Speltz M L (1988) 'Attachment and the ontogeny of conduct problems', in Belsky J and Nezworski T (eds) *Clinical Implications of Attachment*, Hillsdale, NJ: Lawrence Erlbaum Associates, pp. 177–218

Grossman K E, Grossman K and Zimmerman P (1999) 'A wider view of attachment and exploration: stability and change during the years of immaturity', in Cassidy J and Shaver P R (eds) *Handbook of Attachment: Theory, research and clinical applications*, London: Guilford Press, pp. 760–786

Grotevant H, McRoy R G and Ayers-Lopez S (2004) 'Contact after adoption: outcomes for infant placements in the USA', in Neil E and Howe D (eds) *Contact in Permanent Family Placement*, London: BAAF, pp. 7–25

Hadley Briefing Paper (2002) *Matching Children and Families in Permanent Family Placement: Research summary*, Bristol: Hadley Centre for Adoption and Foster Care Studies

Harter S (1987) 'The determinants of global self-worth in children', in Eisenberg N (ed) *Contemporary Topics in Developmental Psychology*, New York: Wiley Science, pp. 219–242

Hesse E (1999) 'The Adult Attachment Interview', in Cassidy J and Shaver P R (eds) *Handbook of Attachment: Theory, research and clinical applications*, London: Guilford Press, pp. 395–433

Hill M, Lambert L and Triseliotis J (1989) *Achieving Adoption with Love and Money*, London: National Children's Bureau

Hobson P (2002) *The Cradle of Thought*, London: Macmillan

Hodges J, Steele M, Hillman S, Henderson K and Kaniuk J (2003) 'Changes in attachment representations over the first year of adoptive placement: narratives of maltreated children, *Clinical Child Psychology and Psychiatry*, 8:3, pp. 351–367

Holmes J (1993) *John Bowlby and Attachment Theory*, London: Routledge

Howe D (1996) *Adopters on Adoption*, London: BAAF

Howe D (1998) *Patterns of Adoption: Nature, nurture and psychosocial development*, Oxford: Blackwell Science

Howe D (2005) *Child Abuse and Neglect: Attachment, development and intervention*, Basingstoke: Macmillan

Howe D, Brandon M, Hinings D and Schofield G (1999) *Attachment Theory: Child maltreatment and family support*, Basingstoke: Macmillan

Howe D and Feast J with Coster D (2002) *Adoption, Search and Reunion: The long-term experience of adopted adults*, London: BAAF

Howe D and Steele M (2004) 'Contact in cases in which children have been traumatically abused or neglected by their birth parents', in Neil E and Howe D (eds) *Contact in Permanent Family Placement*, London: BAAF, pp. 203–223

Ironside L (2004) 'Living a provisional existence: Thinking about foster carers and the emotional containment of children placed in their care', *Adoption and Fostering*, 28:4, pp. 16–26

Jack G (2001) 'Ecological perspectives in assessing children and families', in Horvath J (ed) *The Child's World: Assessing children in need*, London: Jessica Kingsley, pp. 53–74

Jacobsen T, Edelstein W and Hofmann V (1994) 'A longitudinal study of the relation between representations of attachment in childhood and cognitive functioning in childhood and adolescence', *Developmental Psychology*, 30, pp. 112–124

Jacobvitz D and Hazen N (1999) 'Developmental pathways from infant disorganisation to childhood peer relationships', in Solomon J and George C *Attachment Disorganisation*, New York: Guilford Press

Kearns K A and Richardson R A (2005) *Attachment in Middle Childhood*, New York: Guilford Press

Kestenbaum R, Farber E and Sroufe L A (1989) 'Individual differences in empathy among pre-schoolers: Relation to attachment history', in Eisenberg N (ed) *New Directions for Child Development: No. 44 Empathy and related emotional responses*, San Francisco: Jossey – Bass, pp. 51–64

Lanyado M (2003) 'The emotional tasks of moving from fostering to adoption: transitions, attachment, separation and loss, *Clinical Child Psychology and Psychiatry*, 8:3, pp. 337–350.

Lewis M, Feiring C, McGuffog C and Jaskir J (1984) 'Predicting psychopathology in six year olds from early social relations', *Child Development*, 55, pp. 123–136

Lieberman A F and Pawl J H (1988) 'Clinical applications of attachment theory', in Belsky J and Nezworski T (eds) *Clinical Implications of Attachment*, Hillsdale, NJ: Lawrence Erlbaum Associates, pp. 327–351

Light P (1979) *Development of a Child's Sensitivity to People*, London: Cambridge University Press

Liotti G (1999) 'Disorganisation of attachment as a model for understanding dissociative psychopathology', in Solomon J and George C (eds) *Attachment Disorganisation*, New York: Guilford Press, pp. 291–31

Logan J and Smith C (2004), 'Direct post-adoption contact: experience of birth and adoptive families', in Neil E and Howe D, *Contact in Adoption and Permanent Foster Care*, BAAF

Lord J and Borthwick S (2001) *Together or Apart? Assessing brothers and sisters for permanent placement*, London: BAAF

Lyons-Ruth K and Jacobvitz D (1999) 'Attachment disorganisation: unresolved loss, relational violence and lapses in behavioural and attentional strategies', in Cassidy J and Shaver P R (eds) *Handbook of Attachment: Theory, research and clinical applications*, London: Guilford Press, pp. 520–554

Macfie J, Cicchetti D and Toth S (2001) 'The development of dissociation in maltreated preschool children', *Development and Psychopathology*, 13, pp. 233–54

Magai C (1999) 'Affect, imagery and attachment: working models of inter-personal affect and the socialization of emotion', in Cassidy J and Shaver P R (eds) *Handbook of Attachment: Theory, research and clinical applications*, London: Guilford Press, pp. 787–802

Main M (1991) 'Metacognitive knowledge, metacognitive monitoring and singular (coherent) vs. multiple (incoherent) model of attachment: findings and directions for future research', in Parkes C M, Stevenson-Hinde J and Marris P (eds) *Attachment Across the Life-cycle*, London: Tavistock/Routledge, pp. 127 159.

Main M (1995) 'Attachment: overview, with implications for clinical work', in Goldberg S, Muir R and Kerr J (eds) *Attachment Theory: Social, developmental and clinical perspectives*, Hillsdale, NJ: Analytic Press, pp. 407–474

Main M and Goldwyn R (1984) *Adult Attachment Scoring and Classification System*, Unpublished manuscript, California: University of California

Main M and Hesse E (1990) 'Parents' unresolved traumatic experiences are related to infant disorganised attachment status: is frightened and /or frightening the linking mechanism?' in Greenberg M T and Cummings E M (eds) *Attachment in the Preschool Years: Theory, research and intervention*, Chicago: University of Chicago Press, pp. 161–182

Main M and Solomon J (1986) 'Discovery of an insecure-disorganised/disoriented attachment pattern', in Brazelton T B and Yogman M W (eds) *Affective Development in Infancy*, Norwood, NJ: Ablex, pp. 95–124

Marvin R, Cooper G, Hoffman, K and Powell, B (2002) 'The Circle of Security Project: attachment based intervention with caregiver-pre-school child dyads, *Attachment and Human Development*, 4(1) pp. 107–124

Massiah H (ed) (2005) *Looking After Our Own: The stories of black and Asian adopters*, London: BAAF

Miens E (1997) *Security of Attachment and the Social Development of Cognition*, Hove: Psychology Press

Miens E, Ferryhough C, Fradley E and Tuckey M (2001) 'Rethinking maternal sensitivity: Mothers' comments on infants' mental processes predict security of attachment', *Journal of Child Psychology and Psychiatry*, 42, pp. 637–648

Murray L and Cooper P J (eds) (1997) *Postpartum Depression and Child Development*, New York: Guilford Press

Neil E (2002) 'The reasons why young children are placed for adoption', *Child and Family Social Work*, 5(4) pp. 303–316

Neil E (2004) 'The "Contact after Adoption" study: face-to-face contact', in Neil E and Howe D (eds) *Contact in Adoption and Permanent Foster Care*, London: BAAF

Neil E, Beek M and Schofield G (2003) 'Thinking about and managing contact in permanent placements: the differences and similarities between adoptive parents and foster carers', *Journal of Clinical Child Psychology and Psychiatry*, 8:3, pp. 401–418

Neil E and Howe D (2004) 'Conclusions: a transactional model for thinking about contact', in Neil E and Howe D (eds) *Contact in Adoption and Permanent Foster Care*, London: BAAF, pp. 224–254

Oppenheim D, Emde R and Warren S (1997) 'Children's narrative representations of mothers: their development and association with child and mother adaptation', *Child Development*, 68 pp. 127–138

Owusu-Bempah J and Howitt D (1997) 'Socio-genealogical connectedness, attachment theory and child care practice', *Child and Family Social Work*, 2:4, pp. 199–208

Pearson J, Cohn D, Cowan P and Cowan C (1994) 'Earned and continuous-security in adult attachment: relation to depressive symptomatology and parenting style', *Development and Psychopathology*, 6 pp. 359–73

Perry B, Pollard R, Blakley T, Baker W and Vigilante D (1995) 'Childhood trauma, the neurobiology of adaptation and "use dependent" development of the brain: how "states" become "traits"', *Infant Mental Health Journal*, 16:4, pp. 271–291

Phillips R (ed) (2004) *Children Exposed to Parental Substance Misuse: Implications for family placement*, London: BAAF

Piaget J and Inhelder B (1969) *The Psychology of the Child*, New York: Basic Books

Quinton D and Rutter M (1988) *Parenting Breakdown: The making and breaking of intergenerational links*, Aldershot: Avebury

Robertson J (1952) *A two year old goes to hospital* – film, London: Tavistock

Rogers C R and Stevens B (1976) *Person to Person: The problem of being human*, London: Souvenir Press

Rubin K H and Lollis S P (1988) 'Origins and consequences of social withdrawal', in Belsky J and Nezworski T (eds) *Clinical Implications of Attachment*, Hillsdale, NJ: Lawrence Erlbaum Associates, pp. 219–252

Rushton A, Dance C, Quinton D and Mayes D (2001) *Siblings in Late Permanent Placements*, London: BAAF

Rushton A, Mayes D, Dance C and Quinton D (2003) 'Parenting late-placed children: the development of new relationships and the challenge of behavioural problems', *Clinical Child Psychology and Psychiatry*, 8:3, pp. 389–400

Rutter M (1999) 'Resilience concepts and findings: implications for family therapy', *Journal of family Therapy*, 21, pp. 119–144

Ryan T and Walker R (1999) (second edn) *Life Story Work*, London: BAAF

Schofield G (1998a) 'Inner and outer worlds: a psychosocial framework for child and family social work', *Child and Family Social Work*, 3:1, pp. 57–68

Schofield G (1998b) 'Ascertaining the wishes and feelings of insecurely attached children', *Child and Family Law Quarterly*, pp. 363–376

Schofield G (2002) 'The significance of a secure base: a psychosocial model of long-term foster care', *Child and Family Social Work*, 7:4, pp. 259–272

Schofield G (2003) *Part of the Family: Pathways through foster care*, London: BAAF

Schofield G (2005) 'The voice of the child in family placement decision making', *Adoption and Fostering*, 29(1) pp. 29–44

Schofield G, Beek M, Sargent K with Thoburn J (2000) *Growing up in Foster Care*, London: BAAF

Schofield and Beek (2005) 'Providing a secure base: parenting children in long-term foster family care', *Attachment and Human Development*, 7:1, pp. 3–26

Schofield G and Brown K (1999) 'Being there: a family centre worker's role as a secure base for adolescent girls in crisis', *Child and Family Social Work*, 4, pp. 21–31

Schore A (1994) *Affect Regulation and the Origins of the Self: The neurobiology of emotional development*, Hillsdale, NJ: Erlbaum

Sellick C, Thoburn J and Philpot T (2004) *What Works in Adoption and Foster Care?*, London: Barnardo's/BAAF

Sinclair I (2005) *Fostering Now*, London: Jessica Kingsley

Sinclair I and Wilson K (2003) 'Matches and mismatches: the contribution of carers and children to the success of foster placements', *British Journal of Social Work*, 33, pp. 871–884

Sinclair I, Wilson K and Gibbs I (2004) *Foster Placements: Why some succeed and some fail*, London: Jessica Kingsley

Solomon J and George C (1999) *Attachment Disorganization*, New York: Guilford Press

Solomon J, George C and DeJong A (1995) 'Symbolic representation of attachment in children classified as controlling at age 6. Evidence of disorganisation of representation strategies', *Development and Psychopathology*, 7, pp. 447–464

Spangler G and Grossman K (1993) 'Biobehavioural organization in securely and insecurely attached infants', *Child Development*, 64, pp. 1439–50

Sroufe L A (1983) 'Infant-caregiver attachment and patterns of adaptation in preschool: the roots of maladaptation and competence', in Perlmutter M (ed) *The Minnesota Symposia on Child Psychology: Vol 16 Development and policy concerning children with special needs*, Hillsdale, NJ: Erlbaum, pp. 41–83

Sroufe L A (1989) 'Relationship, self and individual adaptation', in Sameroff A and Emde R (eds) *Relationship Disturbances in Early Childhood: A developmental Approach*, New York: Basic Books, pp. 70–96

Sroufe L A (1997) 'Psychopathology as an outcome of development', *Development and Psychopathology*, 9(2), pp. 251–266.

Steele H (2003) 'Holding therapy is not attachment therapy: Editor's introduction to the Special Issue', *Attachment and Human Development*, 5:3, p. 219

Steele H and Steele M (1994) 'Intergenerational patterns of attachment', *Advances in Personal Relationships*, 5, pp. 93–120

Steele H, Steele M, Croft C and Fonagy P (1999) 'Infant–mother attachment at one year predicts children's understanding of mixed emotions at 6 years', *Journal of Social Development*, 8, pp. 161–178

Steele M, Hodges J, Kaniuk J, Henderson K, Hillman S and Bennett P (1999) 'The use of story stem narratives in assessing the inner world of the child: implications for adoptive placements', in *Assessment, Preparation and Support: Implications from research*, London: BAAF

Steele M, Hodges J, Kaniuk J, Hillman S and Henderson K (2003) 'Attachment representations and adoption: associations between maternal states of mind and emotion narratives in previously maltreated children', *Journal of Child Psychotherapy*, 29, pp. 187–205

Stovall K C and Dozier M (1998) 'Infants in foster care: an attachment theory perspective', *Adoption Quarterly*, 2(1), pp. 55–87

Stovall K C and Dozier M (2000) 'The development of attachment in new relationships: Single subject analyses for 10 foster infants', *Development & Psychopathology*, 12, pp. 133–156

Sunderland M (2003) *Helping Children with Feelings* (resource pack), Bicester: Speechmark Publishing

Thoburn J (1996) 'Psychological parenting and child placement', in Howe D (ed) *Attachment and Loss in Child and Family Social Work*, Aldershot: Avebury, pp. 129–145

Thomas C and Beckford V with Murch M and Lowe N (1999) *Adopted Children Speaking*, London: BAAF

Thomas N (2005) 'Has anything really changed? Managers' views of looked after children's participation in 1997 and 2004', *Adoption and Fostering*, 29:1, pp. 67–77

Trinder L, Feast J and Howe D (2004) *The Adoption Reunion Handbook*, London: Wiley

Triseliotis J (2002) 'Long-term fostering or adoption: the evidence examined', *Child and Family Social Work*, 7(1), pp. 23–34

Troy M and Sroufe L A (1987) 'Victimization among pre-schoolers: the role of attachment relationship theory', *Journal of the American Academy of Child and Adolescent Psychiatry*, 26, pp. 166–172

van IJzendoorn M H and Kroonenberg P M (1988) 'Cross-cultural patterns of attachment: a meta-analysis of the Strange Situation', *Child Development*, 59, pp. 147–156

van IJzendoorn M H, Schuengel C and Bakermans-Kranenburg M J (1999) 'Disorganised attachment in early childhood: Meta-analysis of precursors, con-comitance and sequelae', *Development and Psychopathology*, 11, pp. 225–249

Vygotsky L S (1978) *Mind and Society: The development of higher mental processes*, Cambridge, MA: Harvard University Press (original works 1930, 1933, 1935)

Walker M, Hill M and Triseliotis J (2002) *Testing the Limits of Foster Care: Fostering as an alternative to secure accommodation*, London: BAAF

Warren S L, Huston L, Egeland B and Sroufe L A (1997) 'Child and adolescent anxiety disorders and early attachment', *Journal of the American Academy of Child and Adolescent Psychiatry*, 36, pp. 637–644

Weinfield N S, Sroufe L A, Egeland B and Carlson E A (1999) 'The nature of individual differences in infant–caregiver attachment', in Cassidy J and Shaver P R (eds) *Handbook of Attachment: Theory, research and clinical applications*, London: Guilford Press, pp. 68–88

Wilson K, Sinclair I and Petrie S (2003) 'A kind of loving: a model of effective foster care', *British Journal of Social Work*, 33, pp. 991–1003

Winnicott C (1964) *Child Care Social Work*, Hitchin: Codicote Press

Winnicott, D (1965) *The Maturational Process and the Facilitative Environment*, New York: International Universities Press.

Index

Compiled by Elisabeth Pickard

Author index

Compiled by Elisabeth Pickard